PROPERTY OF
NEWBURY FREE PUBLIC
NEWBURY, NEW HAMPSHIRE

P9-CQA-374

ST. PAULS SCHOOL

ST. PAUL'S

*The Life of
a New England
School*

ST. PAUL'S

*The Life of
A New England
School*

AUGUST HECKSCHER

Charles Scribner's Sons • New York

All photographs herein come from the archives of St. Paul's School, with the following exceptions: no. 5, courtesy New Hampshire Historical Society; no. 13, from Mark A. de Wolfe Howe, *John Jay Chapman and His Letters;* no. 15, from Bliss Perry, *Richard Henry Dana, 1851–1931;* no. 18, courtesy Trinity College Library; no. 20, courtesy Mrs. Emily M. Beck; no. 23, from James Knox, *Henry Augustus Coit;* no. 34, courtesy New Hampshire Historical Society; no. 37, from John Davies, *The Legend of Hobey Baker;* no. 42, courtesy Trinity College Library; no. 47, from John Davies, *The Legend of Hobey Baker;* no. 52, courtesy Mrs. Emily M. Beck; nos. 40, 57, 61, 78, courtesy Toni Frissell; no. 60, courtesy *Holiday* Magazine; no. 84, courtesy Tom Jones Photo; no. 85, courtesy R. L. Dothard Associates; no. 86, courtesy Bradford F. Herzog; nos. 65, 66, courtesy Roger W. Drury; no. 45, courtesy Mrs. Richard Eaton; no. 68, from an oil painting by Harold Brett.

Endpapers by William Abbe

Copyright © 1980 August Heckscher

Library of Congress Cataloging in Publication Data

Heckscher, August, 1913 –
St. Paul's: the life of a New England school.

Bibliography: p.
Includes index.
1. St. Paul's School, Concord, N.H.—History.
I. Title.
LD7501.C822H42   373.742'72   80-17096
ISBN 0-684-16607-0

This book published simultaneously
in the United States of America and in Canada—
Copyright under the Berne Convention

All rights reserved.
No part of this book may be reproduced
in any form without the permission of
Charles Scribner's Sons.

1 3 5 7 9 11 13 15 17 19   Q/C   20 18 16 14 12 10 8 6 4 2

Printed in the United States of America

DEDICATION

ILLIS PUERIS SCHOLAE SANCTI PAULI
QUI FELICEM IN PUELLARUM ADVENTUM
CXIV ANNOS PERSERVABANT

A.H.

Contents

Illustrations

Introduction

This history of St. Paul's in Concord, New Hampshire, covers the life of the school from its beginnings in 1855 to the eve of its one hundred twenty-fifth year. Among the first of the New England boarding schools (as distinguished from the earlier academies), St. Paul's has had its influence on American secondary education as upon the lives and characters of the thousands of its graduates. Such considerations should suffice to justify this book. But perhaps its chief interest will be found in the detailed, chronological account of the development of a community—a small community but one served by unusual and often exceedingly able men and women; bearing within itself a strong sense of destiny and a conviction that what it did, or failed to do, was important in the ultimate search for truth in learning and for goodness in life.

St. Paul's history falls into three periods, each covering a period of approximately forty years. The nineteenth century marked its founding and growth; saw it rise to a remarkable preeminence under Henry Augustus Coit; and then, as the impetus of its first rector waned, decline in self-confidence and sense of direction. In the twentieth century, under the long rectorship of Samuel S. Drury, the school found itself again and achieved a period of classic equipoise.

The second great war and its aftermath saw St. Paul's and the world of which it was a part undergoing drastic stresses, until the school, following the perturbations of the late 1960s and early 1970s, emerged as a modern, coeducational institution. The author, entering as a student in 1927, knew at first hand a part of the second of these periods; and as a trustee for more than twenty-five years, knew the third from a different perspective.

In writing about St. Paul's, I have felt at times that I was dealing with a minor nation, a small country replete with the problems and experiences that have traditionally preoccupied historians. A student of the 1870s, indeed, put the matter succinctly. "Every school," he wrote in the school magazine, "is a commonwealth in miniature."[1] The commonwealth of St. Paul's has had its appointed rulers, its intellectuals, nobles, and plain citizens. It has had its pastoral age and its time of development. Rectors and trustees, alumni, faculty, parents and students, have acted and reacted upon one another in subtle, changing ways and through a diversity of institutional arrangements.

Within the compact society of the school one can trace out the way religious beliefs, work habits, leisure-time pursuits, systems of justice, and many other categories of human activity adjust themselves to varying times and circumstances. The diminutive country has had the task of achieving secure boundaries, defensible against external encroachments; it has had its international problems as it coped with other powers—rival schools, recalcitrant universities—impinging upon its life. One thing can be said with assurance: no small country, and few among the larger, have been served—and loved—by so vital an assemblage of characters. Few have had a ruling class, and indeed a body of plain citizens, too, capable of handling the native language with such clarity and force.

Writing this book at the request of the trustees, I have been given the freedom to deal objectively with aspects of the school that in most "official" histories are glossed over. Documents ordinarily private have been opened to me. I trust I will be recognized as having been frank without being needlessly harsh to particular persons. I am partial to the school; my affections embrace most of the varied company that has composed it, and most of its aspects, worldly and unworldly; yet I have wanted to present an objective picture. A group of three, comprising Roger W. Drury, editor of the *Alumni Horae,* Benjamin Neilson, president of the Alumni Association, and Philip Burnham, vice rector emeritus, have read the manuscript carefully, helping me draw the line between candor and indiscretion. While I have the final responsibility for whatever is said or not said here, I have profited from their discerning comments, as I am grateful for their general approval of the text. Dr. Douglas Marshall, of the St. Paul's faculty, not only made it possible for me to eliminate errors of fact or interpretation but enlightened me in many conversations, as well as in a stimulating course on the school's history.

Acknowledgments and Notes at the end of the book record further specific instances of indebtedness. Two men, however, must be thanked here. William A. Oates, Rector, extended me many courtesies during the work; and Samuel R. Callaway, while chairman of the board of trustees, encouraged me to begin the book and made it possible for me to bring it to a conclusion.

I could not, if I wished, deny that the task has been enjoyable. The abundance of original source material, in its richness of detail sometimes giving the sense of being actually present at a distant event; the picturesque scene, bounded and brightly lit; the variety of the principal characters, often greatly gifted; the pathos of young life with its eager claims and basic decencies; the opportunity, not least, to live within the school during extended periods of research: all this has created rewards unusual for an author. At the start of the work, a letter from one of the school's older alumni came to cheer me on. "Whittle your history, churn it, chill it," he wrote. "Something within you will respond to the gaiety of the challenge."[2] I hope that I have indeed responded, as I dare to hope the reader may do in the same spirit.

The polity of St. Paul's has moved from the theocracy of the first Coit, through Drury's splendid monarchy, to the limited republic of the eighth rector. Whatever the changing form of governance, it has been a community of the young—of, and for, the young; and that in itself should infuse the narrative with life, and color the end of it with hope.

August Heckscher

At "High Loft," Maine
September 1979

CHAPTER ONE

The Founding
1855

Into the Valley

A watcher in Millville one early spring day in the middle of the last century might have seen a carriage come down the road leading into the hamlet's shaded valley. On the surrounding hills the snow lingered in white patches; the skies were overcast, dark and blustery. Two boys and a dog were passengers in the carriage, together with a young schoolmaster and his bride.[1]

At the summit of the little hill an armed garrison had stood in Colonial times to protect the inhabitants from Indian raids.[2] Now, near its site, was the pre-revolutionary cottage where Moses Shute plied his trade as blacksmith, and behind a white fence across the road, smothered in vines and under the shadow of tall trees, was the house of William and Mary Shute, the blacksmith's brother and sister. To one coming down the slope, ponds revealed themselves through the screen of pine and elm.

Turkey River, beginning in swampy waters to the southwest and making its winding way to the Merrimack, paused in this valley to create two small bodies of water, the larger fancifully shaped with islands and bays, miniature peninsulas and capes. Between the ponds the road led westward across a plank bridge; on the near side of the bridge a fork branched sharply to the left, passing the dam where the wheels of a mill had been turning since the eighteenth century. Immediately beyond was the miller's house and, on the left, the house of the farmer.

At the juncture of the two roads rose a square stucco house of imposing proportions. Built by Jacob Carter in 1803, the first to be made from brick in that region of wooden structures, it had originally served as a tavern. Ten years before the beginning of our story it came into the possession of the well-known Boston physician George Cheyne Shattuck. He gave it to his son, George Cheyne, Jr., then thirty-four, who used it as a summer residence for his growing family. In front of this house the carriage with its precious cargo came to a halt. Out tumbled the boys and the

I

dog, to be greeted by William Peters and his wife Lydia, keepers for the Shattuck family of the homestead and the surrounding farm, and by young Frederick Shattuck, who had been staying with them.

Their arrival signified the beginning of St. Paul's School.[3] "It was a small beginning which we made on the third of April, 1856; but all things, large or small, must have a beginning." So wrote the first rector, Henry Augustus Coit, when the school had reached its quarter century mark. A small beginning—but, he added, with a big end in view. Like the prophets of old, the little band had set up their landmark. With gratitude for the past and not without hope for the future, they said: "Hitherto hath the Lord helped us."

A Question of Origins

What was the objective that had inspired the young schoolmaster and led the owner, George Shattuck, to make a gift of this land and its buildings? That St. Paul's was fashioned upon the model of English schools has long been assumed; so that to imitate them, and to create a new Rugby or a new Eton on these shores, might be supposed to have been their purpose. In fact it could hardly have been more different. The English schools at the beginning of the nineteenth century were not considered models by anyone. Debased by the corrupt society of the Regency, their students licentious and rebellious, they were passing through a "time of turbulence" comparable to that faced by our own institutions in the late 1890s or again in the 1960s. Arnold's task at Rugby was as much that of cleansing an Augean stable as establishing an ideal. Later, many English customs were grafted on the sturdy trunk of St. Paul's. But the first impetus was of another sort.

Nor was the objective to follow in the line of the well-established and then flourishing American academies. Set up to prepare young men for college, they provided adequate training for the rather primitive entrance requirements of those days. These academies were something more than day schools, for their students traveled from relatively distant places to attend them; but they were less than the "boarding schools" of which St. Paul's was the precursor and St. Mark's, St. George's and Groton later examples. Students at the academies lived with families in the small towns where they were located, attending the institutions only for their studies. At best the town provided a wholesome environment, and the families—serving *in loco parentis*—were a moderating influence upon the passions of youth. Exeter, Andover and Deerfield were among the most prominent of this type of institution. They had been founded in the eighteenth century and by the 1850s were performing an essential educational function.

Difficulties arose as the college entrance requirements became more strict, or when, as with Exeter toward the end of the century, the environment of the town declined. The academies would then build dormitories and gather their students within protective walls. Becoming in time true boarding schools, they kept much of the free atmosphere and the democratic spirit that characterized their origins. By contrast, St. Paul's, amid growth and under the spur of new social conditions, would undergo successive liberations. The paths of the boarding schools and the academies converged, but they began under different stars.

Out of Yverdun and Hofwyl via Round Hill School, out of Flushing Institute on Long Island and St. James College in Maryland, came the impulses that were to start St. Paul's on its course. Our inquiry leads to these places, rather than to Eton or Exeter.

An Idyllic Community

First to be considered is Round Hill. This school at Northampton, Massachusetts, had a short life, but it exercised on its students and on American education generally a decisive influence.[4] Founded in 1823, it was the brain child of two young Harvard graduates, Joseph Green Cogswell and George Bancroft. Both had traveled immediately after graduation to observe the latest educational experiments. At Yverdun in Switzerland ruled Johann Heinrich Pestalozzi, an innovator, a destroyer of idols, and in his own epoch the intellectual heir of Rousseau. His school embodied a revolt against the tyranny of the printed book. Children, he believed, should be educated by direct experience of the senses—by what they themselves saw, felt and did. But Pestalozzi was old when Cogswell visited him; the school was poorly organized and run down. At nearby Hofwyl, the disciple, Emmanuel von Fellenberg, presided over a happier scene. A complex of institutions had been created for the rich and the poor, caring for the youngest student to the most advanced, where all learned by actual experience of living and working. Of Von Fellenberg, Cogswell wrote: "Nothing could resemble more a tender and solicitous parent, surrounded by a family of obedient and affectionate children." He resolved on his return to America to become such a "parent" himself.

Meanwhile George Bancroft, the future historian, was conducting his own researches, mostly of German schools, on a scholarship from Harvard. The two young men met in Gottingen to discuss their impressions and to shape a dream for the future. On his return to the United States in 1822, Bancroft expressed the dream with the jubilant confidence of youth. "I am going to turn schoolmaster," he wrote.[5] "Mr. Cogswell has seen so much of the world, that he knows it and its folly; he will join me in my scheme. We are going into the country and we shall choose a pleasant site where nature in her loveliness may breathe calmness & inspire purity. We will live retired from the clamor of scandals and the disputes of the irresolute. We will train up a few minds to virtue and honor. . . . I *like* the sound of the word schoolmaster," he added.

At Northampton in 1823 the great experiment was begun. "Constant supervision, salutary restraint, competent guidance and instruction, and affectionate intercourse," were seen as the means by which young scholars would be held to their duties and led from evil propensities. The students were to be kept constantly busy, and to be diverted by sports, games and festivals. The situation of Round Hill, upon a slope overlooking the broad Connecticut Valley, gave students a chance to become intimately acquainted with nature. They were encouraged to build houses of their own in the pine woods. Their studies went beyond the classics and mathematics to which the conventional curriculum of that day was limited, the teaching of the two young headmasters being supplemented by a faculty, many of them drawn from European countries, representative of a wide range of learning.

To this idyllic community in 1827 came a lad of thirteen, George Cheyne Shattuck, Jr., destined to be the founder of St. Paul's. He was the descendant of William Shattuck, who in the seventeenth century came from England without family or resources to settle in Massachusetts.[6] Four generations of Shattucks were farmers, ministers and local officeholders. Then Benjamin Shattuck (1742–1794) took up a career of medicine. His son, George Cheyne, followed him, the second of five generations to become outstanding Boston physicians.

Of George Shattuck's six children all died young except the oldest, his namesake. That the latter's education should have been a matter of his father's utmost concern and solicitude can well be imagined. He was evidently a charming youth. "His dispositions are most amiable and his principles excellent," reported his schoolmaster; but there was also in his nature a welcome strain of independence. "Mr. Cogswell had reason to find fault with me last week for firing a cracker in the dining hall," George wrote his father.[7] (Cogswell, also reporting the incident, assured the father that although such "occasional excesses" deserved punishment, "they do not forebode anything evil for the future.")

Another of George's letters speaks volumes—especially when set against the brutalities and floggings visited upon most students at this time—of the care with which at Round Hill a youth's better tendencies were encouraged. The letter, written to his father, describes a visit to an off-bounds tavern. "I went to find out where the tavern was," he wrote; "I found it and went in." At this point Mr. Cogswell arrived upon the scene. Afterwards George was called into the master's study. No thunderings, no corporal punishment. The lad promised he would not go off bounds again, and upon his saying he was sorry to have entered the tavern in the first place—his motives, it was evident, had been innocent and vague—he was "scolded some." No further penalties were invoked, and the boy passed blameless through his subsequent school and college life. The free intellectual atmosphere at Northampton, the enjoyments derived from the school's rural surroundings, the discipline enforced more by persuasion than punishment, became a lasting memory of the young George Shattuck.

The days of Round Hill were, unfortunately, numbered. Bancroft was never as happy at schoolmastering as he had supposed he would be. He was already chiefly interested in his literary pursuits, and mischievous boys, taking advantage of his abstraction, "crept out of the schoolroom while he was thinking about something else."[8] Frustrated and discouraged—doomed, as he wrote, "to bear the petulance, restrain the frivolity, mend the tempers and improve the minds of children"—he went back to Harvard. Cogswell, the beloved father figure, struggled on against increasing financial difficulties and against the refusal of Harvard and Yale to adapt their entrance requirements to the advanced curriculum of Round Hill. In 1834 the school closed its doors. "It seemed to die," wrote Dr.

The beloved father figure. *Joseph Cogswell of Round Hill.*

A churchman with a strong aesthetic sense. *Dr. Muhlenberg of Flushing Institute.*

Frederick Shattuck, George Shattuck's son, a hundred years later. "Rather it fell asleep for twenty years or so."[9] It slept until his father, facing the education of his own boys, established in St. Paul's a school where the ideals of Round Hill could be reincarnated.

The Beauty of Holiness

A second formative influence at the birth of St. Paul's was the Flushing Institute of Flushing, Long Island. Through its founder, William Augustus Muhlenberg, the Institute encouraged the religious piety that put its strong mark upon the school. Thus, two traditions, the Jeffersonian and the Pauline—the secularism of Round Hill and the other-worldliness of Flushing Institute—have coexisted at St. Paul's; the school has been at its best when each was playing a vital role. Round Hill has stood for the love of nature, the sense of community, the cultivation of the humanities, which persisted even in such predominantly religious periods as the 1880s. And if in the third quarter of the twentieth century the chapel exerts a potent force, it is because the influence of the old, forgotten Flushing Institute is still somehow at work.

In February 1845, a boy of fifteen arrived at this school, having made a five-hour trip from New York to Flushing in "a wretched old rack of an omnibus" filled with dirty straw.[10] He was given a supper of tea, bread and butter. Sitting alone in the parlor afterwards, he heard coming down the long uncarpeted corridors the screams and hoots of the boys. "Whether they were reading or studying at the pitch of their voices I didn't know," wrote the young student to his father, one hopes with a glint of conscious humor, "but I was quite alarmed." Dr. Muhlenberg took the lad into his study, talked with him until ten, and then showed him into a little chamber of his own, furnished "with a prayer book and other necessaries." Thus Henry Augustus Coit, future rector, came to the school which was greatly to affect his own views of education and of life.

It was to Muhlenberg's Flushing Institute that Cogswell advised parents to send their sons when his own school was about to close. Indeed, the two schools had much in common. Both exercised a parental discipline, stressed physical as well as moral development, and aimed to create a total environment within which a youth could fulfill his own tendencies. Flushing Institute added, however, an intense religious life. A churchman with a strong aesthetic sense, Muhlenberg celebrated "the beauty of holiness" in chapel services marked by ritual and ceremony, by color, imagery and music. He also looked closely into the souls of his young charges. "My dear Dr. Muhlenberg spoke to me last evening," wrote one of these; "he asked me what was my besetting sin." On being told by the young man that he did not know of any in particular, "Ah," said the good doctor, "that is because of your ignorance." "Alas, it is too true," concluded the youth.[11]

The institute developed along broad lines, to include both a grammar school and a college. In the end this range became a fatal weakness. The older boys proved unamenable to the discipline suitable for the younger; the depression of 1837 caught the institute financially over-extended. Dr. Muhlenberg closed down the experiment and went on to other tasks. In a long and useful life he founded St. Luke's Hospital in New York, established the first Episcopal religious order for women, and created St. Johnland, on Long Island's North Shore, a utopian colony for the aged. Inventive and lively in spirit, he never lost the qualities which in his earlier years had appealed so strongly to young scholars. Through the formative period at St. Paul's his portrait hung in the study hall. He was revered by Coit, he became a friend of Dr. Shattuck, and on at least one important occasion visited the school of which he could claim to be in a real sense the godfather.

A Faltering Start

The separate strands of Round Hill and Flushing Institute now join; we return to the scene with which this narrative opened, the little caravan descending into the valley at Millville.

The year is 1855. George Shattuck, the student of Round Hill, is now himself a successful physician. After graduating from Harvard, he had accompanied Audubon to Newfoundland and Labrador; he had studied for several years in Europe under the famous pathologist P. C. H. Louis, and had returned to Boston to carry on a career as a medical practitioner, teacher and administrator. In 1840, he married Anne Henrietta Brune, a devout Episcopalian and member of a prominent Baltimore family. Two sons, George Brune and Frederick Cheever, were now at an age where their education must be seriously considered.

The father's thoughts turned naturally to Round Hill, the scene of his own schooling, and to the Flushing Institute, with which he had become familiar. Both had ended their existence. With the instinct for benevolence which marked the great generation of Boston Brahmins, and with a shrewd perception of his own need, he determined to establish a school patterned on these examples. Like them, it would be in the country, "exempt from the annoyances and temptations of towns and villages";[12] like them, it would concern itself not with intellectual pursuits alone, but with the whole man—or at least the whole boy. It would teach by example, discipline by persuasion, and bring nature's ministrations into the making of the good scholar and the good citizen. "Green fields and trees, streams and ponds, beautiful scenery, flowers and minerals, are educators," Shattuck wrote.[13] "The things which are seen are very valuable, and may be used to tell . . . of the things unseen." Finally, having been converted to Episcopalianism following his marriage, he conceived a school which would serve the church.

The property at Millville was the ideal setting for such a school. "It was," said Bishop Carlton Chase of New Hampshire, one of the early trustees, "in the right part of the Northeast, in the right part of the diocese, and in the right part of Concord."[14] It had easy access to the new railroad, and yet was sufficiently far from the state capital so that it would have to constitute a community in itself. Beyond all this, and no doubt paramount to Dr. Shattuck, was the beauty of the place, enhanced in his eyes by summers spent there with his young family.

In the winter of 1855 the first steps were taken toward founding the school. A charter was approved by the state legislature. A board of trustees was set up, mostly personal friends of Shattuck. (He himself, neither then nor later, thought it appropriate to be a member.) Among the board members were churchmen, the rector of the Church of the Advent in Boston (which Shattuck had helped found) and of St. Paul's Church in Concord; there were colleagues among Boston's lawyers and physicians; a noted Concord citizen, its postmaster Jacob Carter, and the chief justices of Vermont and New Hampshire. In June 1855, the act incorporating St. Paul's School was signed by the governor of New Hampshire.

That September, a first meeting of the trustees of the school was held in the Shattuck home in Millville, in the front parlor around an oak table which Shattuck's father had bought in France and given to the son as a wedding gift. All trustees were present. They accepted from Dr. and Mrs. Shattuck the deed of gift conveying to the new institution about fifty-five acres of land, together with the dwelling house, grist mill and farmer's and miller's cottages. The gift was accepted "with expressions of respect and gratitude befitting the joyful occasion."[15] To Dr. Shattuck the new board would offer ceremoniously the right to visit freely at the school so long as he lived.

Two trustees who were added to the original board played a crucial role in the negotiations which now took place. They were men of contrasting temperaments and gifts. The first was the bishop of New Hampshire, Carlton Chase, a pleasantly human man of strong enthusiasms but varying convictions, given to pious hopes and to quick disillusionments. Judge Samuel H. Huntington, prominent Connecticut churchman, was the second addition. A hearty man, stubborn, worldly and skeptical, he refused to be taken in by appearances. He was one of those men, declared his colleague Chase, "who when they take hold of a thing, are apt to shake out its folds."[16] In the ensuing months these two led in the search for a first rector, their opposing humors lending quiet drama to the pursuit. Shattuck remained in the background, sage in his advice and keeping the disparate personalities in harness.

Even before the act of incorporation had been signed, the search was set afoot.[17] The great difficulty, wrote Huntington to Shattuck in February, would be to secure the right man—"a gentleman, a scholar and a Christian," whose daily life "shall be the most effective admonition to the indolent and wayward." Shattuck no doubt agreed with this prescription, as with the judge's priorities. But where was such a one to be found?

A Mr. Riley, headmaster of St. Thomas' Hall at Newburgh, New York, was the first to come under consideration. He appears from this distance in time to have been not a very prepossessing character. "I do not see why a personal interview is necessary," he wrote to Dr. Shattuck, at the same time insisting the school open in May rather than in October as planned, "so as to give me *personally* something to do." Huntington wisely counseled more thorough inquiry, and after a visit to the Newburgh school in March, he reported to Dr. Shattuck that it was "not at all such a one as would suit you or in which you would for a moment think of placing a son." Such a school, he added, "is more productive of evil than good." That was the end of Mr. Riley. Indeed, he withdrew on the spot, saying he would not consider giving himself exclusively to teaching and that he would demand a fixed salary.

So the winter passed without a rector in view. In Millville, the Shattucks' farmer and his wife, William and Lydia Peters, carried on their work as if unaware of the approaching new order of things. "I have got in the coal for the furnice [sic]," wrote William. "I have all your summer wood carried over near the kitchen and piled to season." The last of the turkeys would be sent to Boston for Easter. But he was sorry to add that Master George's rabbits were all dead—"and I cannot imagine what the matter was with them."

In May the trustees turned their thoughts to C. H. Seymour, headmaster of the school in West Hartford which the young George was attending. Here, too, the prospects were far from encouraging. Seymour was under pressure of financial and family matters; and he was not, at best, a very efficient man. Letters regarding the new term he had entrusted to an omnibus driver who neglected to mail them; "and this has caused much delay in the opening of my school," he wrote rather pathetically to Dr. Shattuck. Huntington had two sons in Seymour's school, and he expressed himself as being quite uneasy. "I fear that Mr. Seymour fails most in attaching the boys to him *personally,* that he feels it easier to rule through fear than love." Meanwhile young George was having an altercation with the headmaster, the result of "a frolic" the boys had begun after swimming.

All in all, the signs were not propitious. It seemed well to look to the church in addition to the schools. A clergyman being interviewed was judged by Bishop Chase not to have "the preaching arts and gifts"; he lacked "a certain mellowness and pliancy." Another was an elegant preacher, but outside the pulpit was considered to have "a yawning, sleepy way—he wants life and animation of character." The church, Bishop Chase was ready to conclude, possessed its share of "drones, hypochondriacs and eccentric persons." By now Judge Huntington was growing impatient. Chase, for his part, began to fear that "the providence of God will not soon turn up just the very man we want." Resignedly, he wrote Shattuck in July: "I am thinking Seymour will be our man."

But the good bishop soon had a different view. Seymour, he concluded, was boorish in his manners. "Now he ought to mend his manners in any case, whether he engages in our work or not." But in Bangor,

Maine, known to Chase's son, resided a schoolmaster by the name of Roger S. Howard whose manners, apparently, were not boorish at all. "Now Mr. Howard has the appearance of a gentleman in all respects. . . . I am strongly impressed with the notion, that he may be the very man for us."

Whether there were further inquiries is not clear, but at the trustees meeting on September 5, Mr. Howard was elected rector. A few days later, the Reverend Newton E. Marble of St. Paul's Church in Concord made a trip to Bangor, spending forty-eight hours with the rector-elect. At the end Mr. Howard was prepared neither to accept nor decline. He appeared, reported Marble, "to have a self-distrust amounting almost to an infirmity." He was also subject to fits of despondency. In a letter of September 19, Howard declined the appointment. "Well—it is as it is," wrote Bishop Chase to Shattuck; and then, in an historic understatement, "It may all be for the best."

Nevertheless, the rebuff was disappointing. The new venture seemed to be foundering before it had even begun. At a trustees meeting in October, there was no quorum; there were no members from "abroad"— i.e., from Boston. Even young George began to be concerned. "Have they thought of a teacher for Millville?" he wrote his father from West Hartford. He had sent off one letter, "but perhaps it went crooked"—a letter, we may presume, which did not carry an enthusiastic endorsement of his own headmaster.

One day that autumn Bishop Chase, making a slight detour upon his rounds, passed down the road through the hamlet at Millville.[18] All was in readiness, and yet all seemed strangely quiet. The ponds were at full height; the grass was green and cropped all around; Peters and his men were busy digging potatoes. But the great mansion, where the sound of boys' cries should have been echoing by this time, stood with its blinds closed, brooding in solitude.

The Young Henry Coit

Early in October, the name of Henry Coit entered the discussions, apparently brought up by Dr. Shattuck. Upon hearing the name, wrote Bishop Chase, "it struck me he must be too young, that he would hardly have experience and weight of character equal to the dimensions of so important a post." Coit was in fact just twenty-six, and had shown little in the way of conventional achievements. But he had been, as we have seen, a pupil of Dr. Muhlenberg's, and he had gone on to spend a term under Dr. Kerfoot at St. James College. Shattuck had undoubtedly received favorable words from these two mentors. Now the irrepressible Bishop Chase had another of his sudden illuminations. He would write Joseph Howland Coit, the young man's father, with whom he had an acquaintance. "He is a plain, honest, downright, jolly man and will, I think, give an impartial expression."

By this time even Chase showed some signs of apprehension: "O how I wish we might be heaven-directed in this choice." Little did that man of God suspect that amid the flailings of himself and his colleagues, some large force was actually at work. They were on the path of a decision that would ensure—beyond any man's knowing—the success of their undertaking.

At the October meeting the board, again lacking a quorum, formed itself into an executive committee, and from the list of candidates selected the young Coit as rector, subject to the full board's approval. The committee were not exactly enthusiastic, only vouchsafing their belief that, "all things considered," his was the most promising name before them. A letter from Joseph Howland Coit, Sr., received some days later, was helpful only to a limited degree. He spoke with the kindly indulgence of a father upon the merits of his son's character. The lad's "money-gumption," he admitted, had not been tested. Given his common sense, however, his "prudence, economy and strict integrity," the father had no doubt he would succeed in "financeering."

"It struck me he must be too young." *Henry A. Coit just before he became first rector of St. Paul's.*

Doubts of various kinds persisted. Writing to young George Shattuck, Huntington "presumed" that the committee had acted wisely, "doing the best thing that probably could have been done under the circumstances." When the elder Shattuck met Coit for the first time, he was generally pleased, but was struck by the young man's hesitancy of speech, a rather painful groping for the precise word to express his feelings. Chase—optimistic as he almost always was—responded that modesty and self-distrust were not necessarily a sign of poor qualifications. "Quite the contrary," he declared. "I do not like your bold self-assured men, who lay claim to all manner of qualifications, and before whom ordinary and varying judgments have to keep silence." But he still questioned whether so inexperienced a man would find it congenial to run the farm and the mill in addition to running the school—in short, to be the organizer and manager of a considerable community.

To make matters worse, Judge Huntington began to have second thoughts. Was Coit the best man? Was he really known to anyone, and had not disproportionate weight been attached to the father's testimony? "Few men have firmness enough to resist a recommendation, when asked for it by a respectable gentleman," he wrote. The judge still seemed to think the choice would fall in the end on Seymour at West Hartford; the fact that he had two sons at that school, whose removal he would find embarrassing, encouraged him in this opinion.

Matters nevertheless went forward. In November, Coit accepted the provisional appointment. He visited Millville, going over the buildings and discussing possible arrangements with the farmer, William Peters. The latter had some difficulty in accommodating himself to the idea that the place of his kindly master, the great Boston doctor, would be taken by this fledgling, who seemed to have some quite definite ideas of his own. "Going into the cellarway to wash"—as Coit was ready to have the boys do—"it strikes me as not so adviseable . . . sometimes the snow is five and six feet deep around where the door is. . . . You had better bear that in mind yourself, Sir." So wrote Peters sternly to Boston.

Somewhat grudgingly he was prepared to accept the coming of the new school, which now was projected for spring. He was laying in five cords of very fine oak wood—"it is like iron, so hard"; also considerable supplies of food. "I think 7 hundred pounds of pork ought to be enough for the summer . . . and I think very handsome from you." Meanwhile, the snows were coming on fast. The farm's ancient mare, a favorite of the boys in the summer vacations, was hard put to it hauling enough sand to pile around the base of the house. "As quick as myself and old Kate could go," wrote Peters, the vegetables in the cellar were being protected against the frost.

Newton Marble of Concord's Episcopal church talked with the visitor at the same time, being surprised at the sense of authority with which the young man contemplated the work. On several issues, Marble wrote, he had ideas rather different from those expressed by Dr. Shattuck and by some board members.

In great matters there is an impetus which seems to go beyond the designs of men. Such a force was now at work, and despite the doubts, despite the rather haphazard way in which the search had hitherto been conducted, the trustees at a meeting in Boston on January 13, 1856, formally voted to make Henry Augustus Coit the rector of St. Paul's School. He was, as we have noted, in his mid-twenties. He was tall and slender, with an unmistakable elegance in his manner. His feet were invariably clad in long pointed shoes impeccably shined; he looked out on the world through eyes that took in every near detail, yet seemed, like those of a sea captain or an explorer, to be gazing upon a far horizon.

The eldest of eight children, Coit was the descendant of an old Connecticut family. Levi, the grandfather, embodied the practical virtues of his heritage. A prosperous merchant and stockbroker, he emigrated to New York, where his oldest son joined the financier August Belmont in business. But in the youngest son, Joseph Howland, another strain asserted itself. Joseph was the dreamer and the man of God. After attending Princeton Theological Seminary, he was, like Shattuck, converted to Episcopalianism. In Plattsburgh, New York, he served a parish for most of his life. Here Henry Augustus was brought up. The young boy has been glimpsed upon his entrance to Dr. Muhlenberg's school—docile, pious, devoted to his family, already showing a certain natural competence in meeting the problems of life.

From Flushing Institute, Henry Coit went to the University of Pennsylvania, where at the end of his freshman year illness interrupted his courses. A period in the South in the family of the bishop of Georgia was followed by tutoring Greek and Latin at St. James College, where he continued his studies and received his B.A. degree. Preparations for the ministry were made in Philadelphia, and thence the young man proceeded to Lancaster.

This Pennsylvania town was to be the scene of important developments in Coit's life. In Lancaster, he was ordained a deacon; here he began his career by teaching in the parish church; and here, most importantly, he found his bride, Mary Bowman Wheeler, a niece of the rector, Dr. Samuel Bowman.[19] The engagement fixed, Coit left Lancaster and took up missionary work in western New York State. Over the next years he preached and proselytized, establishing several new congregations. It was while he was engaged in this work that St. Paul's called him to its service.

Coit had been briefly a teacher; he had shown himself to be a young man of ambition with a developing sense of authority. Yet little in the first twenty-five years of his life seemed to have prepared him for the task into which he now entered. That Henry Coit should have heeded the call from Concord seems as much a matter of destiny as that the men who searched so long for a rector should have settled their choice upon him. They had shown themselves uncertain in their quest, considering laymen and clergymen, schoolmasters and pastors. They had come perilously close to compromising on a second-rate figure, and, in the case of the self-doubting teacher from Bangor, had placed in another's hand the choice which, if it had gone differently, would almost certainly have doomed their venture to a short life. Yet in the end—or perhaps it should be said at the beginning—all things worked together for good. Henry Augustus Coit turned out to be a great schoolmaster, one of the rare figures who in every generation meets with the unique opportunity that has been prepared for him, growing with the work into someone the world notes. Until his death he would continue to serve St. Paul's, impressing himself so deeply on its life that when he departed it seemed the foundations themselves had been shaken.

Some Remaining Business

Certain pieces of business remained to be concluded before the new school could be said to be fairly under way. Coit, who was promised no salary, asked for $300 to be advanced to him to put the enterprise into full operation, giving assurance that he would repay it within a year. As for any opinions different from those of the trustees, "I do not know," he wrote, "that I have any *set* notions." With modest good sense he proposed that the new institution should be gradually organized, that all details should be put to the test of experience "before we run the risk of petrifying them into an established system." For the founder he had words which in all their long association would never be gainsaid: "I am so poor a hand at expressing my feelings," Coit wrote to Dr. Shattuck, "that I shall not attempt to thank you, my dear Sir, for your very great and considerate kindness."

The main elements of the structure in place, Dr. Shattuck planned to get off for an extended visit abroad. But a gnawing problem beset him. His farmer, William Peters, was drinking to excess. This would be awkward for Coit and could be demoralizing for the students. Besides, his youngest son, Frederick, was to live during his absence with William and his wife Lydia. In this delicate situation the correspondence on William's side is worthy of one of Shakespeare's rustics.[20] "Doctor, you ask me if I have now been in the habbit of taking strong drink," wrote the good man. "I answer no not as a beverage but I have taken at times during the year a little, when I got wet or had a cold." He adds, on second thought, that "in some unguarded hour I may be tempted, but I feel that by the help of God I will be able to perform as a Christian Man all you have mentioned in your letter."

Dr. Shattuck was evidently not satisfied with these assurances, and shortly after took up the matter again. Now William confessed that his bad habit had developed many years before in England, when he worked in a brewery where the best of porter and ales were made. "I therefore always found it hard not to be able to get a little something." But he was resolutely determined to reform. "Doctor," he wrote touchingly, and with a fine command of the King's English, "accept my grateful thanks for the kind way you have spoken to me for my good. If you asked me to do some great thing I would do it, and this I will do through God's grace."

For the young rector, too, there was a final matter to be attended to. On March 27, in the Church of the Epiphany in Philadelphia, he married the girl who had waited for him while he wandered as a missionary around New York's western lands. We have already seen them, a bare seven days later, descending with their pupils into Millville.

Henry Coit was not one to leave any hour unimproved. Frederick Shattuck, who was only nine, was allowed to go fishing upon the group's arrival. But the two older boys were immediately put to work. At a table in the front parlor, the same where the trustees had gathered for their first meeting, George B. Shattuck and Horatio R. Bigelow were assigned compositions, the former on "Adventures of a Lion," the latter on "Strength of Purpose."[21] Upon completion of these tasks, one can imagine them bursting outdoors to examine their new domain. George Shattuck would be showing his companion the scenes with which he had grown familiar over past summers. Behind the mansion, now suddenly transformed into a school house, a rough lawn stretched down to the pond. The lawn seemed to have been made for games; and along the shore turtles and snakes nestled in the reeds and rabbits scampered through the high grasses. On the far side of the road running in front of the big house, the saw mill and grist mill sent forth their steady hum. Near these a rustic arbor, covered with grapevines, promised to form a dark and mysterious retreat.

So the day drew to its close: a simple meal, Mrs. Coit reading aloud (as she would so often in the years to come) and the rector saying evening prayers. All this was on April 3. The psalm appointed for the date included the text, "The lot has fallen unto me in a fair ground; yea, I have a goodly heritage."[22] We can imagine Henry Coit speaking these words in that small gathering, on that first evening of the first day. The tense, vibrant voice, which would become familiar to generations of St. Paul's boys, must have lingered over them, as his small charges yearned for sleep.

PART I

CHAPTER TWO

In Arcadia
1856–1866

The School Under Way

Dr. Shattuck left in March on his European travels. If he had any doubts about the progress of the school at Millville, he was reassured when Bishop Chase reported to him upon a June visit.[1] All was going well. There were now six boys—the "dear fellows" were "as happy as the day is long"; and another six would be arriving shortly. George Shattuck was working at his studies with satisfying diligence; Frederick was prospering in the care of the "worthy dame," Mrs. Peters. The best news, however, was the bishop's favorable impression of Coit. "If I am not greatly deceived," he wrote, "we have reason to rejoice and bless God that our choice fell upon this gentleman." It was hard to believe he had been in charge only two months, so in command was he of all details of the school's business. As for the hesitancy of speech which had disturbed the Shattucks on their first meeting with Coit, that had entirely disappeared. During the day's visit he appeared "animated and fluent . . . and very intelligent."

There was good news, too, about Mrs. Coit. "The lady, I judge, is in no way behind the rector in qualifications." Mrs. Peters had been impressed by how much she knew about housekeeping. And no less a doubter than Judge Huntington was ready to admit that things were turning out rather well.

With the founder away and the trustees dispersed and relaxed, the good ship St. Paul's could now be said to be fairly launched. A few matters from the founding period remain, however, to be disposed of. The little dog, a passenger among the first arrivals, was swept downstairs by a hasty servant and died soon after school began. Old Kate, so quick and ready when need arose, and so gentle when Frederick rode her bareback, died of advanced age, "very much lamented by those who knew her." She was buried in the woods with due respect for her many years. William Peters passed away soon after.[2] He had known the end was near. The

21

Saturday before his death, Coit wrote to Dr. Shattuck, he received Holy
Communion, and seemed truly penitent of the past. The rector could be
forgiving, knowing the circumstances that had played upon the old
farmer's weakness, and having formed a working accommodation with
this relic of a departed order at Millville.

The Household

The school's opening years saw a pattern set in studies, in worship, in
sports and ceremonies that was to mark all its future development. With a
sure hand Coit grasped the essentials of education and community life; he
set precedents which a hundred years later would still be a force. The
demise of Round Hill and Flushing Institute, and soon the tragic end of St.
James College, cast a shadow of mortality over the infant school. The
permanence of the experiment at Millville could never be taken for
granted; yet Coit seems not to have doubted but that he was building
toward a distant future. At the first celebration of the feast of the school's
patron saint, less than two years after the founding, among the declamations was one presenting "a nice epitome of the *history* of the school."[3]
Significant, too, was the fact that from the year 1856 into the first decade
of the twentieth century, a record of school life, of its festivals, events,
visitors and weathers, was kept daily in large leather-bound volumes for
the benefit of after-times. All things might fail, as the grass withered and
the flowers faded; but St. Paul's would not fail for lack of a powerful sense
of mission.

Fifty years later John Jay Chapman, the reformer and classicist,
caught the sense of fragility in these beginnings. "When I think of that
passionate fountain of life," he wrote,[4] "rising and bubbling in the remote
New Hampshire wilderness, in a solitude as complete as that of Abraham
on the plains of Mamre, I cannot but be moved. Here was faith indeed!—a
project all aim and no means."

Certainly, the opening years show modest means—essentially a
Christian household: "a farmhouse, a family group, and the intense soul
of the doctor." All dwelt together under one roof, studied there, prayed
there, and in the hours of relaxation supplied their own entertainment by
reading aloud, playing charades or giving simple musical performances.
This was the pastoral period, before the school expanded to take over the
surrounding village, before the work was divided among many hands and
the students were scattered into a neighborhood of dormitories. At first
Coit was alone as pastor, father, teacher. Before the first masters arrived,
he set the example of "toiling terribly." He dreamed, wrote one old boy
looking back in his imagination upon this period,[5] but he also worked.

The confidante of boys, and hostess to a stream of visitors. *Mrs. Henry A. Coit in her middle years.*

"He taught, he advised, he presided, he fulfilled a hundred appointments during the day—and he left the rest to the hand of God."

He left it, also, to Mrs. Coit. The young bride took to this life as one born to it. She became quickly the manager of the growing household, the confidante of boys, and hostess to a stream of visitors. She did all the marketing, and her surviving cookbook[6]—including recipes for turtle bean soup, wheat and Indian bread, apple pudding, Federal cake and sugar gingerbread—indicates that she was not sparing of either the hearty or the succulent dish. When illness cast its shadow over the boys, she watched with her husband at the bedside.

We must think of the young Coits as being not only in the first flush of a new enterprise, but young and in love. George Shattuck, Jr., many years later marveled that these newlyweds could have suffered with so much patience the interruptions and demands of their charges.[7] Mary Coit teased and bossed her husband. "She talks to him as if he were a little boy and was hardly able to take care of himself," the observant youngster had noted. Accustomed to the carefully groomed Boston ladies of his acquaintance, George was startled by Mary's youthful, windblown appearance. "As for her features," he wrote, "she looks as if she had stood out in the rain about six months without any bonnet on." She talked to everyone, he added, "in a most motherly way."

For the students of the time there was a strict regimen. The rising bell rang at five; breakfast, preceded by prayers, followed at six. Studies ran from seven until one thirty, when "dinner" was served, after which the boys were free until tea at six thirty. Study and a conversation period brought them to the bedtime hour of nine. The long afternoon, set between work and prayers, gave them time for the informal games of that period, for hunting in the woods and exploring the wide domain surrounding them. The terms were long. At the beginning there was but one brief vacation in the late autumn, and the school was in session through the summer. But holidays came frequently and often unexpectedly—to celebrate good weather, to mark some national or local event, or to satisfy a request of the bishop.

Dr. Shattuck often visited the school, as the trustees had formally empowered him to do. Even in winter his sturdy figure could be seen going on foot from the railway depot to Millville. His good sense, his salty wit and his stories of the great world made his comings an event for the boys. Often accompanying him would be his daughter Emily, whose tales of the strange and the supernatural, related in the dim parlor after supper, sent the younger boys creeping off terrified to their beds. For the first summers, the Shattucks took up residence at the Shute cottage. The oak table, around which the trustees had first gathered, would be removed from the front hall of the school house and restored for the season to its former owners.

The immediate environment confronting the students in their daily rounds, the rooms that bounded studies and prayers, mealtimes and rec-

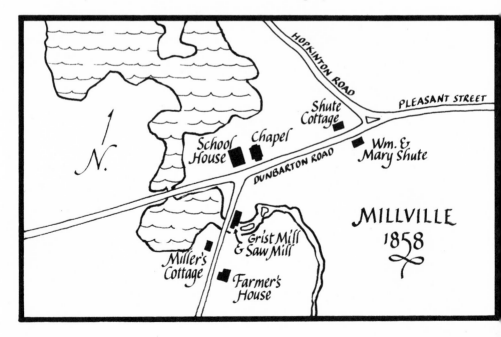

reation, lay behind a facade foursquare and darkly painted. Indeed, the whole building must have been gloomy within as it was certainly forbidding without.[8] To the right on entering was the study room; to the left the parlor, where visitors were received and Mrs. Coit would often be found. The dining room at the back of the long entrance hall was somber, with windows giving no access to the view. Here the household gathered, with the rector and Mrs. Coit sitting at one end of the central table. At the meal's end the rector rose and bowed in a stately manner, dismissing the boys, who filed out quietly to the common room or study where prayers were said after breakfast and supper.

At the top of the long flight of central stairs was the Coits' apartment, with the rector's book-lined study looking out toward the pond. Around it, and on the upper story, were rooms for the boys, for masters as they were gradually recruited, and an infirmary. In the cellar was the lavatory and the space where the boys daily blacked their boots.[9] The building was to undergo almost constant alterations and extensions; but the scene as drawn here represents it in its earliest stage, when it still kept the character of a private residence.

Within the various public rooms, art works appropriate to inspiring young scholars adorned the walls—engravings and photographs of the Bridge of Sighs, the Ca' d'Oro, the Duomo, the Leaning Tower of Pisa, the Laocoön, the Sistine Chapel, and Lord Strafford on his way to execution. The school motto, early chosen by Coit, hung in illuminated lettering over the master's desk in the study hall: *Ea discamus in terris, quorum scientia perseveret in coelis.*[*][10] Shelves containing books, and a cabinet with natural curiosities, were also placed in the schoolroom.

In the cupola of the building hung the school bell. It had once called the nuns to their worship in a Spanish convent and had stood for some years in a Boston railway station. From this latter degradation Dr. Shattuck rescued it, had it recast, and presented it to the school in 1858. It bore on one side the monitory inscription:

> *Tempus fugit*
> *Ars cogit*
> *Dulce ludendum*
> *Vita decrescit*
> *Futura instant.*[*]

---

*Let us learn those things here on earth, the knowledge whereof will continue into the heavens.

*Time flies/Art spurs us on/We must play sweetly/Life ebbs/While future events press upon us.

Farmers as distant as Bow[11] claimed to hear the bell's peals as in fair weather and foul it urged the schoolboys to hasten their tardy steps. A young victim of its tyranny confessed to wishing it "anywhere but where it is," on being awakened at dawn by its ringing or, on some Saturday afternoon in the midst of a pleasant walk, being faintly overtaken by its rude sound. But the bell had a more musical tone on other occasions. How welcome its annunciation of noonday at the end of a morning's laborious study! And how sweetly at 4 a.m. on the day vacation was to begin did it rouse the young scholars! "There are then no imprecations on the bell," our young scribe concludes,[12] "no wishing it in Dixie, but it is received by all as a jolly sound, and all previous faults are lost sight of in this good act."

For those who attended the school in the first decade, it was easy to see the days through a film of sentiment. There was a force working at once potent and touching. "The ideal, if the Lord prospered its growth, had really no earthly counterpart. It was the vision of an almost perfect home, where old and young, masters and scholars, should dwell together in entire confidence and affection." So wrote Joseph Howland Coit, Jr., the rector's brother, in 1897.[13] His words came close to what Henry Augustus had been seeking, as he labored in his youth "when the evil days come not."

Concord and Its Environs

The school, as had been noted by Bishop Chase, was ideally situated— two miles east of where Concord lay at a bend in the Merrimack River. In 1815, this river had been made navigable by a system of locks and canals, providing a water route to Boston, eighty-five miles to the south.[14] The Concord Railway Corporation, chartered in 1815, was to open a new epoch for the city; but when St. Paul's was founded, log rafts and smaller vessels under sail still plied the Merrimack, while cows grazed along its shore, oblivious to the occasional locomotive puffing busily along.

As the state capital, Concord had a quality of its own. Not destined to grow into a thriving manufacturing town like Manchester and Nashua to the south, it was nevertheless the beneficiary of economic activity generated by numerous small mills dotting the banks of the Turkey River,[15] one of the tributaries of the Merrimack. Saw mills, shingle mills and grist mills were still in operation at mid-century; Millville boasted, indeed, that besides converting grain and making lumber, it had once sent penknives to Washington to sharpen the quill pens used in Congress. The local millers at the center of these small-scale activities—wise men like Woodbury Flanders at Millville, who knew their neighbors' business as well as their own—were the kind of citizens Concord liked to consider typical. It was

At the bend of the Merrimack River. *Looking north to Concord and the New Hampshire hills. A painting by Josiah Wolcott, 1847.*

fitting that Concord's contribution to the presidency of the United States should have been the good, solid Franklin Pierce, holding office when St. Paul's was founded.

After the 1850s, many of the mills closed down. Granite quarries, their abandoned ledges one day to form sylvan swimming holes for the St. Paul's boys, provided a new source of employment. On Concord's Main Street was a large coachworks, and various smaller manufacturing plants were developing. It was in merchandising and the providing of services, however, that Concord was to find its prosperity. The focus of its life was trade: the trading of political opinions around the State House and the Eagle Hotel; the trading of goods on Main Street, where the farmers brought in their produce.

Steady work and perseverance counted for more than large ambitions; education for more than natural brilliance. The high school in Concord was established early, in 1857; and the educational experiment at Millville, though always a somewhat alien presence, attracted its share of sightseers, their carriages on a Sunday driving down the dusty road past the school house. It also attracted the friendship and the moral support of some of Concord's leading citizens. Meanwhile the farming population prospered along with the city folk. To lands long cultivated, in the possession of a single family since the Revolutionary War, were added new fields and orchards, the region maintaining a healthy balance between the central town and the outlying areas.

St. Paul's stood at a fork where Pleasant Street, leading westward from Concord, branched out toward Hopkinton on the right and Dunbarton on the left. These two villages, remaining to this day almost unchanged from the nineteenth century, came into an early relationship with the school, their church services conducted by clergymen from St. Paul's and their inns forming agreeable objectives for the students' holiday outings.

More important than such settlements were the natural features of a countryside unusually rich in topographic interest. Southwest of Millville, about one hundred seventy acres in size, lay Turkey Pond, its name derived from its rough similarity in shape to the native bird, with an ample body and bent neck. Dark waters indicated the pond's origin in swamps and shallows, where mysterious tributaries, not to be fully explored by St. Paul's boys until the next century, wandered through dense underbrush. By way of a short stretch of river this pond fed Little Turkey, in the summer seasons of the 1850s a place of "delightful resort" for the local people. In turn this led down by a stream, lazily trickling in a dry season, swift and turbulent after rains, into the two ponds at the heart of the school. This chain of waters formed a source of unfailing adventure for St. Paul's boys over the years, and in the twentieth century was to provide the school with its own rowing course.

Standing apart, some two miles from Millville, was Long Pond, a mile and three quarters in length, half a mile in width, a beautiful sheet of water fed by pure streams from the surrounding hills, clear as crystal and abounding in perch and pickerel. It was said by Concord's historian of the 1850s that in these benign waters no man had ever drowned. "Should the city of Concord," he added, "ever require 'Croton' or 'Cochituate' water, like the smaller cities [sic] of New York and Boston, we cannot doubt it will be supplied by Long Pond."[16] His prophecy was fulfilled, with consequences for the school that will be seen in due course.

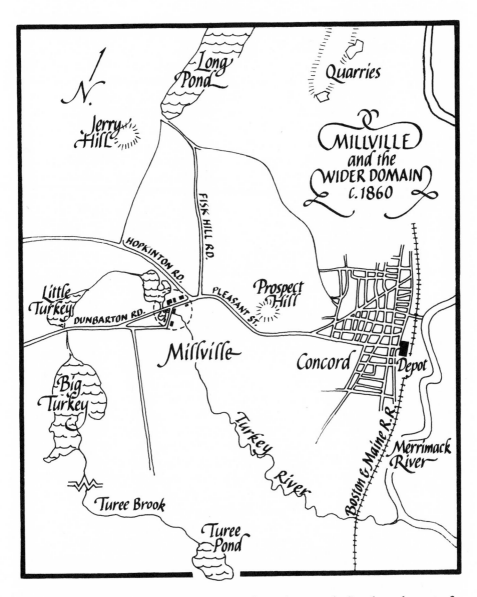

One further topographic feature is to be noted. South and west of Long Pond rose Jerry Hill, so called in honor of Jeremiah Bradley who owned the land. Thickly wooded, it gave to the walker an impression of considerable height; and at its summit it opened to grand views. New Hampshire's Franconia Mountains lay exposed to the northeast, noble Monadnock to the southwest. Man or boy coming home to Millville, at the end of an afternoon by the waters of Long Pond, could by taking a slight detour mount to these exhilarating perspectives; and indeed in all seasons the best of scholars and athletes did, and have been known to do so to this day.

Over this landscape with its works of man and nature played a climate remarkable for its variations and its extremes. It was a climate, the local historian claimed, "favorable to health and longevity." In winter the thermometer would descend not infrequently to twenty-five degrees below zero, and the cold was accompanied by storms leaving the countryside under several feet of snow. Good sleighing could be expected from the middle of December, and often from November, lasting into the middle of March. Spring came late, and then with a burst of fierce beauty as the long-delayed leaves opened almost before a man's eyes. Droughts and floods were accompanied by celestial displays, sometimes of amazing brilliance; and on numerous occasions earthquakes shook the granite hills. Records of the 1870s and 1880s show a half dozen shocks, ranging from mild to severe.[17]

In Concord, William L. Foster, father of a noted St. Paul's vice rector, for forty-one years kept official track of the local weather. At St. Paul's, for almost its entire first fifty years, temperatures taken at three different times of the day were painstakingly recorded for posterity.

Early Times

The winter of 1856–1857 was one of unusual severity and put to the test the hardihood of the new settlers. By December, it was already fifteen below. In January, the temperature descended to minus thirty-seven, a record to stand at least until 1900. Walking on Sunday to the Episcopal church in Concord, the boys—according to the keeper of the *Rural Record*—had from one to sixteen falls apiece on the slippery ice, while one "brave little son of Pennsylvania" froze half his right ear.[18] In the school house the furnace, and a stove kept red hot, did not suffice to make the rooms even tolerably warm. Yet the boys seemed a sturdy lot, and they bore their discomforts uncomplainingly.

Pleasures of a special kind unfolded in such a time. One day the students walked to town to visit the coachworks of Downing and Abbot, established in 1828. Mr. J. S. Abbot's boy was then at the school. Piled high among the vehicles in various stages of completion were the long boards of oak and elm waiting for seasoning; garrets were filled with hubs and whiffle trees. Afterwards Mr. Abbot entertained the boys at his house, and as the chronicler of the day put it, crowned his kind deeds by providing one of his own conveyances to save the weary legs of the boys the walk home. Notable among the afternoon's gleanings was the sight of the skilled artists who made the Concord coaches famous by their scenic decorations. Afterwards the boys' sleds blossomed with their own efforts to rival the masters of Mr. Abbot's shop.

On another occasion the rector offered a sleigh ride to the boys, passing through Concord as far as a little town called Fisherville. In overcoats, shawls, furs and buffalo skins—and with dry feet to start upon the journey (the rector particularly insisted on dry feet)—the students reaped the full pleasure of their excursion. Canterbury was another destination for such a winter ride. Here existed one of the numerous Shaker villages, in that epoch at the height of their prosperity and with a population they were not afterwards able to maintain. Standing at the top of a sharp hill, in a countryside even today devoid of any jarring intrusion, the little community with its neatly laid out white buildings, its shops and enormous barn, offered endless fascination to young visitors.

Best of all was the Shaker hospitality, a table spread with rich abundance happily at odds with the sect's self-denying rule of life. Warmed and well fed, after giving three cheers for the elders and eldresses, and singing the carol "Good King Wenceslas," the group made the return journey, a ten-mile ride to Millville through rural scenes. The boys sang nearly all the way home.

Even that first winter, harsh as was its weather, came to an end. On March 17, Dr. Coit reported seeing the first robin, and soon afterwards the ice began to go out, crashing in large cakes over the miller's dam. Spring and summer brought their own pleasures and rewards. The ponds came to life, a paradise for the hunting of small animals and birds' nests. The densely wooded islands provided shelter for young explorers, who soon had names for every cove and jetty in the larger pond's mysterious configurations. Here was the Gulf of Mexico, the Isthmus of Panama, the Everglades. The arbor by the mill was now rich with the fragrance of the ripened vine. Its deep shade, with only the murmur of the millstream breaking the quiet of a June afternoon, made it a favorite haunt of romantic youth.

Sports during the first decade were largely of a sporadic, informal nature: kicking and throwing balls on the lawn behind the school house or in winter on the ponds, walking, or making expeditions into the surrounding fields and woods. Much time was spent in carefully observing and in gathering natural objects. In close vicinity to the school botanical species abounded. Among minerals, tourmaline and beryl were to be found nearby, and a little farther afield, specimens of silver chalcedony, jasper and iron pyrites. Prizes for the best collections of plants and minerals were offered, and were avidly competed for.

In the earliest years, nevertheless, a more organized form of athletics began to emerge. The field between the school house and the pond was a natural cricket ground. As early as 1857, the Fourth of July was marked by a cricket match. In that same year occurred what perhaps should not be called the first of the school's Race Days (that would wait until 1871), but was certainly an omen. It was like the dumb show in *Hamlet,* foretelling the action of the play in imagery and gesture. Two old flat-bottomed boats, the *Niagara* and the *Water Lily,* were brought out onto the pond, and in these competed the school's chosen crewmen. The day's prize was a bouquet presented by Mrs. Coit. "The boats looked very prettily," commented an observer of that day,[19] "as they left the bridge with flags flying, oarsmen pulling with all their might, and spectators on the shore cheering them on." The race was followed by the inevitable "collation," consisting this time of strawberries and cream.

On July 23, 1857, a holiday was set apart to mark the founder's birthday. "Long may the day be celebrated in his honor," exclaimed the recorder. Unfortunately, it stormed that July day, but a week later the planned expedition to Long Pond took place. Every man, woman and child of the household took part, their number being twenty-nine in all. On arrival, the boys immediately set to fishing, with young Albert Bigelow taking fifty-two perch and sunfish in about twice as many minutes. These made a delicious fry which, along with the sandwiches, crackers and cakes that had been brought, "kept the whole company from suffering the slightest pangs of hunger." There was a sailboat nearby, in which boys put out by detachments; others went a little down the pond to swim. "At four we returned home (on foot, most of us, as we went) having had a most delightful day."

The recorder's wish, that the birthday of the founder be regularly celebrated, was to be fulfilled. The trip to Long Pond was, in effect, the first "Anniversary." Still the chief holiday and major ceremony of the St. Paul's year, Anniversary was to have its date changed when the long summer vacation was established. But in June every year, in war and peace, the birthday of Dr. Shattuck has been a time of sports and holidays, kept faithfully even after its origins had been lost from mind.

Term drew to its close in October. Dr. and Mrs. Shattuck had returned from abroad and made their first visit to the school for the closing exercises. A cricket match was canceled because of bad weather, but in the study that evening several boys offered declamations; a group enacted the judgment scene from *The Merchant of Venice,* and the rector awarded scholastic honors. A silver medal was presented to the "best boy"—the one who had done the most for the school, "all things considered." It went to a frail lad, diminutive in stature, who had not been among those with the highest grades. Yet the choice was not regretted. "Nothing," it was reported,[20] "could exceed the enthusiasm of the whole school at this announcement." The winner of the medal was named John Hargate. He was to stay on at the school after finishing his studies, becoming the rector's close associate and alter ego. Fifty years later, he died at the school he had never really left. We shall meet him again in these pages.

For the rector, it was a moment of quiet thought. "We hope that no boy goes away from here unimproved," he wrote late that night.[21] "God keep them all from harm. . . . Tomorrow at this time all will be gone and for the next six weeks old walls will re-echo with faint footsteps." The boys walked to the station next day at dawn, and climbed happily aboard the train for home.

A Chapel Is Built

Significantly, the first major act of building was the construction of a chapel. St. Peter's Day, 29 June 1858, marked the laying of its cornerstone. It was such a June day as the poet called "rare" and which New Hampshire now and then provides as an antidote to its unmerciful winter climate. A light breeze was blowing as the temperature rose to eighty degrees at midday. Bishop Chase officiated and a dozen other clergy (beside two or three already at the school) were on hand. From Boston, according to the contemporary account, came "the noble founder and his family," along with an assortment of ladies and gentlemen.[22] Twenty carriages and coaches drove out from Concord to make an assemblage of almost three hundred persons.

Precisely at four thirty the procession started from the school house, the boys singing Psalm 122: "I was glad when they said unto me, we will go into the house of the Lord." Following prayers by the bishop, a stone was placed at the southwest corner of the foundations. Within it was a prayer book, a church almanac, a journal of the New Hampshire convention of 1830 and a small plate bearing the names of the donor, the rector and the bishop. Later there was a collation and a cricket match, and at evening the Boston visitors departed.

Nineteen months later, on St. Paul's Day, the completed building was consecrated. Once more there were visitors, prayers, a light collation; but now it was winter, and after the services most of the company adjourned to the ice, where its older members found enjoyment in being drawn swiftly over the smooth surface on sleds. Bishops and clergy were not neglected by the boys—"dignity for a while forgotten, and heads reverend by years and wisdom growing young again."[23] One bishop was observed attempting three times to leave the ice, but was twice tempted back by invitations for another ride.

The chapel had been set just east of the school house, near enough so that in all weathers the boys could walk easily—and often—from the door of the study hall. The gift of the founder, and the work of the Boston architect George Snell, the chapel at first formed a simple rectangle of brick. With the later addition of transepts it still stands, a lone survivor among buildings of that earliest period, a reminder of simpler days and ways. The weathervane and the hinges of the doors bear Dr. Shattuck's initials. Several of the windows are memorials to members of his family and friends. From the old Church of the Advent came the silver candlesticks for its altar.

The building of the chapel was an act of faith, visible affirmation that the little school intended to endure and to grow. It also marked an important period of development within the life of the school. No longer the cold and slippery walks to Concord over winter's ice; no longer the sense of the school's being an outpost, and Millville a congeries of unrelated structures. The cupola pointing symbolically toward heaven (it was placed, unfortunately, too close to the massive school house to permit it to dominate the physical scene) indicated that here was a true community with its ideal as well as its practical aspects. In the early years of the chapel almost as many neighbors as members of the school household were in attendance, the total congregation numbering more than a hundred. At the first Confirmation service in the chapel, Dr. Shattuck's eldest son George was confirmed, along with Woodbury Flanders, the neighborhood's farmer and miller.

The school's essential character was also strengthened. "A good school," said Coit roundly, "is a Christian school," and he was determined to make St. Paul's so, outwardly as well as inwardly. The daily morning and evening prayers were now supplemented by impressive services on Sundays and saints' days, and the festivals of the Christian year found an appropriate and beautiful setting. Judging St. Paul's by the austerity of its daily regimen, some were inclined to call it a Puritan institution. But this was to misread the nature of its worship. Shattuck, a convert to Episcopalianism, was a moving spirit of Boston's Church of the Advent; Coit had absorbed as a boy the aesthetic ritual of Muhlenberg's services. The church of the Puritans had held chanting, wreaths and Easter flowers to be anathema. "Who dared chime the bells?" recalled one of the new breed of churchmen.[24] "How few had organs! We sat when we sang and wore no surplices over the plain black gowns."

The chapel services at St. Paul's, by contrast, appealed from the beginning to the boys' feeling for music and color, to their instinctive enjoyment of ceremony; and they kept the worshipers awake by the various responses required of them. At Christmas and at Easter the chapel would be verdant with wreaths and garlands set in place by the students during long evenings of preparation.

Within this setting, the rector impressed himself on the community in ways for which household prayers had not provided scope. The building, then and in its later expanded form, was perfectly suited to his voice, vibrant and with a subdued intensity; and his form, as he walked slowly to the pulpit or the lectern, stamped itself upon the flock in a dominating and unforgettable image. Masters, as their number increased, included a majority of clergymen, whose prayers and sermons were events in themselves, adding to the topics of the day's conversation and provoking commentaries not invariably solemn or respectful.

The school's religious life had a less attractive side in the restrictions of its Sunday schedule. Beginning with the earliest days and continuing into the next century, the Sabbath was set apart by prohibitions against reading any but prescribed books, playing any sort of games, and wearing anything but the most formal clothes—including a Sunday hat. All this was in addition to two morning chapel services and a service falling directly athwart the leisure of a Sunday afternoon.

These sabbatarian customs must be judged against the background of the times; they must also be seen in the light of youth's patient and often touching indulgence toward its elders. Dr. Coit comments on one service, evidently of several hours' duration, at which an early master, the son of Bishop Chase, was ordained. At least on this occasion there was the satisfaction of a morning ride to Hopkinton. The September day was bright and fair. "The fresh invigorating air," wrote the rector,[25] "the green verdure upon hill and valley, the trees laden with fruit, all tended to lift the thoughts to Him who crowned the year with goodness." Then came the ordination service. Even the rector had to admit that it was long. But the boys, he wrote, were "much interested and evidently impressed"; none of them seemed wearied, and they received the commendation of the bishop on their behavior.

On the return to Millville, the boys nevertheless gathered as usual for the afternoon service.

Traditions and Institutions

A society with its recurring events was in the making through these early years. It is surprising how many "firsts" were being established as the school started upon a period of steady expansion. Coit had a sure instinct for tradition, insight into what would seem significant to the boys, and a lively remembrance of practices at Flushing Institute and St. James. He was still a very young man. The sterner aspects of his nature were shot through with gleams of sympathy and imagination. If he could not bring himself to enjoy—or to admit that he enjoyed—the lighter distractions of daily life, he could nevertheless create with much care the conditions that brought enjoyment to others.

The Christmas celebration of 1861 suggests the spirit of the school at this time and was to have unexpected consequences for the years ahead. Among the masters was one we have already met indirectly through his comments as keeper of the *Rural Record,* John T. Wheeler, recently graduated from Hobart and then teaching Latin at St. Paul's. It is his account we now follow. From December 18 of that year, work went forward every evening preparing the garlands and wreaths for the chapel. A group of ten boys were detached from the study, with John Hargate in charge of operations at the Shute cottage. Amid steadily falling snow, the trimming of the chapel began on December 23; the arches of its windows were draped and the room adorned with complexly fashioned pendants of evergreen. As the great day neared, a tree was hung with decorations in the front parlor of the school house and carols were practiced.

For Christmas Eve a vigil was determined, with Mr. Wheeler and one of the boys staying up all night. Partly they were recalling in this way a traditional observance; partly they wanted to be sure of getting the school's carolers awake at 4 a.m. Armed with lanterns they went to the Shute cottage, where a blazing fire was lit. Four watches were kept through the night, and long before dawn the little party went down to the school house. Other students were up; Merry Christmases were exchanged in the clear star-lit air, and the old carols sounded forth. There was, according to the recorder, much appreciation expressed from within, and then the carolers went back to their warm beds.

It was on this occasion, in that frosty dawn and among the traditional songs, that *Salve Mater* was first sung. The quaint Latin verses were Mr. Wheeler's Christmas present to St. Paul's.[26] Mr. Wheeler retired in 1872 because of failing health, but a window in the chapel testifies to his contributions in the school's formative period. To this day, when the older St. Paul's graduates get together, drunk or sober they sing *Salve Mater,* moved by its hallowed associations even when they do not understand a word of its Latin.

Anxious to direct some of the enthusiasms of young scholars into durable institutions, the rector in 1860 created the Missionary Society. Elias L. Boudinot was its first president; its motto, *Non nobis sed aliis.* The society was seen as a way of interesting the boys in charitable and religious works. Its progress was dear to the rector, and its officers late in the twentieth century were still among the top leaders of the school. Meetings would be addressed by visiting clergymen, usually fresh from adventures in remote parts of the world. These meetings often held lively interest; and the society was saved from becoming self-righteous or solemn by the methods resorted to in efforts to raise money. Entertainments of various sorts, and especially a highly popular fair at Thanksgiving, gave its membership a chance to make full use of their worldly talents.

One means of raising money, conceived by Dr. Coit, was publication of a school literary magazine. During vacation he broached the venture in a letter to one of the students, Robert Hale Bancroft. "It occurs to me to drop you a line," wrote the rector,[27] "about the occasional paper which you suggested and which seems to me a very feasible plan if properly managed. . . . You will have to help us about a name." Coit suggested *The Launch,* "as it is the first attempt which most of you will make in the high seas of literature, in which some may, I hope, by and by, have many a useful voyage." On second thought he considered the name overly ambitious: "A good caption might be *Horae Scholasticae.* Let me have your opinion." The letter is interesting for showing the tact (and suggesting the tone) in which the young Henry Coit approached the students; and his readiness to seek—or at any rate to seem to seek—their advice.

Horae Scholasticae the new paper became. One of its first editors was a youth from Hartford, Connecticut, Henry Ferguson, who was to play a major role in the school's history. "No board of editors ever undertook their important responsibilities with so light a heart," said one of them later.[28] It was not difficult to seize upon material being produced in the course of things—compositions, translations from the classics, poems and orations delivered on school occasions. Besides, the school generated a certain amount of news, to be recorded in the pages of the new journal. When the first generation of students began to make their way in the world, reports from alumni became a regular feature.

The opening issue contained the account of a cricket match. Among the "pretty catches" was one made by little John Hargate. A batsman referred to as "Dr. Coit" suffered the frustration of being unable to score.[29] Some years later, the editor was to boast that in the pages of the *Horae* were to be found no vulgar advertisements—no haberdashers, no importunate tailors, no sporting goods agencies:[30] "We have from cover to cover simply the *Horae.*" Nevertheless, in that first issue there are curious notices—to the effect, for instance, that anyone bringing "two fresh partridges, crow, whip-poor-will or bank swallow's eggs will receive a compensation." There is also a notice betraying what seems a curious lapse in arithmetic or in business judgment: to wit, "Eggs will be sold at 4 o'clock on Saturdays, at 3 cents apiece, and 15 cents a dozen."

The *Horae* gave opportunity for students of that early generation to record their close observations of the immediate environment. No physical aspect of the Millville scene escaped their attention. Like the school bell that set the pace of their daily round, the lamp that lit their nightly studies or the bench they sat on in the schoolroom provided occasions for descriptive prose. The mill was always an object of fascination, with its turning waterwheels and millstones, its carpenter shop; and in the loft, the strange collection of crippled machinery, one-legged chairs and old iron pieces covered with dust and cobwebs.

The miller's cottage (built in 1845) was even more wonderful. "I think it would be called a cottage," said a young author, one of the few fortunate boys having their room there; "but it is a very peculiar one, being so long for its width."[31] The pigeons of the house were in a very flourishing condition, as they would go to the grist mill nearby to eat all the corn they wanted, "much to the annoyance of the worthy miller." A great many rabbits ran about the house; they could be bought for 37 cents apiece in the wild state—"that is, whoever buys them at that price is expected to catch them." In the miller's cottage, in short, "you will find a specimen of nearly every kind of animal that inhabits this part of the country, both biped and quadruped. No building of our day can be fairly compared with it, unless it may be Barnum's world-renowned museum."

As naturalists, the prose writers of that period excelled. For exactitude and authority it would be hard to surpass the unsigned article on insects in the *Horae* of July 1860. The author warns he will take up only the coleoptera, or beetles, "as the boys seem to think more of them than any other kind." A discussion ensues of the five-spotted tiger beetles, the Stag beetles, the May and Capricorn beetles, as well as several other species. But it is the *Macrodachtylus subspinosus* that especially arouses the author's thirst for vengeance. "He spoils the appearance of the most beautiful flowers, and on that account should be killed whenever met with."

The rector kept an eye on the *Horae,* as he did on everything else, and yet he seems to have sensed shrewdly that a degree of confidence in the young literary aspirants would be rewarded. A later editor tells of bringing the proofs of each issue to Dr. Coit's study, but he merely patted the rolls and proceeded to converse about school matters—"and about my prospects as to college, which in his view were evidently unpromising and gloomy."[32]

Impact of the Civil War

Into this guarded community the outside world rarely penetrated. It was said of Dr. Coit that he thought of the President of the United States and

"I think it would be called a cottage." *The original miller's house.*

The mill was always an object of fascination. *The dam site, with the miller's altered house in the background.*

others in authority only when the Episcopal service required that he pray for them on Sunday.[33] This was, of course, an exaggeration. When the Atlantic cable was laid in August 1858 ("God prospered the work," said the recorder, "and brought the ships safe to land"), he gave the school a half holiday. Messages were exchanged between Queen Victoria and President Buchanan; while, plainly audible at the school, a hundred guns were fired at the State House. In June 1860, ex-President Pierce passed through Millville. The boys gave him three cheers as he went by. He acknowledged the compliment by raising his hat.

More somberly, the school was affected as relations between the North and South deteriorated. Lincoln's election in 1860 was noted by the recorder: "The Lord of heaven and earth alone knows how the trouble will end." For the students the outbreak of hostilities was not, at first, altogether displeasing. Catching the spirit of things, they erected a fort on a large rock in the woods near the school, stocked it with green apples for ammunition, divided into two factions and fought it out. Soon they were practicing military drill, achieving a "tolerable discipline," while the Confederate armies were attacking Fort Sumter in Charleston Harbor.

A drillmaster came out from town to instruct the boys. His departure shortly afterwards brought home the actuality of war. He was an early casualty, for "he fell from the car in passing through New Jersey and was run over."[34] At the school, the flag was lowered to half-mast. The unfortunate drillmaster was not to be the last of the state's casualties. Two years later the 2nd New Hampshire regiment returned to Concord to be received with tributes to its hard-won and well-deserved honors. Of the thousand men who had departed two years before, only ninety-five lived to return.

In the summer of 1861, news came from the first St. Paul's boy serving with the Union troops, Fletcher M. Abbot, son of Concord's hospitable coachmaker. "He thinks," reported the *Rural Record,* "he would hardly be able to sleep in a house, he has been so long sleeping outdoors." A lieutenant young in years, he had volunteered in the cause. Soon the masters became vulnerable to the draft. John Hargate was rejected because of his small stature; another was accepted but, securing a substitute, was exempted for three years. For a while it looked as if Dr. Coit would be drafted, an alarming prospect for the school still dependent for its progress almost wholly on his genius. "All things considered"—as Coit himself liked to say—it was fortunate he was not required to serve.

Within the school a spirit of patriotism took over, imparting a new tone to celebrations that had already become traditional. The first Washington's Birthday in wartime saw the Stars and Stripes raised solemnly to the firing of a single gun. "The ceremony was prolonged and made more memorable by the cheer on cheer which went up for the old flag.'' The evening reception, ''marked by the peculiar interest which attends in these times of trouble,'' was lightened by a reading from *Pickwick* and by several charades.

The ensuing Fourth of July was the occasion for a poem and oration, both outstanding, delivered by two students.[35] The day had dawned fair after a rainy eve; the foliage had taken on a rich green and showers had laid the dust of the road. The breeze was gentle, ''scarcely enough to shake out the folds of our national banner, as it hung proudly from our new flagstaff.'' A cricket match had been played in front of a small tent pitched on the playground to shelter visitors from the summer sun; and then there had been boat races.

Guests and scholars sat down to a good dinner at six thirty. Afterwards, in the schoolroom decorated with bunting, Robert Bancroft, poet of the occasion, delivered verses reflecting upon the fate of nations, not without their moral for the divided and struggling American republic. The philosopher surveys a vast panorama:

> *And while he traces, in the times gone by,*
> *The course of Kingdoms, or of Empires high,*
> *Still is he able to discern in all*
> *The Hand of Wisdom in their rise and fall. . . .*

The orator, J. Louis Stebbins, struck home more directly. He conjured up a broad continent—a civilized and intelligent nation, commanding the respect of the world. ''We are possessed of every species of soil and climate, supplying us, in addition to the necessities of life, with the luxurious products of a southern sun. . . . The waters of two great oceans foam and rage on either side of us; beautiful cities smile on the ocean coast and on the banks of princely rivers, and hills and valleys of exquisite beauty and charming verdure teem with the beneficial supplies of nature.''

Thus the orator continued, with many animadversions upon the future and warnings to avoid the fate of other peoples. His peroration was a plea for the restoration of unity. ''At the tomb of Washington we wept,'' he said, ''and the heart of the nation overflowed with sorrow.'' That young prophet could not foresee the occasion, within a very few years, when St. Paul's, along with the nation, would mourn the death of Lincoln.

The Legacy of St. James

Wartime events that were profoundly to affect the school were occurring far off in Hagerstown, north of Baltimore, in the shelter of the Blue Ridge Mountains. Here in 1842 St. James College had been established, an institution to be linked with the history of St. Paul's. The Civil War would cause its demise, and shortly afterwards would come two men, Joseph Howland Coit and Hall Harrison, who were to play significant roles at the school. In all, eight of the masters found their way sooner or later to Millville, bringing with them the customs, traditions and values of a notable institution.

St. James College was, to begin with, an offspring of the Flushing Institute. Bishop William R. Whittingham, the founder, sought Muhlenberg for its first head; the latter sent to him one of his favorite pupils, the Reverend J. B. Kerfoot. The institution was modeled on the college for advanced students that Muhlenberg had created alongside his school for younger boys at Flushing, and carried over an educational philosophy aimed at developing all the faculties and qualities of young men.

"The notion that education is complex and many-sided," wrote a Kerfoot biographer,[36] "that it is an art requiring not merely the power to teach the use of certain languages or sciences, but also requiring skill, tact, knowledge of the world, generous sympathies with human infirmities, ability and quickness in comprehending the special needs of individuals, genuine literary instincts and enthusiasm, and a high moral and intellectual standard, has only begun to be comprehended in this country." It was comprehended at St. Paul's, Henry Coit having been a young instructor at St. James and Shattuck an admiring visitor. "I am glad," said Bishop Whittingham, when all was over at Hagerstown, "that St. Paul's is to keep the old Jacobean team together."[37]

Most of the students at St. James were southerners, and from the beginning the war had a devastating effect. Enrollment fell from two hundred to forty or fifty, but Kerfoot and his chief lieutenant, Joseph Coit (the next younger brother after Henry), carried on against the odds. Two great battlefields, Antietam and Gettysburg, lay within a few miles of the college; the soldiers of both armies crossed and recrossed its grounds. By 1864, the situation had become critical, and on August 7 of that year the danger was evident. "All that day I had a lurking fear of evil," wrote Joseph Coit.[38] Returning to his study after dinner, he was about to light the lamp when there was a knock at the door. An officer placed him, and simultaneously Dr. Kerfoot, under arrest as prisoners of war. They were made hostages for the Reverend Dr. Boyd of Winchester, allegedly seized by Union troops and cast into a common jail. After a night of wakefulness and prayer, the two were parolled on the understanding they would procure Dr. Boyd's release.

Kerfoot and Coit now started on a forlorn odyssey. At Harpers Ferry they sought in vain an interview with General Sheridan. In Washington, armed with letters from influential friends (including one from Dr. Shattuck), they made daily visits to official agencies. No one could find any record of the arrest or the whereabouts of Dr. Boyd. Finally the two arrived at the White House, sending in their names and letters to President Lincoln. Through the open door they glimpsed the war leader, sitting at his office desk, looking "very haggard and weary." A shabbily dressed janitor came out:[39] "The President says he is too tired to run the machine any longer, and you must call tomorrow."

The next day was a repetition of the former ones—wearisome rounds of official agencies. At one point they glimpsed Lincoln again, walking from the White House to the War Office. The form seemed more than ever angular and ungainly. "He had a great stoop in his shoulders," Coit remembered. That night there was again a loud knock at the door. An orderly delivered the message that Dr. Boyd had been found and freed, and the two were released from their parole. The friends met next morning; they reminisced sadly about their past life at St. James and with a handshake went their separate ways. Kerfoot (once more the beneficiary of Dr. Shattuck's friendship) would go on to become president of Trinity College in Hartford and later a bishop. Coit became vice rector at St. Paul's for thirty years, and ultimately succeeded his brother as rector.

April 10, 1865, when peace came, saw drizzle and wet snow all day in Concord. Bells rang out and at the school bunting was liberally displayed. Unfortunately the flagpole was inoperative because of a broken rope, but a banner was strung across the road; another floated from the school house cupola. The various owners of guns were mustered and they fired several rounds. A procession marched around the outside bounds of the school, pausing for occasional cheers.

A few days later, on the morrow of Good Friday, came the news of Lincoln's assassination. "We paid a slight tribute to the deceased," wrote the recorder, "by placing a draped flag over the door of the chapel." He described the scene at the state capital, noting a public behavior which seems characteristic of all national crises. Standing at various parts of the broad main street were "knots of terrified and appalled citizens, seeking to learn the details of the terrible truth." On April 18, rites for the fallen President were held simultaneously across the country, at the same hour as in Washington, D.C. Dr. Kerfoot arrived with Dr. Shattuck at Millville, the two having come on foot from the depot.[40]

A first former's letter conveys the remaining events of that day: "We had additional drapery on the house and at ten we marched into Concord and went to the episcopal church where there were six ministers, and after the service there was to be a great procession of all the congregations to march up to the State House where the governor was to make a speech, and we went as far as the State House where we left and walked home."[41]

The road back to Millville was very dusty. The succession of excitements had fatigued everyone, and all were grateful to retire early.

At the End of an Epoch

Over the small community came the inevitable sense that the days of beginning, the pastoral age of high hopes and slender means, were coming to a close. A school more than most institutions is subject to constant change; for a generation of students is brief, and passes like a watch in the night. By 1862, Coit was writing to Dr. Shattuck, "I miss the old faces, few of which are left now." The newcomers were—or to the rector seemed to be—younger and less mature than those who had forged with him the first stages of the undertaking. "There is a certain sadness to me in all this, but I hope to work as earnestly for these, and perhaps more wisely."[42]

That same year the rector began to feel that financially the enterprise was on an even keel. "Owing to your past kindness and liberality," he wrote the founder in February, "the school, I think, will require no more pecuniary aid." Coit added the hope that, as time went on, Dr. Shattuck's interest would not diminish. "The work will always owe much the larger part of any success it may have to you."[43] Of course the school *would* require more pecuniary help, and Dr. Shattuck would respond as in the past; but in the mind of the rector, at least, a turning point was at hand. St. Paul's was growing up and learning to spread its wings.

Coit, too, was growing. No longer the obscure and inarticulate young man on whom the first trustees had gambled, he was beginning to be recognized as an individual of weight. In 1865 he was made doctor, *honoris causa,* by Columbia, giving him reason to be known to subsequent St. Paul's generations simply as "the doctor." When two years later he was elected president of Hartford's Trinity College, it gave the trustees pause.[44] "I hope he takes it," wrote Bishop Kerfoot to his old friend Muhlenberg. But Coit knew where his work lay, and the trustees acknowledged his decision to remain at St. Paul's with a handsome tribute addressed: "Reverend and dear Sir." "On our part we assure you," they said, "that we along with all the friends of the school, support an obligation to do our best that your situation is made as favorable as possible for the application of your powers and influence."[45]

Within the school family was being nurtured the earliest of the notable alumni masters who were to play so large a part in St. Paul's development. Among the students in the 1860s was James C. Knox, already skilled at playing the organ and piano, a champion cricketer and bowler, and adept at graceful curves and figures on the ice. He won the school medal and the prize for the best all-round athlete. At his graduation, the recorder noted that "much time was spent after breakfast in saying good bye to Jimmy Knox." On another occasion it was reported that the prize for declamation—a fine copy of *Ivanhoe*—went to a lad by the name of Augustus Swift, because of his youthfulness as well as the excellence of his performance. These two were to become outstanding faculty members.

But that was still a few years in the future. During the first decade the faculty included John T. Wheeler, whom we have met; the Reverend Thomas C. Valpey, whose name was to live in an annual award but who was in his time an unreconstructed pedant; and John Hargate. The last, despite his many virtues, was hardly an intellectual light. There now arrived Joseph H. Coit and Hall Harrison, refugees from the ill-fated St. James. These were figures of a different caliber and their coming marked a new epoch in the school. Scholars and men of the world, trained in the fires of a unique educational experiment, they were the first to set up spheres of interest not wholly subordinate to the rector's (yet completely loyal to his rule); and to implant their own interests in the receptive minds of students.

A Virginian, Hall Harrison remained faithful to the Confederacy's lost cause. Even his dog responded dismally to Lincoln's name, and from the school library, to which he otherwise contributed so much, he barred *Uncle Tom's Cabin*. With dark beard and eyes, he was known for his quick wit and social charm. To his teaching he brought gifts of temperament and style such as invariably intrigue the young, and to which the best students respond with delight.

"Tolerant up to a point," writes the historian Arthur Stanwood Pier, "if there was too much laughter or conversation in class, he would spring to his feet, slam his book on the table, and denounce the offender furiously." The story is told of the student who one day asked Mr. Harrison whether he could go to his alcove. "Yes," he replied with deliberate emphasis. "You can go." The next day the boy was surprised at finding himself reported for being in the dormitory without permission. "You asked if you *could* go, not if you *might*," was Harrison's rejoinder when appealed to by the aggrieved youth.[46]

This was, of course, a kind of play-acting. More significant was Harrison's genuine love of literature, which he encouraged his young students to share. He was a graceful writer, and as a conversationalist drew the boys into discussions where even the more mature would not ordinarily venture. In the 1880s he responded to a call to a parish in Maryland, and his departure was much regretted by the whole school community.

The Reverend Joseph Howland Coit was of another temperament and aspect. Easygoing, deliberate in speech, he searched a well-stocked mind for the exact phrase and telling fact, in the end appearing to have experienced all things and to hold well-considered opinions upon them. When no more than a boy, he had seen on his father's table a catalogue of St. James College. Immediately he had formed a strong desire to attend. The prospect of life in a large community of companions and equals attracted the spirited lad, and he engaged directly in a correspondence with Dr. Kerfoot. His father complying, he entered the college at the grammar school level, the youngest and smallest of his class. After graduation he spent two years in Paris, studying at the Sorbonne under the noted chemist Chevreul. A boarder in the home of a lady of the Old Régime, he met at her salons on Sunday afternoons the leading artistic and literary figures of the Parisian scene.

The man who in 1865 came to St. Paul's was mature and genial, more worldly than his brother and able to reach certain students out of the range of Henry's fervent spirit. Years later an old boy recalled bidding farewell to his father at the lower school and trotting down the boardwalk past the school house, until he reached the bridge separating the two ponds. There he sat down and contemplated the water: "If the truth be told," he wrote, "I wept." He had been there for some time when looking up he saw an open, sunburnt face looking down at him. It was Joseph Coit, the vice rector. The man spoke to him "in the easiest, most matter-of-fact tones," calling his attention to a good-sized pickerel that hung motionless in the shadow under the bridge. By this encounter one lad was saved from the worst pangs of separation.[47]

In 1864 the opening of term was delayed two weeks to allow completion of major enlargements to the school building. Students returned in late September to find the grounds ditched where new utility lines had been laid. Piles of lumber and bricks stood around, and the sound of the carpenters' hammers rang through the building. Almost every room in the old place had been altered; a new study, a new dining room and reading room waited to be put to use. The form of the structure, once a square, had in early changes become an "L." It how harbored a sizeable quadrangle within its many extensions.

All this was a sign of progress; but in a community which still kept vividly the sense of its origins, and where traditions were strong, such changes could not but bring a tinge of regret. The keeper of the *Rural Record* may have spoken more sentimentally than most, yet he was expressing a common mood when the customary evening celebrations and

Mature and genial when he came
to St. Paul's. *Joseph H. Coit,
probably in the 1870s.*

partings of the term's end were held for the last time in the old schoolroom. It had long been the center of daily life, he wrote, "the scene of the
dramas of many treasured years . . . a place endeared by the sorrows as
well as the joys it has witnessed."

A few more years and the chapel, too, took on a changed aspect. In
1868, again through the founder's generosity, the little building was quite
literally cut in two. Its northern end was moved toward the pond and a
transept inserted. That a brick structure could be maneuvered in this way
startled the inhabitants of Millville. It was said to be "an excellent instance of the power gained by scientific management of mechanical principles and appliances." The rector may have observed that it was an instance, too, of the workings of a watchful providence.

The end of the school's first decade brought reminders of change in
the grim forms of illness and death. Dr. Coit's father, who had visited the
school on several occasions and had a chance to observe his son's success
in "financeering"—as well as in other spheres—died in 1868 at the age of
sixty. A year earlier death had struck nearer home, signifying, as it were,
the end of innocence, the passing of the Arcadian days. The little com-

munity had borne the harsh winters and the cold indoors (the new schoolroom proved particularly difficult to heat) without grave sicknesses. But
in February 1867, pneumonia took hold.

In Dr. A. H. Crosby, the school had an excellent physician, but it had
no infirmary and no trained nurses. Night after night the rector and Mrs.
Coit sat up with the sick boys. Masters, themselves often sick, took turns
at keeping the vigil and administering medicines; and Dr. Shattuck came
down several times from Boston. The rector's oldest son Charles, then
seven, was among those whose life was feared for. "The weight of anxiety
upon the head of this household, with the exhausting and wearing suspense
and watching night and day cannot be estimated," wrote Mr. Wheeler.

On March 12 the long-feared blow struck. Tolling of the school bell
announced the death at noon of Louis Fouquet Miller. To appreciate the
sense of affliction that fell upon the school one must remember its close
intimacy, its isolation from the outside world, and the deep religious sense
pervading it. Death for the first time had struck at its heart, in the cham-
bers where all lived and worked. The young body was guarded in the
school house through the somber afternoon and at evening borne to the
chapel. After the funeral next day the boys followed the hearse into town
and saw the body placed upon the train for the journey home.

The anxieties and the physical exertions of this time, coming on top
of long years of unremitting toil, seriously affected Dr. Coit. He fell ill that
spring and was absent from the school for a month. The next school year
he pursued his duties intermittently. He needed a rest; the fact that he
could be persuaded to take one shows the degree to which St. Paul's had
become a stable institution. His brother Joseph was now vice rector, and
could be effectively in charge during a long absence of the head. A corps
of masters carried on their work in a pattern that had become accepted
and traditional.

The Coits sailed for Europe in May, not returning until the following
January. In Edinburgh during the summer a daughter, Mary, was born.
Dr. Coit visited English schools, including Rugby and Westminster,
stayed briefly in London and, with his family safely settled in England,
traveled with members of Mrs. Coit's family to Italy. On their return to
the United States, the Coits received an emotional and heartfelt welcome.
A subscription of $1,150, a large sum for those days and well in excess of
the projected goal, had been raised by boys and masters. A portion of it
was used for the gift of a silver service, specially made for the Coits in
Baltimore; the remainder purchased a new altar for the chapel, the enlargement of which was just then being completed.

As for the arrival at the school of the Coits' infant daughter, "Health
and promise," it was noted, "sat upon her little face."[48]

CHAPTER THREE

Vintage Years
1866–1874

The Household Divides

The new age at St. Paul's was given outward form by the building program of the early 1870s. Hitherto one family in fact and ideal, the school took on a tripartite form that was to characterize it for the next seventy-five years. No declaration of policy heralded the change. Dr. Coit used the old words, still speaking of the "household" even when the student body was physically divided and rather widely separated. More room was needed than with all its additions and rearrangements the old school house could supply; and new physical accommodations were quietly provided.

In fact the changes went to the heart of the school's organization, subtly altering its nature and putting a strain on the system of one-man rule that had largely prevailed up to that time. The process was not only one of growth but of maturing, bringing pains as maturation inevitably does. St. Paul's emerged in the 1870s as a pluralistic society, a small world with its diverse elements kept in balance and reacting upon one another.

A few boys had lived previously outside the school-house walls—in the miller's and the Shute cottages. Now across the Turkey River where it flowed out of the school ponds, in a broad field of its own, an upper school was erected. Built of gray granite blocks, a simple rectangle with small rooms opening off central halls, devoid of any amenities or common spaces, the building might have been judged unappealing. In fact it came to be much esteemed, its isolation giving to the older boys a feeling of superiority. A series of strong figures, beginning with the vice rector, Joseph Coit, were put in charge, contributing to the impression of a separate domain with its own life and style. Two wings had been originally planned, one of them to contain a dining hall. But the structure remained stolidly rectangular until it was torn down in the 1960s. Instead, a new dining hall and kitchen were fashioned from the house where the unhappy William Peters had once lived, and from ramshackle old barns behind it.

In these facilities the sixth form achieved for the first time an identity and a dignity of its own.

The Shute cottage was made into a lower school, harboring eighteen of the younger boys, while the old school house remained the residence of an intermediate age group. Thus for the first time each pair of forms had its own building, and each boy his own alcove.

A new hall, to be known as the Big Study, was also constructed, on the Millville street to the east of the chapel, a brick building in a vaguely Tudor style. The windows of the Big Study, as one young scholar observed,[1] were placed ten feet above the floor, "which will effectively prevent anyone from being disturbed by what may be taking place on the outside." This precaution was reinforced at the dedication, when it was prayed that all "evil spirits" might be driven from the place. Finally, and perhaps symbolically the most important of these changes, a rectory was built. The Coits moved from the close intimacy in which they had lived with boys and masters during the early years, to establish a center of their own within the enlarged framework of the school. The rectory, soon to undergo successive additions, stood directly across the street from the study hall, where the rector now had his office.

Old Boys and Orphans

A new element in the school's life, one to become powerful and even dominant in the years ahead, began to manifest itself in the form of an organized alumni body. Former students had from the beginning been subject to the rector's special solicitude. At the first St. Paul's Day celebration in 1858, he established the custom of reading communications from old boys. He followed their careers with hope, if not always with approval.[2] The *Rural Record* regularly noted the return of alumni from business or college as important events in school life.

In the 1860s alumni were few, and were at too early a stage in their careers to be expected to give practical aid to the school. But after the dedication of the new study building, a group of them who had come back for the occasion met in the rector's study and established an association. The immediate objective was to strengthen bonds between themselves and to keep fresh the memories of what the rector called "their boyhood home." They returned, after that eventful day, to the places where they studied or made their living; but at future anniversaries old boys would regularly hold meetings, enlivened by long poems and addresses. They would soon be raising substantial sums of money for a new chapel, and by 1906 would be sufficiently strong to offer a serious challenge to the authority of the rector and the board of trustees.

It came to be much esteemed. *The upper school in its original setting.*

It was prayed that all evil spirits might be driven from the place. *The new study building, before additions.*

A further element in the development of St. Paul's from a simple to a complex organization was establishment of the orphans' home. Its original inspiration was twofold. After the Civil War many local children were left destitute and homeless, and Dr. Coit responded to a pressing practical need. But there was a deeper, perhaps partly unconscious motivation. At the model schools in Switzerland studied by the founders of Round Hill, the poor had been educated alongside the rich, separately but in proximity close enough to provide a sobering moral for the more fortunate. At St. Paul's the orphans' home served this purpose, bringing to the students a sympathetic involvement in the lot of the poor, and permitting the community as a whole to bear in some measure the image of an ideal Christian brotherhood.

Established on the Hopkinton road by Dr. Coit in 1866,[3] the home was moved a year later—the orphans journeying in a hayrack under the supervision of the faithful Woodbury Flanders—to a site on the rising ground just west of the school. A new building had been erected where a one-room school house once drew children from the surrounding community of farmers. By the 1870s the home and its charges had become woven into the life and imagination of St. Paul's students:

> *The little orphans, who are they and where*
> *Their origin and home?—O muse, declare!*

So queried a *Horae* poet,[4] and continued with a vivid, if somewhat chilling, description:

> *The mansion stands upon a lofty height*
> *Where all the school may see it day and night . . .*
> *Northward the building faces, and defies*
> *The wint'ry blasts that whistle through the skies;*
> *While from the lofty lookout it commands*
> *A view of Millville and th' adjoining lands.*

St. Paul's boys did not only behold the home from afar. On Sundays the orphans would file into the chapel, "a heterogeneous band of little ones marshalled by two severe-looking women, the whole company stumbling and shuffling into their seats."[5] The students began to take an interest in the group, an attitude condescending at first, but later with some inklings of true charity. A group known as the Shaker Brotherhood, taking names inspired by the settlement at Canterbury—Brother Nehemiah, Brother Hezekiah—began to solicit contributions.

As one of their members recalled later,[6] they were "six friends who wanted some fun in an eccentric way together." Without any serious in-

A dark image of St. Paul's. *The Orphans' Home, c. 1890.*

tention of doing good, or even of raising money, they held a meeting enlivened by comic poems and songs, and then went about the school crying, "Please for a cent for the little orphans!" On the first occasion $1.20 was raised, which was used to buy rubber balls for the children. Later the stakes became higher. "These boys have screwed a dollar out of me for their miserable orphans," a new student of the 1870s complained in a letter to his family.[7]

Activities of the Shaker Brotherhood were expanded over the next years. Donations of various practical kinds—a barrel of flour, a bushel of apples, a pig—were brought to the home annually by the students. The delivery of this fare was an occasion for the upper forms not only to compete in the kinds and amounts of their gifts but to engage in a good deal of physical combat as the rival groups of schoolboys marched up and down the hill. A presentation address would be read to the matron, and if they were lucky, the organizing committee would be invited in and asked to sit down to an appetizing meal.

Members of the faculty were more deeply engaged. Over the years they took responsibility for managing the home and raising funds. Dr. Coit personally looked after the religious life of the orphans, baptized them, and for many years prepared the older ones for Confirmation.

In a strange way the orphans' home was a dark image of St. Paul's: the very poor caught in the same web of circumstances, and under the same moral order, as the very rich. Coit described the home's function as giving to the needy "the elements of a good education, habits of industry, punctuality and obedience, and those principles which are profitable in this world as well as the next."[8] He might have said the same things about the boys in the lower forms at the school. The discipline of the orphanage was that of the school, but in an exaggerated and circumscribed form; the restrictions placed on the inmates were not essentially different from those on the students.

Both institutions went through good and bad days together, knew sickness and death and physical disaster. But in the end, when the one faded because it no longer met the needs of the times, the other reconstituted its inward being, reshaped its methods, and went forward to fresh accomplishments.

Two Outlying Settlements

In the new rectory, Dr. and Mrs. Coit saw visitors come and go as at an inn. For boys it was always an open house. Scarcely a day passed without the rector's bringing home to dinner or tea a homesick boy, or one needing encouragement or guidance. Mrs. Coit held parties for the various forms, the boys coming in after supper, spending the evening with her and with any ladies who might be present, playing games such as "black art," "mesmerism" and "twenty questions." On these occasions the rector would remain in the adjacent study, coming by at the end of the evening merely to look in. Masters and trustees were more formally entertained, while from outside the school came a stream of clergymen, alumni and travelers.

The Coits presided over two societies—that of the world at large, which came increasingly to call upon them as the fame of their work spread; and the little society of their immediate environment. From Concord itself came several special friends: Judge Carter, descendant of the Jacob Carter who had built the original school house; the Abbots, owners of the coachworks; Judge W. L. Foster, father of the future vice rector; and the Reverend James Henry Eames, rector of the Episcopal church, were their special friends. Westward of Millville, down the separate roads which came together at the school, the villages of Dunbarton and Hopkinton fell within the orbit of that day's social life.

Regularly a buggy drawn by a tall, gaunt, dun-colored horse named General would be seen approaching the rectory; in it was Miss Charlotte Stark, coming to make a formal call. Miss Stark hailed from Dunbarton, seven miles to the southwest. To this day the village remains with no more inhabitants than it had a hundred years ago. Its green is almost unchanged and the building still stands in which the innkeeper opened hospitable doors to excursioners by sleigh or wagon from St. Paul's. Standing, too, is the little church of St. John the Evangelist, where Joseph Coit and other masters went on Sundays to conduct the services. The church was exposed to the worst winds of winter and was too far from the center of the village ever to draw a large congregation. Nothing could be done about these inconveniences. The land had been presented by Miss Charlotte Stark and her sister; and there, whatever the practical disadvantages, the church had to be.

Descended from the Revolutionary War hero General Stark, the Misses Stark ruled Dunbarton from their ancient manor house. Their imaginations, the while, inhabited a larger universe. In their youth they had received LaFayette, and they had been devoted admirers of Emperor Napoleon I. The house contained mementoes of the latter—a little bronze statuette, engravings of scenes of his life and battles; and at their door was a willow tree grown from a slip brought from St. Helena. Miss Charlotte lived on after her sister's death, a handsome old lady attended by young nieces, nephews and cousins. Calling at her house for tea, the visitor of the 1870s would be offered "with a tremulous hand her own sponge cake and currant wine"; proposing her health, he would be favored with a curtsey "more worthy of the *Ancien Régime* than of the Empire."[9]

Five miles down the other branch in the road lay Hopkinton, also largely preserved in the 1970s as it existed a hundred .years before. "Those that have never been to Hopkinton," wrote one of the masters, "have missed a great deal. It is deeply to be regretted that Charles Dickens did not visit it when he was in America. The world at large would have been the gainer if that delineator of character chanced to spend a few days there."[10]

Even the students were fascinated by Hopkinton's antiquity and its odd inhabitants. "First you must know that Hopkinton is a very *old* place," wrote one of these in the *Horae*.[11] It was reputed to have been briefly the seat of the state capital, and indeed men and women had once gone there to observe the latest fashions. But the place "soon became too old for political affairs. . . . The young people have all married, and moved with the tide of population to the western cities." Now it was linked to civilization only by a rickety and uncertain stage, leaving once a day from the Concord depot.

The Hopkinton church of St. Andrew's, like Dunbarton's, was served for many years by the school clergy. The rector himself sometimes officiated. One Sunday morning in a winter vacation, after driving through deep drifts and a bitter-cold wind, Dr. Coit arrived at the church door to find it locked. The sexton informed him that he considered it too cold a

day to open the church and build a fire. The occasion was saved by Dr.
Coit's being received, and given refreshments and a warm welcome, in
the handsome house of the Lerned family, diagonally across the street
from the church. This family possessed vivacious and talented members.
Miss Catherine, the elder of the two sisters, was an accomplished musician, the organist at St. Andrew's and an artist who made delicate illuminations on parchment. Miss Lucy seemed to have an acquaintance with
all the modern languages. They and the Coits frequently exchanged visits.
This angered another villager, old Mrs. Chase, who declared that if the
Coits did not call upon her when they called on the Misses Lerned, she
would ring a bell at her front door to remind them of their duty. The
feelings evidently extended to her husband. "I don't want *her* playing the
organ," whispered the dying Mr. Chase into the rector's ear, "when my
corpse is carried up the aisle."[12]

College and the Curriculum

The school session of 1871–1872 saw the arrival of sixty new boys, the
largest number up to that time. Even with the new and remodeled
facilities, the place was more than full. "Some bitter tears may moisten
unseen pillows," mused the recorder; but even the homesickness would
pass, "if kindness and discretion are able to put the spirits of sorrow to
flight." For most of the boys the opening was an exciting time and the
crowded conditions seemed to arouse fresh anticipations. Besides, the
"dear old pond" was brimming with water; after years of drought the mill
pursued busily its wonted round.

There was now no lack of applications for places at the school. Parents rarely, as in the earlier days, had trouble in making up their minds,
or sticking to a decision once reached. From this period date the first
letters appealing for an available place.[13] Dr. J. B. Kerfoot to Dr. Coit: "I
would be very glad to have my nephew under your care. He has no vices
but needs only mental culture. . . . You will find him a pleasant and docile
pupil." From Samuel Seabury, descendant of the first Episcopal bishop
on these shores: "Mrs. James Livingston, a cousin of mine . . . wishes to
put her son under your charge. She has delayed from the natural reluctance of a mother to send her son so far from home." From the rector of
the Church of the Advent in Boston: "My son Edward is a very good boy
. . . and his religious nature is already so settled that I have no doubt
he will choose the ministry for a profession." Another writes about
Robert, a superior scholar who claimed to be already prepared for
Harvard. "I hope better things of him," said the father "—that after a
year with you he may be willing to go to Trinity."

Letters from Edward L. Godkin, editor of the *Nation,* and George William Curtis, editor of *Harper's,* attested to the school's strength among leading intellectuals of the day. And one of Dr. Coit's fellow clergymen supports an applicant on the grounds that his parents are the most liberal donors of his parish. He would "esteem it a personal favor" if the parents could be gratified by the boy's admission.

Some of these letters present obviously eccentric views. The main reason St. Paul's was coming to be a highly desirable school was its success in preparing students for the universities. It will be recalled that in the beginning St. Paul's was not primarily interested in this objective; indeed, of the first seventy graduates all but five went directly into business or upon extended travels. Unlike the academies, whose training was keyed to the low entrance requirements of the colleges in the first half of the century, St. Paul's could take a broader view and prepare scholars of more liberal dispositions. Those who did go to college found the curriculum repetitious and dull in comparison with their work at Millville. A graduate of Round Hill in the 1820s boasted that most of his classmates had been made ready for senior year at college, though the colleges were not disposed to admit it; and St. Paul's students, too—if entrance requirements had been more flexible—would have found their natural level in the advanced classes.

In these conditions—and given the additional reason of Dr. Coit's mistrust of the Unitarian heresies being fostered on the Charles—St. Paul's started out with a detached relationship to the universities. Better for students to face the world, to begin their careers directly, than to waste time in the dull and dangerous backwater of college life.

By the 1870s, however, a change was coming over the university scene, and the attitude of the St. Paul's constituency changed with it. This was the start of a period which saw at the head of universities a new breed of reformers, of whom Charles W. Eliot at Harvard was only the most prominent. At the same time the age level of college students was being progressively raised, so that a Yale class having two-thirds of its seniors sixteen years and under in the 1820s, had two-thirds seventeen or over a half century later.[14] In these circumstances the intellectual standards of the colleges were raised, sterner qualifications applied to admissions, and a spur was laid to the whole field of secondary education. The relationship of the private school and the college was being reversed: it was now the latter that asked for more effective training and proved ready to advance students according to their qualifications.

St. Paul's thus found itself in a favorable position. Its tradition of advanced liberal training put it in the forefront of institutions capable of meeting the new standards. The academies proved slow in adjusting, and the public school system, which one day would provide an important rival, was still in its infancy. The trustees of St. Paul's recognized their opportunity. An 1865 statement welcomed "the advance in requirements for entering the great universities"; it urged comparable advances in secondary education. "It will be to a great extent in the [preparatory] schools hereafter," declared the trustees, "that the foundations of scholarship will be laid."[15]

For their part the colleges were not content to rely wholly on such an example as St. Paul's or to await passively the development of similar schools. They began to take an active role in fostering "feeder" institutions. It was thus that Yale participated in the establishment of Hotchkiss in 1892, and Princeton in the 1893 revival of Lawrenceville.

What was the curriculum, and what the spirit of teaching, that St. Paul's students experienced in the1870s? The school might be becoming a royal road to college; but it remained, as it had always been, a community of traditional learning. Its curriculum was based on the classics and mathematics, and had for a major objective a lucid and expressive use of English both oral and written. The old routines had been brightened by the introduction of courses in history and modern languages, while Latin and English literature provided the students with the stone on which they sharpened their wits. "We were driven back upon the Bible, the Prayer Book and Shakespeare," recalled a student of the early days,[16] "and these, with Vergil and Horace, provided our more or less archaic nourishment." Yet Vergil and Horace—to say nothing of the other great texts—could fire the imagination as well as form the style of young men. An "eclogue in the Vergilian style" from an early *Horae* reminds us that they could answer, also, to the romantic fancies of youth.

> *Ye gentle Muses, may my mournful strain*
> *Bring cruel Phyllis to my arms again . . .*

So sang the young poet,[17] indicating that life and scholarship were not in this period entirely divorced. Had Dr. Coit nodded—or did he show for the desires of youth a more instinctive sympathy than was commonly attributed to him?

French was another subject having intrinsic rewards, but possessing some peculiar complications. "I like French very much indeed," one young scholar advised his father.[18] There was, however, something "very hard to remember"; it was whether "they" were "masculine or femanine [sic] and it is very important to know." The modern languages, after having been taught for a time by instructors brought in from Concord for the task, fell to Mr. Edward Schindelmeisser, who assigned the disorderly boys in his class to what he called "the bad, or naughty bench," with consequences that may be imagined. He was also remembered because of his rule for the pronunciation of the French *u:* "Form your mouth as if you were going to whistle, and say *e*."[19] Though other subjects were remorselessly pursued through all the years, from the lowest form onward, the oldest boys had the option of dropping French. The assumption was that by this time the students had learned all the French that could be taught by Mr. Schindelmeisser; perhaps there was also a suspicion that to advance further in the language would be to enter dangerous waters.

The curriculum of the 1870s appears, at least to the modern eye, distressingly uniform. From the first to the sixth form *English, Latin, Greek, Mathematics, History* alternated grimly with *English, Latin, Mathematics, History, French.* Sacred Studies once a week was also a fixture. With the addition of Science, this curriculum remained largely unchanged for the school's first hundred years. The emphasis within separate courses, however, and the methods of teaching, could be as changeable as the individual genius of the teachers involved. Dr. Coit had set from the beginning an example of lively teaching, passing lightly over difficulties of syntax to get to the meaning of a text. His own translations in the classroom were recalled as being elegant as well as precise, and in advanced courses in Latin and Greek he encouraged his students to similar achievements. Other teachers emulated his example.

If there were drillmasters like Mr. Valpey—it was said of him that although he had great gifts, he lacked the confidence to make others aware of them[20]—there were also teachers who could evoke a sense of pleasant anticipation on entering the classroom. Two of the best of these, as we shall see presently, cast their spell upon St. Paul's in this favorable decade.

Keeping the Peace

Over the activities of the school throughout this period there hung the hand of a heavy and unrelenting discipline. To understand the system, we must recall conditions as they had existed in schools in this country and abroad. What a schoolmaster called "the ebullience of schoolboy impetuosity" was highly developed in the early nineteenth century. In Britain boys were regularly drawn up in battle array against their masters. At Shrewsbury[21] a considerable group, disguised as peasants and foreigners, fled the school, the ringleader writing back that the headmaster was "a paltry and despicable pedant." The boys were fired, but turned up again at the school anyway, and the headmaster, Dr. Butler, applied to the mayor for a constable for his own protection.

The reaction among schoolmasters to such unruly conduct was a heavy reliance on corporal punishment. Dr. Keat, headmaster of Eton, may have provided an extreme example; but it was said he flogged everyone for even the most minor offenses. On one occasion, "by a trifling oversight"—no doubt he was near-sighted as well as absent-minded—he flogged the members of a class that had been brought to him to be prepared for Confirmation.[22]

Nearer home, the St. Paul's trustee Richard Henry Dana, Jr., recalled his own experiences in his school in Cambridgeport, Massachusetts. "Each misdemeanor was written down, and flogging was the punishment for every offense." When the morning's classes came to an end, books were put away, the names of the delinquents called out, the chest unlocked and the long pine ferrule produced. Dana recalled masters "dragging the boys about by their ears and over the benches."[23] Concord's educator, John C. Ordway, reported in 1896 that there had been progress in the discipline of the local public school; but there was still what had been called "a want of subordination . . . a constant tendency, almost uncontrollable, on the part of many pupils of all ages to indulge in mischievous pranks."[24]

Whispering, talking aloud or smothered laughter were endemic in the classroom; while bent pins or steel pen points were regularly placed in the seats of those rare boys who were considered "staid and sober." Worse befell the teachers. If they were found wanting in courage or physical strength, they would be overmastered by the older boys and pitched headlong through the window into a snowbank. Matters were not helped when parents not infrequently were found taking sides with the offenders.

At St. James, generally enlightened though its educational methods were, severe repressive measures were the rule. A multitude of regulations combined with constant supervision harried the students. The system, suggested Joseph Coit as he looked back upon it, made too scant an allowance for the follies of youth, and treated peccadilloes as mortal sins. It seems unlikely that the students of St. James, or later of St. Paul's, were ever upon the threshold of actual rebellion; but they were treated as if, the proverbial inch being given, they would take a mile and more. The example of the great Dr. Arnold was followed in this regard. He ruled Rugby, it was said, as if it were a remote province constantly on the point of mutiny.

One solution was to expel the unruly members. " 'Til a man learns that the first, second and third duty of a schoolmaster is to get rid of unpromising students," said Arnold, "a great public school will never be what it might be, and ought to be."[25] Muhlenberg was scarcely less severe. "I hear you have been packing off lots of boys," he wrote to Kerfoot at St. James; "there is no other way."[26] Coit, like future rectors of the school, faced the problem equivocally. He let boys go, sometimes in anger, more often in sorrow, and always with a sense that he had somehow failed in his pastoral duties. For a church school there was a theological complication lying below the surface. If the community was a little Eden—and there were certainly times when St. Paul's seemed to be that—expulsion bore an uncomfortable resemblance to Adam's lot. Dr. Coit in his most high-and-mighty moments, and Dr. Drury, his successor, who in so many ways resembled him, were never quite ready to play God.

The easier solution was to fall back upon surveillance, and upon regulations scrupulously and continuously enforced. This was true of performance in the classroom as well as of general decorum. Each Saturday afternoon at St. Paul's, just before supper, the marks of every boy in the school were read out in the study hall. From a large roll were intoned the names, in alphabetical order, from the first to the sixth form. Not only the averages were read but marks in each subject, while the rector by meaningful pauses, or piercing glances, indicated his pleasure or displeasure. Marks in punctuality, industry and decorum supplemented those in academic subjects. Delinquents paid for their failures in scholarship or conduct by being assigned Latin lines to be copied out during their free afternoon hours. In addition, after chapel each day the rector would read out "reports," stating the offenders of the day and the punishments meted out to them.

The writing of "sheets"—a quarter sheet meant copying the same Latin lines over and over for fifteen minutes, a full sheet meant copying them for an hour—was a form of punishment tedious and demeaning in itself, but also hateful because of the incursions upon free time which might better have been spent in other ways. This was particularly true in the case of classroom failures. To compel the student to write out sheets, when he might have been studying to improve his marks, had precisely the degree of logic which once led society to put men in jail for having incurred debts.

In one way or another the students found ways to circumvent, or at least to abbreviate, this form of mental torture. Boys wrote out sheets in advance, for barter or for sale. The more ingenious lashed three or four pens together, thus perfecting an early form of copying machine. The physically hardened would actually submit to corporal punishment as a substitute for the time-consuming sheets.

The system of justice was not without its chance for appeal. This meant going to the rector's study, where an excuse could be offered, considered, and according to something close to divine dispensation, accepted or refused. On one occasion a student confessed to a horrifying combination of offenses. He had been reported for having ink on the floor, being out of order, disorderly, and in constant neglect of his Greek. Confronted by this list of evils, the rector took pity and is said actually to have laughed.

Exceptional Masters

At St. Paul's the need for disciplinary measures was eased by the natural authority of the best masters. Coit set the tone: he had but to enter a room to silence conversation and to quell any incipient disorder. It would have been inconceivable for him to fall into the difficulties of an English headmaster, who finding himself unable to control the study hall, was advised to add to his dignity by wearing a wig. (The boys found out where the wig was stored and purloined it.) Others at St. Paul's, unlike the ineffectual Mr. Schindelmeisser, were able without apparent effort to maintain perfect decorum in their classrooms.

John Hargate was at this time the school's principal disciplinarian; he was extremely popular despite so thankless a role. Though not qualified to teach any but the most elementary subjects, and in church orders never rising above the diaconate, he possessed a quick intelligence and a piercing eye. He seemed to be everywhere; and the boys knew that in his presence disregard of rules could not easily be got away with. At the same time he could share their interests, laugh at their jokes, and during the holidays was a favorite visitor in many of their homes. A student recalled one occasion when a well-known bully was getting his due from a classmate. The fighting was plainly out of order, but Hargate, with sound instinct, turned quietly away and let the boys settle things for themselves.

Two masters arriving at the school at about this time solved the problem of discipline by transcending it. James Knox and Augustus Swift were the kind of men whom it seemed a satisfaction to follow and even to obey. Both came from within the school, having had successful student careers. Knox was of a delicate constitution and deeply conservative by nature, factors tending to blight his charm in the bud. He seemed to grow old before his time, and being old, was querulous and narrow. Nothing that happened at the end, however, should dim the excitement attending him in his heyday.

A handsome man with pale moustaches, invariably dressed to the nines, Knox was a skilled athlete and a charmed musician. In chapel he trained a choir that boys took delight to sing in; on school occasions—and often when there was no occasion at all—he would take to his piano and lead the students in their familiar songs. Of his classes it was remarked that no hint of disorder had ever arisen.

One of the dividends of Dr. Coit's visit to England in 1869 was the friendship formed with the Reverend Derwent Coleridge, son of the poet and a man of exceptional culture and wise ways. Dr. Coit persuaded him to admit, from time to time, chosen St. Paul's boys into his rectory at Hanwell, to finish their education or to prepare them for the university. Augustus Muhlenberg Swift was the first of these, and his residence at Hanwell, as Charles Coit relates in his memoir, produced a marked effect upon the young man.[27] Musical, artistic, open to all impressions of beauty, he provided congenial soil for the culture of the English rectory. He read the classics and English literature with Coleridge; he had opportunities for training his fine baritone voice and perfecting his skill with pencil and brush. His social nature, meanwhile, responded to the advantages of educated English society.

In 1872, he returned to the school as a master. With his many artistic gifts and his joy in their employment, his coming, wrote a colleague, fell "like an April shower upon the arid soil of our Puritan foundations. Henceforth the beautiful was to be part of our inheritance."[28]

Swift was a man who might have been the object of some amusement had he not, by the testimony of all, been so warm, so affectionate and so unselfish by nature.[29] He dressed in the height of fashion, on Sunday wearing a frock coat and a high silk hat. His rooms, opposite the rector's study on the second floor of the new study hall, were furnished in a style to which Millville was not accustomed. The walls were papered in a rich dark green with dragons of gold superimposed. Rows of books in hand-

"His coming was felt like an April shower." *Augustus M. Swift, a master.*

some leather bindings filled the low bookcases, on top of which were rare pieces of china and bric-à-brac. Engravings and watercolors (some of them his own, reminders of his sojourns in Scotland and Wales) hung one above the other to the ceiling. The writing table was that of an artist, with its neatly laid out pens and brushes; and the chairs, in that school where almost everyone sat on hard wood benches, were comfortably padded.

He and James Knox were inseparable friends. Back of Swift's many gifts, Knox wrote of him, there was so Christian a spirit that "his rather sensuous contribution did not strike us as altogether too pagan." The boys loved him. He coasted and skated with them, led them through English literature as through an enchanted wood, and on the school grounds would be at the center of a laughing crowd. No stir troubled the big study when he was in charge. At school entertainments Swift shone, obviously enjoying himself as he walked to the platform amid the boys' expectant hush. They could count on his throwing himself energetically into his songs, managing his voice with the skill of a trained professional. *The Wreck of the Hesperus, Nancy Lee,* Sullivan's *Will He Come?* were never rendered to a more enthusiastic or warm-hearted audience.

Some Gifted Students

St. Paul's in the late sixties and seventies graduated an unusually interesting group of boys, each of whom responded in his own way to the school's life and challenge. The *Rural Record* of 1866 reported a new arrival in the first form—Francis Marion Crawford, twelve years of age, from Rome, Italy. "So fresh from the classical land," said the recorder, "his arrival may well be regarded as an event." The youth could converse in French and Italian as well as English, and spoke German with considerable ease. He was possessed, besides, "of most interesting information and experience." Crawford published his first pieces in the *Horae* and went on to become the author of more than forty books, the most widely read novelist of his generation. His style might seem over-exquisite, but a modern critic describes his *Ave Roma* as "the most perfect" book about Rome—"accurate, swift, adroitly planned and heightened by a careful rhetoric."

Crawford was a genuine romantic, living most of his life in Italy. For one of his returns after a brief visit to the States he purchased a large schooner, which he navigated himself across the Atlantic. New York shipmasters, looking on him with some disdain as "a gentleman who wrote books," were astonished as they saw him train for a full master's certificate, licensing him to command any ship in any part of the world.

In 1892, Crawford returned to St. Paul's, rich and famous, bestowing upon the school the honor of being the second audience in the country to hear one of his much-anticipated public readings. (Boston, of course, provided the first.) His appearance, it was said, was of strength and active vitality; an intellectual, cultured, serious man, reading from his works "not as if they were great things, but as if they were little things and yet worthy of some consideration."[30] The tone was perfectly suited to his St. Paul's listeners; indeed, he seemed the epitome of the civilized virtues the school sought to inculcate. The reading was a success, and the proceeds (after deduction of the noted author's fee) went to the benefit of the school boat clubs.

John Jay Chapman had a lifelong affection for St. Paul's, peculiar in that he began by finding the place thoroughly uncongenial. He came in the mid-seventies, a youth of brooding temperament. "I have always had perfect confidence in you and have found you faithful in duty and anxious to do right," Coit told him.[31] But the chapel services and the general religious tone imposed too great a strain upon a nature already unworldly to an exaggerated degree. To the amazement of his fellow students, Chapman was seen praying by his berth in the night train bringing him to Concord, and when on the cricket field he kneeled down in a state of religious fervor, that was too much even for the rector.

Chapman went home in his third year and suffered a severe illness. The school left its dismal memories, "a mysterious and gloomy whirl of things," as he described it, "a vast complex factory-building of clocks, bells and automata."[32] The water froze in his jug at night, he added despairingly. The traditional Sunday night observances, which one of his inclinations might have rejected as merely sentimental or odd, he endured with a monstrous foreboding of the morrow.

Strangely, Chapman could never put St. Paul's behind him. After another severe illness when he was forty, he became aware that the experience at Concord had meant something important in his life. "The school," he wrote, "had somehow been carrying on its work within me through all these years."[33] He became one of St. Paul's most eloquent critics and interpreters, prophetic, irascible, often loudly humorous. Chanler Chapman, one of his sons, followed in his father's eccentric style, in due course writing about St. Paul's one of the small classics of school literature.

In his day John Jay Chapman was a powerful, if neglected, voice. An early leader of civic reform, a battler for human rights, he embraced every new cause with a flaming tongue and pen. Meanwhile he pursued his studies of the classics, writing on Dante and translating Sophocles. Seeking excellence alone, outraged by the commercialism and what he deemed the tawdry standards prevailing in his day, he was to the end an isolated fighter. He saw St. Paul's as the keeper of a sacred flame. It was not, in his view, the child of riches; rather, "it was the child of hunger and thirst,

He could never put St. Paul's behind him. *John Jay Chapman,
shown a few years after leaving
Concord.*

gaining in character and in vigor throughout a youth of hardy loneliness.''
At every departure from this ideal he roared his outrage.

A contemporary of Chapman's, and as different from him as night
from day, was Owen Wister. Coming to the school as a boy from England,
wearing a Norfolk jacket and knickerbockers, Wister quickly showed
himself to be a fine writer of English, an admirable pianist and a clever
actor. His grandmother was the noted actress Fanny Kemble, who upon
coming into the study on one famous occasion made an unforgettable
curtsey before the assembled school.

Bright, sunny of disposition, cheerfully self-confident, Wister was
destined for success. Letters to his grandmother show his characteristic
style. He writes an account of an afternoon's sleighing: "If you could see
the double runners go down the hill at the rate of at least thirty miles an
hour, you would be astonished''; and he adds a pencil drawing of the
confused mass of legs at the end of the ride. "Often when I have got to the
bottom of the hill, I have not known which pair of legs to remove, as
belonging to me.''[34]

The lad was also enthusiastic as a novice chess player. "When I
come home,'' he tells his grandmother, ''we'll have some games if you
don't object. I intend to have a telegraph communication between the

houses, if I can manage it, and when the weather does not permit you to leave your abode we can play chess by means of the telegraph.'' Again, regretting that the playing of cards is forbidden at the school, Wister hopes that in vacation his grandmother will ''come over to us in the evening, or I to you, and then we can play 'blossoming.''' If the roads are ''impassable,'' he adds, ''you can come over by a subterranean passage that I shall dig under the turnpike, from your cellar to our cellar.''

Wister flourished at St. Paul's, a young animal loose in a congenial atmosphere, making friends equally with boys and masters. Hall Harrison, who left the school shortly after Wister, wrote in 1884 to his former

Owen Wister was destined for success. *The* Horae *board, 1877; Wister seated at left.*

pupil: "Those were pleasant times, and I particularly recall how I enjoyed meeting you and Chapman three times daily (at least) at the table of the lower school. Your table talk was, I must say, to me very entertaining . . . both in its excellent English and its subject matter."[35]

A Young Librarian

Among the interests shared by Wister and Hall Harrison was the library,[36] then being installed in the new study building. It had a sunny room of its own, with engravings upon the walls and busts of classic orators and poets atop the shelves. This installation, combined with the spirit of initiative among the students, led to the establishment of the Library Association dedicated to encouraging literature in all its forms, and to managing and safeguarding the collection of books. It was hoped, said the *Horae,* that in this way the boys' tastes would be improved and their enthusiasm fired. Harrison, then at the peak of his influence as a master, was the principal begettor of the enterprise and its first president; Wister was his enthusiastic lieutenant.

A letter of Wister's to his mother in 1874 states: "Mr. Harrison has requested me to ask my grandmother if she could send some books to the newly organized library . . . with her name in them—so you'll tell her please." Miss Kemble evidently took offense at this indirect approach, and a following letter is sent directly to her. "I beg your pardon for not having addressed you personally, and I now take this occasion of repairing my fault and addressing you *most* personally." This time the appeal was successful. "I must ask you to excuse my haste and bad pen, as the pig said when he broke loose," writes the grandson in a note of thanks. "I will ask Mr. Harrison to write to you in person," he adds, "which you must receive as a great compliment, as he is the President of the Library, & the President only returns thanks for gifts on very special occasions."

A letter signed "Your affectionate old Granny" assures the lad that Miss Kemble does not want to trouble Mr. Harrison with a mere acknowledgment.

This first success encouraged Wister, and he is next found laying plans for raids on sympathetic relations and friends in a coming vacation. "I am going to beg books from everyone with whom I am having any intercourse," he writes his grandmother, though assuring her she will be exempted because of the "beautiful donation" she has already made. The library lists thereafter are indeed dotted with notations of gifts from Owen Wister, including such books as *1,000 Miles in the Rob Roy Canoe,* by John McGregor; *I Will Be a Sailor,* by Louisa Caroline Tuthill; and *Characteristics of Women* (about whom young Wister had already learned something) by Anna Jameson. Not surprisingly, one of his major ambitions is shortly fulfilled. "Knowing my taste for literature," he writes an aunt, "the President has made me a Librarian." And more exuberantly to his grandmother: "Have I told you that I have become a Librarian? Now don't fall off your chair . . . for I don't see anything to laugh at."

Along with the library, the *Horae* became a major concern of Wister's. Here his first literary efforts were published. In his final years at the school, 1877 and 1878, he was editor and managing editor, and the volumes for those years are among the most brilliant in the magazine's history. With the board divided into two teams, successive issues were published by the rival groups, each aiming to excel in the quality of its articles, essays and poems.

Amid the schoolboy's sweet taste of success a genuine love of books was nurtured. Wister went on to become a prolific author, best known for his vigorous western novel, *The Virginian*. ("When you call me that, smile!" is still a standard phrase among young Americans playing cowboy.) Nor did the enjoyment of libraries fail the generation of youth thus initiated at St. Paul's. "I am dwelling in a most desolate place," Chapman writes to his schoolmate Wister in 1878—"worse than a room without a window, worse than a hotel without a bar; ah, my friend, in a town *without a public library*." Hall Harrison had done his work well.

Richard Henry Dana

Richard Henry Dana III, a bright and attractive boy, was the son of Richard Henry Dana, Jr., the author of *Two Years Before the Mast* and a trustee of the school; and grandson of Richard Henry Dana, the romantic novelist, author of *The Buccaneer*. He was the kind of student that entered into activities with zest, the more so because he was impressed by his responsibility in carrying on a family name. He was not allowed to forget having been baptized by Dr. Crowell, the rector of Boston's Church of the Advent. "May there never be wanting a Richard Henry Dana to stand before the Lord," the clergyman exclaimed as he sprinkled water upon the infant's brow.[37]

"I want you to remember these things," the father wrote to the son as a schoolboy, and he admonished him sternly upon the least fall from grace. "I can't imagine your losing a fur cap," he wrote the lad; "I should as soon think of losing a bureau or a bed." "As to self-examination," he admonished on another occasion, "I think you have arrived at an age where you can lay out your faults into classes, putting together those that are cognate, and examine yourself by them."

Young Dana not only suffered from an overzealous father but from

"I can't imagine your losing a fur cap." *Richard Henry Dana III suffered from an overzealous father.*

the normal vicissitudes of a new boy at St. Paul's. His arrival in January was accompanied by excessively frigid weather, so that water froze in the students' rooms and the stove in the study scarcely sufficed to keep the cold out of doors. On his first day the school seemed "very gloomy." "Please send my sled if you can and the soap and various other things that Mother may think of," he wrote to his father in a classic mood of vague disorientation. Even the rector added to his woes. As spring approached he wanted to collect birds' eggs, but Dr. Coit refused permission. "I think that is too bad," Dana wrote home disconsolately. "There are a great many rare eggs here . . . but now all my hopes are gone and all my expected pleasures taken away and I don't know what to do about it."[38]

Things began to look brighter as school activities took hold. A pleasant glimpse of the boy shows him driving a buggy to town, drawn by an old white horse, with Mrs. Coit as his passenger. In Concord, Dana "enjoyed the sights of the capital" while Mrs. Coit shopped for supplies. He began to take a more hopeful view of the rector and, as we shall see, proved to be one of the rare youths who could breast him in his den.

Typical of Dana's brisk competence was his role during the fire in the miller's cottage in 1869. The boys were in chapel at the end of the day when the cry of "Fire!" rang out. The dismissal blessing was given immediately and away rushed the congregation to see what was happening. At this moment the Coits were returning with Dr. Samuel Eliot (the school's long-standing trustee) from Dunbarton. As they approached

Millville, they saw the smoke and found the whole neighborhood in alarm.

At the miller's cottage was a scene of utter confusion.[39] Crockery was being thrown from the second story while pillows were carefully carried down. Each boy and master seized a bucket, rushed to the pond for water, and poured it on the flames. Young Dana with some trepidation (he was still only a fifth former), but braced by a sense of family tradition, took command and organized a line to the pond, with full buckets being passed to the left and empty buckets to the right. This effective effort, the inspiration of one clear-minded boy, confined the destruction to an outside shed and saved for posterity an historic building.

The life of the students was taking on a modern form, with a combination of studies, athletics and extracurricular activities providing the outlet for a diversity of gifts. Dana's record was a model of what the ambitious boy aspired to. Winner of the school medal, he had been captain of the cricket team, had sung in the choir, won the prize for declamation, and in *Hamlet* had played the dual roles of the King and the Ghost. It was a question, indeed, whether there were enough hours in the day for a student to meet his obligations. "Lack of time," said the *Horae,* "is a complaint heard from all sides, especially from those who are in the upper forms, and have many duties to perform in order to regulate the several societies and clubs of which they are officers or prominent members." Even Wister, with characteristic ebullience, sighed over the time-consuming duties laid upon him when he achieved the coveted place of secretary of the Library Association. It was an honor, he said, that he judged "a most grievous burden."

Students, nevertheless, seem to have found occasions for independent quests, for walks and expeditions and for a pleasant degree of idleness. Alexander Mackay-Smith, the first St. Paul's boy to become a bishop, filled his diary with revealing glimpses of a young man's odd pursuits.[40] He was living in the miller's cottage, which in itself gave him a cherished liberty. He records going out one January day with Dana to their wigwam in the woods. It was snowing violently; they dug a hole in the ice before the entrance and, building a fire, warmed themselves and made soup. With another friend he spends a March afternoon sending immense blocks of ice over the dam. Dr. Coit comes by to watch the ceremony.

As spring approaches, he goes "to see about some maple sugar I am hoping to make." He is busy fixing up a boat and prepares an expedition to Little Turkey. (He did not get there because of the heavy logs and boughs.) Throughout the diary there are references to lounging about, engaging in such strange diversions as firing off a cannon, and a good deal of desultory reading. Inevitably, too, there are remarks about the weather which at one time or another has been the despair of every St. Paul's boy—and girl. "This is the most miserable rain," he writes of one March day, "and the most miserable place I have ever conceived."

Toward the end of his life Wister recalled the isolation in which the school of his day existed. "We were still a world within ourselves," he wrote. "Henry Augustus Coit in his way, like the climate in its way, pervaded everybody and everything."[41] In that post–Civil War period outside events faded to insignificance. Chapman, painting a portrait of an earlier, idyllic school period, was undoubtedly influenced by what he recalled of his own brief spell at St. Paul's. "I do not know whether it was the result of Dr. Coit's own prophetic nature," he wrote,[42] "or the result of a more reasoned theory about the education of boys; but the fact remains that at St. Paul's School you were encouraged to dream. You were permitted to wander alone in the woods. You were left much to yourself, and the fact that you were a thoughtful child, slow in development and perhaps backward in your studies, was allowed for. . . . The school was at first a mere country home in which a clergyman conducted the education of boys; and the traditions of boyhood-in-the-country survived as the school grew to more serious proportions." They survived, certainly, into the happy growing period of the 1870s.

From Pageants to Sports

Sports at the school, informal and largely unorganized at first, began during this period to play an increasingly important role in student life. Cricket had long been an accompaniment of ceremonial occasions and a featured holiday event. The first rowing races, as much a pageant as they were a sport, took place soon after the school's founding. Bowling, hound-and-hare races, and a strange contest called "picking" in which the boys propelled their sleds across the ice by the use of pointed sticks, provided early forms of competition. Now significant developments took place in two of the major athletic activities.

Cricket grounds had from the first existed behind the school house on the rough lawn extending down to the pond. With the construction of the upper school on the far side of the Turkey River, in a location surrounded by broad fields, the vision of a more ample cricket grounds possessed the school's athletes. Dr. Coit was not in favor of it. This would ordinarily have been the end of the matter, except that young Dana took his life in his hands, going twice to importune the rector. For the second interview he prepared a memorandum containing statistics and exact measurements. Not without fear and trembling he entered the little, crowded study.

As Dana later recounted, "The good doctor, so firm in his convictions on matters more within his special knowledge, was most modest in his opinion on this. He considered all I had to lay before him and reserved his decision. He said, 'I shall again consult with the trustees and I thank you for the information about cricket which you have written out.'"[43]

In due course permission was granted. Aided by the faithful Woodbury Flanders, students did much of the work of smoothing the rough farmland and removing its many rocks. The resulting playing field, some fifteen acres in extent, was a model of its kind, fit for great battles to be won or lost on. Its practical advantages were supplemented by natural beauty. Turkey River bounded two of its edges, and from its green expanse was a view of Prospect Hill. Known as the lower grounds, this area came to play a significant role in school life. The improvements were the beginning of a new and serious interest in sports.

Of Dr. Arnold it was said that his chief contribution to the athletic craze was that he sometimes stood on the sidelines and looked pleased. Dr. Coit was present at the early games on the lower grounds, and it must be presumed that something close to pleasure was evident. He liked cricket—not, as has sometimes been supposed, because it was an English game, but because it was quiet and gentlemanly and was played without raucous cheering. Baseball was making inroads by this time. It would be tolerated as a subordinate sport; but cricket, wrote one of its devotees, "is the game of St. Paul's. We trust she will never resign this, her peculiar birthright."[44]

Rowing also was ready for a major expansion. On being approached by an enthusiastic group of students, the rector went along with their plans to hold races on Long Pond. "I will consent to the division of the boys into two rowing clubs," he asserted; but he still had reservations about the site, and insisted there be no public notice or advertisement of the races. Heretofore he had insisted that such contests be confined to the private grounds of the school, and had not been disposed to indulge the boys with races on what he called "a distant sheet of water, accessible to the public."[45]

The next question was, what should the two clubs be called? A group of boys suggested the name Shattuck, but there was some doubt as to whether this would prove a proper compliment to the school's founder. Suppose the club never amounted to anything? Suppose it should not win any races? The problem was taken to the rector, who "after some reflection," approved; and then himself suggested the name of Halcyon for the rival organization. Through subsequent years the only form in which the

Shattuck name would be embodied in the school was in this blue-coated rowing club.

Preparations for a serious encounter were now set in train. *The Water Lily* and the *Niagara* had long since outlived their usefulness; the *Ariel,* flagship of the previous St. Paul's generation, had been damaged by vandals. Two new four-oared boats were ordered, and a boathouse prepared. Unfortunately it turned out the new boats would not be ready before autumn, and the old *Ariel* was pressed into service. In the latter part of May 1871, a notice appeared on the school bulletin board: "The Shattuck Boat Club hereby challenges the Halcyon Boat Club to row a race against time, in the *Ariel,* on Long Pond. . . . The race is to come off on Wednesday, June 7 at 3 p.m."[46]

The challenge was duly accepted, and on the day fixed a small regatta appeared on Long Pond, consisting of several rowing and sailing boats together with the *Penacook,* a steamboat carrying a handful of spectators. Three old boys returned for this first Race Day. Under a light rain, the Halcyons first took possession of the *Ariel.* They struck out bravely on the word "Go!" and after a few strokes seemed masters of their oars. Down upon the stake boat they pressed, navigated the turn gracefully, and in what seemed a few moments returned to the judges' boat. Upon their landing, all those wearing pink rosettes applauded enthusiastically.

It was now the Shattucks' turn. Taking over the boat, they were greatly encouraged by the reception of the spectators in blue and white. Starting off with the confidence of men hoarding their strength, they seemed at mid-course to be making the turn in time equal to their opponents. But on the home stretch, when a spurt had been looked for, there was an ominous slackening of speed. It appeared that one of the crewmen had caught a crab. Despite some variation among the timekeepers, it was held officially that the Halcyons had won. The victorious crew were then summoned to receive their prizes, which were presented in a flattering speech by a young lady from Jamaica Plain, Massachusetts. According to the *Horae* account, the captain, Allen Marquand, responded "guardedly." Afterwards all went home and prepared for the annual concert, which took place following tea.

Such was the first Race Day in the school's history, replete with details foreshadowing hard-fought struggles of the future. A few days later, when the Halcyon captain received the school medal, he still wore the glow of his crew's victory. The *Rural Record* expressed the wish that he, and all those aspiring for the trophy in future days, might "wear the laurels of true success in this world and the crown of fidelity in the next." By others it was hoped more modestly that rowing would henceforth have a place in the school equal to ball playing.

The Ariel shown in its early days on the lower school pond.

ROWING WOULD HENCEFORTH HAVE A PLACE IN THE SCHOOL
EQUAL TO BALL-PLAYING.

The flotilla gathered before the Race Day of 1899.

CHAPTER FOUR

At the Turning Point

1874–1878

Financial Worries

"I am most troubled about our finances," Coit wrote in June 1874, to Dr. Shattuck. "The addition of the new school house, and some extravagances, have greatly increased our annual expenses."[1] For the first time the rector at the year's close had not been able to make ends meet. He asked of Dr. Shattuck the use of $2,000 for six weeks or two months, to be repaid at the opening of the school year. "I feel ashamed to ask all this," Coit concluded his letter.

It is interesting that Coit should have brought his troubles directly to Dr. Shattuck rather than to the board of trustees. The two men had remained steadfast friends. Shattuck saw in Coit a man of total dedication, of startling insight into the character of young men; and he shared with him a devout, though more cheerfully temperate, allegiance to religious ideals. Dr. Shattuck's frequent visits, in good times and more often when there was distress, brought cool professional judgment and an instinct for healing. Through the school's annals runs the reassuring note: "Dr. Shattuck came." It mattered not the weather, nor the obligations of his own busy life; he would be there, often walking from the station, and seeking only to be of help. Though persisting in his refusal to be named a trustee, he attended by invitation the annual meetings of the board, where his steady influence could be decisive.

The funds needed by the embarrassed rector were loaned in silence, and were quietly repaid; but a year later Dr. Shattuck made a significant written appeal to members of the board. The school, he pointed out, had amassed debts of $35,000 in the course of its building program; important needs, particularly an infirmary and a gymnasium, still remained to be met. The organization of the school in a village of small buildings was inevitably expensive. Nineteen years, he continued, had elapsed since St. Paul's was incorporated; yet the rector had never received a salary, and

76

no provision had been made for him in case of failing health. It was now time that the school be placed on a permanent basis. Characteristically, Dr. Shattuck ended his plea with a gift from his own funds of $3,000.

Members of the Board

The board receiving this document was composed mainly of friends of Dr. Shattuck, and was habituated to interfering as little as possible with Dr. Coit. "They have been unanimous in their approval and support of the rector," wrote Joseph Coit, himself a trustee, in 1890. "They have been more than satisfied with the success of his administration financially—as well as with the moral and intellectual condition of the school." [2] All this was well merited; besides, Dr. Coit was a man who would not have lightly brooked interference.

During a period of more than thirty years, after the passing of men like Bishop Chase and Judge Huntington of the founding generation, membership of the board had been stable, as the demands made upon it had been minimal. Most of the members served until death removed them, and those in good health seem to have attended only intermittently. "I am still, I believe, (unless my name has been stricken, as it might well be, because of my derelictions) a trustee of that school—and as such I must have, I suppose, some duties": so wrote Bishop H. A. Neely, of Maine, to the rector in 1873. [3] Several others seem to have been absent from meetings over extended periods, as educational or religious duties absorbed them. Some were valued for their occasional gifts to the school, or for their attendance at ceremonial occasions.

Among board members in 1870 a few colorful figures stand out. Richard Henry Dana we have already met with, in his role as father to Richard Henry Dana III. Midway through college the second Dana paused in his studies to take a long sea voyage aboard the brig *Pilgrim* with the hope of strengthening his eyes. The famous record of this voyage stressed the daily duties, the ever-present boredom of seamen, and is as sober as his father's novel of the sea was romantic.

Dana looked upon *Two Years Before the Mast,* published before he came to the bar, as "boy's work," and thirsted for what he conceived to be more durable fame. He was *almost* appointed Secretary of the Navy by Lincoln, and was *almost* made ambassador to England by Johnson. "My life has been a failure," he wrote, "compared to what I might have done." [4] Despite his disappointments, he gave valuable public service in the form of legal assistance to fugitive slaves; and never forgetting his early adventures, he continued to be a friend of seamen.

To his contemporaries on the St. Paul's board, Dana appeared a short, thick-set man, slightly pompous, given to wearing cravats that were thought rather bright for a man of his years. He took himself seriously—in that society where men were not inclined to hold lightly their accomplishments or social position; he carried the airs of one who dined regularly at Boston's Saturday Club, in the company of such immortals as Holmes and Lowell, Emerson, Longfellow, Parkman and Agassiz.

Very different in temperament was Edward Newton Perkins, Jr., of Jamaica Plain. A man without occupation, debonaire in manner, he was given to enlivening school occasions with his puns. (Dr. Coit, who would never have perpetrated a pun himself, was indulgent toward this weakness of his friend.) Charles Perkins Gardiner, of Brookline, came from the same background but brought to the board a sensitivity to the arts, especially to music and architecture. He introduced to the school the architect Henry Vaughan, whose touch was to be on the best of its older buildings. He also concerned himself with the installation of the excellent organ after the enlargement of the old chapel. A modest man, reserved in manner, he was on the board from 1865 until his death in 1908.

A term almost as long was that of Samuel Eliot, a cousin of the Harvard president, who kept a watchful eye over St. Paul's from 1859 to 1898. Like his more famous relative, he was a figure of distinction in the worlds of letters and education. As a young man he had written several volumes on the history of liberty, and in 1860 he became president of Trinity College. His tenure was brief and unhappy. "Discouragement," he wrote in his journal, "is the legend over my gateway to Trinity."[5] The students' irreverence toward religious services combined with poor discipline and the college's financial plight caused his resignation after two years. Later he was head of the Girls' High School in Boston, and then superintendent of the Boston public school system.

Misfortune seemed to pursue Eliot in his career. Poor health caused his resignation from the first of these posts—"Dr. Shattuck says I must resign and I do so under protest," he wrote;[6] and from the second post he was eased out, according to his grandson Samuel Eliot Morison, because he sponsored for youthful readers a highly bowdlerized—but to that generation nevertheless suspect—version of *The Arabian Nights*. Despite these setbacks, and despite the private woes he poured out in his journal, Samuel Eliot retained a smiling disposition, so that at seventy-five he seemed to one observer a far younger man; and to his grandson, growing up in his company in the big house on Brimmer Street, he was a radiant focal point of family life.[7]

Eliot was a finished orator, one of the best in that age of oratory, and his visits on Prize Day, or his addresses on significant school occasions, were worth looking forward to. A devout man, he had thought deeply about the relation between religion and education. "I have been writing an article on our church schools and colleges," he confided to his journal shortly before becoming a St. Paul's trustee, "endeavoring to bring out the importance of religious education. God help the work." God apparently did; at least all Eliot's subsequent utterances on this subject were refreshingly acute. He believed in the importance of young men being both Christians and gentlemen—and then, if possible, scholars. In this he followed Arnold, whom he indeed resembled—as much, said a Hartford admirer, as an American and a layman could resemble an Englishman and a clergyman.

In 1879 the board elected the first trustee to have attended the school as a student, one of the earliest editors of the *Horae,* and a man whose part in the school would be large. Henry Ferguson, clergyman and professor of history at Trinity, had in his youth shared in an adventure that made him famous and that in subtle ways contributed to the quiet courage, the genial acceptance of things, that marked him henceforth. Not yet twenty, he embarked upon a sea voyage which had for its purpose—ironically, as it proved—the restoration of his older brother's precarious health.

He kept a watchful eye over St. Paul's. *Samuel Eliot, trustee 1859–1898.*

Having rounded the Cape, in a windless sea and under a burning sun their ship caught fire and was totally consumed. Two lifeboats put forth together, one shortly to break loose and be lost; the other, including in its crew Henry Ferguson and his brother, to make a fantastic voyage, to this day a classic example of endurance and courage at sea.

In an open boat minimally provisioned, fifteen men traveled for forty-three days across three thousand miles of the Pacific, landing, when all hope seemed gone, upon a South Sea island. The record of this remarkable feat was kept in a journal of the young Henry Ferguson.[8] An 1866 article in *Harper's* was reprinted in 1878 in several issues of the *Horae*. Thus the memory of that exploit was kept alive, and the bearded churchman and scholar, when he returned to the school as an old boy, or took his place upon the board of trustees, was a marked figure, one who was felt to have experienced what other men had known only in night visions.

Such, in part, was the group of men we must imagine assembling in the rectory for the annual meeting. The rector plays the role of host with a courtesy old-fashioned even by the standards of those days; the founder by his presence casts a warm glow over the proceedings. Discussion of school business is brief and is summarily disposed of. After the abundant dinner, an embarrassed discomfort possesses those worldly figures. No cigars to stimulate conversation in the post-prandial hours! By happenstance—or is it prearrangement?—Mr. Swift comes by and invites the company to his rooms in the big study just across the road. Tobacco has already left its odor over that romantic and sumptuous retreat, and now conversation takes its flight on clouds of smoke-laden air.

Upon this group of men were to fall heavy responsibilities, as the school passed through a crisis in 1878 and in the 1890s saw threats to its very existence.

The Specter of Illness

The health of the boys was a preoccupation of which the rector and members of the school household were rarely relieved. Diseases of the young struck swiftly, not infrequently with mortal effects. Pneumonia, scarlet fever and diphtheria were constantly feared, and even measles could be a cause of deep anxiety. Death, when it came, entered a closely bound circle, struck at life in its most appealing stages, and aroused the tenderest, and sometimes the most morbid, emotions. In 1871, on the day when the school was about to disband for the Christmas holidays, a third former failed to appear at breakfast. He was found by one of the masters dead in his alcove, the victim of a sudden attack of membranous croup, which had

"We greatly need a proper infirmary." *The new building standing next to the rectory. Dr. Crosby is on the porch.*

allowed him neither to stir nor cry out. In 1874 and 1875, deaths occurred from pneumonia and rheumatic fever. In the tense atmosphere following these events the rector was severely frightened when he could not find a boy one day at 4 p.m. That mishap had a more fortunate end. For "the young gentleman," as the recorder noted, "appeared on the scene at 5, having been locked up by accident in the report room."

Dr. Coit, in a letter of June 1876 addressed to friends of the school, made a simple but moving appeal: "We greatly need a proper infirmary, or sanitorium, for our sick boys"; he added the hope that he would not be thought presumptuous for thus calling attention to this most urgent of the school's requirements. Samuel Eliot took active charge of a fund-raising campaign; the necessary $6,000 was quickly donated, and by the end of the year a simple frame building, adjacent to the rectory, was completed.

Once again, however, tragedy struck. The matron, a close friend and co-worker of Mrs. Coit's, was to be in charge of the new infirmary; she moved in only to die. Then an epidemic of scarlet fever erupted, and in

November the school was hastily dismissed. Dr. Coit, physically and emotionally exhausted, expressed to parents his hope that the boys, "for their good and gentle ways," would be more than ever welcome at their homes.

At this juncture there arrived on the scene another member of the Coit family, John Milnor, Henry Augustus' youngest brother. Milnor had gone into business in the West, and in Cleveland was generally believed to have suffered financial reverses. Whether it was intended he should stay on at St. Paul's is not clear, but he arrived at a propitious moment, when a gap called desperately to be filled. Taking charge of the infirmary, with his wife he kept long vigils at the bedsides of sick boys, a strong staff in his older brother's hour of need.

Milnor was a heavy-set, florid man, given to mundane enjoyments, about as unlike Henry Augustus as could be imagined. He would slide into a position of great power within the school, still in a hearty middle age when Henry and then Joseph sank into decrepitude. He would make himself useful, and finally indispensable, to leaders grown too weary or too feeble to look outside the family for the unquestioning support they required. However Milnor Coit be finally judged, his watchfulness over the infirmary in this time of trouble must weigh heavily in the balance.

The Girls: An Interlude

The year 1878, which was to be one of disasters for the school, began with an amusing and idyllic episode. In February Mrs. Coit wrote Emily, the daughter of Samuel Eliot, suggesting that she come for "a little visit"[9] over Washington's Birthday. Though the visit would be passed in the quiet of the country, there were "many boys to make it merry"; in addition to which her friend, Owen Wister, would be presenting a play. It would be fine, too, Mrs. Coit suggested, if Emily would come with Mary Brown, Mrs. Shattuck's niece.

The invitation was enthusiastically accepted. The two young girls decided it would be "the wildest spree," and on February 22 they took the train for Concord. Emily Eliot kept a diary of this visit, and her pictures of the rectory and of Millville give a charming glimpse into the school life of this period. Within the severe formality surrounding the rector, and amid the gathering gloom of a new epidemic, the two girls went their high-spirited way, becoming involved with the boys, partly in a maternal but more in a coquettish way, and missing nothing of the surrounding scene.

The day of their arrival was stormy, a matter of minor import to those enchantresses. Dr. Coit, welcoming them at the rectory, was "very pleasant and kind"; Wister came promptly to call. "He has grown a lot since

Emily Eliot in 1877.

"A DELIGHTFUL UNIQUE EXPERIENCE
AND ONE NEVER TO BE FORGOTTEN"

The rectory as it appeared in the period of the girls' visit.

the summer and looked stronger," noted the observant Emily; "he told us about the play which we were to see that night and prepared us for a fiasco." At the rectory were Dr. and Mrs. Coit's two young daughters, Mary and Eleanor; their twelve-year-old son Joseph; and Charles, now a handsome sixth former. In the new-fallen snow walking was impossible, and after tea a sleigh drew up to carry the party a few hundred yards down the Dunbarton road to the school house.

For a curtain-raiser that night, Wister played in a piano duet and Mr. Knox sang *When the Tide Comes In*. Wister, reported Miss Eliot sternly, overdid his part; but J. B. Shober, a fourth former with mysterious dark eyes, seemed "a little beauty." The next day two of the boys received the awful summons to the rector's study where, with a twinkle in his eye, Dr. Coit informed them they could have half the day off to take Miss Eliot and Miss Brown coasting. A sleigh ride to Hopkinton was set for the afternoon—"a very lively time"; and back at the rectory there were more callers, including "Bishop Sherrywhiskey." (The bishop, Samuel I. J. Scherneschewsky, was a well-known figure in the church, fresh from missionary work in China.) The young ladies and their student beaux entertained themselves by singing and playing the piano in the rectory parlor.

That night Emily Eliot looked out from the rectory guest room: "The shadows of the trees swayed to and fro in the window-curtain, and provided a ghostly effect. The sky was as clear as could be, & the stars looked very bright in the cold atmosphere." It was a moment of peace before the storm. On that same day the *Rural Record* had reported that "the dreaded measles" had broken out—and they were soon to be followed by developments even more ominous.

The girls successfully implored Mrs. Coit to extend their visit, and the next days were for them a succession of pleasantly vivid events. Sunday, with its several chapel services, was far from gloomy in their eyes. The choir sang "exquisitely"; at the rectory lunch, "a meek little clergyman" entertained the guests with a discourse on funerals. After one at which he had officiated, a chipper man stepped forward to announce that all were invited to return to the house of mourning and partake of refreshments. The deceased's last words had been: "Victuals—good and plenty of them!"

There were also walks and more coasting, exploration of the Millville sights, visits to classes and to school events such as a meeting of the Missionary Society. The Society gave the whole history of its financial accounts, which amused the young ladies very much. The address by the bishop of New Hampshire was interesting—he told how one poor factory girl out of a weekly salary of $3 had given $1 each Sunday over several years to help build churches. Though impressed, Miss Eliot regretted the interruption. "We should have liked to hear more [from the boys] of their mathematical difficulties," she wrote.

One evening Mr. Knox and Mr. Swift came to call, joining students and the young ladies in an impromptu concert. From outdoors the sound of a serenade suddenly arose. "Mary and I stampeded out of the room," wrote Miss Eliot, "without one thought of Mr. Knox and Mr. Swift, in our eagerness and excitement." Afterwards Mrs. Coit represented to them "the peculiarity, not to say impropriety" of this behavior. Mr. Knox and Mr. Swift, she added, would be surprised at their preferring the boys to their society, "as they were accustomed to being noticed a good deal." Upon which the irrepressible Miss Eliot comments: "For that reason I am a little glad that we *did* show a marked preference for the boysies."

Meanwhile, scarcely observed by the girls, measles was taking its toll among the students. A visit to the boys' rooms in the upper school was aborted, and on February 25 they observed a sleigh proceeding to the infirmary. They were told that it carried Wister, who had fallen ill that day. "So we cheered and waved to a tremendous extent without the slightest notice being taken." When the sleigh arrived at the infirmary, Wister was carried inside "in a very corpse-like way." He was being joined almost hourly by others.

The girls sent flowers to the infirmary, and a few days later, "from our room of sickness," came a characteristic reply. "How shall we thank you?" asked Wister. "We cannot, for the iron hand of the dire sickness holdeth us in a reclining and helpless position. . . . Rest assured that you go away from us, leaving a reminiscence than the which but its authors are more sweet." Wister added that his head was scarce attuned to rhyme, else his thanks would have been dispatched "in the swift iambic."

On February 28 the girls left. "So ended," wrote Emily, "a delightful, unique experience and one never to be forgotten." Escorts accompanied them to the station in their sleigh, and others rode behind with the team carrying their trunks. One of the boys wore crepe upon his arm, purchased at an undertaker's; another presented the girls with a toy china bulldog and a china rooster as souvenirs. In the railroad car all sang *Salve Mater*. Bishop Niles appeared, seeming to be amused, and as the train drew slowly out of the station, two of the more ardent swains followed a short way along the tracks by its side.

A Sense of Doom

A few days after the girls' departure forty-five boys were confined by illness, with part of the school house turned into a ward. Nurses were brought in hastily from the outside, while the measles spread to the orphans' home where all but two were stricken. It was as if an evil fate were visiting these scenes so lately blessed with the sounds of youths' singing and laughter. A boy who had been perfectly well when he went to bed nearly succumbed in the night from an attack diagnosed as rheumatism of the heart. The whole dormitory was awake and watching as brandy was administered and he was barely saved from death by strangulation and spasms. In April a first former, Edward Mason Young, went to the infirmary complaining of a sore throat, but otherwise apparently in good health. Dr. Crosby said on treating him, "that boy is going to be sick."

In the evening the boy seemed comfortable, and was amiable and good-natured as was his wont. But at three o'clock in the morning Milnor Coit noticed a slight change and at daybreak the doctors were sent for. Dr. Crosby at once said that the boy's days, and even his hours, were numbered. He died at a little after ten that morning.

A sense of doom hung over the school. For four days, adding to the misery, rains fell incessantly. The rector, an observer noted, "was completely used up and looked haggard and worn." (It was, said Henry Coit characteristically, the uninterrupted good fortune long attending the school that brought Nemesis.) At the same time Milnor Coit and his wife were, in the words of the *Rural Record,* "unstrung by the terrible scenes through which they had passed." Remaining at Millville through this period, Dr. Shattuck gave his steadying counsel and support.

A letter addressed to the parents of the school on April 27 told of the first former's death and of the unexplainable conditions surrounding it.[10] The risk of infection seemed remote, said Dr. Coit, but the parents must act according to their own judgment. A note appended by Dr. Crosby and Dr. Shattuck gave the opinion that it was in the boys' best interests to remain at school.

This judgment was soon belied. Several cases of scarlet fever appeared among the boys. One boy died at the school, another upon reaching home. No choice now existed but to close the school. Writing to the parents again on May 18, Coit announced that it had been decided not to open again until the autumn. The best authorities pronounced the sanitary conditions at the school satisfactory, he said, and could find no local cause for the recent afflictions. But it seemed wise not to recall the boys until a minimum of several weeks had passed, and to do that would mean prolonging the term into the period of hot weather.

For students graduating that spring, the closing was a harsh blow. For them there would now be no long-anticipated ceremonies, no Last Night hymn, no singing of *Home Sweet Home.* "I have just heard the fatal news," one of these, E. D. Tibbits, wrote to a classmate. "I have been doing what I suppose you think was very unmanly, having a regular cry. . . . When we went away in such a hurry I went back into the chapel to take what I had a feeling was, in a certain sense, a last look. . . . Yes, it is a great trial, but one of those things which, having no recompense, must be gulped down."[11]

To the other reasons for closing the school until autumn, Coit added one of poignant significance. "The great shock and strain to which those of us have been subjected who have the chief burden of responsibility," he told the parents, "makes a longer interval necessary for rest and recuperation." In closing, he spoke movingly of the boys for "their loving and cordial support of himself and the school in this great trouble."

A Bolt from the Blue

The interval of rest to which Dr. Coit looked forward was not to be given, nor was the year to pass without a further disaster. It took the form of a spectacular fire.

The summer of 1878 was dry. A heavy heat lay over the land and the water of the ponds sank far below its normal level. On the morning of July 21, light clouds passed over the little community at Millville; a brief shower of rain fell. A violent clap of thunder ensued, and one sharp flash of lightning. The few people in the school house rushed out of doors to see what damage had been done. Smoke was rising from the dormitory wing. Soon flames appeared, licking the roof edges and extending beyond the wing into the main structure. Deep within the building fire broke out

The old "mother house." *The school's original building with later additions, shown shortly before the fire. The chapel is at the right.*

simultaneously. The bolt that struck the cupola had passed through the house down to the ground.[12]

In hope of securing aid, the chapel bell was sounded. But on that peaceful Sunday in midsummer neighbors assumed it was calling them to church services, and (as one of them later told Dr. Coit) "I wasn't calculating to go." A messenger on horseback was sent forth to summon the Concord Fire Department. Meanwhile farmhands, maids and a few members of the school staff fought valiantly, and in some cases confusedly, to save what could be saved.

The table around which the trustees had gathered for their first meeting in 1855, where the first student compositions had been penned and the first issue of the *Horae* edited, was rescued from the flames.[13] By some miraculous feat of strength, James Knox's piano was carried downstairs and set upon the lawn. The chapel, for a time gravely threatened, survived. But the "old Mother House" in which all had begun, and which still served as a major focus of activities, was reduced in a few hours to some fallen timbers smoking in the July air.

CHAPTER FIVE

The Age of Faith
1878–1895

Out of the Fire

Dr. Coit, that morning in July, after an expedition to the Evangeline country with his son Charles, was returning to Campobello. Reaching the hotel in St. John, Newfoundland, he told Charles to hold the cab while he went in to secure their rooms. "Presently I followed him," the son recalled years later, "and I noticed a change in his manner. He said nothing until we had been shown our rooms and the porter had left us. Then he handed me a telegram."[1] It was thus that Henry Coit learned of the fire which destroyed so much of what he had patiently been building up for more than twenty years. He took the earliest train for Portland, Boston and Concord.

A special meeting of the trustees was called. The prospect before them was grim. A cloud remained over the school after the previous winter's illnesses and deaths; the early closing in itself had imposed heavy financial losses. Now the destruction of the central building, which insurance only partially covered, put a strain on financial resources unbuttressed by endowment funds or accumulated savings. So much to build and to rebuild—and so little except faith to build with! Some counseled delay in reopening the school, but the rector was adamant not only that St. Paul's must go forward, but open on the date in September previously set.

The chapel silver, originally from Boston's Church of the Advent, had been stored in the school house and was found almost unrecognizable among the ruins. Dr. Coit ordered it renewed, with a text from Isaiah in Latin superimposed: *Cum ambulaberis in igna, non combureris, et flamma non ardebit in te.** The weathervane that was believed to have attracted the lightning was also found and placed in the school's cabinet of curiosities. These were the symbols of rebirth. The realities next had to be

---

*When thou walkest through the fire, thou shalt not be burned, neither shall the flames kindle upon thee.—Isaiah 43:2.

dealt with. To assure the opening in September, a small army of workmen were engaged and set to accomplish tasks that in retrospect appeared impossible.

In his history, Pier sums up subsequent achievements. To take care of eighty boys dispossessed by the fire, a new cottage was built, an additional story was put on the miller's house, the ground floor of old Number 3, a nondescript building that had already served many uses, was made a dining room, and its second story a dormitory. A temporary kitchen was erected beside the chapel, a ward of the infirmary altered to accommodate students' rooms, and provision made for lodging six boys in the rectory. The command shown by Dr. Coit in these undertakings was a measure of the force that had gone into the building of St. Paul's from the beginning; and it was proof to all that failure would not now overtake it.

The feat was the more remarkable in that the rector during the period was deprived of the help of the vice rector, his brother Joseph Coit. The latter had been hunting through the summer in the Canadian wilds, out of reach of civilization. Returning to Concord after Labor Day, he asked of the cab driver as they passed the fire station whether there had been any serious fires in his absence. Not since the school burned down, was the reply. Joseph Coit proceeded in silence, without question or comment, preparing himself for the worst.

When the school opened that autumn, 204 boys were in residence, compared with 194 the previous year.

Two tasks remained before the ship could be said to be back on an even course. To assure good morale and to provide some compensation for the discomforts of the improvised arrangements, a new gymnasium was completed in an astonishingly brief period. Begun in the summer of 1878, it was opened to the boys the following January. Replacing a makeshift structure to the rear of the old school house, it immediately became a popular focus of activity. The upper floor—destined to be the auditorium where, on uncomfortable squeaking benches, the school attended plays and concerts until the late 1940s—was converted for the time being into a dormitory, relieving some of the pressure on the makeshift accommodations. Later generations would consider this gymnasium an ugly building, looming heavily over the pond, but to the school in 1879 it seemed a thing of wonder.

In January of that year the Boston architect George H. Young appeared on the local scene, and it was rightly surmised that another building was being projected. The new school house, designed to replace the one destroyed in the fire, rose on the east side of the Dunbarton road, where the rectory and infirmary already stood, but set back about a hundred yards and breaking the pattern of the village street. The building's bulk and height, with its somber tessellated surface, shattered the existing scale and made it at best an uneasy neighbor. Within were alcoved dormitories reaching up four stories into an attic, as well as masters' accommodations, and dining and common rooms institutional and cheerless in aspect.

Joseph Coit was placed in charge of the building, a compensation in human form for the deficiencies of bricks and mortar. Here was moved the founder's table, a warming touch of tradition. The whole derived eventually a sort of patina, if not of age (for its life would be briefer than three-score years), at least of legend and of austerities enjoyed with masculine good humor.

The laying of the cornerstone of the new school house took place on October 18, 1879, and was carried out stylishly, with the picturesque formality the little community had developed through the marking of many good days in its past. A Concord newspaper described the scene as "unforgettable." "The white-robed clergy, the boys—an army of them—all behaving with perfect propriety—the interested faces of the spectators, the voice of melody mingling with strains from the band, the soft haze in the air, rendering indistinct the hills beyond and the valleys between": all this signified in its own way that the school had put its year of trouble behind.

The tall man presiding over the ceremony was as one who himself had come through the fire, whose spirit the flames had not touched.

A World of Wealth

Entering the 1880s, St. Paul's appeared impregnable. Its ascendancy among New England schools was unchallenged, and its unique social order—a mixture of classical studies, competitive athletics, animated Christianity, and community life softened by tradition and often by surprisingly gentle human relationships—was fast becoming the admiration of visitors and journalists. Articles in the national press began appearing at this time. They were full of inaccuracies and often vulgar, sniffed the *Rural Record*, but they would perhaps be of some interest to posterity. The burst of publicity testified to the success of a striking educational experiment, the more interesting to the world at large because of its relative isolation in the remote state of New Hampshire, and because of the extraordinary character of the man who had led it from the first day.[2]

To the rector, preaching on the school's twenty-fifth anniversary in April 1881, the scene presented itself in different colors. After the passage of a quarter century, he said, he had "a full recognition of the manifold mistakes, failures and shortcomings in the past." He could not yet be fully assured of the school's permanency; he felt that the daily cares to be met and surmounted formed, year by year, a constantly heavier load. Coit sensed, no doubt, that changes were coming over the educational world, and over American society, that would make the school's standards ever more difficult to maintain. Despite outward appearance, he may have felt within himself a first diminution of his energies. The burden, characteristically, he placed where in the end he believed all things must rest: "Say of this place also," he concluded, "I the Lord do keep it . . . lest any hurt it, I will keep it night and day."[3]

In the 1880s the material forces of the country were gathering strength. The long travail of Reconstruction was at an end; a new period of industrial growth and power was opening. Over New England in these 1880s still hung the haze of what was to be called its Indian summer; but the rigorous intellectual standards and the close social bonds were weakening beneath the impact of commercial progress. "I see another

As one who himself had come through the fire. *A snapshot of Henry A. Coit.*

antiChrist than that of Rome," Muhlenberg had exclaimed on first witnessing the Morse telegraph;[4] and Coit, though isolated from much that was happening in America, sensed similar apprehensions about the rapid development of technology and big business.

St. Paul's at the juncture faced an inherent dilemma. Its students had been drawn from the beginning from the wealthy urban class. As time went on, they tended to become more wealthy and more visibly connected with the ruling industrial élite. How, in these circumstances, could the school's tradition of simplicity and its strong religious tone be preserved?

Mellons and Morgans were on the lists of those applying for admission. A Concord newspaper would report in 1893 that "A private car of the New York Central and Hudson River line arrived at this city yesterday bearing Cornelius Vanderbilt and party. They went immediately to St. Paul's School, where a grandson of the great financier is pursuing his studies." These sons of the great barons did not appear the most promising soil for the cultivation of St. Paul's peculiar brand of unworldliness.

Coit himself was not prepared to bow before wealth. A representative of big business was met by the rector casually out of doors. Greeting him with reserve, Dr. Coit appeared to be preoccupied and said he would see him later. The great J. P. Morgan, when he sought sympathy from the rector because an impecunious young Virginian was courting his ward, found himself coolly rebuffed. "Mr. Morgan," Coit said, "I suppose there is no better blood in America than in Virginia, and in Virginia I suppose there is no better blood than that of the family to which this young man belongs."[5] The Vanderbilt boys, deprived of the rough pleasures of dormitory life, were segregated in a master's house, but received no special attention from the rector. Indeed a member of the Coit household at this time did not recall ever seeing them at the rectory.

As the possessors of wealth increased in power and self-confidence, the problem of educating them was raised in circles outside Millville's. "The education of the rich is just as important as the education of the poor," declared a writer in the New York *Post* in 1881. They needed to be taught to resist temptation and to become benefactors of society, not a burden upon it. "If we send missionaries among the heathens," queried the journalist with an amusing twist, "have we none for the misguided rich? If we seek to convert our convicts, should we not seek to save from self-destruction our young debauchees?"[6]

St. Paul's recognized that with so many sons of the new élite it had a knotty problem. "Alas," Muhlenberg had written to Kerfoot in 1851, "so long as church schools can receive only the children of the rich, they will be raising crops of weeds."[7] Coit and his colleagues did not look upon

Scudder lived in the lower school. Later, as a master, his rooms were behind the bay window at left. The wing to the right is the original Shute cottage.

A STUDENT'S LIFE AND PREOCCUPATIONS

The Big Study, where Scudder heard the rector lecture the boys on "kissing and such things."

wealthy boys as weeds; still, it was a little awkward to have so many of them.

The way out of the dilemma was for St. Paul's to continue in what had been from the beginning a dream of its own—a dream, said Joseph Coit, like no other that ever had an earthly existence. The school would pass through the 1880s and 1890s turned inward to a greater degree than in earlier decades, ignoring much of what was happening in the world politically and educationally. If it would not serve the new age of industrial expansion, it could at least continue to save souls. If it could not live by works, it would live by faith. The ideal of learning at St. Paul's remained that which would endure into the heavens, even though it might be sloughed off and forgotten during a life passed in the market place.

It was a solution, or a compromise, well suited to St. Paul's wealthy clientele. Parents found their offspring undeniably benefitted by the community life and the intellectual climate at St. Paul's, while being quite willing to leave to fate what happened to them in the hereafter.

A Precocious Student

A glimpse into the student's life and preoccupations of this period—a view from the ground floor and from within—is happily provided through the diary of a boy entering the school in 1882.[8] With rare interruptions over fifty years, as boy and master, Willard Scudder would keep this diary. Through many of its passages it is a collection of trivia: reports on the weather, on the hymns and anthems of chapel services, and on the proceedings of clubs and societies in which he was interested. But at important moments—despite the minuteness of a handwriting which can make it almost illegible—the diary gives us insights not available elsewhere. Through it, Scudder can be seen at various points of his career upon the stage of the school. As a first former he makes his entrance at thirteen, opening his diary with a fine denunciation of his cousin Gaillard. "My cousin Gaillard is an ass," says he; "I have found him to be one after years of acquaintance."

An accusation of larceny having been made by Gaillard against him, young Scudder is determined to create "a great hubbub." But he is soon distracted by other interests and concerns. Precocious, curious, interested from the start in everything going on at the school, with a fastidiousness of taste and dress that was to mark him throughout life, the boy faces up to his inner life as well as to the objective world around him. "I was a little homesick this a.m.," he states matter-of-factly, "but since have not been so at all." His father has been advising him on acquiring habits of decisiveness, giving counsel which the boy endeavors to act on.

"All along I find little places to act right off. Before I think I was of an extremely vacillating temperament, but by practice I can become decided." On one matter, however, he cannot make up his mind. It is the eternal schoolboy dilemma of what one wants for a birthday present. "I answered papa's letter today," he wrote, "and in it I set forth my reasons for wanting the camera. Yet I want those books very much indeed. In fact I cannot decide what to do, and so I have asked papa to advise." The ultimate choice is not known.

Meanwhile, the birthday approaches. "Just think, I shall be fourteen tomorrow. Doesn't it seem queer to be so old?" The pressures of school life increase. "Today in study I squeaked my chair awfully and I guess I'll have to get a report for it." (He didn't; he supposed the master must not have known where the squeak came from.) Extracurricular events become interesting. He is made his form's representative to the library: "So now I have attained one thing I always wanted to be ever since I heard about the library." At the Botany Club he becomes entangled in the most complex of parliamentary maneuvers; or on a botanical excursion—"a very pleasant walk indeed"—he searches for what are called mayflowers at the school, but what to him, he declares firmly, are known as arbutus. A library banquet a year later is "splendid in every way"—"not only were the viands good but the speeches were very nice."

This was a period when dancing became extremely popular at the school, a winter activity rivaling gymnastics as a way of filling the afternoons when the erratic outdoor weather made sports impossible. For young Scudder the opportunity was irresistible. All his life he would enjoy dressing up and cutting a fine figure, and now he went to Concord to order a new suit of clothes. "They measured more things on me than I ever guessed it was necessary to do," he wrote; and one afternoon he donned his new clothes and set forth to the auditorium carrying his pumps in his hand. The dancing class, conducted by a Frenchman, was a success, but later he comments in a slightly disillusioned tone in his diary: "I am not going to dress up for it any more, for I'd have to do it three times a week and it doesn't pay."

On a Thursday afternoon in the study hall, at one of his regular weekly talks, the rector lectured the boys "on kissing and such things—I never heard him so severe before." The lecture evidently had something to do with an incident recounted in the diary a few days later. It seems that a maid in the school's employ wrote to her sister in Concord that a certain student had asked her to go walking with him. The matter reached Dr. Coit's ear and was soon the talk of Millville.

Young Scudder rose valiantly to the defense of his sex. His fellow student, he claimed, was the victim of a most wretched affair, and there was not a word of truth in the vicious charge. Scudder was the picture of innocence, surely; yet it is interesting that when Dr. Shattuck came to talk to the boys on "hygiene," he found the information to contain "nothing new."

So the years run out, chronicled more or less faithfully: the picture of a busy lad, growing, taking his part in the numerous school associations, for his pleasures constantly skating, coasting or walking. The classes and chapel services are events in themselves, and there is plenty of time for reading and talking. One day toward the end of his fifth form year he dressed up again—"as swell as could be"—and went to a *soirée* at the rectory. "Thank heavens," he declares, "I managed to stay near to Miss M. Coit, who is very nice indeed." This was Mary, the rector's youngest daughter, who had been born during the Coits' first trip abroad. It is the first glimpse we have had of her as a young lady, one on whom the fairy godmothers had showered all their gifts, but who was to know dark hours as well as bright.

Two Deaths

Coasting was a major preoccupation of boys more adventurous and daring than young Scudder. The Dunbarton road as it passed between the lower and the new school house was a sprightly scene on a winter afternoon. On one famous occasion twelve double runners and five single sleds were lashed together to carry eighty boys down the hill and across the bridge in a record run. Even more challenging was Tibbit's (or Fiske) Hill. Starting at the top and crossing the Hopkinton road, a skillful driver could penetrate deep into the school property. As a boy, Augustus Swift established a record (to be matched only by Richard Dana) of going from the top of Tibbit's Hill all the way down to the grist mill.

In February 1884, Albert Emery, a third former, was coming down the hill when he ran head on into a sled which a boy was towing up the hill. He suffered a fractured skull and was carried to the infirmary. There he lay for nine days. Scudder, watching from his dormitory, observed early in the morning of the tenth day the shutters closed on Emery's room in the infirmary. He was the first to know that the end had come.

Barely a month afterwards the school received a second blow, peculiarly affecting. In 1884, Augustus Swift married, and obtaining a year's leave of absence, journeyed to Italy for his honeymoon. There he was stricken by a severe fever. On Thursday evening of March 27, in his regular weekly talk to the students, the rector announced that Mr. Swift had died. "I never heard the schoolroom so still before," young Scudder wrote. The man had been completely identified with the school and its boys; he was dear to the rector, who had made him one of his own household when his mother had died in his extreme youth. He was, when death came, at the height of his powers and in the flush of happiness. His remains lie in the Protestant Cemetery in Rome.

In June of that year, his voice shaken in a rare show of emotion, the rector recalled in chapel the student and the master stricken down within a few weeks of each other. As in few places, we hear in this brief passage the very tone of Dr. Coit's voice. "Think of those who, when this term began, were with us," he said, "radiant with vitality and hope and promise, sure of their years, to whom the future was like a pleasant path into blue distances. Yet death came, in such strange ways, in such sorrowful ways, and called them and they had to follow. There was a short resistance, nature pled, and friends agonized, but their eyes darkened, and they reached forth helpless hands, and went into the land which sends back no messages."[9]

Donne himself had never spoken more intimately about death.

The Coit Image

The personality of Henry Augustus Coit was inseparable from the growing fame of the school; or rather, it may be said, the Coit myth was inseparable. An image of the man as he was in his later years cast a backward light over his whole administration, making him, and the school, appear more somber and authoritarian than was the case. A spirit of enterprise, originality and good humor played over the community's life; incidents of the 1860s and 1870s amply illustrate Coit's sympathy and forbearance in dealing with the boys. Yet there was always an absolutist side to his nature. Beneath the practical administrator was the prophet; beneath the affectionate headmaster, the possessed and driven seer. The familiar portrait of Coit in middle age reveals a haughty eye, an abstracted gaze, a mouth beneath the bare upper lip uncomfortably prone to irony, even to sarcasm.

Yet there was another image, a Daguerreotype taken at about the time Coit came to St. Paul's. On the insistence of some old boys, an oil portrait was made from this. Dedicating it in 1912, Owen Wister compared the two images. The official portrait showed the Puritan side of Henry Coit. It was a true likeness—but only half true. In it was nothing of the poet, the dreamer, the delicate scholar and discerning critic. Above all, said Wister, there was nothing of the spirit who "divined and defended the boy in trouble, the mutineer, the scapegoat—and mostly won him." The Daguerreotype, by contrast, showed in the man's eyes "all the young dreams waiting to come to reality."[10]

A haughty eye, an abstracted gaze. *Henry A. Coit in his maturity.*

He seemed quite literally to fill the place.
The interior of the old chapel as Henry Coit knew it.

Puritanical and unworldly aspects nevertheless existed; indeed, as the 1880s gave way to the last decade of the century, they became increasingly dominant. John Jay Chapman, himself a seer, put this side of Coit into words that would remain in the school's collective memory long after the man's more human qualities had faded. Coit was, said Chapman, "one of those saints who come into the world determined to found something: they are predestinate founders. They make and occupy the thing they found, repelling all the world beside, fleeing from all the world except this; and they generally become tyrants within the boundaries of their own creation."[11] The tyrant-founder-saint was a well-known figure of the Middle Ages; indeed, said Chapman (and Phillips Brooks was to echo him),[12] Coit was himself a piece of the Middle Ages: "To have known him is to have come into contact with all the piety, the romanticism, the mystery, the beauty, the depth and power of human emotion which flamed over Europe in medieval times, and which have been temporarily forgotten."

The emotional and romantic sides of Coit's nature were certainly intense and pervasive; but they were confined to a narrow range of expression. They were sensed by the boys, but rarely in forms that could be grasped by the mind. Sometimes, perhaps in chapel service, sometimes in the classroom where translations from the classics would show an unexpectedly poetic strain, most often in his study in the company of a single boy, the depth of a hidden ardor would peep out and transform one's whole feeling for the man.

The Coit who was daily seen, however, who was the subject of such endless comment as informs a small community, was a man a little too fastidious to be wholly admired, too removed from the ordinary affairs of life to be entirely credible. His soul dwelt apart, and where it inhabited there was no human disorder, nor any of the sweat and noise of the market place or playing field. Upon seeing some of the boys in swimming, "The human body," he said, "is not a thing of beauty, is it?"[13] He himself bathed off the Newport beach in the long-sleeved and long-panted suits of the Victorian period. There he sailed, too, in the quiet waters of the bay. "I doubt he would have been comfortable in the heavy weather outside," commented his son.[14] Once, coming down to the lower grounds where football was being played, he was shocked by the apparent roughness of the game. "Tut, tut, this cannot continue," he admonished. When told that what he was witnessing was in the very nature of the sport, he climbed back into his carriage and rode off.

It was remarked of Coit that he rarely walked in the countryside except when he was visiting parishioners or distributing gifts to the neighbors. No one had ever *heard* him sing; yet it was commonly believed he led the congregation in hymns quite as surely as Mr. Knox, though in some different and more spiritual way. Similarly, he played the piano after his own quaint fashion, "a mixture of staccato and trailing arpeggio," judged a critic; and when in an emergency he played the organ in chapel, he never began strictly on time. Coit was not a man to let the musical demands of the service interfere with his private devotions.

This abstracted unworldliness is amusingly set forth in a passage from James Knox's memoir. Knox was a Coit devotee, so much so that he could never adjust himself to anyone who followed after. Certainly he was not intending to be ironical when he wrote that it was probably fortunate the rector had not visited the Holy Land in his travels. He never tired, said Knox, of expatiating on the peaceful reaches of Galilee, on the beauty of the lake of Gennesaret, or Bethlehem and Olivet; but these places were the magic names of his New Testament. "The barren wastes of Judea and the dirty oriental towns might have disquieted him unspeakably."[15] Similarly the ancient cities of the classical world remained for him a marmoreal ideal. Having visited Rome once, he scarcely spoke of it thereafter. We may be sure, said Knox, that had he met Horace on the Via Sacra he would have snubbed him.

The boys he tended similarly to see in ideal terms, and took pains that he should not know them otherwise. The school's strict discipline confined them, as far as possible, to a narrow path; and where the young Adam did break out, others—particularly his brother Joseph—could often reach them in ways outside the rector's powers. Yet his presence was felt everywhere and set the whole tone and spirit of the school. "Whenever I am at St. Paul's," wrote an alumnus after his death, "I still feel as if the old doctor were somehow not far away. I should hardly be surprised to see him step out from behind a clump of bushes or the margin of the stream, or to come across his rapt figure, on the athletic field, standing as I have seen him stand to watch the games, shading his eyes with his hand."[16]

In the long days of his rule Dr. Coit was everywhere, and he would remain everywhere when his physical presence had passed from the scene.

Dr. Coit in the Chapel

A man who had not himself attended the school told a story he considered typical of the St. Paul's boy of this period. A graduate had been involved in a collision between two ocean steamers. Asked what had been his thoughts when he believed both ships might sink at any moment, he replied without hesitation: "I could think of nothing but the last words of the *Te Deum*, 'Lord, in thee have I trusted.' "[17] To the non-alumnus, the deep, unquestioning conviction that the Lord could be counted on, and that believers would not be confounded, was the distinguishing fact about a man who had been trained under Dr. Coit. Certainly Dr. Coit aimed to make it that way. Awareness of God's presence in a man's life he sought to inculcate by precept, by example, and through the chapel services.

It was in chapel that the rector's personality was most publicly and unremittingly impressed upon the school. He seemed in his person quite literally to fill the place, and he permeated and controlled the congregation. Moving majestically from his stall to the altar or the lectern, the folds of his long surplice swaying rhythmically, he focused attention so as to create the feeling that he was leading all to participate in a special moment of holiness. In the act of praying, the intensity of his personal devotion was subtly conveyed to everyone in attendance. He took care that the services should be colorful and aesthetically pleasing (though characteristically he worried lest the boys be distracted by outward beauty); but he was himself, in his absolute concentration on worship, the most dramatic and pervasive element.

His sermons were read from a manuscript; he wrote them hurriedly with a quill pen, amid interruptions, and usually on the Saturday morning before delivery. They were not in a form to make their substance easily remembered: not divided into parts or studded with memorable phrases. Rather they were in the nature of reveries or meditations, creating an impression by the sustained elevation of a vision fixed on values beyond the day. Seemingly artless, their art was in a life lived on a plane different from that of other men. Yet at times he could strike near the central passion of his listeners. The passage on death has been cited; here he is speaking upon a recurring occasion of the school year. It is the Last Night service:

> The hour has passed. The evensong is over. The blessing has been spoken. For the last time the file of boys and men passes through the chapel doors. . . . But the story of their lives here is not yet ended, and for you the Lord is waiting, and in your hearts his spirit stirs, and cries, and listens, and renews the old unchanging and unchangeable lessons.

One can imagine the hush as the final words, full of admonition and the fearsome sense of judgment, fall upon the crowded scene: "Whether you are blest or not, is in your hands. The truth and grace of God outlive the faithlessness and folly of men."[18]

The occasions of the Christian year were acted out with solemnity, and the duties of the church taken on as if they were (what Coit certainly intended them to be) the most important choices in a man's life. With affectionate concern, the rector trained each student for Confirmation.

And then there was the semi-annual Catechism for the whole school, performed with the bishop present and before masters and visitors. Why these occasions should have been made so deliberately dreadful is hard to fathom, except that Coit must have been carried away by what a later rector called "his almost awful righteousness, and his enthusiasm for righteousness in others."

The scene is described by the rector's son Charles, who endured the display with an evident mingling of filial pride and horror. "My father stood, in his surplice, at the front of the chapel. The unhappy boys filled the transepts and the front seats of the nave, while the sixth form were placed in the choir. . . . The atmosphere was tense in the extreme. Some boys were frightened, some were pale, others swallowed with difficulty, with dried lips and anxious eyes. . . . The rector was always in his most dignified and severest manner. Not a smile, not a word of encouragement, not a moment's delay. The answer must be given perfectly, word for word, or else the question was passed immediately to the next. Every boy in the chapel was questioned. Mr. Hargate was present to mark with unerring accuracy the success or failure of the victims."[19] What this ordeal meant for most boys could perhaps only have been described in what Charles Coit called the "energetic words" of St. Paul himself.

The chapel was the focal point of Henry Coit's powers. It was also the fulcrum upon which the whole school balanced. "From what has gone on in past years in this house of prayer, springs all that is, or has been acceptable, here, whether to God or man." So Coit summed up the first period of the school's growth and development.[20] He had no doubt but that religion was at the core of education, as it was at the heart of individual life. The higher the spiritual tone of the place, he said, the fuller and more thorough would be its intellectual development. He had wanted from the beginning to have a *church school*. In the early days, standing upon one of the little hillsides looking down on Millville, he had prayed that this might truly become a *Valle Crucis*. Now at the summit of his career, his determination had borne full fruit.

Building the New Chapel

With dramatic appropriateness the major undertaking of the 1880s was the construction of a new and larger chapel. St. Paul's had closed its gates to the outer world, defying the secularism of the times. Like the cathedral builders of the Middle Ages, the little community found an objective for its efforts, a goal for its common strivings, in rearing stone upon sacred stone—while the rest of the world was rearing temples to Mammon. The end, as so often in human affairs, was darkened by irony. Instead of being the beginning of a new age of faith, the chapel's completion was the beginning of Henry Coit's decline; and it heralded for the school a period of well-nigh fatal difficulties.

In his twenty-fifth Anniversary sermon of 1881 the rector looked ahead, into the school as it might be at the end of its second quarter century. "Will the work still live? Will the flame of this sanctuary still be kept up?" he asked, with that sense of the precariousness of mortal things which underlay all his labors. Nevertheless he permitted himself a moment of hope. He foresaw a time when the number of boys in the school would have doubled, and the great wealth and progress of the times would have provided abundantly for their needs—comfortable lodgings, scientific apparatus, libraries and collections. And then the climax: "In my prophetic thought I enter with the great body of the school into a new and larger chapel." The existing chapel, with its old ornaments and sacred things intact, formed in his vision an ante-chapel. "But the great throng passes through into a more glorious house of prayer."

In 1882 a committee of alumni was appointed to raise a sum of $100,000 for such a new chapel. It was an unheard-of amount and seemed beyond all reasonable possibility. The new school house had cost $80,000; efforts to fund it from contributions had largely failed, and it had left the school encumbered with a debt that had to be paid by strict economies out of annual revenues. Many influential alumni were against the new venture, feeling that maintenance of existing buildings already put a heavy charge on a school possessed of no permanent endowments. Besides there were other, and perhaps more pressing needs.

Nevertheless the drive went forward, at the start not altogether propitiously. With a little over two-thirds of the sum in hand two years later, the boys of the school were called upon. Their efforts, too, fell short of the goal assigned, but contributions from their mite boxes and appeals to parents and friends intensified the feeling that this was an undertaking in which a whole community, working for the school and for the greater glory of God, was joined. On April 3, 1886—precisely thirty years after the founding of the school—Dr. Coit received word from the alumni that the chapel building fund had been completed.

The site for the new chapel was just east of the study hall, to which it was to be connected by a cloister. It was to be set well back from the main street, so as to be approached across a broad lawn, its length and height falling into a middle landscape. Its far side would be set close enough to the pond so that its tower, reflecting in the still waters of the warmer months or rising above the ice in winter, would in future years be an ever-present image.

Design was entrusted to a young architect recently arrived from England who had settled himself in Boston's Pemberton Square. Henry

Vaughan was a high churchman, believing that English Gothic, with its roots in the fourteenth century prior to Henry VIII's break with Rome, was the true style for the Anglican Church. In the course of a solitary, single-minded career he would design some fifty buildings embodying his architectural and religious ideals, mostly churches and school buildings throughout New England, where a design by Vaughan became the standard by which other structures were judged. The chapel for St. Paul's School, the work of his late thirties, was his masterpiece.[21]

On St. Matthew's Day, 21 September 1886, the cornerstone was laid. A whole holiday was ordered. At the service in what was henceforth to be known as the old chapel, Samuel Eliot made the address, the accomplished orator being at his most moving and eloquent. He spoke of the pain of leavetaking: "Here all have been scholars at the Lord's feet." Yet nothing sacred to the memory was to be given up. "Not a member past or present, not a friend near or far away, not they who have ceased to live on earth—we might even add they as yet unborn who are to come here in their youth hereafter—but seem to be with us as we leave one chapel for the other, and say the first prayer on yonder ground."[22]

The foundations on "yonder ground" had already been set, and the walls had risen to a considerable height, when the bishop recited the appropriate words. Dr. Shattuck then struck the stone three times to complete the ceremony of laying.

Gathering Clouds

The year 1888, which should have been one of jubilation and a sense of completion, was instead a time when the shadows lengthened. The epidemics of the previous decade returned in force, with attendance at the study hall decimated by measles and mumps, and all the old vigils and alarms repeated. Several deaths occurred within the immediate households of the school family—the father of one, the wife of another in childbirth; and Mrs. Coit declined under a sickness for which there seemed no cure. That winter, amid severe storms, the rector fell on the ice and broke his leg. He was thereafter a crippled man. In great pain as healing took its slow course, he injured the leg a second time as that sad spring advanced.

Joseph Coit, perhaps weighing what was to come no less than what had already occurred, confessed that he lay awake at night "shedding tears over the calamities that had overtaken the community."[23]

The dedication of the new chapel, occurring in this same spring, took place in beautiful weather. A crowd of alumni gathered, the most numerous that had ever returned to the school at one time. On the morning of June 5 the choir with the large assembly of resident and visiting clergy robed in the old chapel. Here, as the rector had prophesied, was the antechamber for a new house of prayer. But the rector on this occasion had to be helped into the new building by a side door. The greatest day in the school's history saw him compelled to play the role of observer, taking no part in the service for which he had so long prepared. Mrs. Coit, critically enfeebled, was lifted to her seat in the ante-chapel.

The completed structure stood handsomely upon the greensward, its walls and buttresses descending in a cascade of dark brick to the ground whence they had sprung. Within, in an atmosphere of lightness and height, carved oak stalls and benches ran lengthwise, making a fine setting for the processions of the young that through the years would go echoing down the red tile. A carved screen of great intricacy separated the ante-chapel from the nave. Otherwise the chapel was austere and patently un-finished on the opening day. The tower, which had been designed to rise one hundred twenty feet, stood truncated just above the building's slate roof. The windows were bare of stained glass; the altar, the pulpit and many other details were in a rough or improvised condition. It would take the cathedral builders of that little community many years, and would require the accumulation of many sorrows, before the building with its memorials and tokens of thanksgiving became the hallowed icon of later generations.

That summer the long-feared event occurred: Mrs. Coit died at the family home in Newport. It was a blow from which the rector never recov-ered. He had, said their son, leaned upon her completely. Her quiet good judgment, her unfailing support, were the props of his fervid and fre-quently tormented nature. We have a glimpse of her, at one end of the rectory table, cautioning Henry by looks if not by words as he stormed on about the Unitarian excesses of the revered Phillips Brooks. No doubt she was often the force that turned the cloudy weather of his temperament to a shy and fleeting sunshine.

To the school she had made an immeasurable contribution. Through the early years the only woman of a large household, she managed its domestic side, cheered its leisure hours, cared for its sick, and was the hostess whom visitors and returning boys found always kindly and hos-pitable. At the orphans' home she was a godmother to all. Indeed, from its annals is drawn the tribute which better than anything else sums up her gifts in dealing with the young—whether they were the offspring of the rich or the poor. "Children were won by her," said that memorialist, "for they have penetration to see who really cares for them; and she had the brightness of mind that gave her insight into their peculiarities."[24]

The new chapel stood handsomely upon the greensward. *The building in its original form, before the tower was completed.*

LIKE THE CATHEDRAL BUILDERS OF THE MIDDLE AGES

Within, an atmosphere of lightness and height.

Carved oak stalls and benches ran lengthwise.

Despite domestic tragedy, the rector's schedule did not change. When the school reassembled, he would still awake in the earliest dawn and be at his study desk before the rising bell. An immense correspondence with parents of boys and prospective students he carried on without secretarial assistance, tracing out his letters in the fine line of an old-fashioned pen. The door of his study was open to all comers. After an early lunch he would frequently be driven to Concord, where he bought provisions for the aged or infirm of his parish, distributing them himself to their homes. At the lower grounds, if a cricket match was being held, his carriage would pause briefly.

Following tea at the rectory, and again following supper, he would return to his study. "I have [often] found him sitting on a low rocking chair," wrote Charles Coit, "near the radiator, reading a volume of sermons."[25] He usually read a sermon a day, and wrote the date in pencil in the margin. On certain evenings favorite masters would read the New Testament in Greek with him. Promptly at nine the study light would be extinguished and he would go home across the Millville street, where a servant was waiting to massage his fractured leg.

When he was particularly tired, or when the burden of loneliness became intolerable, he would go down to Boston for a few days. "Travel," said his son, "seemed to refresh him." Accompanied by his faithful servant Tom, to wait on him and carry his bags, he would make the rounds of a few of the scenes he had known through the years. He would call upon his old friend Dr. Shattuck, himself now an aged man, or upon trustees within the city.

The ceremonies of school life were pursued meticulously—the Communion services, the Confirmation classes, the intimate Thursday evening talks to the boys. But the new chapel never was to him what the old chapel had been. He had filled the old with his presence, dominated its mood and spirit; now he seemed the performer on a large stage, entering almost surreptitiously from a side door, and not quite at home—as he was not at home in the changing environment of the times—among its unfamiliar and still unwarmed spaces. Frequently he would leave parts of the services to others. The morning prayers, the Sunday night hymn service, were regularly delegated to one of the school clergy.

Increasingly, during these years, Dr. Coit depended for the running of the school upon members of his family. Joseph Coit, long the vice rector, was a firm support at his side. He had wanted his son Charles to serve as a master, but Charles demurred. It had been hard enough for him being in the school as a student with so dominant a father as head. But now, after a spell of parish work, the bishop ordered him back to St. Paul's. A subtly intelligent man, a scholar and ardent churchman, Charles was of all the children most like his father, even while he found himself most seared by that slow-burning flame. Now he served his father faithfully, but was relieved when in 1898 he could once more escape to parish work. A man qualified by natural gifts for a high post in the church, an admirable and touching character, his life was passed in obscure labors.

Of a different caliber was the rector's youngest son, Joseph Coit, 2nd, known as "Bull." Finishing his studies at St. Paul's, he willingly stayed on as a master. Bluff rather than bright, he was drawn from that strain of the Coit family which had produced businessmen and stockbrokers—except that the younger Joseph lacked the innate ability to make money. Like his father he was a visionary, but his visions were of business opportunities which never seemed to materialize.

The first wedding in the new chapel was that of Mary Coit to a young master, James Potter Conover. By that time a lower school was being built on the site of the original school house. (The former Shute cottage then became the *old* lower, and later "the Middle.") The bride and groom were put in charge of the new building. Conover was a passionate devotee of the rector. Bafflingly idealistic, his method of dealing with the youngest boys was not always in accord with their animal natures. Mary, however, was in her element. Lovely in her youthfulness, scintillating and open-hearted, she beguiled even the most wretched of her charges from their homesickness, while she delighted a swarm of visitors coming to her house.

Finally, there was Milnor Coit. This younger brother of the rector had extended his sphere of influence beyond the infirmary. Now he was constantly at the rector's side, a hearty, high-colored man in contrast to his chief's frail demeanor. He would be seen reading for him the morning "reports," or in the traditional Saturday afternoon ceremonies, while the rector looked sagely on, unfolding a long roll to intone the names of all the students together with their marks and demerits for the week.

Meanwhile, the school continued on an outwardly smooth course. The traditions and events established in an earlier time were duly cele-brated as the seasons passed. The clubs and societies, the *Horae* and the *Rural Record,* were carried forward as before. All that was missing was a vital *élan*—the creative impulse in boys and masters that had been re-sponsible for the accomplishments of the past two decades. How much that impulse had been dependent on the rector was evident now that his energies began to fail.

An Observant Master

A young master arrived at the school in the autumn of 1893, the same Willard Scudder whose diary as a student, a decade earlier, provided an insight into the community's life. He had graduated from Trinity College and after a few years had found the practice of law unpromising. Now he took over rooms in the old lower and looked about to judge how the school was going.

At dinner he found several boys who were "disposed to cut up a good deal." He did not know how to deal with them. There was obviously a spirit at work he had not known; they were bent upon making life misera-ble for a new master. For several days he wandered about without much to do, homesick for the busier social life of Hartford and Boston. The idea of getting married suddenly had an appeal for him. He wrote impulsively to an unnamed lady, hoping for a reply. "It would give me such joy as would gladden me for a long time," he confided, thinking of her being so pretty—the golden hair, the gray eyes, the charming complexion and the fine neck and shoulders. "Ah, me," he sighed. Then he worried because at the school there were no accommodations for married masters.

"I have always had a thought I might be a good teacher." *Willard Scudder in his middle years.*

Perhaps that could be taken care of, but then: "As to that, do I wish to marry?"

One must assume he did not. Single, he would stay on at the school, in the same rooms of the "Middle," or in rooms nearby, until he died there one June evening in 1936.

In this first of his autumns, while the old order was imperceptibly dissolving, Scudder got to know his fellow masters and the boys in his house and classroom. "I have always had the theory I might be a decent teacher," he mused. One boy to whom he had been asked to give special attention he finds "quite uncouth"—but he was of "a good heart and affectionate nature." Another boy is caught in some minor infraction of the rules; he hesitates to report it to the rector, as "the rector would treat it in but one way—by expulsion." Puzzled, he errs on what he fears may be the side of leniency. By such tests he begins to learn the trade of schoolmastering. In the afternoons there are long walks, up Jerry or Prospect Hill; and in the quiet evenings are opportunities to talk with congenial souls among the masters. They would find their conversation turning to the future of the school, to their own futures, to the rector's successor.

"Indeed the Rector seems very frail," Scudder wrote that October. And again, "The Rector was so tired that the hymn [service] was given up. It has been necessary very often of late. It is not as Sunday nights once were. The day is incomplete. . . ."

The Kings Depart

If one looked for symbols of the passing of time one could find it in the death in 1893 of Woodbury Flanders, the old miller and school farmer. The substance of things was made evident in the death that same month of the founder, Dr. Shattuck. "A prince has fallen," said the *Rural Record*. "To think of him," said Samuel Eliot, "was to be a part of bright scenes, vivid converse, hearty merriment. . . . His presence was a gift over and above all his other gifts."[26] Yet in material ways he had been munificent enough. Not alone the school's original house and lands had been given by him, but the first chapel, and its enlargement and furnishings; and afterwards, when the school had been in need of help, he had stepped forward unquestioningly.

"A prince has fallen." *George C. Shattuck in old age.*

Perhaps never had a founder played his role with such magnanimity combined with such tact. In spite of worldly honors he was unassuming and modest; in spite of varied pursuits he remained faithful to his first love. The begettor of much that had grown nobly old, he never closed his mind to what was new. It was like him, when the larger chapel was proposed, that despite his affection for the first and the embodiment within it of so many memorials to his friends and family, he gave unstinted support and counsel to the enthusiasts of a new generation.

At the school the founder's portrait was draped in black and the flag flew at half-mast. Boys and masters took the train down to the funeral in Boston, going on foot from the North Station to the Church of the Advent. A thoughtful alumnus entertained them afterwards at luncheon in the University Club. The rector, on the following Sunday evening, preached in memory of the dear friend who had not failed him in word or deed. His text: "Abide with me, for it is toward evening and the day is far spent."

During the school's Christmas vacation, just two years later, an owl ominously took up its abode in the cupola of the old chapel. The ancient verger, attending to his duties in the choir, fell in the new chapel and was seriously injured. The rector stayed on through the holidays, reading, writing his endless letters—it was said he wrote five hundred in those brief weeks—and attending to the needs of the local parish. On January 20, 1894, after the boys' return, he delivered what was to be his last sermon. The words he chose to speak on, "Walk ye as children of light," might be taken as the epitome of all he had been trying to teach for forty years. A few days later, at the service of Holy Communion, he became unwell and had to be helped out of the chapel.

Dr. Shattuck came; but now it was George, the founder's son, who carried on the family tradition, the same George who had been present as a student on the school's first day. He pronounced the rector a gravely ill man, suffering from influenza. Withdrawn into himself, seeming to want to cast off the cares of the world, Dr. Coit lingered for a few days and then sank into a coma. He was in his sixtieth year.

On the night of February 4 the thermometer fell to sixteen degrees below zero and the wind was rising. At the door of the rectory, very late, James Potter Conover found John Hargate. The two old faithfuls kept the last watch. "We stood together upon the steps in perfect silence," Conover recalled later, "just waiting, with no account of time, just waiting. . . ."[27]

Next morning, gathered in the Big Study, the boys heard the rector's brother announce that Henry Augustus Coit was dead. "His idea was that the school should be a family," Joseph Coit said, in words of simple eloquence, "and that when one suffers all the others should suffer and feel the sorrow. He felt for every one of you and loved you in sickness and when you were well. He entered into the trials and sufferings of each of you, and you have lost a friend the like of which you have never known."[28] Dr. Coit's body was moved from the rectory across the street to the old chapel, and boys and masters remained by it throughout the night.

The day of the funeral was one of the fiercest of that or any winter. Falling snow piled into deep drifts; winds howled across the ponds and through the tall pines. Many of the old boys who would have wanted to be present were kept away by the storm. It was not thought wise for the students to take part in the funeral procession, climbing the hill that led out of the little valley to the burying ground at the school's western border. Those who did stand by the grave never forgot the wild ragings of the tempest. It was, thought one, like being on a storm-battered ship. The sense of loneliness, of utter isolation on that hillside, did not seem out of keeping with the nature of the man who was laid to rest.

Henry Coit loomed large in death, as he had at the height of his power and activity. Men were struck by the contrast between the force of his character and the constricted stage upon which his life had been played out. He had turned from the path of advancement—to a college presidency, to more than one bishopric—in order to rule over a small kingdom of boys. More than that, he had labored remote from the large centers of population, in a community hidden away—as the elegiasts liked to put it—in the bleak New Hampshire hills.

In part it was an ineluctable fate that had called him to this role. St. Paul's, as Bishop Potter of New York said at Coit's memorial service, might seem bounded in the world's eye, but it was "large enough for service, and faith, and courage; and mighty in these, he put his hand to the work and wrought." More significantly Coit had deliberately set himself, and set the school he nurtured, against the main currents of his time—against commercialism in all forms, against current concepts of publicity and social mechanisms, against all that was identified with America's throbbing urban life.

The idea of Coit's being apart from the contemporary world was firmly planted at the time of his death. A few years afterwards John Jay Chapman would come back to the theme, stating it in words that could not be forgotten. St. Paul's, he declared, seemed not to be a part of modern American life. The valuable and wonderful part, Chapman thought, was that there should be somewhere in the United States the atmosphere of another world. "To plunge a boy for even a fraction of a year into this pot is to give him a new outlook on humanity." Dr. Coit might have been an ecclesiastic, "rustling with dogma and vestment," but he appealed to a whole class of persons who at first sight did not seem to resemble him at all. "They were straightforward, god-fearing burghers; they were warm people, he was a hot person."[29] But they took him and his little world on trust; they sent him their boys—and that was what the old doctor had wanted.

"If a strange quietude lies over St. Paul's today," Chapman concluded, "it is because in this place a man once wrestled with invisible antagonists and saw ladders going up into heaven, with the angels ascending and descending upon them. The school is a monument to his vision—a heap of stones cast there, one by one, by followers and by witnesses."

CHAPTER SIX

This Troublous Life
1895–1906

Joseph Coit Takes Over

In June 1895, the trustees elected Joseph Howland Coit the school's second rector. It was perhaps inevitable that they should have done so. The board was not in a mood to take a long look at the school's needs, to conduct a search or to accept risks. The Coit image still dominated their thoughts, as it did those of all the masters and old boys. A work remained to be done, as a century remained to be finished out, and the natural course seemed to put in charge the man who more than any other represented the ideals and knew the methods of Henry Augustus.

When elected rector, Joseph Howland Coit was sixty-four years old. The Coits aged early, and he seemed a man of more than his years. Slow-moving, where his brother had been compact of motion and nervous energy, he formed his words deliberately and seemed to project his thoughts from a cavernous interior. He was physically massive, smooth-shaven in an age when hirsute countenances were the rule, and the ample brow crowned a face whose habitual expression was one of kindliness and mild amusement. For thirty years he had been in a second position as vice rector (as he had been chief assistant to Kerfoot before that), deliberately subordinating himself, devoted to his brother and absolutely loyal to his policies. He had never married.

A letter to Samuel Eliot, 4 February 1895, suggests the mood in which Joseph Coit took up his duties. Written while he was still under the shock of his brother's death, it suggests the handicaps to be overcome before he could provide effective leadership. "I feel lost without him," Joseph wrote, "and it is with painful effort that I take up various parts of his labors and duties. To be doing the things which I have been accustomed to see him doing for so many years is a hard task. . . . I am trying to honor his memory by a faithful, untiring but humble effort to keep alive the methods, the traditions, the spirit with which he conducted the school. I have no ambition to serve, and I have gone on with the work in accor-

His habitual expression was one of kindliness and mild amusement.
Joseph H. Coit as rector.

dance with the wishes of the trustees, and with grateful appreciation of their confidence, because it was my plain duty to God, to my brother's memory, and to my fellow men to do it.

"I assure you, dear Dr. Eliot," Coit concluded his letter, "I would willingly change places with him who is gone—and I thought and prayed so, many times during the last week of his life."[1]

In the spring the new rector moved from the school house, of which he had been the head, to establish himself in the rectory. There three Coit nieces—Eleanor, Jane, and Ruth—presiding as hostesses, added to the number of Coits already in positions of influence at the school. Eleanor, Henry Coit's younger daughter, was soon to enter a convent; of the other two only Ruth, the daughter of Edward W. Coit, emerges from obscurity. A lively, formidable woman, she would emigrate to Texas and found a school of her own. Under the three nieces, as they followed each other or overlapped, the rectory again became a center of hospitality, bustling with expected and unexpected guests. Joseph Coit could be a charming host. The well-stocked mind that in the classroom gave him an air of authority and lucidity, in the home circle relaxed into the contemplations of a worldly philosopher, familiar with the latest literature and the major currents of contemporary thought. A taste for travel, carrying into the early period of his rectorship, added yearly to his stock of observations and anecdotes.

Coit's Views on Education

In a discussion of schoolmastering, written a few years before he was called to take charge of St. Paul's, Joseph Coit elaborated the principles underlying his brother's regime; but more accurately he indicated those that would underlie his own. The impression one gets from these pages is of a man open and liberal in disposition, keenly tuned to the boys' need for freedom, choice, undisciplined amusements and kindly toleration.[2]

Little in what Joseph Coit writes deals with the saving of souls, but much deals with the making of useful citizens and decent human beings. The good school he saw as having within it elements of the parental sys-

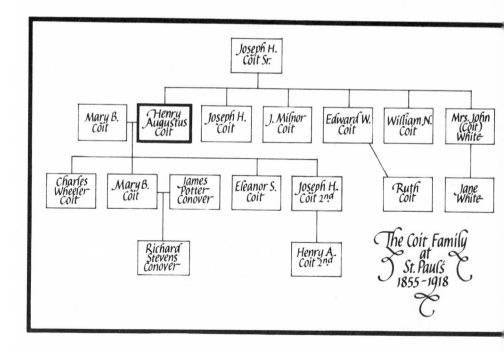

tem of governance; of "a free system" under which little restraint or surveillance is exercised; and of the military system under which "the soldier is the type cultivated after a fashion." In a right mixture of these three he saw the key to a school's success. That the second Coit leaned much toward the free system cannot be questioned.

As for the aims of education, he placed first the cultivation of such basic qualities as truthfulness, fidelity to trusts, honesty, courage, generosity—adding, in a pleasant phrase, "respect for sacred places and things." The fruits of scholarship, like the effects of daily communal life, were seen mainly to be the development of these virtues. A careful reading of such works as the *Aeneid,* the *Iliad,* the *Anabasis,* brought to the young mind a knowledge of great literary works: more than that, when handled by capable instructors, such works had power to form the habits of attention, intelligent observation and clear expression of thought.

The instructors Coit considered a paramount element in any school, second in importance only to the character of the headmaster. "The temptation in all boarding schools," he wrote, "is to overdo or underdo the care and watchfulness expended upon the boys." To tread the delicate line between too much freedom and too much repression was the task of a score or so of men whose experience could only be gained by years of trial, guided by a hopeful and genuinely affectionate spirit. Coit took much pride in the longevity of service attained by a large proportion of the faculty of his day, attributing it generously to the respect felt for his brother. But Joseph in his own way did much to keep good relations, and to achieve an absence of discord, among a group of men united more by their individuality than any other characteristic. Alumni of the school through the 1880s and 1890s certainly kept a cordial remembrance of their teachers, counting many of them among their lifelong friends.

To one of such genial instincts the later years of his brother's administration must have been trying. Only an unwavering loyalty could have kept Joseph Coit from questioning the restrictions and banishments that became increasingly prevalent. The Sunday regimen at the school showed him most clearly on the defensive. He admitted there had been criticism of this aspect of the school. Some of it, he maintained, was based on exaggerated accounts of what actually took place. The hours spent in chapel on Sunday during obligatory services he totaled up to not quite two and a half. The splitting of the morning service into two parts, one at 9 a.m. and one at 11:30, he defended as making the conventional worship of the period less burdensome to the boys. Even considering the devotional time spent in Sunday study and recitation, he found ample intervals for walking, letter-writing, visiting and reading. Though Coit never altered this Sunday routine, one gets the impression that he would have liked to extend the time provided for these activities, even at the cost of lessening the religious tension.

Upon the nature of the rector's role Coit had clear convictions. He saw it as having changed drastically since the earlier years when he could know each boy personally, as a father would. Now he gained knowledge of individual students by the less personal method of observing them as they performed in clubs and societies, on the athletic field, and at formal school occasions. In other ways, too, his responsibilities had grown diffuse and onerous. "Besides a large and exacting correspondence," Coit wrote, "there devolves upon him the oversight of the instruction, health, morals and manners of three hundred boys, and the general care of a great estate." In fact, he added, so numerous and arduous are the duties the rector must discharge, "only a man of vigorous constitution and large mental powers can hope to fulfill them with any degree of success."

Such were the views of the man who now took up the reins of leadership at St. Paul's. One could have hoped for precisely the kind of leaven the school needed, a liberation within and an opening toward the world of the day. Up to a point, and for the first years of his rectorship, these things occurred. But the times were adverse to the second Coit's easy ways and civilized views on discipline. His own constitution, moreover, was not up to the task he had set himself; his body would fail him tragically in the health and vigor which he had defined as essential to the work.

A Mixed-up Time

The 1890s and early 1900s formed a strange period at St. Paul's, with students showing a mixture of conformity and rebellion, conventionality and strong individualism. More than at most times they could seem at once very young and unexpectedly mature. Boys still wore the narrow, pointed shoes of the time, stiff collars and scratchy woolen underwear; informal dress, even for athletics in the afternoon, was rigidly controlled, and hats (the students actually wore hats!) had to be tipped to each master as he passed. Permission was required to go on a walk or into town. Yet beards and side whiskers were grown, and as the years of the second Coit administration passed, drinking and smoking were common, not only among the sixth formers but throughout the school.[3]

The New England scene to which St. Paul's had always been linked was changing, too, and was marked by discordant strains. Like massive oaks, a generation of Brahmins, writers and scholars had shaded a business civilization, softening its contours and humanizing its ambitions. Now the generation was passing. "The bells," wrote Van Wyck Brooks, "tolled every year for a great name gone."[4] Of such sages as those with whom Dana had lunched regularly at the Saturday Club, Lowell died in 1891, Whittier in 1892, Parkman in 1893 and Holmes in 1894.

In Boston, as in Millville, a new generation was taking over, what Brooks called the Alexandrians, an élite that could no longer claim the simplicity and homogeneity of the lost Athenian spring. For these, Brooks said, the gods still lived, but they were as mere men, more revered for earthly than divine power. "Like all Alexandrians they had lost touch with their origins, as they pursued the tradition in mechanical ways."[5]

Even in Concord the breath of a different world could be felt stirring. The capital city was becoming a busy place, with as many as a hundred passenger and freight trains coming or departing on a single summer's

The capital was becoming a busy place.

day. In 1890 the old Eagle Hotel was enlarged and rebuilt, to become the focus of the devious political maneuvers described in the American Winston Churchill's *Mr. Crewe's Career*. Main Street was a scene of activity, with automobiles beginning to take the place of carriages and buggies in the first decade of the new century.

Radical winds were threatening encrusted beliefs. A speaker at the St. Paul's Anniversary service in 1894 inveighed against the dangerous tendencies of contemporary politics. The true economic theories must be taught, he declared, in order "to exorcise the foreign demons which French and German laboratories have conceived and sent here. . . . We need a check to socialist heresies." Religious innovations were also occurring. Mary Baker Eddy came to Concord to live on Pleasant Street, near the entrance to the school, where she received a stream of Christian Scientists visiting her home on pilgrimages. Through the 1890s until her death in 1908, she could be seen going about in her buggy, often driving down the Dunbarton road through the school, an aging lady of penetrating eye and precise speech, dressed invariably in black.

For schools, and especially for the New England private schools, it was a time of pervasive unrest. By the middle of the decade, Cecil Patch, the famous headmaster of Andover, was lamenting that "we cannot maintain a higher standard of self restraint and moral worthiness."[6] The recently introduced trolley was upsetting old ways; and Patch, prowling around the town at night, often in fear for his own safety, found his students in the midst of strange and dubious activities. St. Mark's, having modeled itself on St. Paul's and having grown along with it, now found itself in a time of troubles. Against a background of mounting debt, disharmony among the alumni and local unrest, the headmaster, William E. Peck, went off to Pomfret, taking with him a considerable number of boys and masters.

St. Paul's was not immune to the general sense of disorientation. In the last years of Henry Coit's administration, relations between masters and boys had already deteriorated. A previously cited passage from the Scudder diary suggests that students were not averse to tormenting a new master. Now they prided themselves on having been able to reduce to one year the term of several recruits.

In pervasive ways the decline of standards manifested itself. An older master, W. W. Flint, noted in his diary of 1897 the "very remarkable fact" that the lower school boys seemed to be allowed to spin their tops on Sundays. "I had to step almost clean out of the sidewalk to go around spinning tops," he added reprovingly. A fire broke out in the woods of the school property where boys had been camping. It was fought for three days by students and masters. "I noticed at different times as I was carry-

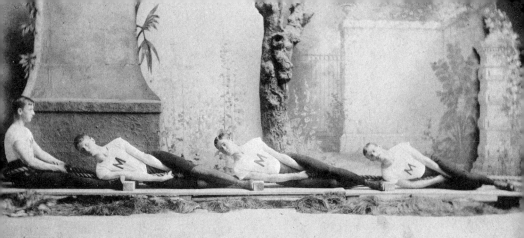

An archaic form of competition.

THE "PLUCK AND GRIT" OF THE ST. PAUL'S BOYS

A professional was brought in to coach. *The St. Paul's football team of 1895.*

ing water," said Mr. Flint, "a coffee pot, empty cans of condensed milk, tumblers, a mug, and at the center was a little phial that smelled like laudanum."[7]

The New Mood in Sports

From the start, sports had been indicative of the school's character, changing as they did from the informal scrimmaging of the 1860s to the more organized pageantry and the livelier contests of the following decade. Now, as one more sign of the times, they showed increased variety and competitiveness and assumed an altogether novel importance among the values of school life. Sports rivaling the traditional rowing and cricket were introduced, though often they led short lives. Boxing contests, introduced in 1884, were barred two years later by Henry Coit because of their strenuousness and sanguinary results. Long-distance walking races were abandoned when, not surprisingly, it was found impossible to draw the line between walking and running. More serious was the tug-of-war, which became highly popular.

This seemingly static and archaic form of athletic competition was said by Malcolm Kenneth Gordon, master and sports enthusiast, to require a degree of technique, precision and rhythm comparable to that of a well-trained crew. At either end of a rope seventy-five feet long, teams

He took to all forms of athletics as to a natural heritage. *Hobey Baker (with Willard Scudder).*

would engage in various sorts of heaves, "some long and steady, some short and jerky, some with irregular impulses which required much study and practice."[8] A pull of five minutes without the slightest chance to relax a muscle constituted so severe a test of endurance that young men collapsed or fell in a dead faint. The contest was ultimately banned at St. Paul's because of the strain on the heart.

Football was destined to have a longer history. By the 1890s it was being regularly played at the lower grounds, notwithstanding the disapproval expressed by the first rector on beholding the nature of the game. Three athletic clubs, Delphians, Isthmians and Old Hundreds, took form in 1888.[9] Established primarily for intramural football games, they were soon extended to almost all sports within the school. The football players, however, looked for larger conquests.

By 1895 we find a St. Paul's team playing Harvard seniors. The visitors were heavier and more experienced, noted the Concord *Patriot,* but "the pluck and grit" of the St. Paul's boys was very obvious. The growing popularity of sports at the school was evidenced by the fact that, although played in a driving rain, the game was witnessed by five hundred spectators "who enjoyed it to the utmost." A few years later a professional, fresh from grid iron victories at Yale, was brought in to coach the St. Paul's team.

Like baseball, football was a game that aroused the passions of the onlookers no less than of the players, provoking displays of questionable manners. "We are sorry of late there has been too much disputing and needless talking," complained the *Horae Scholasticae.* Among opposing teams a regrettable tendency had been observed of each seeking to have the opponent disqualified. As for the practice of giving voice to club cries and yells, "it should be stopped," the *Horae* advised sharply.

Hockey, meanwhile, was taking on something like its modern form. At first it had been an informal scrimmage on the ice, gradually settling into a more organized contest with eleven men to a side, playing with a square piece of wood for a puck. In 1896 the Canadian version of the game, with seven men on each side, was adopted. That same year the school team played for the first time on the fabled St. Nicholas rink in New York against a group of alumni. The alumni won, 3 – 1. But the encounter was a spectacular event, and the school was off upon a long career of hockey playing, which was to make it known in the sports world and to fill many of the places on the top college teams with skaters trained upon the Millville ice.

In 1903 a first former appeared at the school who took to all forms of athletics as to a natural heritage, but made hockey his first love. The lad's name was Hobart Amory Hare Baker. As Hobey Baker he was to become famous in his time and to impart to St. Paul's the luster of his fabled achievements.[10] At this stage he was a portent merely, and we leave him, a tiny figure, a treble in the school choir, practicing at all hours on the ice, weaving in and out among the crowded players and onlookers, twisting, dodging and turning, learning never to have to look at his puck . . .

Not surprisingly, the staid and gentlemanly game of cricket began to lose out. In the early 1890s the rector forbade baseball, a provocative and generally unpopular decision. But baseball was the great American game; it was also better suited than cricket to expressions of the schoolboy's competitive spirit and his enjoyment of loud yells and catcalls. That cricket should have disappeared from the lower grounds in 1903 was an indication that the rector's fiat could no longer control all the impulses of schoolboy life. It suggested, too, that the invisible walls which had once isolated St. Paul's were being penetrated by the styles and values of the day.

Secrecy and Power

Another sign of the times was the growth within the school of secret societies, patterned on those existing on many college campuses and especially at Yale. Occult proceedings have always held an attraction for immature minds, and at St. Paul's as early as the 1870s this aberration had taken picturesque forms. Two deliberately obscure clubs were formed, "half literary and half convivial," the purpose of which was to do honor by readings and other ceremonies to the illustrious character of Mr. Pickwick. They died out shortly; but a note in the *Horae* of 1875 remarks that the Natural History Society, an early outcropping of the scientific spirit, was gaining a reputation as their successor. Though dissimilar to the earlier societies in many respects, "it resembles them in the paucity of its members, the profound depth of its investigations, and the unfathomable secrecy of its proceedings."[11]

In the last years of Henry Coit's administration, when his grasp on the details of school life was loosened, the tendency toward secrecy, combined with a new emphasis upon worldly success, took a less benign form. Rival societies, known as the "Bogi" and the "Hoi," were established to capture for their respective memberships the chief athletes and officeholders of the school.[12] The student heads of the Shattuck and Halcyon boat clubs, the hockey and football teams, the missionary society and the dance committee were competed for in an atmosphere of political skulduggery that might have put to shame veterans of the Concord State House. At first entirely secret, these societies met in the fields and woods around the school, usually at the same hour as that in which the masters held their regular meetings. Deliberative sessions were supplemented by large teas or "feeds" in the students' rooms.

A report that the rector had got wind of these activities caused their hasty suspension; but Henry Coit let slip the opportunity of putting a permanent end to organizations that were potentially mutinous as well as inherently divisive and snobbish. When he failed to act, the societies resumed with the tacit, if not overt, support of the faculty. The minutes of the "Bogi" provide a glimpse of the political shenanigans carried on with the naïve connivance of Milnor Coit. Pressure was put upon him to postpone elections to the athletic committee so that the "Hoi" would have a better chance of winning places for its members. Coit refused the request, but the "Hois" won out anyway; for Coit, noting the stuffed ballot boxes, "didn't pull out enough stuffing" to ensure a fair election.

Such was the school in the 1890s and in the opening years of the new century: an institution beginning to show signs of internal disorder, fastening upon athletics and secret societies as channels for the expression of a strong current of student independence. The spark of disorder flickered threateningly, while authority at the top gradually slackened.

Reform and Rebuilding

Joseph Coit's first years, from 1895 to 1901, showed a firm and lucid direction of school policy. He overcame the attitude of deliberate self-effacement cultivated during his brother's long administration. In disciplinary reforms and academic reorganization his ability was unquestioned, nor did the long-range financial problems of the school lie outside his concern.

A first act of the new rector had been to mitigate the severity of the disciplinary rules. In his brother's last years the system of discipline had congealed; its administration had grown almost ludicrously inflexible. Dismissals were frequent and routine. Punishments were meted out for the most minor offenses, and students found themselves entangled in lengthy procedures of absolution. In ruling that demerits would only be given for serious misdeeds, Joseph Coit followed the natural benignity of his nature and set the tone for his best years as head of the school.

Academically, too, he strengthened St. Paul's. Faculty members who had been autonomous chieftains, setting their own examinations and determining much of the content of their courses, were for the first time made responsible to department heads. The long reliance upon alumni masters, sometimes eccentric and often financially well off, he curbed by the appointment of a strong group of outsiders, expert teachers and rigorous disciplinarians in the classroom. Within a few years of each other in the 1890s, four men were engaged by Coit who were to play an important role in raising the standards of scholarship at St. Paul's. F. Beach White, Theophilus Nelson, Robert E. Peck and Frederick E. Sears remained faculty mainstays through the 1930s.

Joseph Coit saw clearly the school's basic financial problems. Tuition had deliberately been kept low by his brother. With no endowment to fall back on, annual expenses increased while the school's physical facilities called for enlargment or replacement. The rector set before the alumni in 1896 a strongly reasoned case for the raising of endowment funds. An appeal was launched, not very successful in its results but setting the precedent for more effective drives in the future.

Improvements in plant had lagged during the decade when all efforts were focused on the building of the chapel. A new lower school, on the site of the original school house, had been completed in the last year of Henry Coit's life; apart from this, building projects awaited the coming of the second rector. Joseph Coit was responsible for a major enlargement of the Big Study; a complete reconstruction of the old lower school, henceforth to be known as "Middle," which involved raising to a second story the original Shute cottage but leaving its timbers embalmed among the improvements; and a wing joined to the gymnasium. In addition, important new buildings were erected. A pleasant inn known as the Alumni House was situated at the entrance to the school grounds. An enlarged home for the sixth form was, however, to prove more controversial in its design and location.

The wave of construction, and particularly the need to find a site for a new upper school, called attention to the haphazard fashion in which the physical plant of the school was developing. What had begun as a series of small-scale buildings along a village street was in danger of losing its character without achieving a new ordering principle. Seeking advice on an overall plan, the school turned to the foremost landscape architect of the day. Frederick Law Olmsted, designer of Central Park in New York, had already withdrawn into the darkness that shadowed his last years; but the firm of Olmsted Brothers continued and was now requested to deal with the problem at St. Paul's. Significantly, it was the Alumni Association that initiated and paid for the plan, indicating the increasing role former students were prepared to play in the school's affairs, and suggesting, too, the relative inactivity of the trustees.

The Olmsted report of 1898, brief and generalized though it was, stands as a major school document, an example of imaginative thinking applied to the form and structure of a community. Schools and colleges, its authors noted, had long been accustomed to growing "in a pleasant healthy fashion, with a natural disinclination to anticipate great changes."

The image of a village street. *St. Paul's along the Dunbarton road about 1890. The middle school is at the right.*

For St. Paul's, the planners proposed a few seminal ideas. The best way to group buildings, they pointed out, was around an outdoor central open space—"be it long and narrow like a street or a canal, or be it broad like a quadrangle or a lawn."[13]

The image of a village street had hitherto served the school: along it were strung the original school house (now replaced by the lower school); the old and new chapels, the study hall, the Middle and, on the other side, the rectory and the infirmary. This pattern had been broken, however, by "an inconclusive quadrangle" where the school house was set back, and also by the broad lawn in front of the chapel. The street had lost its clear visual impact; in any case it offered little chance for expansions since it narrowed to a bridge where the two ponds were joined.

How, then, was additional construction to be organized? The smaller pond offered attractions as a body of water on whose surrounding shores new buildings would stand. For various reasons, this solution was discarded as impractical. What remained, in the view of the Olmsted planners, was the charming small valley through which ran the Turkey River after it flowed over the miller's ancient dam. To take advantage of this natural feature, trimming the trees that obscured its form and siting buildings around the valley's rim, seemed to them to offer a delightful prospect. They urged that the next project of importance be thus located.

In accordance with this advice, the old upper school, massively constructed of stone, was moved back sixty feet to accommodate the dormitory planned for the sixth form. Amid the confusion that often overtakes building plans, the new upper school was then placed in an entirely different location—upon high ground beyond the larger pond, remote from the center and unrelated to any of the existing buildings. Not only had a substantial structure been moved (at costs which must have been considerable) but it had been awkwardly placed, so as more than ever to remove it from the center of the community.

Meanwhile the new upper school went forward, an immense and compendious pile of brick in the collegiate Gothic style. Designed, like the chapel, by Henry Vaughan, it showed that an uncertain client can be responsible for a good architect's producing a poor building. It possessed no visible entrance, no outward expression of the various dormitories and masters' apartments within it, and—worst of all for the students and faculty—no closets. (The architect was said to have "forgotten" these, though he may have had in mind some form of medieval armoires.) The high cost of the building put the school heavily in debt, while the poor standards of construction materially increased annual maintenance costs. A dining hall, rivaling the chapel in the beauty of its oak paneling and vaulted ceiling, crowned the work. That, at least, spoke for Vaughan at his best.

Perhaps more serious than the economic or design defects of the building were its consequences for the morale of the sixth formers who inhabited it. The original upper school, in its field across the river, had given sixth formers a feeling of separation from the rest of the school; but at least the style of life it imposed had been Spartan. The new upper school added to the exclusivity of its remote hilltop location the luxury of separate studies, suites of rooms and (of all things!) modern plumbing. Much of the trouble within the school, from the time of the building's completion in 1901 through the 1920s, was incubated within this citadel.

A New Library

A final project of the second Coit was a new library. Not actively sought or planned for, it was the offer—gladly accepted—of William C. Sheldon and his family. It was placed at the site of the miller's cottage.[14] An odd fate seemed to favor the choice, for in the school's early days one room of

An immense and compendious pile
of bricks. *The new upper school.*

"A Taj Mahal of the Western hemisphere." *The library in a modern
photograph. The original roof of red
tile has been removed.*

the building had provided quarters for a library of sorts. As the school developed in the twentieth century, moreover, the location became agreeably central to the students' daily activities. Designed by Ernest Flagg, the donor's chosen architect, the library was situated at the pond's edge, a Renaissance temple—or, in the words of a *Horae* wit, "a Taj Mahal of the Western hemisphere"—constructed of rough-hewn ashlars and topped with a roof of bright red tile. Within, a lofty central chamber gave into reading rooms of spacious dimensions. The interior walls were decorated in green with dark red above the wainscotting, and from niches under the high dome the busts of classic authors looked down.

At various times thought to be a thing of splendor or a monstrosity, the library was perceived by the 1970s as one of those eclectic oddities dear to the hearts of architects and laymen. Dedicated in 1901, without substantial later modifications, this building would continue to serve as the school library through at least four-score years, though the number of

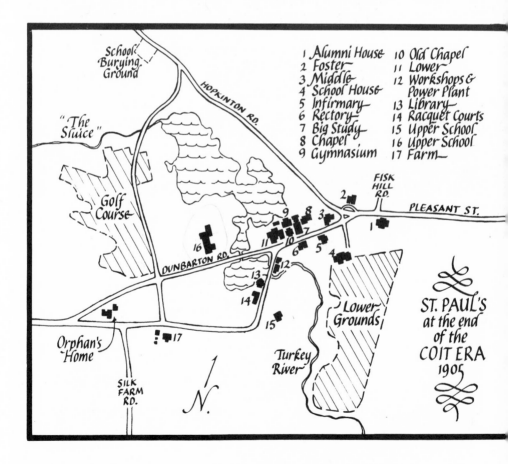

its users almost doubled and the choice of courses in the school's curriculum was multiplied many times over.

The granite-walled terrace of the library became, a few years after its completion, the setting for a memorial to the St. Paul's men who fought in the Spanish-American War. This war (1897–1898) roused Millville to a high pitch of patriotic fervor and struck a responsive chord among St. Paul's alumni wherever they were. It was a St. Paul's graduate, Hamilton Fish, Jr., serving under Colonel Theodore Roosevelt, who became the first American to be killed in action. Roosevelt wrote of the tragic event in a style that seems almost a parody of that period's naïve sentiments. "As we talked over the morrow's fight," Roosevelt recalled, "I said, 'Well, Fish, we have all got to die sometime, and after all, we cannot die in a better way,' and he nodded and said, 'That is just how I feel, Colonel, and it is one of the reasons that made me come.' "[15] Later Roosevelt visited the school at Anniversary and expressed in person his admiration for the six St. Paul's graduates who had served in his regiment.

Altogether one hundred twenty alumni took part in the brief conflict, and all connected with the school seemed to think it was one of history's noble causes. Only Samuel Eliot, cogitating in his great house on Brimmer Street in Boston, now too feeble to attend meetings of the school's board of trustees, groaned at what he considered the hysteria and jingoism of the times.[16] His grandson, Samuel Eliot Morison, was not to forget the old man's independent attitude.

The war memorial was dedicated on a rainy June day in 1906. James Knox made a patriotic address, proclaiming "the noble and unselfish ardor aroused by our nation's interference in the cause of Cuba." The memorial itself, a bronze statue by Bela Pratt, showed a soldier at ease but tense, committed but with an air of youthful insouciance. It seemed the perfect tribute, and typified the attitude toward war of that innocent generation. Three-quarters of a century later the statue remained the focal point of Memorial Day observances at the school, after several other wars had been fought and bitter disillusionment had replaced idealism. It did not appear to grow dated or sentimental, but in its youthfulness and a certain ambiguity of posture and regard, spoke freshly to later generations of young men and women. Indeed from the early 1900s nothing quite so alive remained as that faintly unsettled, and still unsettling, figure in bronze.

Growing Disorders

At the Commencement exercises of June 1902, Joseph Coit announced he would say goodbye from the platform and would not return after the Last

Night chapel service to shake hands with the boys in the traditional leavetaking ceremony. The simple change seemed to indicate a growing distance between the rector and the students, as if the ruler should vanish with a wave to his subjects rather than coming down to speak a personal word among them. In fact the departure from tradition was a symptom of long-lasting trouble. In July of that year a printed letter over Coit's signature went out to parents, announcing that poor health would keep him away for several months after school opened in the fall.

During his absence, he announced, his brother Milnor Coit would be acting rector, with Joseph H. Coit 2nd in charge of studies. (The first rector's more scholarly elder son, Charles Wheeler Coit, had already left the school.) Overseeing athletics along with "Bull" Coit would be two young masters, Malcolm Kenneth Gordon, bluff and hearty, and Godfrey Malbone Brinley. Brinley, whose tenure would extend into the 1930s, was decent and tenacious, the eternal deacon whose sermons startled and amused the boys by their vivid Old Testament imagery and the roaring manner of their delivery. It was not altogether a promising team, and it was evident that the rector's return would be eagerly awaited.

But the rector, in a sense, never returned. From 1902 until his death four years later he was a figure tragically defeated by age and illness. Absent from the school for long months at a time, his periods of residence were marked by increasing feebleness. The slow searching for words, once an appealing sign of modesty and wisdom, became a series of embarrassing silences; the unfurrowed face relaxed into passivity.

By 1903 Willard Scudder was noting in his diary that the rector was "seedy" in appearance, and only in the morning capable of conducting business. In chapel he spoke "haltingly and in a weak voice." A reception at the rectory was now "portentously dull." A student during these unhappy years recalled an interview in the rector's study. Suddenly the old man dozed off. "I waited for minutes," wrote Edward D. Toland in his reminiscences, "and then got up and tip-toed out of the room."[17]

Discipline among the boys, already in a precarious state, broke down alarmingly. In the Big Study, when a master rang the bell for silence, "it was the signal for a riot that could be heard at the lower grounds." In the dining rooms, in dormitories and in the classrooms, masters were dealt with as a common enemy. It was not only the unfortunate misfit who was treated unmercifully—there was, for instance, a Mr. Thinn, of whom W. W. Flint noted in his diary that the boys "worried" him, and being of a nervous and morbid disposition he could not bear up under it; far stronger characters suffered comparable treatment. Boys looked upon the faculty, Toland said, as "a necessary evil, who spied at us from behind closed

Dedicated on a rainy June day. *Ceremonies on the library terrace at Anniversary 1906, as the Spanish-American War Memorial was unveiled.*

doors and trees, who trailed us when we went off into the woods, who tore down our huts."

The masters, not surprisingly, reacted strongly. A habit of loud yelling developed in the classroom, and books were thrown regularly at the heads of offending youths. For so slight a sign of disrespect as failure to tip his hat to a master, a lad was bent over backwards and nearly throttled on the school fence. To escape the pressures, members of the faculty took to absenting themselves from the school. A young master, returning from what Pier calls "a night of conviviality" in Boston, "in a condition still far from normal," announced that he would issue excuses for all outstanding reports. The delighted boys gathered round him with their slips, to which he affixed his signature "gravely but with an uncertain hand." Another, having been absent for several days, was searched out by a colleague, who by good fortune intercepted him on his way to the Charles River, where he declared it had been his intention to drown himself.[18]

Among the masters and administrators of Millville, habits of ostentation and high living inconceivable in the earlier days of the school began to take over. Milnor Coit set the example. A driver of fast horses behind sporty equipages, "speeding along snow-covered roads in his gaily painted sleigh, wrapped in furs," he presented the appearance of a Russian grand duke.[19] The school regularly stocked Milnor's house with viands (on one occasion his frugal brother, going over the accounts, complained that even Milnor did not require so hearty a roast as was being regularly assigned to him); while other members of the school community built up large charge accounts in Concord to permit them to live in a similar style. Several of these accounts remained unpaid well into the twentieth century.

The secret societies that had been pestiferous but relatively harmless at their start now contributed to the general disorder and decline in morale. A good deal of drinking was taking place at their meetings. An entry in the "Bogi" minutes of 1902 states resignedly that after such a meeting four of its members were "snagged"—"two of them were badly tanked and the other two were, by no means, in a sour disposition." On a subsequent occasion, according to the same source, "We all started out right after dinner and went to a small hut about a mile and a half from the school. There were three friends from town waiting for us with a great big 'feed.' There were all sorts of things to eat and drink and everything was in abundance. We left at a late hour and wended our way homeward." On this occasion, at least, nobody got "snagged."

A more sinister note is struck in the minutes for 1905. "Some alumni came up and told us about the way some of the masters had been acting toward the school. All along we knew the masters they had mentioned . . . were not fit to have anything to do with gentlemen. Still, we thought them harmless. The alumni . . . said we ought to kick them out." It was thereupon decided that three of the members should go to Milnor Coit and inform him of the situation. Coit received the boys and promised them that the masters in question would not return after the school year. "If we could only take Dr. Milnor at his word," the society's scribe concluded.

These young upstarts, it must be said, were not the only members of the school community having trouble with Brother Milnor. During Joseph Coit's prolonged absences, Milnor was a controversial and often mistrusted leader. According to Scudder, the loyalty that had bound Joseph to Henry Augustus was not reciprocated by the younger brother, who told "droll stories" about the ailing rector. He bitterly divided the faculty by complaining that he was not being given sufficient authority while Joseph was away; and that Joseph, when present, was not capable of assuming responsibility.

The rector clung to such power as remained to him. His case was hopeless, Scudder confided to his diary: "One grows irritated at everything he does or says, for thinking of him in the old days." Yet he was resolved to be in office for the fiftieth Anniversary of the school, due to be celebrated in 1906. A pathetic recollection shows him in his study in one of these later years, receiving students coming to him, as they had come since the time of Henry Augustus, to seek excuses from punishments administered by the faculty.

Now a long line of students, counting upon the old man's indulgence, fills the corridor and runs down the stair. When a master later reproves him gently, asking how discipline can be enforced if he countermands all the penalties, he gazes vacantly at the slips bearing his name. "Did I sign all those?" he asks.[20] To this sad parody had come the generous instincts that in days of strength made Joseph Coit a beloved figure.

The rector would rarely be seen out now, and when he did appear it would be on the arm of his valet, Edward King. Despite this precaution, he tells in one of the few surviving letters,[21] "I have had the misfortune to slip on the ice three weeks ago, and have been very slow in recovering." Slipping upon Millville's treacherous ice had also been a fatal omen for his brother.

Last Days of Joseph Coit

For two years the trustees sat through these events, taking no action, while authority lapsed or gravitated in the direction of the alumni. Of the older members of the board, Perkins, Eliot and Dana had died by 1902; Gardiner was soon to pass away. Former students of the school were now in the ascendancy, including Alexander Mackay-Smith, bishop of Pennsylvania; Frederick Shattuck, younger son of the founder, present at St. Paul's opening day; and Henry Ferguson of the long sea voyage. Finally in 1904, Joseph Coit's condition being apparent to all, the board voted the election as rector of Anson Phelps Stokes, Jr., a learned young churchman who was to make for himself a celebrated career. He was named to take office when Coit should decide to retire. Perhaps wisely in the circumstances, Stokes did not accept. The board then turned to one of its own members.

Henry Ferguson had every reason to resist the call that his fellow board members put to him with extreme urgency. He and his wife lived within a congenial group of friends and colleagues at Hartford, in a large house suited to their wealth, surrounded by books and all the allurements granted to Trinity's favorite professor of history. To abandon in his sixtieth year the familiar scenes and the circle of lifelong friends, to take up a task that was sure to be vexing and onerous and of which the outcome was at best uncertain, required peculiar dedication to the school. It required of his intelligent and charming wife qualities of devotion rare even in that day. That the Fergusons should in the end have accepted—on the understanding they would remain at Concord for a period limited to five years—put St. Paul's for all time in their debt.

Ferguson, an ordained Episcopalian and a scholar who carried his learning with a light touch, looked on the world with an air of cool sanity. As a man he showed something of the steadfast ways that had sustained him during the long ordeal of his youth. Accustomed to the management of his wife's considerable financial interests, he seemed the right man to straighten out the school's confused and haphazardly managed accounts. It was hoped besides that as an old boy, intimately familiar with the school's affairs, he would be able to appease the jealousies and relieve the anxieties within the faculty. How this quiet scholar was expected to deal with the vagaries of several hundred schoolboys, a species of animal with which he had little first-hand acquaintance, is not clear.

The fiftieth year began with Joseph Coit still keeping his enfeebled hold. At the beginning of October he left the school, spending some weeks in a hospital in Boston and then being taken south. Meanwhile John Hargate, having been absent most of the previous year, returned to carry on his work. But Hargate was obviously a dying man. He was moved from his rooms in the school house to a small wooden dormitory known as the Farm, where it was hoped he would find the stairs easier to climb. There he never asked for help and always protested when it was given him. But his old friend James Potter Conover would slip in the door and, quietly picking up the small figure, would deposit him outside his room. He struggled feebly, Conover wrote, "like a child."[22]

When he died that January, it seemed that a whole epoch of the school's life and history had passed with him. "Johnny" Hargate was always an appealing figure, from the time he first appeared as a boy at the school. Loved by the boys for his jests, for his severity mixed with an unfailing cheerfulness of spirit, he was cherished by the first rector as a principal aide and an adopted son. His firm grasp on the business policy of the school, his proficiency at raising funds, supplemented Henry Coit's gifts and made him indispensable in more than one major crisis in the school's development. "Where is your home, Mr. Hargate?" a visitor to the school once asked. Before he could answer, the rector put his hand on the little man's arm and said, "His home is wherever I am."[23]

It had always been assumed that John Hargate was an orphan, although the rumor persisted of a younger sister's having been seen once near the school. Actually more than one sister turned up for the funeral, rather to the dismay of John Hargate's devotees. He was buried next to his old chief. "So long," it was said, "as men remember the one, the other will not be forgotten."[24] Hargate left his entire estate to the school, after a life interest for his sisters. It was a sizeable amount, approximately

$50,000, due to careful investment on the advice of one of the trustees; and this, together with an equal amount that was given through him by an alumnus shortly before Hargate's death, was the real start of the St. Paul's School endowment.

Hargate died in January 1906. In March, word came from the South that Joseph Coit was sinking. "The odd thing," Willard Scudder wrote in his diary, "is to find oneself glad that this is the end. Such is the result of five years of more or less continuous trouble, and a man who ought to have gone out respected and revered, goes with little regret." When Coit passed away on March 17, he had outlived the memory of his ability and charm; he had failed to survive until the school's fiftieth anniversary; he had even been upstaged in death by the more poignant blow of John Hargate's end. "All tragedy," sighed Scudder.

The trustees named Milnor Coit acting rector to serve until the end of the school year, and the fiftieth Anniversary found St. Paul's at a low ebb in its history. The weather for the occasion was dark and rainy. Boat races, the sixth-form dance, the chapel service and other rites were performed as had long been the custom at Anniversary; the local deities did their best to celebrate the present and to recall the past. But the school and its alumni, as Brooks said of the Alexandrians, "pursued the tradition in mechanical ways." At the Anniversary lunch the presence of two formidable headmasters of neighboring schools, Endicott Peabody of Groton and William G. Thayer of St. Mark's, may have suggested to some that St. Paul's, too, would find its foreordained leader; and a prophetic eye might have seen a good omen in the number of girls attending the sixth-form dance. "Hitherto," said the *Horae,* "there has generally been a scarcity of the gentler sex, but this time it was different, and no one who attended ever had much spare time on his hands."[25]

Chapman alone was capable of the elegiac mood; and he only from a little distance in time, and by skipping over "the great disturbances" which he saw as having followed the first rector's death. The fiftieth Anniversary, he wrote, "brought together all the school's adherents and fosterers and old boys, and peopled Concord for a day with the gentle burghers that had followed the Doctor. It was a touching assemblage because here in these people was to be found the peace which he had all his life preached so much and found so little. He had attained it in others. He had left it as a dower and an inheritance to the institution that he had loved almost too passionately. Out of the strong had come forth sweetness."[26]

Peace, perhaps. Peace for the moment. There would be a good deal of storm and stress before St. Paul's found its way again, under a new leader as strong, and in the end as creative, as the first Coit.

PART II

CHAPTER SEVEN

Interregnum
1906 – 1910

Year of Upheaval

For many in Millville who had known him since his youth, it was difficult to think of "Fergie" as the head. But it was reassuring, thought Scudder, as the third rector took office at the beginning of the academic year 1906–1907, to have a live and single chief at the helm. It was an agreeable change to have the rectory peopled by "humans." The closing years of the Coit regime he judged to have been a time of deceptions. Now there was the bracing atmosphere of truth. Students, too, felt the change in the air. The sixth form of 1907 was anxious to make things run successfully and on its own formed a committee to control the hitherto prevalent smoking.[1]

The first necessity, as Ferguson saw it, was to get the school's accounts in order. This involved him in personnel changes that shook the institution to its roots. During the long years of the first Dr. Coit, finances had been handled informally by the rector; he would himself, in effect, pocket the receipts as they came in and disburse the necessary funds. As the school grew and the reins of responsibility loosened, the primitive methods of bookkeeping failed to keep pace with the size and complexity of the school's operations. By 1907 it was not only impossible to control expenditures, but fees and contributions became difficult to trace. There was no record, for example, of a major gift which a noted financier was reputed to have given the school. Fortunately the financier was as vague in regard to his philanthropy as was the school in regard to its receipts.

Ferguson's practical mind was particularly disconcerted by what he deemed incompetence in the management of the power plant. A. H. Campbell, an early St. Paul's graduate, held the position known as the school's "curator," or business manager, and the trustees on Ferguson's recommendation forced his resignation. Campbell had support among alumni; his case aroused sympathy among faculty members who found the dismissal abrupt—and perhaps feared that they might themselves be purged in the same way. In part to appease the old guard, Ferguson gave Milnor Coit, now once again in the role of vice rector, many of Campbell's duties.[2]

Milnor Coit remained a highly controversial character. The name of Coit was revered in the school; on the other hand, many resented what they considered to have been Milnor's disloyalty to his ill and failing brother. He had never been a person inspiring general trust, and stories of his business adventures before coming to the school, and of his ostentation and extravagance while there, clung to his name. Dropping by the rectory for tea in October, Willard Scudder had a heart-to-heart talk with Mrs. Ferguson upon the subject. Ferguson, Scudder commented, "knows the whole story and trusts him no more than we." But Ferguson needed Milnor Coit's knowledge of school affairs and his admitted managerial experience.

The alumni now entered into the fray. The standing committee of the Alumni Association introduced and passed a resolution criticizing the rector and the trustees for their dismissal of Campbell and their unwillingness to dispense with Milnor Coit. The move failed; the trustees held firm. At the school James Knox, whose influential support had been expected to back the dissidents, weakened at the last minute. He showed himself (according to Scudder) "plaintive and vague," taking pity on Milnor Coit and urging that he be allowed to stay on for at least another year.

The case of another Coit was equally delicate. Joseph H. Coit, 2nd, younger son of the first rector, was in charge of the upper school. He had exercised considerable power during his uncle's administration, with a large principality under his management and with the general field of studies as his responsibility. An engaging extrovert, he was a favorite with the boys, for whom at Thanksgiving he would compose popular musical shows. More than most, he was bound to feel the chill winds of change. He became seriously ill during Ferguson's first year, and then conceived a longing to escape from the school's constraints. He and his wife, he wrote the rector, wanted "to be free of the noise and annoyance of boys."[3]

Complicating the situation were debts which young Coit owed the school. Apparently under the impression that household supplies would be paid for out of general funds—not altogether unreasonable given the previously existing customs at the school—he had run up charges, beginning with the year of Joseph Coit's illness, for vast amounts of firewood, eggs, milk and blacksmith services. Fortunately prices were low in those days, and the 300 quarts of milk consumed by the Coit household in an average month cost only $15, while a monthly cord of firewood cost $6.10.

Ferguson was unrelenting in presenting young Coit with the bills due, but at the same time he was insistent that he stay on as master, to preserve what he deemed a necessary continuity within the faculty. "In this period of transition," Ferguson wrote him, "it is of the very greatest value to the school that the old masters, who have had so much to do with it in the past, should keep with it and carry it over." But Coit did leave in the spring of 1907, and a subsequent letter, written from New York, confesses, "My debt to St. Paul's is a perfect nightmare to me. What with poor business and heavy living expenses it has been impossible for me to pay it."

Milnor Coit, meanwhile, had caught the drift of the standing committee's resolution. He resigned that same spring, going abroad to found a school for boys in Munich. In his early days at St. Paul's he had served the first rector well and become a merciful presence at the bedside of sick boys. If he was a rascal, he was at his best a jovial and colorful one. A pleasant last glimpse of him at the school shows the guestroom of his suite in the school house brilliant with the parchment and red ribbons of the diplomas he was in the habit of conferring, while he hands to his successor the baton upon which they were traditionally rolled.[4]

To the trustees, Ferguson referred to 1906–1907 as "a trying year."[5] That was a characteristic understatement. In November Scudder found the new rector "beaten by little things." He was overtaxed by the heavy burden of correspondence, by financial problems, and by worries about discipline. We see him starting for Boston for the April meeting of the

The bracing atmosphere of truth. *Henry Ferguson as the school's third rector.*

board "still fretting." Everyone was telling him something different: "We must brace him," Scudder averred. James Knox and his brother Charles, inseparable pillars of the old establishment, were said to be upsetting him with their irresponsible talk (he was not the last rector to be thus afflicted); Deacon Brinley was complaining that the rector did not understand him, and Malcolm Gordon was threatening to resign unless his salary was raised immediately. Even the sixth formers were forgetting their good resolutions of the autumn.

At the end of June, when the question arose of who would take the younger Coit's place at the head of the upper school, Scudder was "amazed" to hear Mrs. Ferguson suggest that she and her husband might go there. It would be helpful for them to be closer to the boys, she indicated; it would be an example of economy, and it would give them a chance to be alone, away from the constant distractions of the rectory. How those two, at the end of that first year, must have longed for Hartford and for the quiet life of a professor and his wife!

A Strange Choice

That same June the trustees elected Frederick J. Kinsman as vice rector, with succession to the rectorship assured when Ferguson had completed his major work of reorganization. Kinsman had been a student at the school in the 1880s, returning for two brief terms as master in the next decade. From the beginning he was doubtful about being rector, questioning his own fitness for the post. Dropping by at Willard Scudder's rooms to discuss the offer, he found his friend harboring some reservations, but encouraging him on the whole. Kinsman, Scudder thought, had a feeling for the old ways, was a scholar, and would undoubtedly gain mellowness with the years. After considerable reflection, Kinsman accepted.

Once again, dissension broke out. Joseph Coit, 2nd, was strongly opposed to Kinsman—his animosity no doubt going back to intrafaculty quarrels of the previous decade. He found an ally in the chairman of the Alumni Association's standing committee, and an anti-Kinsman motion was introduced on July 1. The alumni resisted the dangerous course of opposing the trustees on so important a matter and the resolution was defeated.[6] Kinsman, in the meanwhile, was having second thoughts. Though writing in midsummer that he was "pledged" to the office,[7] he withdrew shortly afterwards on the grounds that his preference was for a wholly ecclesiastical post.

The school was thus spared a rector who would certainly have led it into troubled waters (and who, incidentally, had one of the least legible handwritings to be encountered anywhere). A solidly built man of impressive scholarship, a rower, walker, and prodigious woodcutter, Kinsman went on to become bishop of Delaware. He resigned because he did not approve of the church's ritual. Subsequently he withdrew from the Episcopal Communion and became a convert to Catholicism. His entrance into the Catholic Church was, in his phrase, "the last act of a life that is ended."[8] A final letter in the school's file, dated 1924, suggests removing his name from the mailing lists, as he was departing on an extended journey. He had traveled already a long way.

In 1855, in the case of the depression-prone Mr. Roger Howard, the withdrawal of an elected rector had saved the trustees from an embarrassing choice. Kinsman was of a caliber different from the Bangor schoolmaster; unlike him, he was a powerful intellect. But as Kinsman said of himself (no doubt with an excess of biblical humility), he was "a double-minded man unstable in all his ways."[9] Howard's refusal had had the effect of bringing in the youthful Henry Augustus Coit. If providence was again to intervene, it was now up to providence to lead Ferguson toward one who would have something of the first rector's longevity and stature. St. Paul's could not survive further misjudgments by erring, if well-intentioned, powers of this world.

Clearing the Air

The school Ferguson took over was in many ways dark, musty and unkempt. Plumbing leaks, problems with the sewers and central heating engaged his practical mind. Dormitory facilities for the school of 325 boys needed renewal and enlargement. The Middle, scarred by years of service as home of the lower school, embodying the bones of the old Shute cottage, was still highly popular but so dilapidated that the rector refused to let visitors enter. The trustees must recognize, he informed them coolly, that St. Paul's was beginning to be considered antiquated and behind the times.[10]

Combined with the debts, the bookkeeping deficiencies, the poor maintenance of the plant (and symptomatic of the whole state of the school when the rector took over) was a lack of ventilation in the classrooms and the chapel. Ferguson confessed that he himself had the greatest difficulty in controlling his drowsiness during chapel services; "and the boys are frequently absolutely unable to do so." That the air should be asphyxiating was, in his judgment, "neither desirable nor reverent." The aged sacristan was lured into dangerous acrobatic exercises in an effort to open as many as possible of the chapel's stained glass windows.

Ferguson took especial interest in the farm, upon which the school had long depended for dairy supplies and fresh vegetables. Its acreage provided a green belt isolating the grounds from the intrusions of Concord's growing population; its farmhands performed indispensable winter chores. But the farm, like so much else, had been poorly managed. Its barns were inadequate and unsanitary—one can imagine that the cows were sleepy, too, like the boys in their classrooms and chapel. "We have to buy hay for the cattle," Ferguson wrote despondently, "as well as potatoes for ourselves." Among the reforms in the school for which he was responsible, scarcely anything so satisfied his practical sense as that, under his direction, the piggery should have been put in a thriving condition.

The same mind, with its cool penetration, applied itself to problems of scholarship and discipline. In these matters Ferguson had the day-to-day help of a vice rector, like himself gentle and unassuming, whose life would be woven like a warm-colored thread through forty-five years of the school's existence. William Hamilton Foster, an old boy from the golden crop of the 1870s, son of the well-known Concord judge, had come back to teach shortly after his graduation. His path to influence and power within the school was taken by quiet steps. One scarcely finds the record of his name in school affairs from the year of his arrival, 1883, until the early twentieth century. But by 1901 he was sufficiently secure in his position to build upon the high ground near the entrance to the school a mansion of red brick in the Georgian style, more commodious than the rectory, that was soon to become a center of social life for the school and its visitors, and would serve after his death as a dormitory for twenty boys. Smiling, judicious, untroubled in appearance, Foster was such a man as appealed to Henry Ferguson; and the two made an effective team. Some, indeed, claimed it was Foster who was running the school.

To Foster, Henry Ferguson gave praise for the sensible reform which for the first time introduced the "carrot" into the school's disciplinary system. Based on the assumption that the worst of boys are capable of reform, or at least subject to temporary remissions, it now became possible to work off by good behavior the demerits that had been accumulated by bad. That a favorable tone in the school could be attributed altogether to this change seems unlikely, but Ferguson was happy with the results. "I have been and am constantly amazed," he wrote in 1908, "at the good spirit and cheerful good behavior of so large a number of boys of different ages and individual characteristics."

The comparatively low level of scholarship was a more difficult matter to contend with. Admission to college was by now the overriding aim of the school's educational efforts, and the entrance examinations were the supreme test for all concerned. For success in this competitive field, St. Paul's counted upon a well-organized and elaborate academic structure that had grown up with the school and that ran largely alone. It worked, unfortunately, only moderately well. "At examination time," wrote Ferguson a little ruefully, "parents blame us for their sons' inattention and idleness, which we have been struggling to overcome throughout the year." One trouble was that the student body, composed so largely of sons of the rich, did not have the "invaluable incentive" of looking forward to earning a living. The leisure class, he said "are at a great disadvantage" in the competitive spheres of life.

The current emphasis on athletics was another problem. Athletics, Ferguson commented, "are useful servants but bad masters." Sports developed the character; they were to be cultivated, besides, for reasons of "hygiene and morals"—the sound old belief that if the students exhausted themselves in athletic contests they would not, in the circumlocution of the school's patron saint, "burn." But if sex was thus kept off the boys' minds, sports filled them too completely. St. Paul's boys had been known, said Ferguson, "for their good manners, their fine physique and their sense of honor." He hoped that "before too long we can include in the list a broad and accurate scholarship."

The word "broad" was revealing. A humanist himself, a faithful student of history, Ferguson did not believe that all wisdom could be found within the confines of traditionally prescribed courses. With satisfaction he introduced the substitution of German for Greek at the advanced levels, and he looked forward to providing the same "honorable treatment" for Latin. Noting a growing disenchantment with Latin studies, he asked that "the ancient language be relieved from its degrading employment as a grindstone upon which dull minds are sharpened." At the same time he deplored the constantly changing curriculum of the colleges. They were demanding for entrance nearly double what they had a generation before. The higher learning had been revolutionized, he said with a nod toward Harvard; now the "vice" of the colleges was their indefiniteness, "exaggerated in some cases by a great diversity of unrelated electives."

In such ways the rector pushed along, seeing the large picture, making small improvements where he could, and keeping the whole community in a tolerant and hopeful mood. The year 1909 he characterized as "one of those happy years that have no history"—a fact, in his view, permitting the school to prosper and to grow. Yet the burden was beginning to tell. At the end of the third year of the five that he had consented to serve, he admitted he found "the constant daily hurry and the close attention required, both irksome and wearing." It was time that a new rector be chosen and installed. On this front, too, Ferguson had not been idle.

A Young Missionary

In the Philippine Islands, on March 11, 1906, a young missionary not yet ordained preached at the cathedral for the first time in the presence of his bishop, Charles Brent. It was a significant moment in the lives of both men. The missionary, Samuel S. Drury, had been languishing in Manila, frustrated by inactivity while he waited for a primitive school house to be completed in Baguio, two hundred miles to the north, and for his eight Igorot pupils to be transferred from a more remote station in the hills. Two weeks later, on the eve of his departure for the new school, the bishop engaged him in a long and heart-searching conversation. "He is very reserved (which I like—I mean to be so myself),"[11] Drury wrote to his mother, "but he showed enough affection in the interview to carry me along with him for many a day."

While the missionary's mind was focused on his tin-roofed school house and his little native students, the bishop suddenly opened to him wider horizons. "He told me in confidence," Drury's letter continues, "that he hoped I should some day be elected as 'rector,' or headmaster, of St. Paul's School in Concord, New Hampshire!" The very idea, the young man said, "took my breath away."

Brent evidently wrote to Ferguson, suggesting that Drury might be employed as a master at St. Paul's after his return from the Philippines. Ferguson's reply, positive in tone, was enclosed in one of the bishop's letters to Drury. "My first judgment," Brent wrote, "is to go to St. Paul's as Dr. Ferguson suggests you may and let the problem work itself out." If Drury's vocation was to be with boys, a year of trial would prove it. "But the *where* is of small importance just now," the bishop added characteristically. "Get engulfed in God's will and the rest is easy."

A year later Drury returned to Bristol, Rhode Island, his boyhood home. The sojourn in the Philippines had been, in a way, his making. He had got out of the family circle, breathed alien airs, felt the spur of the extraordinary man who was to be a mentor so long as he lived. Now he felt the need to be nearer his roots. He would study and train—"You will not forget," Bishop Brent had admonished him, "that just because God has endowed you with gifts beyond the average you must make extraordinary effort"—but further than that he had no plans. Others, however, were watching the young man. He served briefly as curate of Calvary Church, Providence; and then unexpectedly, in the autumn of his return, he was called to be rector of Boston's St. Stephen's Church. At about the same time he received from Henry Ferguson an invitation to come up to Millville as guest preacher.

St. Stephen's in 1908 was an unusual church. Founded by Phillips Brooks, with Charles Brent as third in a notable line of rectors, its congre-

His little students in loin cloths. *Samuel S. Drury as a missionary
in the Philippines, 1906.*

gation consisted largely of Boston's South End, the poor and the dispossessed, who found in its Episcopal services a balm and a challenge. In
addition, a considerable staff helped meet the social needs of the poor
with educational and health facilities, a gymnasium, a library, classes in
almost everything from carpentry to dancing. For a young man still at the
threshold of ordination, the call was an extraordinary one. After some
weeks of doubt and self-doubt, Drury accepted.

The matter settled, and less than a week after he had written to the
St. Stephen's committee accepting their call, Drury made his first journey
to Concord. Dr. Ferguson was evidently taking his measure, but the

community at large had little sense of the visit's import. "On Sunday, December 8," the *Horae* reported, "Mr. Drury, of the Philippine Islands, preached and in the evening addressed the Missionary Society." In his diary, Drury set down brief impressions of the visit. He had gone from the railway station "by a little motor" to the Fergusons' house—automobiles at that time were still a novelty—"Homey people. Lovely time." He had long walks with Dr. and Mrs. Ferguson; the chapel awed him.

The diary entries seem, for so historic an occasion, surprisingly flat. But the inner struggle preceding his acceptance of St. Stephen's had tired Drury physically and emotionally—twenty years later he would recall the headaches and dyspepsia of those days.[12] Besides, the choice had been made. St. Paul's had been put into the background of his life.

With these brief notations Drury's diary-writing ceases and is not taken up again for several years. He now had a big job to do. He would be dealing with the world of outward things, contending with the needs of a complex and diversified parish. He would be (as Bishop Brent had urged) "immersing himself in God's will." It was a time not for introspection but for deeds.

The Quest Succeeds

Dr. Ferguson did not give up. If he had rendered no other service to St. Paul's, the school should remember him always because of the patient, humble and undiscourageable way in which he pursued his candidate. In the May following Drury's taking over St. Stephen's, Ferguson wrote him, specifically mentioning the vice rectorship, with accession to the post of rector assured upon his own retirement. Would he consider such an offer if it were made? Was there any "insuperable objection"? To this Drury replied—chillingly from Ferguson's point of view—with a reitera- tion of his commitment to St. Stephen's. "God helping me, I shall stay by it, without respect to the years, doing my best."

Ferguson ignored the apparent finality of this position and then went down to Boston. The two men had a frank talk, the gist of which was summed up by Ferguson. He went away, he said, with the feeling that Drury would like to come to St. Paul's—"in itself considered"—and that he did not "absolutely insist on 'never.'" There was another letter, writ- ten in long hand immediately after this meeting, which shows Dr. Fergu- son's modesty and the utter simplicity of his spirit. "I do not know why I was so stupid and voiceless and unable to say what I felt and wanted to say this noon," he wrote to the man young enough to be his son. "I feel so much the need to help here, and am so anxious to have the dear old place find the right man, that I am disgusted with myself for having made so poor a plea. I feel, however, we were near enough together those few moments for you to understand what I wanted to say."[13]

In response, Drury still refused to be encouraging. "I am sure that we do understand one another. . . . An opportunity so rare will ultimately attract the man to fill it." From Bishop Brent now came words of support and counsel, heady wine for a young man at the start of his career. Brent was delighted, he said, that Drury had declined St. Paul's—"not because I do not covet for you the opportunity, but because in the circumstances it looks as if you could not have gone without a distinct loss of power. . . . Never be the victim of opportunity, Sam. Many a brave eager life has been smothered by opportunity. Whatever you do, do as master. . . . To those who have the high responsibility and thrilling inspiration of many talents like yourself, opportunity is as plentiful as the sands of the seashore, and its best openings lie at one's feet."

Perhaps Drury had "declined" St. Paul's, but there was that at work which could not allow his relationship with the school or with Dr. Ferguson to be entirely broken off. The following Thanksgiving he preached again in the long chapel full of boys. This time the *Horae* referred to him, oddly, as "Mr. Stephen Drury." But Scudder in his diary judged the sermon "capital," and within the faculty there was now a growing sense that this was the man fated to be Dr. Ferguson's successor. For Drury the situation was awkward. He did not consider himself a candidate for the rectorship; if the trustees were waiting for him to express an opinion regarding his connection with the school, they would, he wrote Ferguson, "wait indefinitely."

Ferguson replied with tact and with a delicate humor that deflated a mood in danger of becoming self-righteous and pompous. "I have been working," he told Drury, "to prevent the question being put to you in such a way, that you would be compelled to say 'no.'" He would make no move until there was reasonable hope of getting an affirmative answer. "So, my friend, do not trouble your conscience about your honor. I shall be as tender of it as my own, and I want you here so much that I would not do anything to scare you away."

A season passed. At St. Stephen's Drury was making a deepening impression, not only on his own congregation but on men and women who came to hear the young preacher who spoke to his people in an unusually direct and moving way. In Concord Dr. Ferguson carried on his work, hopeful as always, a little wearily, watching the winter with its familiar rituals give way to the swift revelations of a New England spring. He persuaded Drury to come for a day as a visitor at Anniversary. And to the steamship on which Drury was sailing for an August vacation in England, he sent a wistful note of *Bon Voyage*. "We are keeping close watch over you," he said, "and wish to keep ourselves in your memory."

The pieces were falling into place. Patience and infinite tact were winning their rewards. When the trustees, in October 1909, unanimously elected Samuel S. Drury vice rector, to follow Dr. Ferguson as rector, his acceptance followed within a month. "Whatever you do, do as master," his mentor had advised. Now, at thirty-one, he held a foremost position in the church and in education. And St. Paul's, for all the troubles it had passed through, was the oldest, the largest, the most deeply influential of the church schools.

In his letter of acceptance, Drury asked of the trustees three things: that the date of his becoming rector be made firm; that he be assured a secretary; and that he be expected to use his own judgment in regard to absences from the school. All three were granted. The third of these was to become a rock on which his rectorship nearly foundered.

Charles Brent may be allowed the last word at this point. He had watched the youth in whom he had such faith, and in whom he undoubtedly saw a reflection of his own ardent spirit, move from awkward gropings into mature self-possession. Behind the scenes he had played a key role in making his qualities known in the appropriate circles. Most of all, he had goaded, checked, inspired and taught his protégé. Now he had his hour of triumph: "Rejoice, rejoice, rejoice that God has given you such a wonderful work to do for mankind. You are favored as only one man in a generation is favored. . . . Again, I say rejoice!"

Two Final Anniversaries

For Henry Ferguson there was also satisfaction. The "dear old place" had found what seemed indisputably the right man. The school where he had been happy as a boy, which he had revisited often as a young man and served as trustee and rector, had through his efforts and skill come now to a new chapter in its history—one, he believed, opening unprecedented avenues to growth. He could relax a little and enjoy life in Millville.

Anniversary, 1909, was a particularly brilliant occasion. The day was fair, the crowd of visitors unusually large. Three score girls were on hand, attending the sixth-form dance on Saturday night, lending their bright presence to the scene at the lower grounds—eight records were broken in that year's track meet—and gathered around the flagpole when the Shattuck crew rode down in the first barge singing their songs of victory. For the next day's luncheon, in the lofty dining room of the upper school, Ferguson had invited Woodrow Wilson, president of Princeton University, to make the principal address.

Wilson was then in the midst of battles with Princeton's alumni and trustees that would lead him to resign a year later and to enter New Jersey politics. Elected governor in 1910, he would be elected President of the United States two years later. The man who rose to address the assemblage of alumni and guests on Anniversary was a vibrant figure, at the turning point in a remarkable career. His appearance, as described in the *Horae*, made the most profound impression: "The tall ascetic figure, the deeply chiselled and beautifully modelled features, the brow of the scholar, the eyes that flashed as he drove home his points. . . ." He enthralled his hearers at the outset, said the observer, and held them to the end with the spell of a great orator.[14]

One can hear today, in the meager accounts surviving, the passion of the man's words. Wilson had begun with a pleasing reference to the date of the school's founding, which he had observed carved upon the paneled walls. The year 1856 was also the date of his birth. Then he launched into a profession of his beliefs on the nature of education and of the contemporary social order.

The danger surrounding modern education, he said, was that of wealth: "I am sorry for the lad who is going to inherit money; the object of college is to make young gentlemen as unlike their fathers as possible." "You cannot distinguish yourself by pleasure," he continued; "I fear that the kind of men who are to share in shaping the future are not largely exemplified in school and college." Throughout was an emphasis on values other than those that education in places like Princeton and St. Paul's seemed to be fostering. "So far as the colleges go," he said in a phrase to become famous, "the sideshows are swallowing up the circus." The world, he insisted, must be governed not by inherited prestige but by intellectual power. "The only man who is a master of the modern world is the man who is master of things he never saw."[15]

The speech, with its derogatory references to inherited wealth, caused a sensation in the public mind and among Princeton alumni. Wilson issued a denial of the extracts printed in the Concord *Monitor*, but the tone and accent of its account bear the stamp of authenticity. We do not know whether wealthy alumni in his St. Paul's audience took offense, but for one young man the speech had particular significance. Drury was among the luncheon guests; that morning he had walked with Wilson around the school pond, fascinated by the brilliant and audacious play of his mind. His own evolving commitment to education was undoubtedly strengthened by that encounter. Perhaps then, in an unconscious way, the die was cast that brought him as rector to the school. In any case the St. Paul's alumni and trustees would, often to their dismay, hear from Drury in the years ahead sentiments like those of Wilson in the Anniversary speech—the same questioning of wealth and insistence on spiritual values, in words remarkably similar to those Wilson had used.

For Ferguson there would be one more Anniversary. This time his young successor was at his side, the man he had searched out and persuaded, and whose acceptance had been his proudest achievement. A portrait was unveiled of the scholar who at so large a cost to himself had brought the school safely through a period of transition. Ferguson, always modest, said little; his farewell was reserved for his annual report of 1911, where his words were a final testimony to the man's humility and charm. Here was no list of accomplishments, no self-congratulation, only a quiet recognition that in the years of his rectorship the school had passed "from a personal, almost proprietary institution" into "an organized, general corporation." "Yet in this transition," he maintained, "there was little for anyone to do, but keep quiet and steady, and allow the natural causes to work themselves out."

The greater part of the farewell was a gentle apologia, dealing with the boys of the school, those strange creatures Ferguson had never been able fully to understand. "I trust," he wrote, "that what I have done or left undone have been of no injury to any of the boys that have been under my charge." The folly of youth is proverbial, he noted, and one has to see with sorrow and remorse young lives becoming warped in the wrong direction, losing the bright promise they had shown. Yet there were occasional compensations. Nothing could be more rewarding than to witness "the gradual development of character, the strength of moral principle and the steady growth in stature of the boys one has learned to love."

Toward his relative lack of success in encouraging higher standards of discipline and scholarship, Ferguson was humorously resigned. "I suppose there will never be a time when all boys will be diligent and studious continuously," he said. "The unwillingness of the simple to receive instruction is a complaint as old as the Hebrew sages."

There followed a few words for his successor: "I hope he will not allow himself to be hampered . . . by the specter of any exaggerated conservatism, in alumni or trustees." And then: "Thanking you again, gentlemen, for your many acts of kindness and forbearance, there is nothing left for me but to wish you goodbye."[16]

CHAPTER EIGHT

The Way Restored
1910–1919

The New Rector

Samuel Smith Drury, though his abilities were widely recognized, was not in these years an outwardly appealing figure. The first time we find him referred to in print, he is cast at eighteen in a play—a three-act comedy presented in Bristol for the benefit of sick soldiers and sailors—in the role of "Mr. Dismal."[1] He was thirty-one when he arrived at St. Paul's in February 1910, to take up his role as vice rector; but to the boys in the upper school where he lived, he was known immediately as "old Drury."[2] Something reserved and cheerless in his manner, something solemn in the watchful eyes: these with a solid but not graceful build and strong features—a large nose and large ears, a mouth wide and firmly set, crowned by hair parted at the center of a broad forehead—created an aspect more formidable than prepossessing.

Drury's image, in thirty years as rector, would stamp itself indelibly upon St. Paul's. Time would soften the features and bring them into a more pleasing harmony. Time would preserve—indeed would appear to accentuate—the springy step, the swinging carriage that seemed to have been born of going on foot in all weathers. As he grew older, he smiled more often, but the impression could not be escaped that this figure, authentic and rough-hewn, had been born old; and in 1910 it was hard to think of him as being young.

The man who all his adult life would be in charge of boys had himself never really been a boy, at least not with a boy's carefree ways. His father, a Bristol physician for whom he was named, died a few months after his own birth. He grew up in the care of his mother, Hannah, the daughter of Daniel Goodwin, a minister five of whose sons followed in his steps. Hannah had dreamed of being a missionary herself, but after her marriage turned to teaching, and as a young widow—"an inescapable figure in bulky black widow's dress and lace cap, cheerful but not

157

optimistic"—ruled the house in Bristol "like a provincial Queen Victoria."[3]

The darling of four older sisters, with an older brother too separated in age to be accessible as a playmate, Sam Drury in his youth knew few of the ordinary pleasures of boyhood. In the house on High Street there were serious readings, maternal lessons in botany and geography, but no games, no outdoor sports and few social diversions. His uncle, Daniel Goodwin, rector of a nearby church, received dutiful letters from the young man, but he was scarcely such a one as could replace a father. Drury remembered later "his erect bearing, his great propriety of dress, his approaching figure in a gleaming top hat"[4]; not features to induce confidence or to provide inspiration for a searching, introspective youth.

Not surprisingly, Drury matured slowly. When Hannah moved her large family to Boston, there was the further disadvantage of a city apartment and of rather unhappy years at the Boston and Roxbury Latin schools. A Bristol friend of the family remarked later that the boy had turned out to be "an agreeable surprise." He had been as a lad "entirely unobjectionable"; "nothing in particular" had been expected of him. Like another member of his family, he might well have turned out "crotchety, queer and impractical."[5] But something within Sam Drury was ripening, and fortune provided the focus his life needed. Within a few blocks of the Drury apartment off Copley Square lived a youthful priest, Charles Brent, whom Phillips Brooks had installed in 1891 as rector of St. Stephen's. One Sunday, Drury heard Brent as a guest preacher in Boston's famed Trinity Church. Thereafter, as he entered Harvard and formed plans for his career, Brent became his confidant and friend, the spiritual father to replace the small-town doctor the son had never known. St. Stephen's, more than Harvard, became the center of Drury's life.

Years later, when Drury wrestled with inward and outward problems at St. Paul's, those who watched him closely were often puzzled by what seemed contradictions in the man; they complained that his decisions were unpredictable and his course erratic. Had they known Brent, they would at least have had a clue to Drury's personality. "Few things about Brent were more difficult to understand," wrote his biographer, "than the basis on which he made important decisions. . . . It was hard for even his closest friends to follow his mental processes, and practically impossible to predict accurately what he would eventually decide to do. And yet his formula was very simple. He was always striving to obey the will of God and to subordinate his will to divine purpose. To ascertain God's will seemed to him as difficult as it was important."[6]

The words could have been written about Drury in the crises of his later life; and the final summing up of Brent's strength and weakness could likewise have been written with entire accuracy about the rector of St. Paul's. "A tremendous vision struggled against the consciousness of tasks poorly performed. . . . Limitless aspiration and a painfully acute conscience fought with pride which wanted recognition, a strong man's desire to have his own way, and a hot temper." Brent's biographer added—what was to be true of Drury (though only his diaries reveal it)— that he knew periods of "unutterable despondency."

The young man went from Harvard to two years of teaching at Pomfret. "Before we were aware of what was happening," a Pomfret student later recalled, "a large ungainly youth whose voice sounded like the notes of an organ and who spoke every word as if he were mentioning the name of a cherished friend, made us hungry for things we did not know existed between the covers of books."[7] From Pomfret, Drury went to the Philippines, to St. Stephen's and to St. Paul's.

Along the way he discovered his gift for preaching. It was to bring him fame, to deepen his personal influence, and yet to entice him into many of his later difficulties. The voice that sounded "like the notes of an organ" was to cast its spell over the long chapel at St. Paul's; but its very appeal made its possessor restless and often led him to crave the larger audience that called for him in churches and colleges across the country. It would be easy to presume that with such a gift he spoke with the grandiloquence of the old-fashioned pulpit orator. The exact contrary was true. Simply, without gestures, without seeming to reach for any climax, he spoke directly to men's hearts; in the largest church or chapel there might have been but one soul to be reached.

The rector of the Episcopal church at Bristol, he who was so "agreeably surprised" by the young man's development, described listening to him preach immediately after his ordination as deacon. "The sermon was without notes, brief, delivered with perfect ease, as if he was talking to Pomfret boys. . . . The impression on my own mind was a wish that I could preach like that." Scudder, who was a good judge of sermons—on one of Dr. Ferguson's he would comment, "Good matter, but, alas, too long, and no voice"; or on the efforts of a visiting clergyman: "Preached in odious sing-song a very vile sermon"—would invariably praise Drury's early sermons for their lucidity and brevity. "Strikingly simple and clear," "Drury capital again; boys perfectly held throughout," are characteristic diary entries. The man had the gift of tongues, a gift perfectly attuned to one seeking a direct relationship with his listeners.

When Drury agreed in November 1909 to leave St. Stephen's and come to St. Paul's, he was single. When he took up his rectorship eighteen months later, it was as a married man. A volunteer worker at St. Stephen's had caught his eye. Tall, angular, shy, Cornelia Wolcott was the daughter of a former Massachusetts governor, member of a wealthy and socially prominent Boston family. They became engaged in the autumn of Drury's year as vice rector, and the wedding, six weeks before Anniversary in 1911, was an event of the Boston season. "In the midst of our beautiful life together," Drury wrote to his bride-to-be, "let us be . . . very thoughtful, and never gaily act as if we were darlings of the gods."[8] Bishop Brent interjected into the midst of their private happiness the sense of his protégé's inescapable calling. "Anyone who has his native talent," he wrote to Cornelia Wolcott, "in a peculiar sense belongs to society at large. It is for you to make Sam ready for those sacrifices which are the core of great service."[9]

Cornelia Wolcott never flinched from duty, then or later, and she undoubtedly took the bishop's words to heart. But there was another side to her, a quality swift and intrepid, not always evident to those who knew her as a highly disciplined presence in the little community of Millville. There must have been times when she longed for a stage on which she could herself play a leading role, and when even the family, as it grew to two sons and a daughter, could not absorb her restless energies.

St. Paul's boys recalled her dashing appearances, side-saddle, on her favorite horse, "Waffles." "She is a glorious and almost mischievous horsewoman," her husband confided to his diary. In an automobile she was also known for her fast speeds. After her death a school driver recalled how he would be urged on by the rector—"Mrs. Drury would make the journey in an hour, or an hour and a half: could he not equal a woman's record?"[10] Even so they would be stopped, and twice were saved from a ticket only by the rector's clerical collar.

One observer, a romatically inclined lower schooler, observed Cornelia Wolcott through his own eyes when, at twenty six, she came to the school. He saw a young bride; and she, he wrote, was "lovely beyond our fondest hopes and expectations."[11]

Taking Charge

When the young couple moved into the rectory in the autumn of 1911, the old building had for the first time been wired for electricity, and it had been turned from dark gray on the exterior to gleaming white. (Drury would later arouse a hubbub in Millville by suggesting that properly the rectory should be *plum-colored*, and by having it thus painted.) For a year, as second in command under Ferguson, the new rector had watched and waited; now he stepped confidently into full control. In the chapel, and on daily school occasions, he was a powerfully felt presence. In the masters meetings he was all business, ready to listen to comments or suggestions, but cutting short diffuse or vague discussion. "It is the only way," remarked Scudder; and "it's odd how men like being ruled." Once again, Scudder noted with approval, there were receptions and tea parties at the rectory.

The students felt the lash of a new whip. One was suspended for possessing a shotgun, another for smoking. "If it goes on like this, boys will sit up and think," Scudder commented. It was "a grand thing" for discipline; and behavior did, in fact, noticeably improve.

Drury's first report to the trustees, submitted immediately after assuming office, was composed in what he called "a conservative spirit." His modesty was sincere. "Quite obviously," he wrote a friend at this time, "I am entering into other people's labours, reaping where they have sown."[12] He recognized, too, that he had much to learn. Schoolmastering, he told the trustees, is a science in which a man gradually becomes skilled. Experience would fit him for the task of being rector of St. Paul's School. That sounded reassuring, but the next paragraph indicated that the new rector had no intention of remaining silent or diffident while he was in the midst of learning.

Schoolmastering, he declared, involved the art of ruling men. Modesty might be an innate virtue that a headmaster shared with other good people: "The head of a school, however, must banish his natural self-distrust and steer a course which often provokes dissent and the charge of autocracy." Justice to the community would frequently stand against kindness to the individual. Machiavelli could hardly have put the matter more knowingly; but the pastor in Drury was never far from the surface, and he warned now, as he would in later difficult choices, that "the fortunes of the individual" must never be unnecessarily harmed.[13]

In the name of "science" the new rector proceeded to outline concepts that would mark and agitate his regime. The scholarly tone of the school would have to improve, he said, even though parents might prefer for their sons the honors of varsity athletics to a Phi Beta Kappa key. The craze for athletics had "lured us clean away from the cultivation of a rounded education"; that craze, he said, getting into form, was "the acrid fruitage of a scholastic collapse." The wealthy classes needed to wake up. "City high schools are filled with young people desirous to learn, while our boarding schools fit their pupils for the pleasurable arts of an idle existence." And why, he asked, must the coast of Maine be filled with tutors during the summer season? Their ministrations were an indulgence, an extravagant prop, unnecessary if the boys would do their work in term time. As for the faculty, "We cannot provide the best education from the hands of gentlemanly amateurs."

If this was an example of the "conservative spirit," what could be expected when the rector hit his stride? Seated in their comfortable chairs around the parlor of the rectory, the trustees listened in amazement as Drury read out his ringing phrases. They were accustomed to a passive role, but one of their members now bestirred himself to question whether it was good policy to set before the public an account of the school's shortcomings. Tension gripped the little company. For a dangerous moment the prestige of the rector and the authority of the board were counterpoised. Dr. Frederick Shattuck, the founder's son who had been present on the first day, broke the heavy silence. He blew out a cloud of cigarette smoke; he smote the table; he declared he would "rather send his boy to a place where defects were not only recognized but publicly faced," than to one where weaknesses were glossed over.[14] This was not to be the last example of Dr. Shattuck's vigorous good sense, nor the last occasion when Drury would be deeply indebted to his support.

One of Drury's first moves was to alter the time of the Sunday afternoon chapel service. For sixty years that service had come at 3 p.m., causing a sharp break in the day's activities. Now it was moved to the early evening. There would thus be time for long walks, informal games, uninterrupted reading. The Sabbath, Drury said, was *made for boys.* "Is it not better to risk two boys getting into mischief than to make two hundred tired of church?" Even more significantly he sought to change the tone of the chapel services, to make them brighter and less arduous to follow. He also wanted them to be briefer.

"Worship resembles other emotions," said he sagely, "in that it cannot be long sustained." A certain freedom from formalism, which he saw correctly as marking the next twenty years, he felt could nowhere begin better than at a boys' school. "Boys are religious," he told the board of trustees, "but seldom wholesomely ecclesiastical. They pass through phases of dumbly resenting a formal approach to God."[15] And so by his sermons, by the choice of hymns and anthems, and above all by the example of his own presence—visibly dominant, and audible in the unforced tones of his naturally resonant voice—he shaped services pleasing in themselves and at their best animated by a quality of sincere emotion.

Along with spiritual health, physical health became one of the rector's overriding preoccupations. The winter of 1912 was unusually cold, with temperatures dropping as low as thirty-four degrees below zero and a record number of uninterrupted skating days. The school suffered at the same time a record number of severe cases of grippe. In one week fifty-four sick boys taxed—and overtaxed—the school's facilities, recalling epidemics of the 1870s when the Coits had kept their anxious vigils. That same winter a lower schooler, Edmund Armour, died of infantile paralysis. The crisis put Drury's leadership to an early test. He rejected strong pressures to end the term before the time scheduled for vacation; and for those who questioned his decision, he had stinging words. "Parents who are bewildered by a moral problem in their boy's life," he wrote, "or who are none too militant about his studies, become in many instances fearsomely definite when he has the mumps." He went on to assail "fashionable doctors who fan apprehensions by agreeing with every fear." The wave of ill health he attributed to "depleted constitutions resulting from careless holidays."[16]

A resolution in the spring meeting of the trustees backed the rector, expressing "complete assent and approval in favor of the rector's action in regard to recent sickness at the school." At the same meeting they took note of the offer of a gift, the largest up to that time made by one person, for the construction of a modern infirmary.[17]

The first new building of Drury's administration—but definitely not the last—thus came to be Armour, rising handsomely on a site a little apart from the daily life of the school but near enough to be reached by the familiar chapel bells, or the sound of skates on the ice in winter. Its thirty-odd beds looked west across the school ponds; large solariums opened at either end; special rooms were set aside for parents visiting their sick sons. A chapel, along with an operating room and a modern dispensary, was provided. Drury, often accompanied by his dog Taffy, made the rounds of the infirmary daily. His visits to sick boys, frequently concluded with a bedside prayer, became as much a part of his ritual as the chapel services.

A few years later, preaching before a Princeton congregation, Drury referred obliquely to this crisis of 1912 and to his own rather authoritarian role. He had faced, he said, difficult choices almost alone. "Truth sat at the table and for once did *all* the talking. Facts that as head or administrator one had denied or banished, as disciple one almost embraced."[18] They were words that Princeton's Woodrow Wilson would have understood, and indeed in this early test of his leadership Drury had shown firmness and sagacity. But the lesson he drew from it—the idea that a power outside himself could direct the ultimate choice—reads disturbingly. It would return to haunt him in later decisions leading to less happy results.

The Conovers Leave Millville

Unknown to all but a few insiders, the school became the scene at this time of a complex and moving human drama, involving the trustees, one of its best-loved masters, and the rector. Within the limits of human fallibility all played their parts admirably. Drury, in a kind of test he had not previously been called to meet, revealed the sympathetic and kindly side of his nature.

After Milnor and Joseph Coit, 2nd, left the school at the start of Ferguson's administration, there remained in a white cottage at the top of the hill James Potter Conover and his wife Mary. Daughter of the first Coit, Mary had been the favorite of the rectory in earlier days. Her marriage to a young master of whom the rector was particularly fond was an outstanding event of the 1880s, and their installation in the new lower school promised a long pro-consulship. They were displaced, however, by the second rector, and nothing afterwards seemed quite the same. Teaching Sacred Studies and acting as the pastor of the old chapel's congregation of neighbors, Conover pursued his gentle and unworldly ways. But Mary dreamed that one day her husband might become rector and she once more the mistress of the recto.y. Her home was still a center for students and returning alumni; her "winsome, mysterious beauty"[19] cast a spell upon a wide circle of admirers.

In the summer of 1915 it became known that Mary, without her husband's knowledge, had been running up heavy debts and borrowing substantial sums of money from various members of the board of trustees. Drury was privy to these facts. Vacationing at Northeast Harbor, Maine, he hesitated, however, to make any move. Conover, as a member of the faculty, was directly within his field of responsibility; but the problem of a master's wife was more complicated. Then Mary was so imprudent as to write Drury a letter criticizing his administration of school affairs. This was too much to bear in silence, and with considerable heat Drury wrote Conover. Mary intercepted the letter and concealed it.

The ensuing complications, the awkward misunderstandings and puzzlements, could provide material for a novel. Here it is only important to note Drury's wise management of the affair which kept husband and wife together, saved the school from embarrassment, and continued unbroken the cherished links between the school and the Coit family. Writing as if he were the older of the two men, Drury in a series of letters urged Conover not to be "too upset" by his wife's actions. She was suffering more from a "mental twist" than from moral obloquy; undoubtedly she had been affected by the habits of extravagant living that had taken root during the final years of the second Coit's administration. He urged gently on Conover his acceptance of a call to a small church in Rhode Island.[20]

"My wife is coming to herself," Conover wrote back, "as these barriers recently set up between us are broken down." He was himself, he averred, ready to take full responsibility for all his wife's debts. "For the sake of truth and its accompanying love, I am willing to endure any shame

and inconvenience. It will not hurt my children a bit to be penniless."
Conover went on to confess that he had been trying for years to break his
connection with St. Paul's for the sake of his wife and children, but that
Mary would not hear of it. Loyally, he took his wife's side. Born and
nurtured at the school, she could not but think of herself as an inseparable
part of it; when cut off from the lower school, she kept open house summer and winter, and borrowing (as she saw it) "was just a calamity to be
borne by the school."

In the autumn the couple left Concord, aided by a gift which Drury
had discreetly collected on their behalf. One cannot judge either of them
harshly: not James for his unworldliness, nor Mary for her aberrations
following the awakening from hopeless dreams. The two, as the old
stories have it, lived happily ever after—she, indeed, until the school had
reached the age of more than a hundred years. In 1932, after James's
death, Drury wrote a touching memorial in which he treated the old master's thirty-three years at St. Paul's as "but a chapter, not the most striking or the happiest," of his career. His last years had been the best. He
had found fulfillment, Drury wrote, "on horseback, riding from cottage to
cottage for friendly visits throughout his wide pastoral domain. . . . At
length as God's freeman he could magnify his office in a simple rustic
round of bearing big burdens inconspicuously."[21]

More will be heard of James and Mary Conover. Their debts, such as
they were, were paid many times over amid the common sacrifices of
World War I.

A Shrewd Disciplinarian

"Since I've been here there have been several rectors around this place,
but only one good, straight, all-around man, and you're it."[22] The words
were those of George P. Milne, a Scotsman not lightly given to praise, a
small wiry man with a bristling moustache, the school's chief disciplinarian, blunt, laconic, sometimes unexpectedly humane and wise. Drury
took to this man with an easy affection, seeing in Milne an indispensable
ally in his struggle to renew order at St. Paul's. He was also won by the
frank humor peeking out from so unpromising an exterior. It was a delight, among so many tender sensibilities, to have one master who could
take a detached view of himself. "Dear Sam," Milne wrote when the
question of his being chairman of the history department was at issue,
"Titles don't bother me, so juggle it any way you wish to . . . I should
enjoy being a martyr."

Drury complimented Milne on his good sense. "What should a
Scotchman have if not sense," Milne replied, and added his appreciation

of working for "an honest, genuine man." Drury went well beyond the formal courtesy he extended to loyal masters. In 1916, we find him attesting to Milne's "profound judgment expressed in honest language." "This letter requires no answer," he continues, "but I take pleasure, at the end of a long day, in telling the truth to a good man." Much later, when differences of opinion and approach had separated them (but not diminished their respect for each other), Drury wrote to Milne of the "unique and brotherly helpfulness" he had given through nineteen years. "I could not have done my part without your loyal and undeviating assistance. It has meant everything to me personally to be by your side."

The new rector in his approach to discipline insisted on close observance of the rules governing communal living, combined with basic confidence in the maturity and good sense of the students. In both of these positions—though perhaps more the first than the second—he had Milne's reassuring support. What Drury called "unflinching and strict standards" did not mean endless punishments and heavy penalties. Several of the young masters seemed inclined to hand out large numbers of demerits for trivial offenses. A more modest dosage, along with a private reprimand—"a word of sternness *and* encouragement"—would, in Drury's view, be quite as effective.

But in reserve there hung always the threat of the ultimate punishment: dismissal if all other measures failed. A certain awe and even fear seemed healthy. At the end of one expedition in the company of boys, Milne commented on their favorable conduct; it reflected, he told Drury, the boys' consciousness that the head was a man who "meant business." "The sword of authority," he wrote the rector during his absence from the school in a period of illness, "does not perhaps smite with such a trenchant edge." That sword was seen as indispensable, however sparingly it might be used.

Disorders following World War I and the changed morals of the postwar world—disorders that Drury would deal with when his own inner world was in turmoil—should not obscure the nice relationships, the delicate moral balances, maintained at the school in these relatively innocent days. An unintentionally amusing indication of how subtly the scales of justice were weighted is given in a letter of Milne's to the rector, discussing a boy who had taken his own way on a departure from the school. The boy, it seems, did not obey instructions to go to Boston, but "evaded them by going to Hooksett." "If many boys treated the rules that way," said Milne, "we could hardly exist as we do." True, the boy had gone away by train; but he had gone only about a tenth of the distance he had been expected, or rather told, to travel. "He needs to be in a place where he cannot lose himself quite so easily, or escape attention," Milne concluded.

Another troublesome boy was treated more gently. He was told by his father, in an interview at which Milne was present, that he was "pigheaded, immature, and a jack-ass." "It was very satisfactory," Milne wrote the rector, "to hear the father speak so sanely." He did not know how firmly the rector was set on dropping the boy, but he was himself inclined to leniency. He had been against him for a year and a half, thinking him more malicious than stupid, but "when the little one said 'he'd try,' I told the father I could not tell you how to run the school, but that if the boy were here next fall, I'd do my best with him." The boy turned out to be one of the most active and loyal of St. Paul's alumni.

A Famous Prize Fight

An image of discipline at its most humane and enlightened is provided by the case of Chanler Chapman, son of John Jay Chapman, whose own years at the school had been marked by excessive religiosity. Chanler was as independent and eccentric as his father, but an excess of religion was not his problem. With Chanler it was a desire to frustrate the system without resort to such commonplace misdemeanors as smoking or drinking— and, if possible, without getting expelled. Having conceived an intense longing to own a motorcycle, he decided that the best way to raise money for its purchase was by organizing a boxing match for which students would be charged admission. To satisfy his sense of honor, and also to assure a maximum "gate," Chanler selected for the major contestant one of the school's most powerful physical specimens. He then made himself the challenger.[23]

The affair was arranged with great secrecy, but the shouts of the spectators, coming on a Sunday from the depths of the old gymnasium, drew a master to the scene in time to avert the worst consequences of the ill-matched contest. Chapman was summoned next day to the rector's study. Drury evidently had a liking for the boy. He admonished him upon the gravity of his offense—obviously, he said, he could not countenance boys' fighting each other for money; that was nothing less than "commercial prize-fighting." Then to the lad's astonishment he let him off with the injunction that he return to each of the spectators the dollar that had been paid, and the solemn wish that he might reduce his accumulation of demerits.

Chanler was touched by the rector's kindness—"a most Christian gentleman," he wrote, and he never lost a sense of gratitude for the toleration the school showed toward him and similar nonconformists. "Although I abused it," he said, "I respected this toleration." Still, he mused, perhaps the rector made a mistake in not getting rid of him. His own father had recommended such a course on more than one occasion. Was "this cavorting animal," he had written Drury, "surrounded by such sympathetic experienced and loving people as you, his mother and myself," to be permitted to try their patience forever? As for the ill-gotten dollars, young Chanler did his honest best to return them, but was not displeased when he found that many of his schoolmates, feeling they had gotten their full money's worth from the brief show, refused to accept reimbursement.

The book in which this and other of Chanler Chapman's adventures at St. Paul's are recounted is dedicated to G. P. Milne. It was Milne who at the end of Chapman's fifth-form year, after having spoken to him less than half a dozen times during his time at the school, placed an arm on his shoulder and remarked quietly that he was glad the boy was coming back to finish out his course. "He would deal with matters of discipline without moralizing," Chapman wrote; "indeed, without comment."

Aboard the SPS Special

The journey to New York at vacation time, aboard the St. Paul's School Special, was invariably a test of discipline and an arena where masters and boys matched their strength. With the tensions of the long term relaxed, yet still under the school's surveillance, the boys in resourceful ways displayed their capacity to be boys, while the romance of the train ride, the race against time and the conquest of distance, stimulated their imaginations. At Millville the rector waited—it must be presumed anxiously—to learn the precise time of the train's arrival and to be reassured that all had passed safely. "A good run. The special arrived three minutes early" (or three or a dozen minutes late) was the substance of telegrams sent back at the end of each trip by more than one of the accompanying masters.

Subsequently there would be more detailed reports. "The trip was as good as any I have ever made," Milne wrote of one such occasion. "One window was broken, the cause, being, I believe, an attack by Garrison on Jarvis, Jarvis being perfectly quiet at the time, but unfortunately pushed into unfavorable prominence."[24] On that occasion the train's ticket collector was plainly under the influence of liquor. Milne took him in charge. "The boys as a whole were very well behaved; the Pullman company got a square deal, and the drunken porter helped to kill the time in a very good way."

Another occasion found Mellon matching coins with an unidentified student. "Mellon's activities," Milne assured the rector, "were merely natural hilarity without malice and need not, I think, be remembered." A second master observed some boys shaking dice. "You probably know," the master explained to the rector, "that dice-shaking is an extremely popular form of gambling at the present time among the youth of America." Happily, the boys desisted. "They seemed to lose interest in their career of crime, and behaved themselves in a very orderly manner for the rest of the trip."

This same journey was made notable by the escapade of three youthful swells who arose at an even earlier hour than the rest of the school and, engaging a taxi, breakfasted at Nardini's, then one of Concord's

The romance of the train ride. *The St. Paul's Special in the 1890s.*

more plush eating places. Boarding the train in advance of their compa-
triots, they took possession of a compartment for which they had no tick-
ets. "They were of course promptly evicted," the rector was informed by
the next post.

The most famous incident occurred in December 1920. The journey
had been without incident until the Special pulled into New Haven. Then
immediately alongside it came the Colonial Express from Boston. The
Colonial was bound via Hellgate Bridge to Philadelphia and Washington,
and several of the boys conceived on the spot the brilliant plan of abandoning their own iron horse and boarding the Colonial, with a view to
beating the rest of the school to Philadelphia for the scheduled hockey
game. This maneuver was accomplished mainly by fifth and sixth formers
in the rear cars. But one second former, sensing what was going on,
grabbed his suitcase and jumped from the moving train.

The disciplinary problem was overshadowed in the excitement of the
race as the two trains pulled neck and neck out of the New Haven station.
The Colonial, at first in the lead, fell slowly behind and arrived a poor
second in New York. Willard Scudder, always debonair, had time to cross
town in a taxicab, pick up his mail and packages at his club, and catch the
four o'clock for Philadelphia. He was in the midst of dressing for his evening engagements when the Colonial, with its small group of dispirited passengers, finally pulled in.[25]

Scholarship–and Teaching

After discipline came higher academic standards. "Gentlemen," said
Drury to the trustees in 1915, "the one thing needful at St. Paul's School
is an improved scholarship." The record of St. Paul's boys in entering
college and during their years as students was not as good as it should be,
and not up to other schools of its type. Perhaps, suggested Drury, more
boys should be dropped back to lower forms. Parents would protest, but
"if the school is good enough to teach a boy, it is qualified to state in
which form the boy will be taught."[26] These remarks were the more
timely because the sixth form of that year was presenting special difficulties. The president of the form had withdrawn for academic failure and
seven or eight boys were on probation.

The public schools were actually doing better than private schools in
the competition for college places. Yet it could not be, in Drury's harsh
phrasing, that "boys at St. Paul's are stupider than those in high
schools." The problem seemed to be one of motivation and ambition.
Even after St. Paul's students had competed successfully for a place in
college, they showed up poorly by the end of their senior year. Was it

some fatal relaxation of effort, some unjustified sense of superiority, that caused them to grow slack?

Not only the boys were at fault. A student's failure, Drury maintained, was fully half the responsibility of the teacher. Most of the teachers at St. Paul's, he complained, talked too much and too loud. An expert he brought in to survey teaching methods confirmed his conclusion that boys cannot work effectively when noise is reverberating from all the walls of a classroom. Also there was too much emphasis on isolated facts. It was not by being crammed with irrelevant knowledge that young people grow wise: "We learn a subject by the slow and arduous process of incorporating it into ourselves." To acquire the kind of teachers who could encourage this process, Drury got permission from the board to raise masters' salaries and to pay them according to the work done, whatever their private resources. He was prepared as well to act decisively toward those who did not perform adequately.

From one of the more influential members of the board Drury received not only support but helpful prodding. Charles D. Dickey, Sr., wrote to the rector of the many complaints he was hearing from parents. Compared to Groton, St. Mark's and Hill, they told him, St. Paul's was taking second place. Dickey put his finger directly on the vital spot. "The conclusion I have somewhat reluctantly reached," he said, "is that we have a number of decidedly inferior *teachers*. I put emphasis on the word teachers, for among those I have in mind are warm personal friends and [those] most popular among the boys."[27] Drury asked permission to read the letter at the next trustees meeting, and then added his own revealing comments. During the first two years of his rectorship, he said, he had been more concerned with trying to improve the tone and discipline of the place than with trying to raise its academic standards. He had been more concerned, in a word, with "deficient and lazy boys" than with "incompetent teachers."

The problem of ensuring good teachers was, he admitted, the more deep-seated and far-reaching. "You can easily understand that a new and somewhat young man, coming into a community of masters . . . should feel a hesitation in questioning their work." The hesitancy, however, was not to last long. Drury's long-hand notes for comments to the trustees at the meeting of April 1914 provide a militant defense of his right to dismiss inadequate masters. He had failed to reappoint two and had taken "considerable criticism" on the ground that if a man has done his duty he is entitled, regardless of competence, to continue at the school. This Drury could not accept. Moreover it was not possible for him to give explanations when a man's service no longer seemed in the best interest of the school. "It is impossible," he told the board, "to do these delicate personal things in town meeting." A school, he continued, "is a very small place and schoolmasters are sentimentalists." Accordingly, he would not explain in detail why a certain master might fail of reappointment, "partly because such explanation is inexpedient and partly because it is uncalled for." What constitutes the good of the school must be judged by the rector, "who alone knows all the facts."[28]

The doctrine Drury expounded was dangerous at best, and showed him in his most imperious mood. Whatever might be its long-run effects in improving the quality of teaching at St. Paul's, it was bound in the short run to cause trouble. Drury admitted to a sentiment of "unrest and resentment" within the faculty following his decisive, but essentially arbitrary, action; he declared himself prepared to bear the burden. But feelings of resentment lingered, and three years later they were fanned by a controversy not directly of Drury's making but having its roots in the declaration of 1914.

Malcolm Kenneth Gordon had been discontented during the Ferguson regime; now, under Drury, he resigned abruptly. He sent an intemperate letter directly to the trustees, expressing general disillusionment and bitterly reviling one of his fellow teachers.[29] The trustees, wisely or not, accepted the resignation. Within the coterie of older masters, and among the surviving Coit loyalists, the matter was angrily discussed, with Drury mistakenly taken to be behind the resignation, if not the principal cause of it. Gordon was an alumnus of the school, had been a master for twenty-eight years, and was a popular figure among students and old boys. A sports enthusiast and adviser to the *Horae*, he was a brisk and busy figure on the school scene. His departure was a blow at the roots of the old order. Scudder found himself at the center of the resulting agitations and intrigues. "No end of a row among the old boys," he wrote in his diary, "unless a way is found to keep him on."

But Drury was resolved that a way should not be found. He had had no hand in promoting the bitter and ill-considered resignation; the board, not he, had accepted it. Nevertheless, by the middle of summer he was deeply involved. Writing in an adamant spirit to one of the protesting masters, "After careful consideration," he said, "Mr. Gordon saw fit to resign from the school. After deliberation equally careful his resignation was accepted. There the matter stands and there it should be left."[30]

More profitable than open breaks with faculty members were Drury's efforts to stimulate and encourage the best of the teachers then at the school. Under the second Coit, a group of men previously unrelated to the school had joined the faculty, bringing with them a cool respect for hard work and tangible results. To these Drury now turned, goading them, praising them as their students began noticeably to improve their college entrance scores.

Among these was Theophilus Nelson, dry and peremptory in his teaching of mathematics, giving no quarter to the laggard and insisting that a large number of boys repeat the course. "The school has been criticised in the past for lack of scholarship. It is better for the school to be criticised for zeal in maintaining a high standard," he wrote to the rector when his severity had been challenged. The rector was delighted. To Robert Peck, a tough-minded Latinist, Drury was quick to dispatch an approving letter when failures in his course fell below the 27 per cent which had been accepted as normal. "I feel that every one of us should make the scholarship of the school his primary thought," Drury wrote to him, "and 'without haste and without rest' should work away at it." And in a later year to Milne, "It is characteristic of you and your teaching, not to allow any failures."[31]

New Recruits for the Faculty

In the end it would be the new masters Drury recruited who made the difference between a school where classes were required drudgery and where the attraction of true learning began to be felt. The men Drury went after were apt to be quiet men, speaking not as drillmasters but as participants in a common search. However effectively they prepared boys for the ever-looming college examinations, they were concerned with what lay beyond the day's assignment and the bounds of their particular discipline.

There was, for instance, John Richards. The offspring of well-known writers—Julia Ward Howe was his grandmother, Laura E. Richards his mother—he taught English as if some important revelation lay just beyond his ken, and as if the least brilliant student might be as likely as he to grasp it. "He has a singular moral power with boys," Drury wrote of him. "His influence with them is not of the superficial kind, but is deep and permanent."[32] Richards roamed the New Hampshire hills, wrote gentle verses, coached the rowers, and gave Drury the kind of eager loyalty a man gives to the captain of a ship making a difficult passage.

Another such recruit was John Gilbert Winant.[33] Always afterwards Winant would consider his arrival at St. Paul's as a student, one autumn day in 1904, the most important event of his life. He took naturally to the place. He made friends in Concord—the sons of a railroad engineer and the city's bookbinder were at least as important to him as his Millville schoolmates.

A strong ethical sense gave Winant weight among his peers. In 1909,

With his odd humors and latent powers. *Henry Kittredge in his thirties.*

DRURY RECONSTITUTED HIS ADMINISTRATION.

He put his lasting mark on the school. *John Gilbert Winant in World War I.*

when Ferguson found himself baffled by poor discipline in the sixth form, he made the surprising suggestion that the faculty wait to get advice from a Princeton freshman who would be returning to the school for Thanksgiving. That was the same occasion on which the rector of St. Stephen's in Boston was coming for a first appearance at the school. Drury and Winant met on that important weekend, talked, and formed an immediate friendship.

After Winant's graduation, though he had fared poorly in his studies, Drury prevailed upon him to come back to the school as a master. "I believe a life with an aim and some definite work to be done in attaining it," Winant wrote to Drury, "is necessary to hold the respect of others as well as of oneself. Boys through intuition feel this even more quickly than men." At St. Paul's Winant found his aim, at least for a while. In the classroom his long, lean frame, the penetrating eyes beneath a craggy brow, gave him the appearance of a young Lincoln. While others still made the classroom walls reverberate, he talked on in low tones, sometimes scarcely audible, each word seeming to be drawn from the deepest level of his being. American history came alive in strange ways; even a tariff bill could seem important and exciting. In his rooms students would gather at all hours, finding their places in the small apartment where piles of books covered the floor, climbed into the chairs, and seemed to take possession of the bed itself. Here the visitors would talk of school matters and dream of the larger world outside, until a striking clock reminded them all that the hour had long passed when students' lights should have been put out.

For the rector, Winant was an indispensable support. "He is doing uniquely valuable work at St. Paul's," Drury wrote to the young man's father. "His quiet strong principles, tempered by deep sympathies, enable him to carry out certain personal measures which no one else on the place can effect." Drury leaned on Winant for advice in dealing with the boys, made him ambassador on delicate missions, and rejoiced to see him grow in self-confidence and strength. Supporting Winant's entrance into politics, he adjusted the young man's teaching schedule so that he could make himself known to the voters of Concord's seventh ward.

At the Adirondack-Florida School in 1915 was a master in his mid-twenties, the son of Harvard's famed Shakespearean scholar George Lyman Kittredge. "Probably the most successful teacher the school has ever had," is the way the principal characterized Henry Kittredge. Drury's desire to see Kittredge at St. Paul's was not, however, to be easily satisfied. With a persistence and tact equal to that which Ferguson had shown in pursuing him, Drury set out to win the tall figure, salty in speech and free and easy in his ways, who clearly had a mind of his own. He appealed to the young man's ambition: "St. Paul's is a big place offering ample scope," he wrote, "for people who don't want to be and never ought to be small." He appealed to the father, who replied cannily that Henry was being sought after "very eagerly" by others. "It gratifies me to know that you think so well of my boy," he concluded. "I like him, too."[34]

Something made Henry Kittredge hold back. He did not at that time feel quite free to leave his post; perhaps, too, he sensed a danger in placing himself, with his odd humors and his latent powers, under a man so evidently dominating as Drury. In any case, he put the rector off. "Your decision is undoubtedly a wise one," Drury replied, now playing the role that Brent had played on Drury's first declining the offer from St. Paul's. "Do not forget St. Paul's School," he added. "You and I will probably be in the teaching business for some time. Maybe we shall yet be co-workers."

Co-workers they in fact became, Kittredge arriving at the school as master in the autumn of 1916. That December found Drury writing to the father again, to tell him how "wonderfully successful" Henry's first term had been. "Everybody likes him, everybody trusts him. . . . Everything which Henry has handled has gone well." This was another quiet teacher, who could keep order by the faint wrinkling of his brow, and whose classroom was a theater of unpredictable rewards. Drury had shown perseverance in pushing so hard and waiting so patiently to get him to St. Paul's. But even Drury could scarcely have supposed that nearly thirty years later this independent and not altogether conventional young man would become the school's sixth rector.

World War I

The United States saw the outbreak of the European conflict in 1914 as something far off and only remotely touching its interests. But St. Paul's from the beginning found itself emotionally involved. A romantic outlook, so much a part of its tradition, made the school family particularly sensitive to the sufferings of nations overrun and conquered, and found it quick to answer the call for sacrifice. When America declared war, minds trained in classical learning did not lack words to ennoble the struggle. The youth turned soldier, wrote Owen Wister, was going to the war in the name of an ideal cause. "Not at all for the sake of advancement is he facing it, nor does he blow any trumpets—his eyes are seeing something invisibile and his soul has made a resolve."[35] John Jay Chapman, so often the iconoclast, wrote with burning faith in his *Ode, on the Sailing of American Troops to France:*

> *Awake! the virgins perish, monsters rage;*
> *The earth is mastered by Hell's Overlord;*
> *Accept the manhood of thine heritage:*
> *Behold the shield, the sandal and the sword* . . .

The example of doomed heroism had been provided even before the United States entered the war. George Williamson, an English citizen who had been head editor of the *Horae*, enlisted in the forces of his own country and was the first of one hundred twenty St. Paul's men—as he was the first graduate of an American college—to give his life in the cause. In 1915, André Champollion, an artist whose paintings of the New Hampshire hills and meadows still speak of promise cut off, left a young wife and five-year-old son to fight for the France of his grandfather. At Bois-le-Prêtre, on his first day at the front, he was killed by a bullet in the forehead. The United States had scarcely entered the war on its own before two grandsons of the first rector, Henry Augustus Coit, 2nd, and Richard Steven Conover, 2nd, enlisted.

Young Conover was one of St. Paul's great athletes, a formidable football player, and in hockey one of the few to be mentioned in the same breath with Hobey Baker. In the spring of America's declaration of war he left the school to enter the ambulance service in France. "Believe me, Sir," he wrote the rector in June 1917, "it was indeed hard to go before the end of school, for I had always looked forward to that last night when I should stand with the rest of my form and hear the final words of loving advice and farewell." When the chance came for him to go to France, he continued, "I was greatly at a loss to find where my duty lay. . . . It is very comforting for me that, although I have dropped out of the school's life, and my small part in it is already forgotten, there will be some few who remember me when I return again, if it is God's will that I should ever return."[36]

Conover was transferred to the transport services. "It is very hard, Sir," he wrote Drury in another letter, "for me to go rattling along in a truck, and pass by French troops marching up to the trenches; so many of them are so young." Conover was young himself, not quite twenty, when he met his end as a corporal in the capture of Cantigny. His captain had sent him out into the thick of the fight with a message when he was struck by a piece of shrapnel and fell. "Take this message and deliver it," were his last words to the man at his side. "I am done for. Leave me."[37] His first cousin, Henry Coit, 2nd, was killed in an accident a year later, at twenty-six.

In this way the school that had been born a few years too late to play more than a symbolic role in the Civil War laid its sacrifice upon the altar of a later conflict. The Coit descendants had been among the earliest to volunteer; they were to be part of a swelling stream of graduates, enlisted in all the services, on land, sea and—for the first time in any war—in the air. The athletes, the scholars, the poets left something of themselves at the school where they had found brief happiness. And when the bells tolled, as they did frequently in Millville through the fateful months of 1918, it seemed that the best and most promising of the generation had passed.

The last death of a St. Paul's graduate was, in a way, symbolic of them all; and symbolic, too, of the spirit of a country-wide academic élite that, when the test came, did not fail in heroism. Hobey Baker we left as a lower schooler, a diminutive figure already known as an athlete. He had extraordinary gifts, backed by a spunky determination that enabled him to do well in studies or in the choir and in whatever sport he tried. In his first-form year, hoisted to the horizontal bar, he promptly executed a giant swing. Putting on roller skates for the first time he was, after the first few minutes, performing all kinds of spins on one foot. He played excellent football, won a swimming race, coxed a crew; and in his fourth-form year, at fifteen years of age, he was on the school hockey team. A pleasant recollection finds Hobey Baker as a sixth former getting permission to take "night flights" with friends. He especially liked to skate at night, racing over the pond's dark surface, carrying a puck on his stick without being able to see it.

As a hockey player his fame was won. To appreciate the legendary character of his playing, we must perceive the place held by St. Paul's among schools and colleges in the first decade of the twentieth century. The emphasis on athletics, against which two rectors inveighed, had its attractive side in the schoolboy knights of the hockey rink, going forth to victory after victory. They played the best college teams, and often beat them. The year Princeton won the intercollegiate championship, it lost to St. Paul's, 4–0; another year Harvard lost to them, 7–0. In the St. Nicholas hockey rink in New York, before the glamorous sub-debutantes of the day, they played against teams made up of top players from the big three colleges, often with a sprinkling of formidable Canadians. At this summit of the school's athletic achievements Hobey Baker was without peer, and when he went on to Princeton the national spotlight was focused on him.

An ace flyer in the war, he seemed to burn with the flame of a whole generation's gallant recklessness. "You say Hobey Baker," wrote a journalist many years later, "and all of a sudden you see the gallantry of a world long since gone.''[38] It was a world in which handsome young officers danced away their leaves in the tea room at the Plaza, and, when spring came round, kept their rendezvous with death. Baker knew the romance of wartime Paris as well as the reality of flaming machines at the front. Some said afterwards he treated the war like a Yale–Princeton football game, and wondered whether he would have been able to adjust to the long boredom of peace. He was never put to that test.

When the Armistice had been signed and he had been ordered home, he went out to the field for one more flight in his faithful Spad. Characteristically, he felt impelled to take up for a test flight a friend's plane whose engine had proved faulty. At fifteen hundred feet in the air the engine failed; the plane crashed and Hobey Baker was killed.

December 5, 1918. *Hobey Baker went out to the field for one more flight.*

The Home Front at Millville

At Concord, meanwhile, the conflict was making itself felt in various ways. Willard Scudder had been caught in London—no doubt while dining at his club—when war broke out. The transatlantic cables hummed while arrangements for his return were completed. A more complicated case was that of Edward Spanhoofd, who had come to the school in 1880 to teach German, successor to the unhappy Mr. Schindelmeisser. Spanhoofd was in Germany in August 1914 and decided to remain there for a while. To the rector he wrote naïve apologies for the aggressor's cause. "People used to call it militarism . . . but we only now realize the grandeur, the beauty and the nobility of it and bless it for saving our country." With tact Dr. Drury replied: "It seems to me that many people at St. Paul's School do not regard the cause which you hold with such affectionate interest in the light which you regard it." Nevertheless, he urged the errant master to return. "It will be splendid to have you in your old quarters again and to have your benevolent face amid these familiar scenes."[39]

Drury tried without much success to raise a sum of money for Spanhoofd's living expenses. "Clearly no one would want to give money to a German aiding the Germans. I regard it in the light of helping an old friend, who is temporarily in straits." In due course Spanhoofd did return. "We must all in our school community labor for peace, as the psalmist says," Drury told him, "and we must be very careful not to let any sort of factions develop in the faculty." In the circumstances it was a vain wish. The acerbic Theophilus Nelson was soon advising the rector that he would not think of assigning to Herr Spanhoofd his full quota of teaching hours. That would deprive him of opportunity to win proselytes for the German cause.

The former vice rector, Milnor Coit, stayed on in Germany throughout the war. He explained that his wife's health had not permitted him to leave, and he later told Drury that far from having been a German sympathizer, he had kept in his apartment throughout the war years a large engraving of General Washington, draped in the American flag. With a kindness that never failed him where the Coit family was concerned, Drury did his best to secure credence for this testimony.

The experience of one more of the older masters must be recounted. James Potter Conover, leaving his Rhode Island parish, took up the duties of an army chaplain in France. On many occasions he visited the battlefield where his son had fallen, and from the evidence of army officials and fellow combatants of the young corporal, he established as best he could the exact spot where the fatal bullet had struck. The tides of war had surged over the field many times; in advances and retreats the devastated earth had been reduced to a trampled expanse of clay and mud.

Looking down, Conover drew from the soil a portion of the last letter he had written to his son. "In spite of all the turmoil," the fragment read, "you may be at perfect peace. . . ."[40]

For the students, war brought diversions as well as frustrations. Even before the United States entered the conflict, Gerald Chittenden, a slightly built, aggressively independent teacher of English, called for volunteers. The hundred and fifty boys who responded found themselves immersed in complicated infantry maneuvers, capturing the Alumni House, storming the orphans' home, and capping their efforts with the entire company, led by Captain Chittenden, joining in Concord's "preparedness parade." The next year, with the United States engaged in the war, military drill was intensified; and a major effort was set on foot to redress wartime food shortages by the cultivation of potatoes and beans on the school grounds. Twenty acres of lawns were plowed up. Contingents of boys returned to the school during the summer to cultivate the crops, serving voluntarily and under no restrictions except the long-standing ban on smoking. "We had *Salve Mater* in the potato patch today," wrote Milne. A returning alumnus, startled by what he saw, put the appropriate sentiments into verse:

> *His thoughts are of the granite hills—*
> *He sees a hill of beans.*[41]

Nine hundred bushels of potatoes were harvested that summer; the amount would have been greater except for an August drought and an unseasonably early frost in September.

Half in fear, half enviously, the boys watched their sixth-form comrades departing for war, and news of their fortunes flowed back into the school. In the cloisters connecting the chapel with the Big Study, the names of all alumni in service were inscribed. "Every morning we go trooping through," wrote Drury, "and in chapel, prayers for the safety of our brethren arise with humble and hopeful confidence." For those left behind, the routine of the small school community could be galling. Shortages and cuts in service added to a general feeling of unrest. Drury looked with alarm at the change in the type of servants available to the school. "We need a steady quiet group of women," he told the trustees; "we cannot have flashy nomads." Writing his own letters in long hand seemed to the rector an act of conscience. John Jay Chapman professed to be appalled. "It's as if I should cook my own food," he told the rector. "You'd better get a young woman who knows a little typewriting, or a poor boy, the son of a widow. This Simon Stylites business is not the way to win the war."[42]

Noting the restlessness of the boys, Drury called, not for a more rigid discipline, but for greater freedom and responsibility. "When times are hard and nerves are tense," he wrote sensibly, "a wise method, it would seem to me, is to trust more and expect less. We shall have to leave boys more to themselves . . . and let many disciplinary niceties slide. We must walk, and work, by faith."[43]

A result of this wise attitude was the establishment of an effective school government, based on a council and a sixth-form president, and the concomitant dissolution of the secret societies. The latter had grown more respectable (and less picturesque) than had been the case amid the disorders of the 1890s. They were supervised by the school administration, their meetings were under disciplinary restrictions, and drinking at dinners away from the school was forbidden. They remained, nevertheless, a divisive influence within the school and within the sixth form. They constituted, as Drury told his board, "an inner circle of control; they keep snobbish boys snobbish."[44]

War made a program of self-help necessary and involved the boys' participation in many matters that had been left before wholly to masters. The moment was ripe for a decisive act. At the trustees meeting of June 1917, Drury was able to announce that in the previous week the entire fifth form of that year had presented him with a document embodying their resignations from existing secret societies and pledging themselves not to join any others that might be formed. At the same time they had voted to adopt a school council.

This reform, Drury stated, could not have come about without "the tactful and influential persuasion of Mr. Winant." The young master had in fact penetrated the conscience and enlarged the views of the school's élitist groups. For two years, islanded in his sea of books, he had gathered boys to discuss the possibility of a free social order within the school. Though Drury deserved praise for the reconstruction which two rectors before him had been unable to achieve, he was right, as well as generous, in sharing the credit with his favorite master.

Two Further Events

Two further events of this decade, not connected with the war, wait to be told. In the immediate environs of Millville the exploration of Turee Pond was first accomplished by two intrepid St. Paul's canoeists. Turee lay in the misty marshlands west of Big Turkey; or at least it was believed to lie there, for in Millville some doubt existed about its actuality, as well as about its precise location. Maps of surrounding streams and trails, sold at the school store, omitted the area in which Turee was supposed to be found, thus raising in the minds of many the question as to whether it was not a mythical body of water. One of the older masters, keeper of the arcane facts of local history, was said later to have been fully informed on Turee, but at the time no one thought to ask him. It was in these circumstances that two St. Paul's students decided to establish the true facts once and for all.

These explorers, Hugh E. Rowan and George Riggs, realized that because of the distance of their objective and the time required to cross the school pond by canoe, navigate the sluice, and traverse the two Turkeys with their connecting marshland, the expedition could be mounted only on a Wednesday or Saturday afternoon, when no late classes were scheduled. Choosing their day, they reached the place where Turee Brook debouched. But upon ascending it, they came to a fork. They took the right branch, which dwindled, then vanished from sight. Dusk was falling, and they returned, defeated, to the school.

A second attempt was soon organized. Now the left fork was mounted, and presently the explorers entered upon the still waters of Turee Pond. With a modesty and conciseness worthy of the old chroniclers, they summed up the conclusion of their expedition. "We spent about twenty minutes on Turee, paddling around the pond and inspecting it as thoroughly as we could in the time available. Then we retraced our route to the school, where news of our success created a mild sensation." Today, Turee Pond is to be found on at least some school maps.

In 1917 occurred the great fire at the orphanage, known by then, in honor of its founder, as Coit House. Monday was washday, and in the basement shavings and chips were thrown on the furnace to force steam into the laundry. Some of these chips were drawn up through the chimney and alighted on the wooden roof. It was soon blazing, and the alarm spread through the school. Leaving their outer clothing strewn on fences and bushes, a considerable number of boys were quickly astride the roof, while others saved possessions from the lower floors. The rector, as he wrote to Mary Conover, personally removed the founder's portrait and went upstairs to save the cross in the chapel. By now sparks were threatening the orphanage's old school house nearby. Though the main building was lost, it was the efforts of students in putting out incipient blazes that preserved the old school of the orphanage until a later day.

Coit House was by this time something of an anachronism. The social ideas of the earlier generation were outmoded; protracted institutional confinement seemed the least satisfactory way of caring for children. Concern had shifted from abandoned or impoverished children to those who were disturbed or backward. Still sheltering more than sixty youths at a time, Coit House held them for psychological tests and then sought an appropriate foster home. The "little orphelings" of Henry Augustus Coit, shuffling into chapel and receiving largesse from the school's students, were as much a tale from the past as other ancient features of school life, which Drury had subtly banished or was in the process of transforming.

CHAPTER NINE

Schoolmaster as Prophet
1919–1929

Drury Faces the Old Guard

The war had brought about an almost complete exodus of the younger masters. Those on whom Drury counted most to give form and impetus to his policies—Richards, Kittredge, Winant—were all away, and others who would have been their followers were likewise in training or overseas. This was the moment, if ever, for the old guard at the school to make its influence felt. Several of them, sincerely wedded to the old ways, were grieved by even such popular reforms as the liberalized Sunday schedule. Others mistrusted Drury and feared for their own skins. Malcolm Kenneth Gordon's leaving had shaken their confidence in the unbroken continuity of things; his departure, along with others of less note, had followed upon the upheavals of the Ferguson interregnum. Ferguson was an alumnus. He had come to power in a crisis threatening the school's very existence and could not be effectively opposed. But Drury, an outsider, was another matter.

The school, as Scudder had remarked on first returning as a master, was a small place. Within it existed a society with its hierarchies and its élite, a court with its intrigues and gossip—all of it bounded by Millville's diminutive scale. Formal calls at the rectory, tea parties and entertainments in the masters' homes, were supplemented by the agreeable country-club atmosphere provided by the golf course (laid out in the 1890s) and social occasions in the dining room of the school inn. A walk of less than a mile separated these various points of contact and pleasure. In the summer—and most of the masters remained in residence for at least part of the vacation—the school became a resort of delightful climate and varied resources.

The leader of this little society was James Carter Knox. His association with St. Paul's was the longest—he had been at the school a bare six years after its founding. His contributions to its life and traditions were the most notable; his manners were the most old-worldly. A long silken

moustache illumined the parchment pallor of his face. Now close to his
eighth decade, he moved with courtly grace and spoke in the fastidious
accents of a man who, having seen much of life, found comparatively little
of it to his liking. He was an open and avowed conservative, a loyalist to
men and causes long since faded. With difficulty he had adjusted himself
to Ferguson's being in the rector's seat; at least, Joseph Coit had written
him in a last letter, it was better than having someone "entirely new."
"We shall all do our utmost to aid him," Knox wrote patronizingly, "not
in making, but in keeping, St. Paul's a great Christian school."[1]

Knox stressed what he called "a certain propriety" in personal appearance. The first rector, he noted, believed a boy behaved better if his
boots were blacked—quite the opposite, he said, "of the present fashion
in scholastic attire, half sweater, half rough-rider, with its attendant
cavalierish manners." The propriety he sought extended to other fields,
such as the boys' personal reading. With approval he saw such items as
Fielding's *Tom Jones* and the *Encyclopedia Britannica's* article on sex
barred from the library, along with Sax Rohmer's novels and the Tarzan
series. As for what he called "the Sunday question," he maintained that
any sudden change in the old schedule "would operate as a dissolvent,
and have a tendency to weaken moral fiber."

Charles Sigourney Knox was his alter ego and major ally. Not an
alumnus, and appointed a master six years later than his brother, Charles
Knox nevertheless shared most of James's views, and like him aged into
inflexibility. A brilliant teacher of the classics in his younger days, a scholar of wide interests with a lively knowledge of men and affairs, he had
succumbed by Drury's administration to the pedantry of endlessly repeated exercises. Yet something original, some residual spark, still
showed itself to the perceptive youngster, and when he died in the summer of 1920, a former student, the most accomplished in a long line of St.
Paul's poets, recalled him in moving words:

> *O beauty, more than visits on a maid*
> *And gathers up all garden sweets in her—*
> *Minted beneath a cracked and breaking mould . . .*[2]

Holding an intermediate position, often exasperated by James Knox,
more intelligent in maneuver and rarely unambiguous in his attitude toward the rector, was Willard Scudder. He could not but admire Drury's
firm hand and approve his style. But he felt himself kept uncomfortably at
a distance. "Count upon me," he wrote Drury on his coming to St. Paul's,
"as your steadfast friend—and more, if you don't mind, your affectionate
friend." "I have an incorrigible idea," he added, "that St. Paul's will be

James C. Knox.

A SOCIETY WITH ITS HIERARCHIES AND ITS ELITE

*Edward Spanhoofd and
Malcolm Kenneth Gordon.*

better for your being there."[3] There would be times when Scudder was sufficiently consulted—on the disposition of rooms, the scheduling of lectures and other school affairs—to keep him relatively happy. But his long letters to the rector, typed in his own weird extemporizations, mixing school notes with whimsical comments on life, remarks upon the state of his health and news from the East Coast watering places, were usually answered *pro forma* by Drury.

One summer on Mount Desert Island the two exchanged cards but never managed to meet; Drury on another occasion complained that from his study at Northeast he could hear Scudder's emphatic voice, coming from the verandah of the Rock End Hotel across a considerable body of land and water. Scudder wrote plaintively after a meeting at the school that he understood Drury's having to rush off in the midst of a conversation, "but I would have liked to go on talking for hours." Perhaps better than Scudder, we can understand Drury's need to "rush off."

Criticism of the rector and his policies festered, and during the two years of the war grew in intensity and scope. The Knoxes missed no opportunity to spread their views among alumni. Scudder was more prudent, but shared in the increasing gossip. In these circumstances, Drury decided to strike back. He could not touch the chief protagonists; their roots went too deep and their contacts with the alumni were too close. But there was a younger master, Lloyd Hodgins, who had come to the school

The rector in his study with William H. Foster and W. W. Flint.

in 1907, a colleague and close friend of Scudder's in the Middle, on terms of growing intimacy with the old guard. In June 1919, Drury called Hodgins to his study and notified him that his mastership would not be renewed.

Drury afterwards expressed contrition over the interview. "I am full of regrets for the way I handled it," he wrote a good friend.[4] The rector's manner had been peremptory and his temper short. If on this occasion Truth sat with him at the table, Tact and Compassion had both been singularly lacking.

The deed, and the style of its execution, aroused a furor in Millville. At a meeting of the masters a few days afterwards, such Drury stalwarts as Richards and Milne were among those who signed a statement expressing the faculty's dismay at what they conceived to be a breach of basic understandings on which teachers were hired. Among the alumni, figures as outstanding as Chapman and Wister became embroiled. The latter called on Frederick Shattuck, urging him to receive James Knox. Shattuck hesitated, but in the end refused. Despite an initially unfavorable reaction, Chapman kept in friendly communication with the rector. The Messrs Knox, Drury wrote him on June 27, would probably make trouble all summer—"Charles especially. When aroused, I fear the old gentleman is pretty unrelenting."[5]

Meanwhile, in Millville, the term had proceeded to an unhappy end. The ceremonies of Last Night passed under a shadow that must have been evident to boys no less than to masters. "Recall no service so depressed," Scudder wrote in his diary.

From an unexpected quarter Drury received moral support. Chanler Chapman, organizer of the famous boxing match, wrote the rector from France, where he had gone immediately after graduation. "I am writing you this letter before going to bed," he began, "in the hopes that my sleepiness may make it seem more sane and more happy to you." (The rector was not used to getting letters like that!) "I am behind you and your position all through in the dismissal of Mr. Hodgins," he went on, excusing himself for not having written sooner. "Being only so recently hatched out of the egg I did not want to begin immediately by either approving or disapproving of the policy of my long-suffering brood-hen."[6]

Chapman went on to paint a picture of Hodgins as one who provoked in him as a student "the most indecent and unmanly tricks" as he tried to get even for his slights, his vague sneers, his outbursts of temper. The master's relations with the boys was close but divisive; his criticisms of fellow workers were "rather too frequent, too petty and too pityable [sic] for me to respect them." There was always "the odor of the Social Register about Mr. Hodgins; he was adored by those masters who had not come too close to him." In short, "the school meant too much to him in the wrong way." If he was not a bad man, "at least he was thoroughly bad for St. Paul's."

Such in the eyes of one student who had known him well was the strangely contradictory man at the center of the controversy: a brilliant teacher, a charmer in social circles, a corrosive influence at the deepest levels of community life. Drury must have been puzzled how to deal with this glittering newcomer to the staid company of the establishment. To temporize was to risk new defections, and to cut him off was to invite a many-headed protest. Hodgins went to plead his case before Peabody at Groton and Thayer at St. Mark's. But Drury, however much he regretted the manner of his original initiative, stood fast. "H packing in many boxes—*eheu!*" wrote Scudder on June 26. "So war is on! What next? Who next?" He always feared the next might be himself.

The trustees held together in this crisis and gave Drury their full backing. "Trustees finally accept SSD as leader," was Scudder's realistic interpretation; they were seeing St. Paul's "as the greatest school in the country." The masters still met and threatened a formal protest but to Scudder's disappointment the move petered out. Only the Knoxes continued with what Scudder himself finally recognized to be "graveyard talk."

At the trustees meeting of October 1919, the board took the unusual step of empowering the chairman to communicate with the Knox brothers, to express dismay at their recent conduct. "The freedom with which each discusses the policies of the rector and trustees is damaging to the school," they said, "whether it is expressed to masters and boys, or to parents and alumni." The rebuke was important, not because it struck at two tired and disconsolate old men, but because it was an occasion for reiterating their faith in the rector. "The trustees believe that in Dr. Drury they have been fortunate enough to secure the very best man in the country. With his policies in all essentials they are in enthusiastic agreement. We ask you both to calmly search your hearts."[7]

A New Vice Rector

Thus fortified, Drury went forward to reconstitute his administration. The disruptions of wartime were ending and he sought the return of his best men. Kittredge was hesitant. Once again, and again successfully, Drury applied his quiet, tactful persuasion. Kittredge came back a married man and took Deacon Brinley's place as head of the lower school. Winant, after an outstanding war record as an aviator and a stint at the Paris Peace Conference, was also contemplating wedlock. The hesitancy characteristic of his nature showed itself in matters of the heart no less than of the head. "All our joys are touched with pain," Drury wrote him sympathetically from Northeast, "and the pleasures of a man in your state of mind are bound to be shot through with half-disappointment and tinged with regret."[8] Winant did marry, and Drury asked him to come back to St. Paul's as vice rector.

William Foster was already a vice rector, and it took skill on Drury's part to convince him that his authority would not be undermined by the appointment of a much younger man to a similar position. Foster was accommodating, as always, but when Winant and his bride arrived in the spring of 1920 to take up temporary residence at the rectory (Drury was lending it to them while he was away on sabbatical and the young couple were awaiting completion of a new house), they found him very much in charge of things. Winant complained of "enforced idleness," but wisely refrained from asserting himself. Drury returned to make of the two men an effective team—Foster, always loyal, but with roots in the regime of the first Coit; Winant with his mind moving constantly toward a new frontier.

"The recurring picture of him now," wrote Drury, when a few years later Winant started a political career that was to make him the nation's youngest governor and the only one to have been elected three times chief executive of New Hampshire, "is of a man standing quietly at my office door, asking his characteristic question, 'What can I do for you?'"[9] The picture was also of a man incurably absent-minded. "Your hat was left in the study here," Drury wrote him when he was a national figure. But Winant left more than his hat at St. Paul's. He put his lasting mark on the school as an administrator, as he had been a mysteriously effective teacher. And when the battle proved too hard for him, it was to Concord and the house he had built on Pleasant Street that he returned to put a bullet through his head.

The Lightning Strikes

Drury's methods and personality had, by the beginning of the 1920s, made themselves powerfully felt in the school. Within the board he was the acknowledged leader, a precious resource the members were ready to support and willing to humor when necessary. For the boys he was a fact of life, so grave, wrote one, that one could not be in his presence without feeling abashed,[10] yet given to the kind of dramatic gestures that kept school life fresh and exciting. One boy remembered his having announced in chapel it was St. Crispin's Day, and then launching into a reading of Shakespeare's lines, the voice and presence that of the great actor, so that always afterwards the moment would remain vivid.

Drury's entrances into the schoolroom were felt palpably, like a sudden change in the weather. On his walks about the school, cane in hand, the resolute figure was as a force ready to sweep all before it. He missed no detail, let pass no slightest deviation from order or decorum. The young man who through experience was to fit himself to be rector of St. Paul's School had achieved the first stage of his journey. That he was rector, that he was entirely in command, no one could doubt.

A visitor to the school toward the end of his first decade found it "like St. Francis' idea of heaven—glowing and jolly, merry and joyous." "All this social element, and free talk and development at St. Paul's, is your influence," wrote John Jay Chapman. "At any rate the gaiety of it is due to you—for while it existed before, it was a little sad and embryonic."[11] This is a somewhat unexpected picture of St. Paul's toward the end of Drury's first decade as rector. But evidently that grave man had the capacity to stir the deep places of the institution; his own soberness was a steady force that allowed, and indeed encouraged, the progressive impulses of youth to assert themselves.

In circles outside the school, too, his influence was growing. The annual report of 1917 was couched in a new tone of confidence. Drury was not speaking alone to his immediate constituency, but to educators generally. How, he asked, can St. Paul's best serve America during the next ten years? To fulfill its responsibility, it would have to act "not wholly in the old way." For the school he sought a new spirit, summed up in the words "simplicity and freedom." Simplicity came first. Year by year the students had been provided with additional comforts until they were looked after as if they were "hotel guests." American boys in general tended to be "slovenly, dilatory, inconsiderate and slack." Would men returning from the experience of war find at home a race of leisurely, cleanly youths "with no conception of anything but how to get into college and how to have a good time?"

It was up to the schools—all schools, not St. Paul's alone—to challenge and awaken the new generation of the young. The schools must trust the boys more. When you are afraid of boys, said Drury, when you become nervous about what they will do next, "precepts, punishments and padlocks must abound." As for himself, he foresaw a period at St. Paul's when a larger grant of responsibility would be matched by a correspondingly greater willingness to accept the risks of failure. There would probably be, he said, more dismissals from the school—"free, cheery dismissals, unweeping and unwept." Such a voice could not but be listened to; and in each year afterwards the rector's annual report would be a document eagerly awaited among leaders in secondary school education.

At the same time Drury was keeping a heavy schedule of outside engagements. He was often absent from the school, preaching or taking part in educational conferences. He had a message he wanted to impart. He was resolved, as well, not to become immured in a petty round of duties. How but in a wide knowledge of men and affairs could he attain the sharpened vision which he considered the chief attribute of a successful headmaster? "Avoid, O my soul, the lacklustre, dingy dowdy disposition," he would exclaim in his diary. To be escaped at all costs was a mood of contentment with things as they are; to be dreaded was the administrator "snuggled down into a pleasant, sheltered routine." And when he felt the dull mood coming over him: "Alarum, for you are betrayed!"[12]

So he would journey forth in the cold Pullman cars, struggling with trains that were often late, and returning to the school to deal with a myriad of accumulated details. It was a risky course. Masters at the school complained that they could not find him in his study when they wanted to settle a matter; he might as well be living in Boston, said one. Boys missed the striking presence, the brief, luminous sermons. At the same time he was being marked by the outside world as a man to be watched and sought after. He was out where the lightning strikes; and in April 1921, it struck in the offer of one of the most glittering prizes of his calling.

In that month it became known that William T. Manning, rector of Trinity Parish, would be the next bishop of New York. Rumors were current to the effect that Drury might be his successor. That spring, indeed, he had preached daily during Passion Week from the Trinity pulpit, attracting unusually large congregations. But the choice of a rector from outside the parish seemed unlikely, so that when his election came unanimously and without controversy, the triumph was complete. It was what Drury's son was later to call his "high noon" of worldly success.[13] He had been called to the largest, most prosperous, most famous Episcopal parish in the nation—its original charter having been granted by the English king in 1697 and its wealth extending into some of Manhattan's most valuable real estate. The next day's press took Drury's acceptance as a foregone conclusion and anticipated his assuming his new duties within a few months.

Yet Drury hesitated. He had been ten years at St. Paul's. He had accomplished much, but was his work there completed? For him there were many pros and cons: "It all comes down to a question of divine guidance," he wrote to a friend three days after the event. "I am entirely ready to go and I am quite ready to stay. I truly pray for that light which will lead us to a right decision."[14] His ever-faithful mentor, Bishop Brent, who had not been without a role in the election, counseled Drury in practical terms. He felt that the decade at St. Paul's had "rounded out a period and completed a volume." The previous summer, moreover, he had thought he detected in Drury indications of the need for a new direction. Was it right, in the circumstances, for him to expect a mystical voice to speak to him decisively?

More than ten years earlier, when Drury had been wrestling with the problem of whether to come to St. Paul's, Brent had written him a revealing letter discussing the circumstances and the ways in which God's voice is heard in human affairs. Undoubtedly Drury reread the letter now. Frequently, Brent had warned, it would be difficult, if not impossible, to distinguish the divine voice, and—strangely—this would occur just when it seemed most necessary to hear it. At such times one had to throw oneself back on past experiences and on the wisdom distilled from former victories and defeats. This did not mean that God had abandoned us, "except as it may be said a mother has abandoned her child when she removes her arm . . . that he may walk alone." Again, Brent continued, there would be times when it was impossible *not* to hear God's voice—frequently when one was least desirous of hearing anything but the voice of one's own caprice and interest. "In times of elation, success, strength, wisdom, Good Lord, deliver us." Brent later added that God might be expected to speak when a man's vocation was involved, but not in a matter of mere position.[15]

Upon these uncertain revelations of God's will Drury now cast himself, while the St. Paul's family, and a large public outside it, waited to learn what his decision would be. From many quarters came expressions of hope that he would remain at the school—"Oh Sam, Sam, why are they trying to take you away from us," wrote one old friend, Endicott Peabody of Groton. A delegation from Trinity made a formal visit to the school. Still the rector kept his silence.

May 5 that year was Ascension Day. It fell on a Thursday, when Drury, carrying on a tradition established by the first rector, was accustomed to speak to the school in intimate terms and on matters affecting the school family. After the Confirmation of fifty-six students by the bishop, the rector arose in his seat and in quiet tones announced that he had something very personal to say. In the last few days he had reached a decision, already communicated to the vestrymen of Trinity: he had declined the call and would stay on as rector of St. Paul's.

After Trinity

Perhaps no one could have anticipated the reaction of the school to this announcement. Drury was not loved by the students—"A man's middle life," he wrote of another, "is often too dominant and strident to win the shy heart of youth."[16] Certainly he was not loved in the sentimental way schoolboys and masters are sometimes inclined to regard a headmaster. But Drury was respected; he was looked upon by nearly all as a man who plumbed waters of which they knew only the surface. Now his decision not to leave the school released an emotion long submerged.

Even the youngest boys reacted enthusiastically. "Isn't it slick!" exclaimed one in a letter to his parents—adding, as schoolboys do, an appeal for some of his soft collars if they could be found. "Great stuff," wrote another; "it's the best thing that could have happened to the school." It was wonderful to think of the benefits "every possible thing related to the school would receive from now on," and of how far the act went toward easing the solution of future difficulties. That evening, immediately after the service, masters could be seen fervently shaking the rector's hand, and faithful John Richards was observed by one boy skipping ponderously about the chapel lawn.[17]

The next morning the rector came as usual into the crowded schoolroom to read reports. "For just one second," as a student described the scene, "nothing but the rector's footsteps disturbed the silence; but, in the next, pandemonium reigned." Cheer after cheer arose as the rector stood in unaccustomed silence. "Nothing could be better for the rector or the boys," added the observant youngster; "both are shy, and both want to show their appreciation."[18]

There were other reactions. The New York *Times* found in Drury's reason for declining the Trinity offer—"I felt my work here was not done and that I should stay here to do it"—a spirit "which every school teacher should honor and which honors every school teacher." Chapman wrote Drury he would have been reconciled to the outcome in any case. "To run a school is the greatest thing a man can do—except for the bad effect it always has on the man himself." Joseph H. Coit, 2nd, still wandering in his unhappy exile as a not very successful businessman, said: "I have felt that month by month and year by year you . . . were becoming more and more in touch and sympathy with the atmosphere that existed in the minds of many before your advent." But the old guard still harbored its reserves. "More innovations?" wrote Scudder in his diary. "More restlessness? We shall see. . . ."

From Malcolm Kenneth Gordon in that hour of reconciliations came a long letter, healing the bitterness of his departure. "Four years," he wrote Drury, "have brought many changes, many things have been straightened out, some are forgotten, some have proved false, and others which loomed large have burst like bubbles and left no trace." Perhaps, he admitted, he had been hasty at that time; certainly he had been "badly advised" by friends.[19] It was a sad letter, ending with an assertion that he would have liked to be close to Drury but could not be. It is pleasant to record that this good-hearted but impetuous man founded his own school, to be headed by himself and then by his son and grandson, both St. Paul's graduates; and that at the age of ninety-six he still led the alumni parade at Anniversary. He had become a beloved artifact, a familiar tradition in himself when so many of the traditions he cherished had been eroded by time.

The press was anxious for a glimpse of the man who had turned down worldly honors for a post in an isolated boarding school. It was an awkward position for the school which had long sought to avoid publicity, and for Drury, who was more accustomed to communing with God than with newspaper reporters. After lengthy negotiations, arrangements were made for a *Times* writer to conduct an interview. "That you have made an arduous trip to this remote spot on purpose to see me," said Drury, "is in itself a fact which impresses me."[20] Thereupon he delivered himself of a lengthy disquisition on the philosophical aspects of religious education. The most interesting part of the article, however, was the reporter's impressions as he trailed Drury on one of his regular walks around the school.

Down "shaded paths by little rivers" the rector marched in his swinging gait. The tour was interrupted by a "cheerful shouted dialogue" with a boy in a second-story window who was recovering from the measles; an inquiry of another as to the latest baseball score; a little sermon as to why gravel paths should not be used for running tracks; "and the careful inspection of a small boy—his own—who was periodically falling off a bicycle in front of the rectory." Thus was the lonely searcher for God's truth converted into a yet-to-be-invented Mr. Chips. Drury may well have cried out to his soul once more: "Alarum, for you are betrayed!"

The trustees at Anniversary that year expressed their pride in the rector, as well as their affection. Frederick Shattuck—he who in the first meeting "smote" the table in the rector's defense—consented to withdraw a planned resignation and continue to serve as chairman of the board. That Anniversary, the celebrations were particularly brilliant. "It was a joy," Bishop Brent wrote Drury, "to be able to share in the victory, as I had shared in the struggle. The end of the victory is not yet!"[21]

In the autumn the alumni paid their tribute to the man who had brought the school great honor. They had perhaps never understood him, but they acclaimed him now as a hero. On the night of December 8, the ballroom of the Plaza Hotel in New York was crowded with alumni all in black tie—the largest assemblage of the St. Paul's family ever gathered for such an affair. Around the ornate hall were hung large-scale banners of the athletic clubs, symbols of the school's victories and of its fame. At the speaker's table were James Byrne, representing the Harvard corporation; John Grier Hibben, Wilson's successor as president of Princeton; and President James Rowland Angell of Yale. All the speakers referred in glowing terms to the Trinity decision. Drury, when he arose in turn, made no mention of it, but as the *Herald Tribune* reported next day, "climbed to 'the top story' of his job of education and revealed what he wished the future of St. Paul's to be."

Drury was at his best that evening, modest and human without losing the prophetic note.[22] Immediately he challenged the minority of his audience who still mistrusted him as a radical innovator. "The good old days were always days of ferment and adventure," he said. "Zion ceases to be Zion when its people are at ease." The school was not, and could not be, a place to itself. "The fact which specially interests me is this: St. Paul's School, tucked away up there amid the New Hampshire hills, living in dignified isolation, has somehow got mixed up with the United States at large; and I, for one, am not interested in any method of keeping the two apart."

In more intimate vein, he spoke from the perspective of a schoolmaster. Past his study door at all hours of the day moved the endless crowd—there were "just as many throbbing histories as scurrying feet." Most of it is happy, he said, a little of it is sorrowful, and "all of it is full of hope." For these alumni fathers he had words of sympathetic understanding. All were "banded together" in a sort of secret society of mutually baffled parents, "confronted by stalwart sons and surprising daughters, who daily become more so." Much as he would like to qualify as a good schoolmaster, Drury said, "I know that I qualify as a perplexed parent." He used the phrase he was often to fall back on in troubled times: "the benevolence of the majority." "I used to hammer and scold a good deal," he concluded, "but as the years go by I have come to value more, and I hope to use more, the power of gentle persuasion and loving expectation."

The newspaper headlines next day referred to the seventeen hundred boys on the waiting list for St. Paul's, a figure Drury had let fall in his address. But when the applause had subsided and the lights gone out, it was another St. Paul's that remained in mind: not the school of worldly success and prosperity, but a reservoir of quiet moral force. Drury watched happily the last days of that autumn term go by. "Tomorrow at this time the place will be absolutely still," he wrote in his diary. "The grey squirrels will boldly sit on the fence, the electric bells will be heard no more, and a brooding Christmas peace will flood over the silent school."

Yes, it was to be an empty school. For the first time in memory not a single boy had been kept over a day because of an excess of demerits. In the whole Big Study, indeed, no one had accumulated even half the fatal amount. Drury could well take satisfaction in the thought. And he could enjoy the calm. There would be plenty of strife to come.

Mandate for Reform

The rector looked upon the events of 1921 as the beginning for him of a new period at St. Paul's. If one chapter had been completed—the chapter of apprenticeship and reorganization—another waited to be written. The refusal to take the rectorship of Trinity was not, Brent wrote him, a negative action: "Rather is it a re-choice of a trust committed to you by God ten years ago. The old trust has become new. It is so fine in its possibilities and its importance that for you nothing in the world can compare with it. Fresh power and light will come to meet whatever lies before you."[23] This challenging view coincided with Drury's own convictions, and was confirmed by the expectations of the trustees and of many, within the school and outside, who were watching his career. A "more outspoken way of going forward" was Drury's own evaluation of the charge now resting upon him.

His annual reports for 1921 and 1922 are strongly stated and animated by reforming zeal. His determination that St. Paul's get "mixed up" with the United States, affirmed at the alumni dinner, was reiterated as he attacked the idea of a school "picked and purple," in the disturbing phrase of the *Times,* a school dedicated exclusively to the rich. St. Paul's must be a cross section of America, representative of various races and economic groups. "It is folly," he wrote, "to run a little reform school for the few within the confines of a free society"; and again: "If in our endowments and accumulated backing we are strong, clearly we ought to bear the infirmities of the weak." Not for St. Paul's, any more than for himself, was there to be an "exclusive, ornamental isolation."

In setting St. Paul's on a new course, Drury called for a change in student mores. Demands for a less luxurious life echoed earlier themes of simplicity and economy. His targets ranged from the excessive use of banners in the students' rooms—"an offense against art and hygiene"—to the over-elaborate wardrobes of the boys. All too often a surplus of private possessions led to "pathetic contrasts and unavoidable rivalries." Was it necessary, he asked, that boys be accompanied on their return to school by "huge drays piled high with tremendous trunks"? The arrival of an alumnus in a showy automobile was enough to stir his unconcealed anger, while wearers of polo coats and white buckskin shoes, symbols at that time of exclusivity and extravagance, were admonished by his stern gaze.

Working at another level, Drury sought admissions from a constituency wider than that on which the school had traditionally drawn. To achieve this, a liberal endowment, with ample provisions for scholarships, was a prime requisite. A drive for $2 million launched in 1920 gathered momentum slowly, but four years later yielded $1.6 million, nearly all of it to be used for tuition aid. Next, the "waiting list" came up for reevaluation. What to outsiders might seem a proof of strength, Drury saw as a limitation on the school's freedom to select a varied and representative student body. Places were guaranteed for those on whose behalf applications were made early—birth was considered a fitting time—provided a basic examination was later passed. The quality of scholarship, and the general background of a prospective student, could not be adequately weighed under these arrangements.

Finally, in his militant campaign for a more representative school, Drury conceived the idea of making St. Paul's the leader in bringing foreign students to American shores. His image was of "a league of youth" in which a number of other schools would ultimately share. St. Paul's would show the way, however; it would admit ten foreign students, from the Orient as well as from Europe, on full scholarships. "Here in this little place," Drury wrote, "let us open our door and step forward." The American school must hold itself responsible for producing "not only good Americans, but citizens of the world."

At the meeting of October 1923, the board recorded its "general interest" on hearing the rector's proposal and referred it to a committee of which at least one member could be counted highly sympathetic. The trustees were still in a post-Trinity mood. They expressed "hearty approval" for the rector's being absent for as much of the coming winter term as he might choose to take; they voted substantial funds for adding to the rectory a library for his use. By spring, however, a different attitude prevailed. Assaults on wealth had irked some members of the board; questioning the "waiting list" had seemed to others an attack upon the preeminence of the alumni; and the proposed scholarships for foreigners upset others.

Did not this proposal rest on precisely the kind of idealism that the country had repudiated in the presidential elections of 1920? Did it not echo the discredited Woodrow Wilson? All the latent resentments against Drury's efforts at reform focused on this issue of scholarships for foreigners: it was extravagant, it was not needed, it left many practical details unresolved. When the vote was taken that spring, the motion was defeated.

The objections to the plan for foreign students were accompanied by growing complaints against the rector's frequent absences from the school. To Drury these journeys were the breath of life. His very coming to St. Paul's had been upon the condition that he be allowed freedom to be absent from the school as he judged necessary. In visits to colleges he found the challenge to prepare lectures and sermons reaching beyond the limited attention of boys. In Cambridge, where he was a member of the Harvard Board of Overseers, he was in touch with leaders from the world of business and education. "It helps me mightily," he wrote, "in thinking about affairs of the school." Here were intimate hours with men like Bishop Brent and Bishop Lawrence; and there was President Lowell himself, "a magnetic, mercurial man," with his "dashing humor and adventurous, progressive spirit."[24]

A resolution condemning the rector's journeys was broached at two meetings of the board. Rather than being voted down, it was tabled—a bitter blow. Drury drafted an irate letter to the acting chairman, C. E. Ingersoll, charging that his original agreement had been violated. Only Cornelia Drury's good sense prevented him from sending it.[25] But in his diary he poured out his dismay and frustration. "I am sorry to see in our board materialism, caution, conservatism," he wrote immediately after the vote on foreign students, "visionless routine willingness to let 1924 look like 1884. . . . Better a parish of fifty souls down by the sea." And then: "I refuse to be a club steward acting under a directorate of world-lings."

The Board of Trustees

Who were these "worldlings"? How was the board constituted through the decade when the rector was so often tense and disgruntled? It was a very different body from that which had slumbered passively through the last period of the Coit regime. It was a mixed group, with its share of solid businessmen and a minority of intellectuals. It had also its original, independent characters, some supportive of the rector, some not. And all, in one way or another, saw it as their responsibility to guide the school actively according to their own lights.

In 1914, after having been on the board for forty-one years, Bishop Niles passed away—the venerable "father in God" remembered for having confirmed generations of St. Paul's boys, as if each depended for safety from mortal and immortal dangers upon his ghostly intonations alone. He had been succeeded by Bishop E. P. Parker, elevated from his mastership at St. Paul's. Now in the place traditionally reserved for the bishop of New Hampshire served the sturdy, Scots-accented John T. Dallas. The ex-rector, Henry Ferguson, became chairman of the board in 1915. It is a tribute to this man's extraordinary tact, and to Drury's abiding affection for him, that no conflict arose in a situation that might have seemed made for stress.

Upon his death two years later, Ferguson was succeeded by Frederick Shattuck. With his colorful wit and robust common sense, Shattuck hit it off famously with the rector. "How he did light up the bankers' brass and mahogany room!" Drury wrote with delight after a meeting of the executive committee: a jolly man "in a broad checked gray suit, yellow linen waistcoat, a bright red tie and a bright red carnation, and his hat on the back of his head."[26] A close connection with the school going back to the beginning did not in the least turn his eyes to the past; he judged each new situation as if it were arising on the first day. He was indeed a worldling, but with an instinctive sympathy for the man of vision.

Robert P. Perkins was a second trustee in whom Drury found unfailing friendship and support. It was he who in the crisis over the Hodgins dismissal backed Drury unconditionally, when even Shattuck was tempted to waver. "Without you," wrote Drury at that time, "I should not have survived"; and to him Drury expressed his self-doubts about the way

With his colorful wit and robust common sense. *Frederick Shattuck on the Long Path, 1926.*

he handled the incident, confessing that nothing, save loss in his own family, had ever distressed him so deeply.[27] But Perkins was unable to play a part in the 1923 confrontations. That steady, downright figure, his closest personal friend, Drury saw decline in fatal illness, just when his own internal and external worlds seemed to be falling apart. By 1924, when he needed them most, Shattuck and Perkins had both died.

For the rest, did they constitute what Chapman called disparagingly "a strong lot of men to run a bank"? [28] There was Levi H. Greenwood, a businessman to the core, who quarreled with the rector when he insisted (understandably) that as treasurer he be asked to approve emergency loans. Greenwood had his charming and whimsical side. He made the radical suggestion that women be elected to the board. He complained about the universally hard seats on which boys of that period were expected to sit. In the chapel, in the library, in classrooms, at meals, he pointed out, nothing softened the surfaces on which their posteriors rested; but on entering the houses of masters, what did one find? Furniture stuffed and liberally upholstered! [29] There was also "Judge" John MacLane, clerk of the board for thirty-four years (as his son was to be for thirty-one years thereafter), a solid New Hampshire man, ardent tennis player and skier, collector of first editions of Thomas Hardy.

Charles D. Dickey was a banker whose son was to succeed him, both of them broad-minded men and winning companions. The elder Dickey's correspondence with Drury got off to a rocky start when he addressed him as Dr. *Stephen* Drury.[30] The rector inadvertently evened the score by locating Wall Street in Boston. Two other businessmen, C. E. Ingersoll and Reeve Schley, served as chairman of the board, the former briefly and the latter for twenty-three years. Both came from wealthy backgrounds; both were plainly conservative. Their affection and generosity made them highly useful members.

The pair who formed the focus of opposition to Drury might be thought those least qualified, in Chapman's phrase, "to run a bank." That they were worldlings, however, and that they stood by the old ways, cannot be denied. John M. Goetchius had retired from business to manage the family property, to enjoy golfing and yachting, and to give himself wholeheartedly to the leadership of the St. Paul's alumni. The raising of endowment funds was his chief concern and his lasting contribution. "Now what is it all for?" he asked his fellow alumni in a 1921 fund-raising address. "What is the idea? Well, there we have grounds for debate, but personally I have always regarded that little institution as a sort of jewel—a perfect setting as to climate and otherwise in those New Hampshire hills. But we realize that the jewel [is not] complete. Will it ever be complete? It may be like a cathedral. . . ."[31] Whether jewel or cathedral, the alumni responded affirmatively to Jack Goetchius's appeals, and for the first time placed St. Paul's on a solid financial basis.

Joined with Goetchius in opposing scholarships for foreign boys, and spearheading with him the attack on the rector's absences, was Charles D. Hart. A Philadelphia doctor, Hart's contact with the school was broken for twenty years following his graduation, until in heading the twenty-fifth reunion of his class he experienced a kind of revelation. Thereafter no detail of the school's welfare was too minute for his consideration. His interest in the school was such, Drury's son was to write caustically, that he seemed to think "the school depended on a flood tide [of letters from him] to keep afloat."[32]

Hart's gifts were constant and often unexpected. He provided for the school a shrine where the path around the pond entered the woods; a boulder near the bridge over the sluice inscribed with lines from Shakespeare; numerous autograph letters and signed photographs of presidents and generals; and saplings from rare or famous trees, including the cedars of Lebanon and the Penn charter oak. Perhaps his most notable gift was a statue of St. Paul, presented for the school's hundredth Anniversary, which shows the patron saint as an emaciated fanatic, very different from the stolid burgher of Dürer's engraving that had long appeared on the school's seal. On one occasion toward the end of the donor's protracted service, screams were heard emanating from the study of the sixth rector. The secretary had just opened a large package from Dr. Hart, containing two human heads: Peruvian—and shrunken.

The rector had a taste for the unusual himself. In a rare pun, he once warned the students "not to fall foul of the water fowl"—two swans he had taken special care to obtain; and on another occasion, at the Anniversary luncheon, he gravely thanked an alumnus for the gift of "two bull heifers." (No one in the audience dared to smile.) He and Dr. Hart might have established a friendly concordat except that the latter's conservatism on social and educational issues galled him. "It is wrong, wrong, wrong for me to think about Dr. Hart," Drury exclaimed in a characteristic diary entry. Besides, the endless fussing involved in receiving and placing the gifts exhausted the rector's patience. A trustee (presumably Dr. Hart) arrived at the school "bursting with talkative interest in nonessentials. "I excused myself," Drury confided to his diary, "and took a rest instead."[33]

Two Intellectuals

In an effort to enlarge the board's representation and to increase its emphasis on educational matters, two graduates of outstanding intellectual credentials were elected in the 1920s. They arrived too late to ease the crisis of 1923, but played useful, if limited, roles once the atmosphere had calmed down. Anson Phelps Stokes, later secretary of Yale University (he narrowly missed being its president) and dean of the Washington Cathedral, was a peer with whom Drury could converse freely and from whom he could accept the bitter pill of advice. As late as 1927, a paragraph in the draft of the rector's annual report, referring to foreign students, evoked from Stokes the warning that it would run into the "strong opposition [of] Ingersoll, Hart, and other trustees."[34] Stokes recommended omitting it, though he approved the sentiment, and Drury struck out the offending words. Stokes placed a high value upon advanced degrees for teachers in secondary schools. Drury, succumbing to this plausible enthusiasm, engaged an older master equipped with a Ph.D., who unfortunately turned out to be a long-lived bore.

Stokes backed Drury on his absences. "I hope and pray we may all be guided aright in meeting a serious, though not critical, situation," he wrote Drury on the issue. "I shall of course come up for the meeting." Independent inquiries had convinced him that Drury was entirely within the rights and normal practices of his trade. Dr. Alfred E. Stearns, headmaster of Andover, assured Stokes that *he* accepted outside engagements freely; moreover, he had little sympathy with parents who could only arrange to deal with their sons' business on Sunday.

Stokes was of the opinion, however, that the trustees' criticism on this subject was a symptom of something deeper: the feeling that although Drury had done the work of renewal and reconstruction "wonderfully," he had failed to create within the school family as a whole a solid *esprit de corps*. His summary of Drury's record at this stage was just: "As an organizer, a preacher, an idealist in education you have been and are beyond praise . . . [you] have everywhere respect, almost everywhere loyalty, but in a good many places not that degree of *enthusiastic* support which would make your work most effective." Drury accepted such a judgment with surprising humility.

A trustee coming late in the decade, and serving for a brief four years, brought to the board his particular insights and acerbities. Samuel Eliot Morison was already one of Harvard's outstanding lecturers and known to the academic public as an historian, but he had not yet gathered the popular fame that his sea journeys and best-selling histories and biographies were to bring him. A comparatively young man, he still showed the loftiness of manner and cool air of superiority that age was to soften into a charming courtliness. His credentials as a trustee would have seemed beyond challenge. He was an alumnus whose first writings had been published in the *Horae*. His great-grandfather, William Otis, had been in the founding group of trustees; his uncle, Frank Morison, had been a graduate of one of the first classes; and he was the adored grandson of Samuel Eliot. Nevertheless there was a good deal of head-shaking when Sam Morison's name came under consideration for the board. Was he not known for radical views? Had he not supported the cause of the notorious Sacco and Vanzetti?

Morison lived up to the role of independent critic for which, in the end, he had been chosen. What was needed, he told the rector, was to get boys practicing the arts. "At present the school is so wanting on this side of the fine arts that when I visit it in the football or the hockey season it seems to me like a polite and virtuous lumber camp."[35] Wasn't it "a bit scandalous," he asked, that every sixth former of the previous year had gone to college? "Surely five or ten percent of them will do neither them-

He lived up to the role of independent critic. *Samuel Eliot Morison in the library of the house on Brimmer Street. The books and furniture are almost unchanged from the days when Samuel Eliot, his grandfather, worked in the same room.*

selves nor the college any good in going there.'' Meanwhile so large a part of the school's effort was used to secure their admission to college as to deprive the majority of cultural opportunities.

When Drury supported the idea of having classes taught like college seminars, with the students seated at large tables, Morison was highly skeptical. ''The device of sitting around a table with boys instead of sitting in front of them,'' he wrote, ''is (in my opinion) but another form of that craze for method and paraphernalia which is the leading vice of American secondary education.''

Drury accepted these and other communications with good grace. Morison's fellow trustees, however, had difficulty in accommodating themselves to his views. On one occasion the board was discussing the case of a boy who had applied red paint to the statue memorializing the Spanish American War. No punishment seemed to fit so heinous an offense; firing the lad was to let him off too lightly. Morison sat looking out the window, apparently lost in his own thoughts. ''Sam,'' said one of his colleagues, ''you have not spoken on this matter. What is your opinion of what we should do?''

''I wouldn't do anything,'' was his reply; ''the most damn-fool war we ever fought.''[36]

That was too much for the rest of the board, though they were precisely the views of old Samuel Eliot, when in 1898 he was nodding out his last days in the house on Brimmer Street where Morison still lived.* Morison did not regret his four-year term as trustee; he always kept a warm affection for the school.

A Time of Self-Doubt

The decade following World War I was marked by unprecedented prosperity and growing materialism. The world with which the rector had hoped to see St. Paul's ''mixed up'' was increasingly out of key with the school's ethical and religious values. Drury did not fully grasp the incongruity. He blamed himself, rather than the times, for the school's failure to produce ministers and scholars; he failed to sense the burden of worldly pressures under which schoolboys of that generation were laboring. Men scarcely older than his sixth formers had borne the heat of battle and known the post-Armistice letdown; they were now in the midst of a moral and social revolution. Yet at the school, rigorous codes and restraints were expected to be observed unquestioningly. The mixing of worlds was inevitable, but in ways Drury had not foreseen.

*Morison died there in 1976.

Amid the widespread prosperity, Drury modified his hopes of making the school a representative cross section of America. The school's constituency, at least for the time being, seemed fated to be the rich. But at least that constituency could be prodded and shaken up. "Our function," Drury said, "is not to conform to the rich and prosperous world which surrounds us, but rather, through its children, to convert it." Again: "This is in [no] small part a school of rich men's sons. So be it. Let it then be the director, the converter, the inspirer of rich men's sons."[37] In words reminiscent of Wilson's at the 1909 Anniversary, Drury urged these sons to be better men than their fathers.

That they were different from their fathers could not be denied. On a visit to Bar Harbor shortly after the war, Scudder first sniffed out the new mood of youth. "One matter which occupied the talk of people to an amazing extent," he wrote Drury, "was the free and easy, not to say wild, behavior of youth. One marvels at the stories. Schools will find, *sans question,* more difficulties in dealing with the lads and lassies than ever."[38] It was the kind of letter that must have annoyed the rector, who once called Scudder "a *trivial* man." But it contained a warning he might well have heeded. Drury, however, could not bring himself to believe that his exhortations and his hopes were falling on the stony ground of postwar materialism.

From within the school warnings more serious than Scudder's were being brought to the rector's attention. Under the surface of good faculty – student relations and good morale after 1921, disturbing signs of unrest and rule-breaking were becoming apparent. Beach White, one of the sturdy crop of masters brought to the school in the 1890s, told Drury that "a hard core of upper formers" was convincing those below them that rectitude did not pay in school life. They might not get control of the form in 1922– 1923, White asserted, but their influence could be dominant. "Even if they do not procure the offices for their principal members, they have influence enough to turn the tide in favor of their hangers-on."[39] White recommended the dismissal of five of them, but Drury could not bring himself to face such a course. Later he came to regret it.

On the surface, everything seemed as it should be. In March of that year, a master making his rounds on a Sunday afternoon reported to the rector a scene of healthy and innocent activity. In the library here were about twenty-five boys, very quiet; eighteen were in the Big Study; while others in the classrooms of an annex were playing on various musical instruments. In the laboratory two boys were working with a new-fangled radio, but nothing of interest was received; in the cowbarn two were visiting, but seemed to be causing no disturbance to the cows. A snowball fight was in progress between second and third formers outside the lower school.[40] How could it be that within the charmed circle rebellious forces were at work?

Yet the same spring that saw the rector shaken by the trustees' rejection of his proposal for a league of youth found him in a serious disciplinary crisis. It all began innocently enough. On June 19, the Halcyon Boat Club swept the races at Long Pond. The following evening these victories were appropriately celebrated at a banquet in the Alumni House, the long tables shimmering in white table cloths and candlelight, laden with silver trophies. It was a beautiful dinner, Scudder recorded in his diary; the speeches were excellent, "witty and to the point," and the company was thoroughly convivial. Afterwards, in forms less traditional, the festivities were continued at the upper school. Alone now, the sixth formers passed the challenge cup around, drinking liberally and smoking. Talk of their indulgences spread through the upper school and inevitably reached the rector.

Two days later, Drury summoned those he believed to have been guilty of major infractions. One of the group, captain of that year's hockey team, supposed he was to be complimented on the diploma, *magna cum laude,* he expected to be awarded that evening. To his astonishment, on entering the rector's study, he found gathered there the president of the sixth form and his roommate, star goalie of the school's hockey team; the school's outstanding scholar; and the captain of the Halcyon crew. What followed can only be attributed to Drury's heightened religious sensibilities, combined with the stress to which his crisis with the trustees had subjected him.[41]

As one of those present described the scene years later, the rector asked the boys to pray with him. Then he asked them to give their word that they had neither smoked nor drunk during the school year, whether on the school grounds or in vacation. There was a dead silence. "I think the rector aged ten years in the next minute," recalled that participant. "I am absolutely certain he believed we would all take the oath, and it shattered something in his faith when we didn't."[42]

"Gentlemen," the rector said next, "you shall not receive your diplomas tonight." They all filed out.

The situation was an impossible one all around. An action that would have been welcomed by a large part of the school had it been taken earlier, or after consultation, or on the basis of demonstrable evidence, was judged with incredulity in the light of the bizarre scene described above. A sixth-form meeting was half prepared to censure a president who was believed by many to have betrayed his trust, but as none but the tiniest minority of the class could swear to the oath required of the five, the move fell through. The rector was left alone and vulnerable. Convinced he had acted in the cause of righteousness, he could not retreat from his position. Meanwhile the five young men, deprived of their diplomas, found the door to college closed.

A touch of humor might have set things straight. These young men, after all, had entered school during war years. Older brothers and friends had come back to regale them with tales of the soldier's life, or life in Paris after the Armistice. These were the heroes they sought to emulate in their schoolboy escapades. A cleansing laugh, however, was the one thing not forthcoming. The hockey team captain wrote to the rector on June 17: "This has hit me harder, I think, than anyone expected it would, but I hope it may prove a lesson and perhaps make me worthy of the time and care spent on me by the masters and yourself. It needed a hard blow to wake me."[43] Drury in his anguish let this contrite letter lie two months on his desk unacknowledged. He slipped off to Mount Desert in an unhappy mood, grateful for the end of a hard year. "O my God," he wrote in his diary, "all these days of coastwise shipping are over." Still he brooded. "Give me a right judgment about the boys. I do not want to blight their career or keep them out of college. I only want to be a furtherance of Thy will."

A father, who was to remain Drury's friend until his death many years later, accused him of having broken the fundamental principles of Anglo-Saxon justice in the treatment of his son. "He may be right," Drury avowed. "I have an increasing disrespect for my own wisdom either in what to do or how to do it. *Dominus illuminatio mea.*" In the end the boys were given English rather than the traditional Latin diplomas, thus by a simple stratagem assuring their entrance into college. But for Drury the sum of his defeats was heavy. The adverse vote of the trustees still rankled; what was worse, the voice in which he trusted had let him down. He had labored earnestly to be an instrument of the divine will and had created only a fearful muddle.

For a season the whole fabric of the school seemed to have suffered corruption. Writing to his constituency, Drury gave vent to a sense of angry despair. How could it have been that he was not made aware of drinking among sixth formers, far more widespread than among the few who had been expelled? Did certain alumni and parents know about it? Did the faculty fail him? "Though the school administration is not provably lax," he wrote with astonishing candor in his annual report, "I do feel that not to have known this condition marks a real failure on our part."

There was the question, besides, of how the students procured the liquor, alcoholic beverages being at that time illegal. Did they steal it from their fathers' homes, or was it brought in by "chauffeurs"? The thought persisted that "lawless sources" near the school had been responsible. One master on his rounds had reported, indeed, seeing strangers on the outskirts of the school property—"four girls or so at different times, several young men of sinister aspect."[44] These apparitions particularly troubled the rector, who reported taking legal means to forestall them.

Afterwards there would be difficulties and disappointments, but the dark depths of 1923 would not again be plumbed. Drury had been acting at the same time as prophet and administrator, pastor and disciplinarian. It was a difficult posture to maintain, and there were moments in 1924 when he thought of leaving St. Paul's for another, wholly religious sphere, that mythical "parish by the sea" where he could preach to the poor and visit the sick. Yet he labored on at his "coastwise shipping," and gradually the opposing aspects of his work fell into a happier balance. He learned to listen sympathetically to the troubles of the wayward boy and still to hold him to the standards of the secular community. One reads of his harboring a wish, on an occasion when he was at the climax of a sermon, that he might hurl an iron-bound prayer book at the head of a second former, "lolling" in a front pew.[45] Drury was remembering, what for a time he had forgotten, that spiritual appeals may not by themselves reach the sons of Adam.

The Rector at Northeast

After the toils of a school year, even such a year as 1923, the summers at Northeast Harbor were a balm for the rector. At their home, "Concordia," on the sea close to the large house built in 1895 by Cornelia Drury's father, the growing family took pleasure in the island life, in riding, sailing, mountain climbing, and in expeditions to such nearby islands as the Cranberries or Great Gott. His wife arranged a small retreat, the Lair, where Drury could deal with his immense correspondence, compose his sermons and books, or just think. On the beaches he gathered white stones to set before the entrance to the Lair. White stones, he said, quoting the Apocalypse, are the sign of a secret friendship with God.[46] Or he would pick the blueberries and wildflowers that grew abundantly on the surrounding hills.

St. Paul's was never far from his mind. Several of the trustees, and many alumni, summered on Mount Desert. On a Sunday he would hold a special Communion service for the school flock. Looking out over the Great Harbor dotted with sails of the Northeast fleet, he would guess that half the boats were manned—"or perhaps I should say boyed," he punned, adding his hope that therefore they would be less likely to sink—by students of the school. Too many bishops for his liking gathered on the island: what he called "clerical lunching and munching" was not his preferred way of spending a July afternoon. But there was delight in the company of a summer regular like old President Eliot, gravely discoursing upon such topics as whether the airplane would ever be of real benefit to humanity.

Then the summer turned. "I begin to sniff the coming year," he would write in his diary. "The blue chicory in the vacant spaces, the sight of fresh young faces, the tang of evening air, all speak of September, the springtime of schools." There would be a last trip to Great Cranberry Island. Surely, he thought, from such an expedition one should be able to store up something of the bright sea and air, the wind-swept, rain-washed rocks, against drab and duteous days of the coming winter. By September 1, it was no longer possible to say, "*Next* month work begins." Would he ever grow up and get over the schoolboy reluctance to see the holidays pass?

Finally, in his little Ford, the trip down to the rectory at Concord. "Oh God, as I walk about this house, so comfortable, connected with heat and light and telephone, I pray that I may still be a pilgrim."

Educational Seer

The nightmare of a pervasive corruption faded; those sinister characters whose missions had penetrated the outskirts of the school withdrew like so many shadows. A more cooperative sixth form took over, and Millville returned to its former peace. Perhaps the events of the previous spring had had a salutary effect after all.

Drury turned back to his role as educational seer. The pressures for a college education continued to disturb him, for he saw the process of secondary education narrowed and distorted by the fierce competition for college admission. In 1926, he proposed that the colleges, if they chose to take care of those besieging their gates, should formulate a two-year course of combined cultural and vocational study—an interesting anticipation of the community colleges of the 1950s. "It is foolish," he wrote, "to impose the curriculum of an ancient, learned society on the masses of college candidates in our commercial day." Both the private school and the college were called "boldly to put first things first." For the brighter and more ambitious of St. Paul's students, he urged the taking of the new admissions examinations—general tests, unrelated to specific subjects—at the end of their final year. Such examinations involved risk, but they challenged the best in young scholars, and they gave the school the opportunity to enlarge the curriculum with advanced courses and special classes in the sixth-form year.[47]

He did not forget the average boys, those "who received no prizes and provoked no applause, children of the house who created no history either glorious or shameful." For them, once admitted into the school, there was the duty of attention equal to that given the brighter lads, along with equal affection and appreciation. "Son, thou art ever with me," he quoted, "and all that I have is thine." Yet there remained some who never should go to college. For these he proposed—and for a while seemed to have the funds to create—a new school: a farm where a dozen boys, two teachers and an adviser "could work out the problem of making the unfit, fit." He was not thinking of the backward or the handicapped, but of the boys, many of them the children of prominent families, who would one day have large responsibilities. They deserved "a noble grounding" in the business of living. For them he proposed, not the subtleties of traditional scholarship, but "an unafraid acquaintance with common knowledge."

Drury's views on the running of schools were most fully set forth in his book *Schoolmastering,* published in 1926 and written during the year when he dutifully (yet somewhat grudgingly) cut short his travels and eliminated his absences from the school. It is his best book, the only one apart from a brief anthology of his sayings that has survived unscathed by time. A sunny and vivacious disquisition on various aspects of boarding schools, it has for its theme the ever-present need to keep institutions from falling into a humdrum or commonplace existence. Schooling is a realm, Drury maintained, where the routine must constantly be criticized—and the ideal constantly clarified. For the institution to be at its best, the head must be a man who will "bear the misinterpretation and the loneliness of ruling"; yet he must never let himself become "grand, gloomy, or peculiar." "I'm sure my co-workers get vast amusement and amazement and irritation out of me," he said. "It must be so. It's only the man who is willing to be thought a fool that's fit to run a school."

The frustrations of the early 1920s are taken into the argument and made to come out purged and sweetened. The trustees, he argues, are the housekeepers, but they are primarily men of vision. They must see the school "as a serviceable human tool for the creator's hand." Their job is to be "unlocal," to connect their special work "patiently and broadly with countrywide progressive tendencies."

The masters of the ideal school must be free to be as wide-ranging as they can. They must have sabbaticals, travel, read deeply, know their subjects profoundly, and be cheerful and outgiving in the community. "There can be no sanctity," he warned, "in sticking to a little job and trying to dignify it by dogged perseverance." In return for their services, masters need to be able to marry, have good salaries, and dwell in comfortable, well-warmed houses. As for the alumni, "the school belongs to the boys who are in it," he declared with a fine Jeffersonian ring. Returning alumni must be greeted, their gifts gratefully acknowledged. "But in the heat of the day there is no time for reminiscence."

There was plenty in *Schoolmastering* to make individuals wince, but nothing was personal, and all of it was stated broadly and generously. Its author had mastered the trade which, as a young man, he had known to be infinitely complex.

Elected Bishop

One final occasion, nevertheless, was to test Drury as the decade ran out. Its resolution was to determine the course of the school for the decade to come.

In May 1929, Drury was elected bishop coadjutor of Pennsylvania. "I earnestly want to do what is best for the school and best for the church," he wrote to the trustees. "In many ways the bishopric appeals to me. I have sometimes felt that headmasters do their best work as young men, and that after a certain point, which I may have reached, their contribution decreases." As in 1921, there was a period of uncertainty while the rector pondered his decision. Particular circumstances made Drury hesitate about accepting the post. The bishop whom Drury would serve as colleague and then succeed, Thomas James Garland, was a crusty Irishman of sixty-two who had no intention of signifying when he might retire. He was known as a chief whom younger men disliked serving. "They all seem to be afraid of hard work," he said. "It amuses me."[48] In the school family at the same time strong appeals were made to Drury to continue as rector.

The voice of John Richards was probably as persuasive as that of any other man. "When I think you may take it," he wrote his old friend, "I feel tired and blue. . . . All I can see is the danger that our ship may be left without its captain, in the midst of a dangerous voyage. For we are in a transition at St. Paul's still, and it is you who conceived of it and are guiding us through." A boy wrote to his parents: "Nobody knows whether the rector will accept the job. . . . I hope he does not, and so does everybody else."[49]

One evening late in May the news came that Drury had refused. In Millville the leaves were just beginning to reach their fullness, and the school lay under warm airs, its lawns clipped and all in green readiness for the alumni who would be returning at Anniversary. Passing beneath the elms, a group of boys went up to a master's house where, it had been learned, the rector and his wife were dining. There were three cheers for Drury, and a heartfelt rendition of "For He's a Jolly Good Fellow." The rector, who had come out on the porch, stood for what seemed a long time perfectly still while the boys waited for his response. The man who had never been at a loss for words seemed to have none at this crucial juncture of his career. At last the silence was broken by the chapel bell chiming the hour. Stroke upon stroke—and then silence again. Drury still waited. Then in very quiet tones he said that he had heard many wonderful things in his life, but never anything as beautiful as the sound of that bell. [50]

That was all. But in the applause and cheering which followed, the rector and his constituency entered upon a new phase, one that was to bring the school through nine years of harmonious effort into a period of material and spiritual growth. The man who had so often been at odds with himself and with the school ceased in that hour to be Drury *at* St. Paul's. He had become Drury *of* St. Paul's.

CHAPTER TEN

Augustan Age
1929–1938

New Boundaries Established

Though as a young rector Drury had doubts about the need for physical improvements, a major building program marked his administration. A school should be "the quietest place in the world," with little outward change from year to year; a schoolmaster's job was with boys, he said, not blueprints.[1] But the prosperity of the 1920s created a building fever to which St. Paul's would not remain immune. The rector, when the opportunity presented itself, proved as insatiable in material transformations as in educational projects. "I love the smell of fresh mortar," a student of the 1930s recalled his saying, as he walked with him about the school grounds; and the rector's cane came down as forcefully as if the aging structure before their eyes were instantly to dissolve.

The first concern was that the geographic domain be expanded and its boundaries made secure and defensible. Drury encouraged the board to undertake land acquisitions of several hundred acres, especially west of the school, in the areas surrounding Big and Little Turkey. Long Pond, on whose shores stood the boathouses of the Shattuck and Halcyon clubs, had been made the city water supply in 1870. Although no concern had yet been expressed over the use of these waters for recreational purposes, the fact that one day they might be closed to rowing may have occurred to the rector and the trustees. In any case, Long Pond was a good two miles from the school; the daily journeys (except for the few hardy spirits who always walked, or became joggers before jogging was invented) were accomplished in large horse-drawn "barges"; or later, for the lower crews, in trucks. The concept of an inland sea, suitable for rowing and wholly within the school's terrain, appealed to Drury's imperial gaze.

Next, the heart of the school needed to be reinforced against invasions from the outside world. The road into the valley and through the center of Millville had once been a dusty and little-used thoroughfare. The infrequent passage of buggies and carts provided in the nineteenth century a pleasant diversion. Cattle, coming from the farm at the top of the hill, could consume as much as an hour in making their way, past boys and other impediments, to fields beyond the school. By the 1920s, however, automobiles were becoming a menace. Local "hot rods" roared down the incline. Sightseers and Sunday drivers came to peer at the chapel and other school buildings, while the workaday traffic passing from Concord toward Dunbarton and Hopkinton had greatly increased. Drury saw the possibility of creating a secure enclave, with vehicles no longer passing through the school.

The first need was to get the Hopkinton road moved so that it joined Pleasant Street at a point east of Millville. This was accomplished in 1928, when the main road was made to pass behind Foster's brick mansion, leaving the infirmary, which had stood at the very edge of the property, safely within the school grounds. The second and more difficult problem was to provide means for Dunbarton-bound cars to circumvent the principal buildings. In agreement with Concord, where Drury was well known and always liked, the school constructed a road on its own property, including a new bridge across the Turkey River.

The old Millville street now belonged entirely to the school. How was it to be improved and beautified? The concept of a row of buildings harmoniously related to each other along a village street had been abandoned by Drury's time, partly as a result of the lingering influence of the Olmsted report. Now the old road was narrowed to a drive; the granite fence erected by William N. Coit, "curator" in the school's earliest days, was removed, and curving paths of brick were laid on either side. Shaded by elms, the drive presented a stately and serene effect, though it lacked the picturesque qualities of the former country road.

A further improvement, dear to Drury's heart, was the construction of what he named The Long Path, running at the edge of the larger pond from the infirmary to the upper school. Up to this time the only route through the school was by the Dunbarton road; buildings extending their backs to the water ignored views across the pond and blocked passage along its shore. To achieve a rerouting of pedestrian traffic, Drury filled in part of the shoreline and constructed a new footbridge where the ponds joined. In later years, as older buildings were torn down, the school would become increasingly oriented toward these pleasant vistas. The Long Path, its origin and its name forgotten, would serve as a daily thoroughfare for a large part of the community.

For the newly landscaped areas at the center of the school, Drury had a special dream. The automobile—which he disliked as a symbol of wealth and because it inhibited walking—would be banned. In this he was too far in advance of his time to gain support. It would take another generation

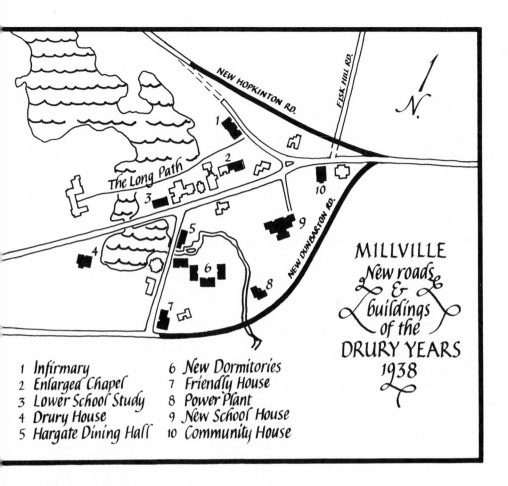

MILLVILLE
New roads
&
buildings
of the
DRURY YEARS
1938

1 Infirmary
2 Enlarged Chapel
3 Lower School Study
4 Drury House
5 Hargate Dining Hall
6 New Dormitories
7 Friendly House
8 Power Plant
9 New School House
10 Community House

before the disadvantages of the unfettered automobile would be fully grasped and the heart of the school freed from either moving or parked vehicles.

Rebuilding the Center

All this was only the infrastructure, the setting of the stage for the major reconstruction of the Drury era. The chapel that had seemed imposing and almost grandiose when completed in 1888 was now too small to contain the enlarged student body (at that time about 315 in number) along with the attendant growth of faculty and staff. Rows of "monkey benches"— chairs that squeaked under the weight of restless lower formers—ran down the length of the chapel, narrowing the aisle and impeding the formal procession in which students both entered and left the services. Ralph

Adams Cram, Vaughan's successor as the foremost interpreter of the
Gothic style, was engaged. He proposed an operation similar to that by
which the old chapel had once been enlarged. The structure would be cut
in two at the choir; the altar, including the recumbent figure of Henry
Augustus Coit, would be moved bodily eastward so as to allow the inser-
tion of two new bays. Along with this provision for greater length would
go such additions as a new choir room, and a chantry designed to receive
a war memorial.

Even the most confirmed enthusiasts were surprised by the ease with
which funds for this costly project were raised. Former students might
grumble about the number of times they had been compelled in their
youth to attend chapel service, but they were generously prepared to provide a suitable religious environment for the generation of their sons and
grandsons. In 1927 the chapel was deconsecrated, and workmen began to
slice through the brick walls. A student, impressed by the Piranesi-like
web of scaffolding in the darkened interior, climbed to the top, slipped,
and only by getting an uncertain hold on a crossbar as he fell saved himself from perishing in that unsanctified place.[2] The school held its collective breath as the eastern end of the vast structure, seemingly too narrow
to hold itself erect, was slid upon tracks to its new location.

The task of reconstruction then went forward as the void between the
two parts of the old building was filled with Gothic tracery. Within, the

A shaded drive replaced the old Dunbarton road.

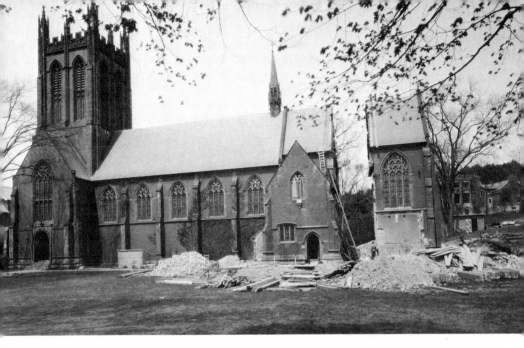

The chapel was cut in two at the choir.

REBUILDING THE CENTER

The enlarged chapel along the new school drive.

added length deepened unexpectedly the sense of mystery. Two sections of seats and stalls, lying between the altar and the pulpit, provided necessary additional seating in an area to become quickly known as "Sleepy Hollow."

Plans for the war memorial in the new chantry had, meanwhile, been going forward. After much discussion in the board, the American sculptor Daniel Chester French was engaged for the work. The result was a composition of two figures crafted in pure white marble: a stricken soldier, his sword broken, falling into the arms of a winged, encompassing angel. The image was the cause of much unhappiness. Ingersoll, then chairman of the board, called it "awful," and expressed privately the conviction that it would never be placed in the chapel.[3] Drury was at least half of the same mind, admitting that he and James Knox, perhaps for the first time since he had come to the school, found themselves in agreement.

Where in this work was the image of Christian death, its heroic militancy, its faith in a purer, nobler realm? So far as the sculpture implied, death was a mere negation and a repose and the cause for which it had been suffered only a fleeting dream.[4] In addition, the white marble figure of the soldier was distressingly nude.

On the latter point, at least, the board was prepared to take action. A resolution in the meeting of April 1926 formally expressed the trustees' hope that the sculptor "would approve the placing of a fig leaf, a scarf or other covering on the figure." French obliged, with a result that left nature and art in precarious balance. By this successful maneuver, the pro-memorialists were able to carry the day. On January 26, 1929, the sculpture was dedicated in a moving ceremony. It remained, like the statue of the Spanish-American War veteran in front of the library, expressive of something beyond its own time. The figures might appear Victorian in their realism, and the white marble stark against the brick and sandstone of the Gothic interior. Yet the image of youth in its physical perfection, with the angel asking no questions and making no demands, spoke to later students as more conventional Christian symbolism might not have done.

Other construction projects could have appeared prosaic after the enlargement of the chapel, but each was marked by the rector's intimate concern and by his sometimes quaint idealizations. A new power plant carried the upward thrust of Gothic details on its chimney—it was a day when the extra cost of such elaboration would be willingly borne; and on its brick walls bore the fine Prayer Book injunction, "O ye Fire and Heat, bless ye the Lord." A dining hall for the middle forms was built on the site where the original mill, and later the school's laundry and first power plant, had stood. It was named after John Hargate, and was carefully

Where was the image of Christian death? *The new war memorial became a matter of controversy.*

scaled so that boys at their meals should feel comfortable and not over-powered.

Here was placed the portrait of the rector by Sir William Orpen, commissioned at this time by a grateful alumnus. "A bright decoration," Drury described it,[5] though the outstanding British painter had presented him in full clerical regalia, and in his most formidable public manner. Here, too, reached by a high winding stair at the end of the building nearest the old mill, was a modest apartment set aside for distinguished (and reasonably spry) visitors. "Let us make a little chamber," had said the biblical widow blessed by the prophet, "and let us set for him there a bed, and a table, and a stool, and a candlestick."[6] So the apartment was named the Prophet's Chamber. It was a typical Drury touch.

With dining facilities for the middle forms thus taken care of, the old school house remained in use only as a dormitory. Now Drury pushed forward with a plan to replace it with smaller-scaled and more homey accommodations. Students had developed feelings of affection for the school house, the replacement, it will be recalled, for the building destroyed by fire in 1878. "A superb specimen of Victorian architecture," it was described facetiously in the *Horae;* the trustees were considering its preservation as a "most precious historical relic." Tradition had it that "the garrets once formed the quarters of Ethiopian menials." Its basement bathing facilities were only to be compared, said the *Horae,* "with the baths of Caracalla, at one time so famous."[7]

Relic or not, the days of the school house were numbered. On the far side of the sluice Drury projected a quadrangle of four dormitories. A sign of the times was the naming of the new buildings for their respective donors—Ford, Manville, Simpson and Brewster—rather than honoring (as Drury had hoped) old worthies of the school's history. The "new buildings," as they were still to be known to alumni fifty years later, did not warm the hearts of the boys. The formal organization of the quadrangle, and the identical plan of each building, contrasted with the random and often peculiar structures in which they seemed to enjoy living.

Other minor touches were in the Drury style. The old gas house at the center of the school was remodeled—not inappropriately—as a circular theater for debating and for masters meetings. A branch of the United States Post Office, the only school post office in the country, was opened in the basement of the Big Study, complete with 564 boxes. Enlargement of a subterranean eatery known as the Tuck Shop recalled a time when all orders for food had gone through John Willcox, a rotund bewhiskered little man, whose "Millville Express," drawn by a scrawny, mouse-colored team, made daily journeys to Concord. One massive stroke, however, still waited to be applied before the school's physical regeneration could be considered complete. The Big Study, with its jumble of offices, administrative and educational functions, and the annex of classrooms darkening the edge of the pond, needed to be replaced.

One July day in 1934, Drury received in Northeast a letter from his vice rector describing the unannounced appearance at the school of "two distinguished-looking gentlemen." "I spotted them," said the vice rector, C. C. Monie, "introduced myself, and asked if I could do anything for them." One, it turned out, had been a boy at the school forty years before; the other was the father of two former students. The visitors were Edward S. Harkness and the architect James Gamble Rogers. "I invited them to lunch," Monie continued, "which they declined; they said they just wanted to look around, and needed no assistance."[8] Soon afterwards began complicated negotiations that were to conclude in a princely gift, providing a new educational center on the former school house site.

The school's physical reconstruction achieved a beauty in land and buildings almost totally erasing the forbidding and gloomy aspect inherited from the nineteenth century. More than ever the school grounds become a world in themselves, cherished and apart. Within this world the inhabitants made their way on foot in all weathers, the distances measured out to the last pace. From the cottage at the top of the hill where James Potter Conover and his wife had lived (now an agreeably ramshackle dormitory) one would walk, in the course of three trips daily to the upper school dining room, a distance of twelve thousand feet, or a good deal more than two miles; from the Middle and the old upper school, the distance was 9,348 feet. Going further afield, the student would walk 11,067 feet to the top of Jerry Hill. Through this wide domain Drury moved, the eternal pedestrian, always curious and probing—as one who walked about Zion telling the towers thereof.

Outposts of Empire

The building program and the enlargement of the endowment fund could not have been accomplished without vigorous support from the alumni. By the early 1930s they were an active and highly organized group, whose chairman sat as a member of the board of trustees. The little realm at Millville was the center of an empire, the chief outposts of which were in Boston, New York, Philadelphia and Pittsburgh. Its power and wealth were reinforced by the tribute coming in from these and from more remote places.

The school had long kept affectionate ties with its alumni, a practice fostered since the days of Henry Coit. The boys of the school were *his* boys, and they did not wholly escape his fatherly concern when they set forth into the world. He read to assembled students the letters they wrote him; he welcomed them when they returned on visits, and encouraged the formation of a society in which their attachment to each other and to the school could be expressed. For twenty years or more after the school's founding, the alumni were still at the start of their careers, able to provide little in the way of material support. But as they grew older, they established their place in society; and they became a formidable, as well as a kindly and supportive, group.

Drury looked somewhat uneasily at the burgeoning of this power. A letter from his friend Anson Stokes in 1924 urged him to be more accommodating to the alumni chieftains. As for himself, Stokes could only marvel that this body of former students should wish to play an active role in the school. Oxford graduates, he pointed out, maintained a constitutional reserve of power. A few years earlier, when the question of entrance requirements in Greek was under discussion, county ministers from all over England had come up to cast their votes. There was something "perfectly splendid," Stokes thought, "in the way Oxford men cared about entrance Greek"—and in the way Yale men felt about a new building being placed on their campus. Drury was not altogether convinced.[9]

Matters were not made easier when Goetchius and a few others of the older alumni, determined to find a place for Joseph Coit, 2nd, made him permanent secretary of the Alumni Association. Ferguson and Perkins had strong reservations; his appointment seemed a coup of the old guard, undoing Ferguson's strenuous efforts after 1906 to set the school on a new course. With the alumni offices established in New York City, removed from the rector's surveillance, it was easy to imagine a meddlesome, countervailing power. As it turned out, Coit was cooperative with Drury. "It has been patent to me for some time," he wrote, "that if the new rector of St. Paul's was to be a really successful rector, he must change the old order to conform to new times and conditions."[10] His cheerful disposition, combined with Drury's efforts at compromise, assured a reasonably cordial entente between the school and the alumni office.

In 1921 the *Alumni Horae* was established, the official organ of the alumni body. Once again New York, not Millville, was the headquarters. The rector was invited to offer a communication to lead off each issue; but he was not loath to go beyond this privilege and give instructions on general editorial matters. A particular cover was not to his liking; the practice of recording the remarriages of divorced alumni was disapproved. As late as 1929, Drury was referring to the publication as one that was "*supposed* to emanate from the school." "I have strong convictions about what would constitute a good alumni paper, but I mean to be pliant and reasonable."[11] Mostly he was.

Funds, meanwhile, continued to be raised. A leap in the school's endowment (from $1.1 million in 1920 to $3.6 million ten years later) took place in the last years of the postwar prosperity. For the rector, participation in fund-raising activities was not easy. After one meeting from which he had been absent, word came from Coit that the affair had been novel, "owing to the fact that the two men who did most of the talking were adorned with ear trumpets and did not hear what the other fellow said."[12] After another such gathering the rector complained privately that his presence was hardly required if the alumni wished merely "a sentimental chat." If, on the other hand, they desired to be seriously enlightened, "I feel quite strongly that they should do the school the honor of drinking considerably less champagne." Coit was encouraging, if a little patronizing. "You are losing the natural diffidence," he told the rector, "which a sensitive man has when he must discuss money matters."

One alumnus, the eternal iconoclast, had his own views about those efforts. "I have been groaning a good deal about the school," John Jay Chapman wrote Drury at the start of a fund-raising drive. "The place is, I fear, going the way of all flesh." Given the trend of the world, St. Paul's was bound to get enough by gifts and bequests "without the hurrah boys." "They'll give you buildings you don't want and cover the place with sentiments not yours. You have the awful warning of Harvard—and Groton. . . . Why, my dear Sir, you're playing with an avalanche."[13] Drury would have liked to agree with Chapman, especially when he urged that "the more masterful and unapproachable you are, the better." But he couldn't quite agree. He was more reasonable, and more basically human than that. Besides, the avalanche when it came brought many welcome rewards.

Beneath the organization, the dinners and the inevitable hoopla, there were ties of generous affection between the alumni and their school. These feelings might be expressed sentimentally, but they originated in deep roots. An alumnus who had been at St. Paul's in the late 1880s declared it was worth a year of one's life to stand again by the old Middle in June, to feel the square white fence rail in one's hand, to see the shadow of the chapel tower stretching across the lawn. At St. Paul's, he said, one is always welcome: "The old masters abide, one sees old friends in the chapel stalls, one breaks bread with kindly and familiar hosts."[14] Chapman, for all his irreverence, had discovered that school meant much to him in strange ways. Of Winant it was recorded by his biographer, "He never escaped St. Paul's." That was the one place where he felt understood and which was always beyond questioning or doubt.

For others the escape might seem complete, but some small incident—a meeting with a friend, the lilt of an old hymn—would flood the mind with memories. A charming vignette recalls F. Marion Crawford, rich and world-famous, dining with one of the school's masters upon the terrace of his sumptuous villa high above the Italian Mediterranean. The night was brilliantly lit by stars, so that candles upon the heavily laden table remained unlit. When the meal was finished and the other guests had departed, Crawford put his arm around the old master's shoulder and together the two sang *Salve Mater*. To Crawford there were to be but few years left, and those marked by misfortunes worldly possessions could not avert; but in that brief interval, amid the glow of recaptured years, life seemed complete and youth eternal.[15]

At the school, the names of old boys were carved on oak panels, and the reunions of their forms were marked by ceremonies and celebrations.

The names of old boys were carved on oak panels. *The cloister of the upper school.*

THERE WERE TIES OF GENEROUS AFFECTION
BETWEEN THE ALUMNI AND THEIR SCHOOL.

A committee of notable alumni gathered to discuss a school history in the house of trustee Frederick Baldwin Adams, January 19, 1928. From left to right: Willard Scudder, William Foster, Arthur Stanwood Pier, Owen Wister, F. B. Adams, J. H. Coit 2nd.

The younger alumnus, perhaps at loose ends and temporarily out of cash, was assured of finding in Millville a night's shelter and a welcome from faculty friends. How many must have felt, as they went out again into the world, that they had touched the springs of hope. At the precise hour when an old boy married, the carillon in the chapel tower played the wedding march. "I wandered into the moonlight," Drury recorded in his diary during one Christmas vacation in the 1920s. A light snow illuminated the grounds as he slipped into the old chapel to kneel for a moment in the silent night. There he prayed for the neighbors, and "for every St. Paul's boy, wherever and however he might be." Of such bonds, tenuous as threads but strong as iron, were woven the ties that kept a far-flung empire together.

Some Old Masters

Masters constituted the nobility of this realm, especially the older masters, toward whom Drury, by the late 1920s, had grown accustomed to show a grave consideration and often a touching affection. His authority no longer threatened, he could reveal a side of his nature that the resentments and insurrections of his first years had obscured. Sitting in the rectory garden one April, he even allowed himself kind thought about the two Knoxes. "The flowers are so lovely," he wrote James; "in half an hour I am taking some to put on your brother's grave in the school cemetery." To Beach White, the ornithologist, he wrote from Maine about seeing chickadees, juncos, purple finches—"and a couple of others which only you could have identified." He tells White "how absolutely I count on your personal friendship toward me, and your chivalrous loyalty, too. . . . I trust you to say quite boldly whatever you want the school to do for you."[16]

Milne was now in Maine, where he had retired early, partly because he was out of sympathy with the new and less authoritarian attitude toward discipline. Yet Drury urged him to return to the school. Milne preferred the company of his "sturdy johnny jump ups, and ladies delight or heart's ease, whichever name pleases most."[17] Being so out of sympathy with recent policies, he added with characteristic bluntness, "I would make a most unpleasant addition to the staff."

Below the immediate sway of the rector, not wholly understood by him, not always wholly approved, was a network of relations between masters, and between masters and boys, that gave St. Paul's much of its special flavor. There were young masters who came and went, illuminating the life of the school in their own ways, often curious or striking, their names later forgotten by all but a few boys and fellow workers. One of these, going on to a rival school, wrote the rector that he saw no reason against the "schoolmaster's honestly gunning for some of the fruits of a manifold prosperity." This was in April 1929, just before the crash; he had been a good teacher of history. A young classicist, his identity lost but his views preserved vividly in a departmental memorandum, rejoiced in sharing Ovid with sixth formers. "No exhumed fossil of antiquity" was Ovid; no "stuffed shirt like Cicero." Ovid was one in whom contemporary youth could recognize their own kind: "a city-bred lad, born in affluent circumstances, discarding the law to find an appreciative audience as a popular raconteur of risqué stories and a participant in amorous adventures." A few favored students must have delighted in that young master's perceptions, before he vanished into some other sphere.

In a bare room in the upper school a young clergyman, balding and rotund, held forth for a few years before he, too, went his way. He had become quickly known as the Friar. In the chapel he was no star, but in personal intercourse he could reach the boys in a way more imposing figures could not. The upper school was in his view a needy parish, and no problem was too small—or too great, for that matter—to be endlessly probed. "He is an individualist in his own line," Drury wrote of him good-naturedly. When the Friar went off in 1936 to minister to St. George's, he left on amicable terms with the rector, and with deep ties among a small circle of boys.

Others among the masters were old in service, and not infrequently old in years. The school had no pension system until the early 1930s, and it was an embarrassment to the trustees and the rector to deal with men whose whole life had been given to St. Paul's and who in their late sixties and seventies had neither anywhere to go nor, often, the means to support themselves. To the students, however, such men appeared hardly more venerable than many in their middle years. A master past his thirties could appear picturesque and authoritative, and was often more responsive to youth's needs than one just out of college and hot on the trail of success. An old boy wrote appreciatively of the variety of men who made the school an interesting and valid place, being "able to tolerate and nourish a band of queer-shaped boys."[18]

There was, for example, old Beirne Lay, still teaching when he should have been out to pasture, who was liked because he was absent-minded in so kindly a way. Covering the blackboard with the symbols of an unresolved equation, he would turn to one of the class to finish it, gently grumbling, "I've forgotten more algebra than you boys will ever learn." Spanhoofd, his aberrations of the war days forgotten or ignored, advanced into old age with an ingenious system of folding spikes upon the heels of his shoes, to prevent his slipping on the ice: a tall ungainly figure with a close-cropped white beard and a mind dry and irreligious. To his rooms in the Big Study boys would repair to enjoy the play of his cool wit, and not a few, even in the last years, carried away in memory some fragmentary verses of Goethe or Heine. At the end, Drury—as he did so often when' he was moved—expressed the sentiment of the community. "He lived for forty years in a very small place, retaining the while a very wide mind. Whoever heard him say anything that was petty? . . . All his communications were cosmic and charitable."[19]

Theophilus Nelson was another of the durable crop harvested by the second rector in the 1890s. An insistence on hard work he tempered with a sarcasm more often humorous than wounding. One day in class, after the bell had rung to mark the beginning of the period, an absent-minded student remained at the open window, his chin in his hand. "Come in, dearie," came Nelson's penetrating tones. "If the architect had wanted gargoyles on this building, he would have placed them there."[20] Sometimes his humor was lost on the less quick-witted. "They are doing something that strikes me as simple," one student wrote irately to his father. "They make us take trigonometry which does not do us the least good because we do not need it for Harvard." When he complained to Nelson, the lad continued, "He said he was giving us this to take up time." More likely Nelson said something like, "The better to keep you busy, my dear"; or, as he is remembered to have said on another occasion, "If your brains were put in a nutshell, and the nutshell were turned upside down, nothing would come out."

Judson Howard, the Greek teacher who had long been in charge of the school house, was of another kind, courtly in his younger days and still cheerful and devout as he grew older. When at the end of a school year a Greek class decided to present him with a silver cocktail shaker, upon which was displayed a Greek inscription they had composed, Howard was delighted. In the midst of his enthusiastic expressions of thanks, he chanced to observe the inscription. "Look," he said, "there is a mistake in the Greek." "O, Sir," exclaimed one of the boys, "give it back to us and we will have it corrected." "No," replied Mr. Howard more cheerfully; "if it were right I should never connect it with you boys."[21]

Beach White was roughly of the same generation—he of the juncos and the chickadees; a graduate of Harvard, a lifelong bachelor and teacher of English, who succeeded John Hargate as head of the old upper school. "I never could make head or tail of his mind in the classroom," Chanler Chapman wrote. "Every time he said anything I disagreed with him inwardly, and frequently voiced my opinion, with the result that I was dismissed from his classes with surprising regularity."[22] But outside—in his apartment in the old upper or on the trails about the school—he was a mine of seasoned humor and detached wisdom.

His rooms were furnished with Moorish pieces, Oriental rugs rising crescendo-like to cover chairs, couches, and even the walls. Tables were littered with books, papers and pipes, and on the shelves—in that citadel of non-smokers—was reportedly one of the best collections of books on tobacco and its uses to be found in any library. Boys dropped in regularly for tea, whether in the afternoon or at less conventional hours; he served them a strong brew in glass teapots, which he insisted removed the leaves' noxious effects. The scene was overlaid by clouds of smoke, and the discussions punctuated by his vehement interjections.

White had developed as a youth a strong interest in ornithology; and coming to St. Paul's in the 1890s he found an atmosphere congenial to his avocation. A cabinet for mounted bird specimens and other natural curiosities had been established at the school as early as 1863. This was supplemented over the ensuing decades by the collection of a local taxidermist, purchased by a student, as well as by gifts of various mounted birds, mostly gulls, ducks, hawks and owls, and including one osprey. Beach White began his own serious collecting in 1918, and with the help of students added hundreds of specimens. These activities encouraged further gifts, some from the famous naturalist Louis Agassiz. Boys taking part in the bird-hunts were rewarded by the stimulus of an original mind, White's company providing in itself many of the elements of a liberal education.

By the 1930s Willard Scudder had outgrown the apprehensions, though not the eccentricities, of his earlier years. Securely ensconced in the dilapidated old Middle, the same wooden structure Ferguson had been fearful of showing to visiting parents, his bachelor quarters were the gathering place of the school's top scholars and athletes, managers of the *Horae,* the Concordian Literary Society and other extracurricular activities. The deference with which he treated the incumbents by itself made election to such posts an enviable mark of success; while over the Halcyon Boat Club he presided as if its victories and defeats could shake the civilized world. Old boys returned to pay him obeisance, or during vacations received him in their homes as they might the overlord of some remote principality. His rule at the Middle, wrote T. S. Matthews, was accomplished "by the obvious assumption that a gentleman would never behave unbecomingly, and that we were all gentlemen." As a teacher, Scudder applied a variant of the same principle: "He taught English literature by raising his eyebrows."[23]

The atmosphere in his book-lined study at the Middle may be imaginatively conjured up. It is a Sunday. A group of fifth and sixth formers have dropped by for coffee after dinner, among them the captain of the school hockey team, the head of the *Horae,* and a half dozen others who have caught his fancy by something original in the play of their mind, or by their relationships to men he once knew as boys. Scudder is elaborately dressed, spats showing above his highly polished boots, and a gold chain across his broad waistcoat. He treats his guests with utmost seriousness, yet with the bantering courtesy of a shy man. He questions them, challenges them, then embarks upon an extended monologue incongruously mixing school minutiae with the things of literature or the great world.

For a while on this particular day it has been the chit-chat of Millville that united them; now the conversation turns to general matters—one's favorite character in history; to the apostles and one's favorite among those. Simon Peter, Paul and Timothy seem at least as familiar in that hour as Lincoln, Cromwell, Sir Philip Sidney. What is a saint? somebody asks. Can one be alive today? And the talk is off upon another tack, until the chores or enticements of the long Sunday afternoon call out the little band upon separate ways.[24]

Scudder's correspondence with the rector, more enthusiastic on the part of the former than the latter, has already been mentioned. A few samples from this source give the tone and flavor of his conversation. "Isn't it a beastly nuisance to be caught with this sort of epidemic?" he writes Drury, then on sabbatical. "There will be no end of withdrawals for a while, one suspects."—"Did you ever hear of any spring in this climate that was not the coldest, or the wettest, etc., known? There's not a tinge of a leaf."

Or this, when the rector was obviously expecting some more helpful approach to the problem caused by a surfeit of admissions for the fall term. Scudder is in "a gloom," he writes to Drury at Northeast. "With characteristic laziness in the summer months I have not been able to happen upon any suggestion which might engage your attention. Now that September has arrived, I shall bend my thoughts, a bit rusty from disuse, upon some way of meeting the situation, so unfairly thrust upon us."[25] "Persons who have boys to send to a school," he continued, "are perfectly relentless in the pursuit and brutal in their methods. When we are already overcrowded why should not a few of them consider our plight and take away some of the superfluities? Only one man off the list since July 1! It is outrageous." One can imagine Drury, in his little Lair, pondering how to deal with such a letter.

A note tossed off to a student, an editor of the *Horae* suffering from chicken pox, further illumines his table-talk. Dated only "Feast of the Immaculate Conception," and addressed to the recipient in "The Al-

coholic Ward, The Millville Sanitorium,"[26] the letter is principally concerned with getting out the Yuletide issue of the magazine. Agreeing with
the student's comments on one contributor, Scudder adds: "He must not
overdo the exotic, and he must write with decent attention to rhythm, if
not to form. . . ." In regard to another contribution, Scudder's comment
was, ". . . though I quarrel with the fate of his little one: I don't care for
freezing the little ones, you know: he has a story; not too bad. He gains in
freedom of expression. But it's rather an unpleasant Christmas, isn't it?"

Scudder then turns to the sad condition of his correspondent. "Mrs.
Stanley [the head nurse] has told me of your woes, and I grieved. She
tho't, however, and one of the Heavenly Twins confirms her view, that
when you'd hatched the chickens you'd be more comfortable. It is a half
century since I was an incubator, and I fear that I've rather forgotten the
sensation!!" And so the letter continues, with many school and barnyard
animadversions, until his imagination fails for looking at the pile of themes
on his window sill waiting to be corrected. He signs himself: "As ever—
and then some, WS," and adds a handwritten postscript for the benefit of
a student not improbably driving himself too hard. "The enforced rest will
do you good: don't forget!"

Reconstituting the Second Echelon

With Winant's entrance into state and national politics, a successor,
Vaughan Merrick, served all too briefly in the post of vice rector before
being called to head another school. Merrick was an appealing figure,
athletic in build, considerate in manner, and with a fine baritone that rendered the school anthem undoubtedly better than anyone since Augustus
Swift—with the possible exception of Carl Lohman, later secretary of
Yale. Merrick had been a student during Drury's first years as rector, and
he was one of those younger faculty members whose going off to the war
left his chief to the mercies of the old guard. Drury was devoted to him,
and counted heavily on his serene good sense.

Something of both men is told in the correspondence surrounding
Merrick's appointment as headmaster of St. George's. "In all I have been
conscious of your firm and kindly support," wrote the vice rector, "of
your sympathy and appreciation of my sorrows and my joy, and especially in the past weeks of indecision. You have understood so clearly,
you have rendered everything as easy as possible."[27] Drury understood
indeed. Merrick was then thirty-four, close to the age at which he had
himself faced the decision of leaving the rectorship of St. Stephen's
Church for St. Paul's.

"All my love goes out to you," Drury replied, "and prayers for your confident development into a sort of task that is happily and obviously too big for either you or me." From Brown's Hotel in London, where he was being painted by Orpen, Drury in his large inimitable calligraphy wrote a letter to be read to the boys of the school. Clearly he was thinking of the anguish he had himself passed through. "It is the part of true friendship at a time like this," he said, "to cheer Mr. Merrick on his way. I *know* that it pains him even to think of leaving St. Paul's—but we must not make it harder by placing vain regrets in his path."

Of his young associate, with that love of recurring rituals which became a reassurance and almost an obsession, Drury asked: "If I write to you every April 23rd [St. George's Day] will you write to me every January 25th [St. Paul's Day]—not confining ourselves however to those dates?" So indeed they did; and Merrick, who never lost interest in his old school, returned as trustee under the fifth rector.

This same year the first vice rector, William Foster, lay dying in the large brick house that, as a dormitory, was to bear his name. At Anniversary he was well enough to receive returning alumni, several of whom shared memories with him reaching back to the time of the first Coit; but the advance of his disease was certain and swift. A midsummer funeral found the faithful gathered. Drury, in a move unusual for him, broke the service with a eulogy, a happy evocation of this exemplary, sunny-minded man. "In driving torrents of rain," wrote Scudder, "the company went on to the school graveyard, where the rector read the committal office and we bade farewell to our beloved friend."[28]

The reconstitution of the administration's second echelon brought into the posts of vice rector Charles C. Monie and Henry Kittredge. Monie, in charge of studies, was upright and meticulous. Bent over long lists of names and numbers, or juggling arcane requirements in the adjustment of academic schedules, he would become familiar to generations of schoolboys. His correspondence with Drury is endlessly detailed, his posture invariably self-sacrificing. That under the rigorously controlled exterior there existed normal human passions is indicated by his surprising dislike of one academic subject, and of the man who was its department head at that time. "Am I right in believing that after all the French are not a great people and never were?" he wrote the rector. "What really great statesmen, philosophers, reformers have they produced? Not one to compare with our own George Washington. After all, why French?"[29] Rarely did Monie state such categoric views.

Kittredge has already crossed these pages. Here we observe him in his middle years, newly appointed vice rector while continuing as head of the lower school. His chief valued him highly, but something in the younger man's native independence, his detached attitude toward men

and affairs, kept him from drawing too close to the burning center of
Drury's affection. On the rector's part the recognition that this was an
irreplaceable man, and perhaps the premonition that he might one day be
his successor—"No man," Drury once declared to a student, "loves
his successor"—promoted a friendly alliance rather than a true
concordat.

The rector was a little envious, and even resentful, of the way boys
returned to the lower school. "Why do you *waste* your time at the Kittredges?" he blurted out to one older student, who found pleasure in the
teas at the master's house, the lively conversation led by Mrs. Kittredge,
the inexhaustible supply of molasses cookies, and the interesting visitors
from the outside. But mostly Drury knew that in Kittredge he had a
unique accomplice, whose singular humors he could not but enjoy.

Kittredge's letters to Drury, usually written from his summer home in
Barnstable, suggest the respect and gratitude of the younger man, and the
wise spirit of concession of the older.[30] Kittredge had already published
his classic history of Cape Cod, and in 1932 was working on his *Shipmasters*. "No schoolmaster," he wrote Drury, "ever had more complete
freedom than I have had." While Monie carried on uncomplainingly the
work of placating disappointed parents and dissatisfied faculty, Kittredge
spent his mornings writing amid the shades of the old sea captains, in the
upper room of the barn; in the afternoon, with his wife or his aged father,
he rattled about the Cape in his Ford, looking for the "local talent" who
might have in their garrets the logs or letters of sea-faring ancestors. As
the summer approached its end, "I find myself engaged in a neck-and-
neck race with the flying days in an attempt to finish the opus." The
writing was completed. It was now, he reported cheerily, "a battle to get
enough impressive references to make the text appear authoritative."

Other summers Kittredge and the rector would be in almost daily
correspondence on the business of schoolmastering. A certain boy, Kittredge suspected, was guilty of far worse offenses than the smoking at
which he had been caught. "However, if he was guilty of such miscon-
duct, it is his good luck that we do not *know* it, and good luck, I suppose,
is a legitimate factor in everybody's life." Drury accepted this humane
good sense; indeed, Kittredge's generally smiling approach to problems
seemed to relax his normally uncompromising stands. "You are undoubtedly right," Drury wrote him in regard to one dubious candidate. "There
comes a time when we must for the sake of very existence, if not for
peace, capitulate." On the administration of the lower, the two men were
in fundamental agreement. "After all," Drury wrote Kittredge, "one of
the glories of the big school is that it can do the delicate and personal
thing, without seeming to, that small schools do."

The Lower in Its Heyday

The lower of the 1930s, its students ranging from twelve to fourteen years of age, had in truth many of the characteristics of a small school standing by itself. Its own athletic teams, its own crews and boathouse, its study hall, dining room and classrooms, made it semi-autonomous. The cubicles in the lower might be cramped and lacking in privacy; on winter mornings the radiators sizzled ineffectually against the encompassing cold of the huge, barnlike dormitory, and the showers seemed a dismal mile from the warm bed. But few who in this period were subjected to the lower school's regimen regretted it afterwards. To have been a first former was to have had a head start upon life, and even those who came as second formers seemed possessed of an indefinable status. They were old boys when many of their third-form comrades were new, and they had been part of a rare experience.

The Kittredges presided over what one graduate remembered as "a community of unadulterated delight."[31] When a group of second formers decided to write, and to produce, a play based on the famous Bulwer-Lytton novel, *The Last Days of Pompeii,* Mrs. Kittredge lent her dining room curtains for the occasion, and both she and her husband carried on as if they saw nothing at all unusual in staging a volcanic eruption in the lower school common room. More regularly, in this common room, Kittredge led the brief evening prayer, his voice marked by a peculiar twang, half Harvard and half Cape Cod. Boys remembered especially words from Robert Louis Stevenson that he often repeated—the plea on behalf of the Samoan household that afflictions might be borne "as if they were straws upon the tide of life." A prayer from some other, untraceable source asked for his young charges that they might "sail up and down these stormy coasts, carrying a heaven-scented cargo of better life to men."

Kittredge kept an eye on the predominantly youthful masters of the lower school, promoting their interests with wily benignity. When one of them received an offer from a rival school, Kittredge counseled him against too quick a rejection. "Negotiate, delay, get a letter," he advised. "You will then take the letter to the rector and say, 'Dr. Drury, smell this!' And he will raise your pay." Over the boys he extended a sway in which humor almost invariably played a part. When a protest was set on foot against the number of times a week squash was served in the lower school dining room, Kittredge rapped solemnly on the table. "Gentlemen," he said, "I have received your petition. But I am afraid I can do nothing about it. It is squash that has made New England what it is. Furthermore, the school has just received a gift of forty tons of squash."[32]

In its heyday it was "a community of unadulterated delight."
The Dickensian austerities of the lower school.

In the classroom Kittredge was unforgettable. He was not (like his father) a performer upon the stage of scholarship, but a genial guide through sloughs and thickets of schoolboy learning. Poor discipline could not be conceived under his civilized expectation that each boy would give his best, and his encouragement to even the least nimble. "Sure," he would say, when an answer had been given or an opinion ventured, and then with a most delicate elaboration he would indicate a more likely version of the truth. The rector, who was always looking for better forms of instruction, sent Kittredge out to investigate what other schools were doing under the name of progressive education. Kittredge was amused by the professional approach to pedagoguery and came back to give his own view of sound teaching.

The trouble with the curriculum, he declared, was not that it had too few subjects of instruction, but that it had too many. "When Galileo invented the telescope," he reported gravely (but one can just see the shimmering of a smile and observe the quizzical wrinkling of the forehead), "schools cut two hours of Latin and instituted astronomy in their place." Nowadays, he continued, even English teachers "get rattled" and suggest abandoning rhetoric with one hand while they welcome new poets with the other. Lower schoolers, as a result, spent "all their academic hours panting from gerunds to frogs, from frogs to *Casabianca* by heart." The younger boys took for granted their instruction in these diverse fields, "without realizing that it is preposterous."[33]

Not a many-sided curriculum, but the many-sided teacher was what Kittredge saw as the answer to a better education at the elementary level. Contrasting St. Paul's with other schools he had visited, "We are far more likely to stroll into the classroom," he asserted, "in the same state of mind as a clergyman I once heard preach in North Perry, Maine. He began his sermon thus: 'As I was coming to meeting house, my friends, I said to myself, "What shall be the subject of my discourse this morning?"' That's the way many of us feel." And then Kittredge went on to give what undoubtedly was a description of his own method, in speaking of a recent English class in one of the lower forms.

"The master came into the room in the properly reflective frame of mind and someone said, 'Let's read a poem.' That struck him as being a sound plan and he told the boys to open their books to *Sennacherib*. When one of the boys had stood up and read aloud, a youthful skeptic questioned the power of the Lord to smite the Gentiles with such ease. Instantly another said he had done it quite easily by means of a plague. The first youth replied that plagues arise from unsanitary conditions and were not the handiwork of the Almighty. And before he knew it, the master found himself with plenty to do in directing a discussion of the power of Almighty God.

"For aught I know," Henry Kittredge concluded, "this may be Progressive Education."

In a day when every outstanding younger teacher coached one sport or another, Kittredge was seen on the athletic grounds only as an enthusiastic spectator. The lank figure seemed better made for roaming the beaches of his native Cape Cod, or for crowding into a diminutive sail boat, than for the highly competitive games of the 1930s. There was one exception. He loved baseball. He loved its lore and its lingo as well as its splendid spurts and relaxed, seemingly indolent, interludes. He had coached baseball teams in his first years at the school, but afterwards was content to appear for rare performances in the games between masters and boys. A story, carrying the ring of authenticity, is told of the day a boy bunted a ball into the masters' infield. As errant faculty throws were lunged over first, second, and third base, the young man stretched his effort to a home run.

"The embarrassed silence that hung on the spring air"—concluded the tale as told by one happy raconteur—"was broken by Kittredge's stentorian tones. 'Throw it around some more, men.'"[34]

Ceremonies and Traditions

The ceremonies and rituals of school life achieved in these years a classic quality, a fullness like that of a perfectly formed water drop, bound to collapse and fall, yet seeming for the moment as if it might endure for ever. The elder Coit, had he returned in spirit, would have found many familiar details in the way occasions such as Thanksgiving, Lincoln's Birthday, Last Night were marked; but all were on a large scale, amid a certain outward magnificence. In the 1920s, the scientific exhibition at Thanksgiving could boast one new marvel—the Teslar coil. "Behold, some brave boy grasps the points of the 175,000 volt coil. The current is applied, the crowd groans; yet the hand is unharmed." (The secret of this "apparently insulated character" was the existence of a mere .0008 of an ampere in the coil.)

But mostly the Missionary Society put on the same show, and sold the same articles, as had benefitted the orphans of the 1890s. The girls coming up for the weekend were now the younger sisters of the "flappers" of the 1920s. Their coming was still a long awaited, strangely terrifying event; the length of their stay, ending with the Sunday evening chapel service, was as a fleeting dream.

The rector added his own touches to the tradition. He revived the celebration of St. Paul's Day, making it a holiday culminating in "Gaudy Night," with the great spaces of the upper school dining room lit only by candlelight and aglow with white linen napery. Cricket, which had disappeared amid the disorientation of the late nineteenth century, was now preserved as a memory in an autumn holiday, its date a well-kept secret, revealed only when in morning chapel the rector read a traditional prayer "that thy holy city Jerusalem shall be full of children playing in the streets thereof." A long sigh would punctuate the service, and then in the unencumbered hours that once had been given over to the stately progress of a cricket match, the boys scattered into the surrounding woods and hills.

The day, always assured of being one of the most beautiful of the New Hampshire fall, saw Drury taking the new boys on a picnic up Jerry Hill or to the shores of Long Pond. After a dish considered his specialty—a mixture of scrambled eggs, bacon and potatoes cooked vigorously together in the same large frying pan—he read some tale of adventure, his fine voice sending chills up the spines of the school's youngest members.

On these occasions one boy was appointed to be the ceremonial bearer of the machete Drury had brought back from the Philippines, now put to the use of chopping brush and small logs for the fire. Another was entrusted with the silver matchbox, etched with the familiar monogram SSD, presented to him on his leaving Pomfret by the boys of his dormitory. One year, by some incredible mischance, the unfortunate bearer of this treasure dropped it into fifteen feet of water off the end of the dock at Long Pond. No record comes down to us of the boy's reaction; but John Richards's account of the sequel is a model of brevity. "I stripped," he wrote, "then dove and recovered it, to Dr. Drury's joy and admiration, for he could not swim."[35] Years later, Mrs. Drury gave the matchbox to John Richards and he, before his death, gave it to the school.

The early enjoyment of charades and skits, that had highlighted so many evenings in the original school house, persisted in the entertainments of an organized dramatic club. On the top floor of the old gymnasium, upon chairs that creaked and were uncomfortably hard, before a cramped and ill-equipped stage, audiences saw productions of such plays as *The Man from Mars* and *Captain Brassbound's Conversion* that perhaps reached the limit of schoolboy art. Drury never really approved of these dramatic efforts; some residue of deep-lying Puritanism made the stage suspect, or could it have been the result of his own brief stage career in the character of "Mr. Dismal"? Being greeted by a student one evening during the holidays at the performance of a musical comedy in Boston, he made haste to explain that the entertainment had been Mrs. Drury's selection.

Interest in nature likewise persisted. As late as 1923, an article in the *Horae* upon "The Winter Habits of S.P.S. Animals" is not, as one might have supposed, on life among the boys and masters, but a minutely observed disquisition by a fourth former on minks (admitted to be rare), skunks, muskrats, woodchucks, porcupines, red foxes—and, of course, squirrels and rabbits. A few years later a boy walking around the school pond in spring could see and name thirteen different flowers, nineteen varieties of trees, and fifty-eight species of birds.[36] Others enjoyed nature without knowing too much about it. The recurring seasons and the never-failing shifts of New England weather, the extremes of cold and snow with certain spectacular events like earthquakes and showers of meteorites, gave even to those least familiar with botany or geology the sense of partaking in an endless show.

In 1936, the most damaging flood in New England's history revealed nature in a less beneficent guise. The flow of water from the two Turkeys had been a source of concern throughout the school's history. In the early years, seasons of extreme dryness had left the mill desolately stranded, with the smaller of the school's ponds a mere mudhole, capable of being crossed dry-shod. To find the water brimming on the boys' return in September would be taken as the portent of a prosperous year. Now the threat was of another kind, that the unleashed waters of March would carry away the dam and flood the power plant at its site down the Turkey River.

By mid-March of that year rains and thaws had carried off the snows
and caused the annual rise of waters around the school. These had begun
to retreat when on Tuesday, March 17, the rains unexpectedly resumed.
All day the puddles deepened and an air of apprehension pervaded the
school. At nightfall the call for volunteers went out. Through that night
and the following days boys of the upper forms piled sandbags and
manned pumps, working with farmhands and assembled groundskeepers
of the school.

The sight of booted figures clad in bright yellow or orange slickers,
their forms magnified in the glare of searchlights and silhouetted against
the unfamiliar machinery, was one long to be remembered in Millville.
The waters came to within a half inch of extinguishing the fires in the
power plant, and as Concord cut off the supply of gas, emergency measures for cooking were taken at the infirmary and the upper school. On
Saturday the floods subsided, but New England would spend weeks re-
storing communications and digging itself out of the damage.

The long-established literary and scientific societies, the *Horae* and the
athletic clubs, were prospering and satisfied a broad variety of interests.
A student unskilled at allotting his time could find himself pressed and
distracted by such extracurricular activities. "I have learned," said one,
"how to make use of the margins of my time."[37] The rector had little patience with those who complained. "There is time a-plenty," he wrote.
"We have always time to accomplish the things we really want to do. The
most careless fourth former has as much time as Señor Marconi or Dr.
Schweitzer or Archbishop Soderblom." It was an invigorating doctrine,
and for the best of students, it worked. In the multitude of engagements
and activities the ambitious youth found his personality extended and
given form, his mind challenged, his friendships enriched.

In 1932, outside football games were abandoned in favor of "paper
teams" comprising the names of the school's best players. The games
between clubs were satisfying that epoch's need for competition, while
the skill of the players was believed to be most effectively perfected in the
long club season under expert coaching by the masters. The St. Paul's
hockey team, however, maintained its schedule of outside games. The
contest against a college freshman team, played in New York's Madison
Square Garden, provided the Christmas vacations with a brilliant start,
often with a school victory (well reported in the next morning's papers)
and with a tea-dance afterwards for the season's most promising "sub-
debs."

Back at Concord the ice on the pond behind the Big Study was divided into a checkerboard of nine rinks. The young and the less skilled
had their chance to play on lower club teams, while the stars, the de-

migods of the first team, "swooped like falcons and clapped together like fighting cocks." An alumnus, T. S. Matthews, many years later could still feel, see, hear, that memorable scene—"the windless, nose-numbing cold, the clear gray light filtered through a leaden sky, the hushed, crowded lines of boys packed along the breast-high boards of the rink, the sudden thunder of hockey sticks clattering applause for a thunder-bolt shot or a gallant save by the goal keeper."[38]

As always in the best of times, laughter and satire trimmed the pretensions of the great. "The main thing about hockey, and the one that makes it so offensive," wrote one of the *Horae* wits, "is that it is played outdoors in the middle of winter. Now almost any sensible man can tell you off-hand that it is better in winter to sit indoors. . . . All the public-spirited enthusiasts don't care if you freeze to death or catch pneumonia, just so long as you're not enjoying yourself somewhere where it's warm."[39] Nor did the *Horae* writers themselves escape the salutary deflation of humor. An editor deplored the fact that in the first twenty pages of one Thanksgiving issue twenty-nine deaths had occurred, mostly by violence—and this allowing for only three among the chimney sweeps of London in 1825, "a very moderate estimate."

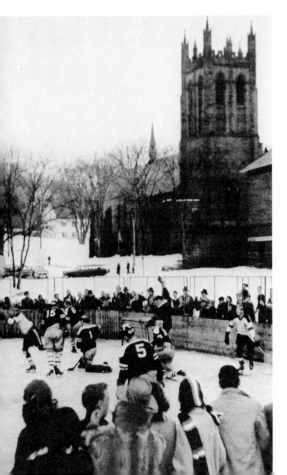

A sudden thunder of hockey sticks. *In the shadow of the chapel tower, a St. Paul's team makes a goal against the Yale freshmen.*

The typical St. Paul's author, it was suggested, was more than "half in love with easeful death." "He has a positive mania for it—if not for himself, at least for his characters." Was it absolutely essential that somebody be killed in order to create an effective climax? The *Horae,* perhaps, should be printed within black borders; or else some other means of disposition might be devised, such as putting the hero in prison, or marrying him off.[40]

Of all the school ceremonies the chapel services were the most regular and pervasive, a distillation through time-honored forms of a community's hopes and perceptions. Students would grumble routinely about "too much" chapel. But in fact the daily morning service was brief—a hymn, a prayer, preceded and followed by thunderous processions as the whole school marched in serried ranks; and after the regular Sunday morning worship, if he had chosen the option of early Communion, the student could be free for the rest of the day. Sunday Evensong, with its familiar music and its prayers—for the alumni, for kindness in daily life, for "a safe lodging and a holy rest"—was a ritual not everyone was eager to escape. Besides, there was always what one alumnus called "the dreamy, irreverent side of chapel," something luxurious and poetic, and there emanated from the services bits of school news and gossip, the little jokes or moments of drama that could light up a school day.

The rector, of course, dominated the chapel. He gave much thought to the nuances of the services, to their pace and liveliness, and to their beauty in words and music. He was himself always a striking figure. When he went from the rector's stall to the pulpit, or down the full length of the chapel to the altar, all eyes were drawn to the robed figure walking. "He strode as if against a wind," one remembered afterwards, "neither sauntering nor hurried. His head at first half bowed, but then drawn challengingly erect, he moved energetically, wholly in motion."[41] In the pulpit he stood four-square and simply. His first words were carefully framed to catch the attention of the congregation, and he proceeded without gestures, his voice, as he enlarged upon an often-repeated text, carrying without strain from Sleepy Hollow to the furthest reaches of the antechapel. "Do not roar yourself into a belief, nor expostulate nor rhapsodize," he counseled himself in his diary; "just calmly explain the living hope—not the dead certainty."

His listeners did not perhaps realize how much he labored to be brief. Mr. Howard would time his sermons, and on one occasion handed him, through Verger Foote, this note: "*Peccavi.* I forgot. As an estimate, 11 min."

"Dear, good Mr. Howard," Drury commented. "He is charitable—and cheering."[42] As a matter of fact, there were some who thought he preached *too* briefly. One was barely led into the realm where his mind moved to its own music, before he turned abruptly and the spell was broken.

The Spring, Race Day, Last Night

Spring came, though sometimes it seemed it might not, and brought with it a new world of sights, smells and sounds. It came to St. Paul's, wrote an alumnus, "in little driblets, in tiny puddles, then big ones, and rivulets running through mud. Here and there, through the thinning snow, croci appeared on the chapel lawn." Spring, wrote another, a cynic surprised at his own emotion, "softened the bleak angles of the school and warmed the cold memories of long winters. The masters, even the hostile ones, seemed to regard us in a new way, speculatively but kindly; we felt the stirring of a specious fellowship with one another and with the school." Nature now made a more direct and vivid appeal. "There was an icy swimming place," one remembered, "an abandoned quarry quite high up in the hills which we used to drive to in a hired buggy. Jogging along a single-track lane through laurel, azaleas, and pink and white dogwood, the downhill side of the lane opened up in places and we looked out on an America just as the first settlers saw it—nothing but trees as far as the eye could see."[43]

For the rowers, spring meant long hours pulling against the dead weight of machines in the dark basement of the gymnasium, and then finally, after weeks of anxious waiting, the first days of practice on Long Pond. The air would be icy, the waters rough; but the leap of the frail shell (or even of the stout-hearted lap-streaked barge) was enough to convince a man that his world was right. The ride back to the school after a long afternoon of rowing was warmed by the camaraderie of friends; and the old songs of the Halcyon and Shattuck crews sounded above the hoofs of horses or the whine of trucks.

Race Day would seem a far-off event, until suddenly, with the lilacs in bloom and everything drawing toward an inevitable close, it would be a reality, part of the larger occasion that brought trustees, alumni, and the girls of sixth formers for the grand weekend of Anniversary. The festivities included a dance at the upper school and a track meet at the athletic fields. And nothing was quite so moving—unless it was the parade of alumni down the Millville road, the oldest first, tottering but cheerful—as the ceremony around the flagpole after the races.

Sixteen eight-oared crews had competed on Lond Pond in the rivalry between Shattucks and Halcyons. Victors of the first crew race rode in triumph under the arched avenue of elms, their oars raised, their blue or crimson blazers resplendent in the rays of the late afternoon sun. The crowd at the flagpole was of such size as must have hailed returning

The air would be icy. *A glimpse of rowing in early spring.*

RACE DAY WOULD SEEM A FAR-OFF EVENT.

The victors rode in triumph. *A Halcyon crew coming down the school street after the races.*

The winning oar was raised . . .

conquerors in medieval towns: not thousands, but the several hundred necessary to magnify an event and give it symbolic meaning. In brief ceremonies the oar of the winning crew was raised, along with the club banner; and afterwards athletic medals and trophies were awarded. Malcolm Kenneth Gordon would make a speech—always the same speech—in a jaunty manner and with a vibrant voice.

Soon even Race Day was over and Last Night came on. Held a week or more after Anniversary, with the college examinations intervening, it was an extremely simple ceremony of graduation and farewell, with no outside speaker, no academic gowns or hats, and few parents in attendance. Yet for sixth formers, especially, it was a moving occasion, one that even the most cynical and hard-boiled found touching their emotions. A seemingly endless bestowal of academic prizes and awards in the Big Study, a few words from the rector, a brief chapel service, and then a handshake from each master standing in line on the chapel lawn. That was all. Yet in the gravity with which these events unfolded, in the almost palpable drama of final things, not least in the beauty of the chapel service, with its Last Night hymn and prayer—and over all the dim glories of

The oldest first, tottering but cheerful. *Alumni classes, accompanied (at left) by the president of the Alumni Association, William G. Foulke, walk in the Anniversary parade. Malcolm Kenneth Gordon is carrying the 1887 sign.*

the building itself, a repository of shadows and half forgotten hopes—there was stamped upon the departing student something at once sentimental and true, and likely to remain with him long afterwards.

Wandering out by the pond's edge when the night's events were over, a sixth former of the 1930s, speaking more to himself than to any listener, shaped words to express the subdued and poignant feelings of that hour:

> *Since we cannot descry*
> *Our grief or gainsay it,*
> *Do not ask why*
> *It is there, or display it–*
> *But you and I*
> *Must quietly say it,*
> *Quietly say good bye.*[44]

Drury's Last Phase

Drury's relations with the trustees had during this period virtually none of the strain that had characterized the 1920s. Goetchius and Hart remained on the board into their advanced age, but were less busy and influential. Reeve Schley, Charles Dickey, Jr., and—toward the end—Henry A. Laughlin, were of the post-Coit era and accommodated themselves to the changed atmosphere of the times. But the most important factor was in Drury himself. After his rejection of the Pennsylvania bishopric, he looked genially upon the school, feeling its organic nature and its inner harmonies. The trustees minutes reflect the growing accord. Scholarship aid was voted for English boys (if not for the Orientals Drury had hoped to see at the school); he was formally congratulated on the greatly improved record of the St. Paul's boys at college. A thorny question was resolved once and for all in January 1930 when Drury asked the board to state its attitude toward his absences. The board asserted that they wished the rector "to feel at liberty to take such leaves of absence in the future as he may deem best."

It was not that the rector ceased to speak out in challenging and often abrasive tones. He had become doubtful of the almost universal desire of sixth formers to enter college. "Onward they go but not upward, often merely to satisfy that parental pride which in turn is engendered by fear of relatives and neighbors."[45] The length of the sojourn at St. Paul's seemed in itself stultifying to some boys. The four last years at Millville and the four at college might be better spent: for example, "two in a high school, two at St. Paul's, one at Exeter, two at Princeton, and two at Grenoble." He even urged at one point that the whole school be placed on a ship and carried for a term to the Holy Land.

"What-we-have-always-done looks venerable and benevolent," he wrote, "whereas it may be sloth." Was the school family developing a fool's paradise within the hurried, mechanistic society of the day? Still far from the Mr. Chips mentality, he would question whether the school, instead of preparing its graduates for life, was not fostering unreality with its "endeared and quaint ways," with its "stained glass windows and melodious, sheltered environment." Always there was the troublesome problem of admissions. "We try to admit every son of an alumnus. We wish to admit every boy with high marks." Between the two aims could be a basic incongruity.

The boys saw a rector at once more wily and more compassionate in matters of discipline. He felt he had been wrong in not making a clean break with certain troublesome elements in the class of 1929. A year later he said in chapel that 10 per cent of the sixth form would probably be expelled if they didn't mend their ways. "Actually he was right, we were a bad lot," said one of them, J. Lawrence Barnard, who admitted that Drury's subsequent actions were remarkable. The bad 10 per cent were, according to Barnard, "gently garnered to his bosom." This took the form of their going to the rectory on Sunday evenings, where he gave each a Welsh rarebit and read passages from *Pilgrim's Progress.* "An open fire was blazing in the hearth, and, in addition to teaching us how to make a really good rarebit, the rector in a black velvet smoking jacket showed us the difference between good and bad book-binding with examples from his extensive library."[46]

Of that hard-bitten crew—some smoked, some drank, some shared an old Buick hidden away in the woods—not one, says our witness, "got away scot free from the civilizing impact of an open fire, Welsh rarebit and Riviere bindings in full morocco leather." Nor from the impact, it might have been added, of an extraordinary man, one who suffered, and learned from his mistakes. In any case, there were no mass firings that year—nor afterwards.

The Great Depression was deepening over the land. School workers were kept employed through the winter clearing the woods, and emergency scholarships were provided for the sons of hard-hit families. Economic difficulties caused a marked slackening of gifts, a postponement of building plans, and for several years a falling behind in payments of tuition. By decision of the board, no student was allowed to graduate until all bills had been paid, but for the boys thus affected the problem was handled as tactfully as possible by giving them blank diplomas, outwardly no different from those received by the others. Applications for admission, which had been expected to fall off, actually continued at a high rate through the 1930s.

With major building enterprises completed or in abeyance, Drury turned to the small amenities that seemed suited to the times and to his mood. The bells in the two chapels bothered him, the one in the old sending forth "an unmelodious summons"; and that in the new, though it had once sounded beautiful to him, now being condemned as "cold and unwelcoming." Both were improved. He dreamed of a natural swimming pool for the boys, carved from a disused quarry near the school, "surrounded by rich vegetation, providing coolness and privacy." "Do you think it would be pleasant," he wrote one master, "to have an informal group of boys and masters especially charged with the look of things, the paths, the gardens and the plantings?" In the future, he said, "we should certainly enlarge our flowering borders and semi-public, semi-private gardens. Let us talk about this." And to another: "Would you agree to omitting all electric bells from the upper school this year? . . . The experiment might well lead further and further into the school."[47]

In June 1936, Willard Scudder died. His passing, seen in retrospect, was a sign that an epoch in the school's life was moving toward its close. He had been the embodiment of many of its traditions and its special virtues, going back to his vividly recorded days as a student under Henry Coit. He had been a young master when the school faced change and disturbance after the first rector's death; a member of the old guard when Drury brought in a fresh broom; the sympathetic elder statesman of more recent years. Now the manner of his going crowned his life.

The eightieth anniversary of the school had been marked that June by the traditional celebrations, the Halcyons sweeping the races at Long Pond. Scudder was there to join in the singing as the red banner was raised on the flagpole. Next day he took part in the early service of Holy Communion; at evening he was in his stall in the choir. He dined with friends at the school inn, returning to his rooms at the Middle accompanied by the newly elected captain of the Halcyon Boat Club and others. While chatting, he leaned forward. Before anyone realized it, he was dead. "He died," said his eulogist, "in harness, in his red coat, and in the presence of friends." [48]

A major project of construction and innovation, deferred by the economic situation, was one designed to lift the whole level of instruction. In its original form it involved ten chairs for additional masters, as well as a new building for classrooms. Drury was encouraged by the trustees to develop the project with the donor, the alumnus Edward S. Harkness, and in 1933, he was provided with extra staff for that purpose. But the plans faltered and lay fallow. Two years later, in a more modest form, with the focus on a new building, they were revived.

The rector set about this climactic undertaking with energy and enjoyment. The building would stand upon the site of the demolished school house, and would be, he hoped, in the Georgian style. (The trustees, however, preferred Gothic.) What was important, in his eyes, was that the classrooms be shaped to small groups of students placed in close relationship with the master, with books displayed upon ample shelves, and, where possible, open hearths. Such, in his belief, was a setting congenial to hard but leisurely work.

Large reading rooms, spacious quarters where masters could meet for discussion or be alone for work, were to be supplemented by the rector's own study—a small room in comparison with all the rest. It pleased him to recall how Dr. Ferguson, "the liberal and the far-seeing," had stored in the school's red barn a supply of virgin pine planks, seasoning for more than thirty years, to be used now in this little chamber. [49] Drury insisted that the study be placed at the crossroads of student life, without the protection of an outer office or waiting room.

By the autumn of 1937 the building was completed, its furnishings and equipment having cost $1 million, an immense sum for those days. It was a building, Drury said, "that we ought to enter with trumpets and banners of high resolve." [50] The center of scholastic activity was shifted from the Big Study; recitations were held in the new classrooms. But still the rector hesitated to leave his old quarters.

There for more than a quarter century, in a little square room, its window seats piled deep in second-class mail and the sills covered with innumerable kinds of flourishing green plants, he had run the school with an eye to every detail. A boy passing on the greensward below would hear

S. S. Drury with Mrs. Drury on the chapel steps.

THE YEAR 1936 WAS THE TWENTY-FIFTH ANNIVERSARY OF HIS BE-
COMING RECTOR AND HIS TWENTY-FIFTH WEDDING ANNIVERSARY.

And in the midst of students.

the mighty voice, like a bolt from heaven, urging him to keep to the brick paths. A boy summoned here would come in fear and trembling, often to be admonished in a few pungent phrases that left him mystified but somehow the wiser. Alumni or trustees entering the sanctum would note the walls crowded with photographs of past school figures and architects' drawings for proposed dormitories, rustic bridges, and the like. Now, when he was expected to move, "I linger," he wrote to a fellow schoolmaster. "I love the sweet disorder of my little study." And to readers of the *Alumni Horae:* "To pull up stakes and move from the old study where four rectors have wrought . . . is, let me repeat, not without pain."[51]

The alumni had had an opportunity to express their own feelings for Samuel Drury at a large dinner in New York. The year 1936 was the twenty-fifth anniversary of his becoming rector (and also his twenty-fifth wedding anniversary). The occasion was a homely affair, warmly affectionate in its tributes to a man who had locked horns with some of those present, and irked or puzzled many of the rest, yet whom they now recognized as a brilliant leader and as a man who was still growing.

Drury spoke that night more revealingly than he had ever allowed himself to do. Recalling that he had been only thirty-two when he became rector, "How old we seem then to ourselves," he exclaimed, "how disturbingly young to others! Somebody has translated the phrase *mens conscia recti* as 'a man who is conscious of being rector.' I was that! I must have been difficult to get on with." He spoke of his own experience as a boy, "a plain second or third rater. . . . I've known the horror of having a rotten report go home, I've known the terror of being dropped. And so, though I have a tremendous respect for the fine schoolboy scholar; that feeling is theoretical."

"My natural understanding," Drury continued, "has always been with failure. . . . A persistent creed that the miscreant is entitled to tenderness, that the so-called bad boy is probably better than yonder ever-so-good man, has leaped over the years, those pompous thirties and those prim forties; and mercy possesses me."[52]

When it was over, Drury in his annual report expressed in moving simplicity what the evening had meant to him. "These experiences," he said, "will remind our children that what their parents worked for and cared for was, while they lived, understood."

A Safe Lodging

He had never really planned for retirement. He used to tell his children that, when they left St. Paul's, he and their mother would "set up a little Mom and Pop grocery by the side of the road and sell Mom and Pop cakes

to passers-by." If he had any dream, it must have been to do as he had
pictured James Potter Conover doing, riding out regardless of hearthside
comforts "to share his vision of Faith with some bewildered pilgrim." Yet
he seemed to know that his years might be numbered. "We Drurys are a
nervous and irritable breed," he wrote a sister who had fallen ill in 1935;
"we push ourselves and other people unduly. The time comes between
sixty and seventy when the Drury bodies either give out or slow down."[53]

Two years later, in his annual report, he struck a similar note: "Thus
the years pass, and while the school at the age of eighty is adolescent,
some of the workers grow old. . . . School is a place for the young, the
young chronologically and the young in heart. There will come a time for
each of us when Mother Nature will assert her claim." Did he have some
premonition, some forewarning? Was he beginning to sense what some
years before he had described as "the pathos of last things"? To his sister
he wrote, "I am in good shape, working hard and enjoying every day."
Yet following his words and actions in these years one senses that, like
Prospero, he was ready to "drown" his book; he was casting off his
worldly spells and magic.

"I shall never expel another boy," he declared in the annual report of
1935. And he told the trustees in the meeting of January 1938, "I have
given up raising money. I do not any longer want to approach individual
donors and try to take their money away." Just as unruly boys would still
be dealt with—though by other means than sudden expulsion—so the
good of the school would still be served, but no longer by waiting in the
drawing rooms and antechambers of the rich. "This walking up and down
Fifth Avenue or Wall Street is over for me."[54]

The man who to the alumni in 1936 had declared himself "possessed
by mercy" now could abjure the old masks and guises of authority. "A
headmaster's strongest weapon is weakness," he wrote at fifty-nine, in
what was to be his last communication with the St. Paul's constituency;
"the subtlest exercise of power is forgiveness."[55]

In this season of last things, his mind turned back lovingly to the
Coits and to the long history of the school in which they had played so
commanding a part. Charles Wheeler Coit, the first rector's eldest son, in
the summer of 1937 responded to Drury's invitation to spend some weeks
in the Prophet's Chamber at Hargate. It was the first time in many years
he had been back. Walking about the quiet grounds, Coit was conscious
that "this peaceful visit has broken down certain barriers in my mind as
long ago as the rather trying period when I was a master here." (That had
been from 1888 to 1898.) In January 1938, from Ruth Coit the rector received the following: "Being a very old lady and at the moment in bed but
not ill, I believe that if you were here I would put my arms around you,

because I am so genuinely happy over what you are accomplishing and have accomplished for St. Paul's School, and I know the position has never been an easy one for you."[56]

On February 8, 1938, Drury wrote Charles Coit again. "The lengthening days remind me that spring will soon be here. . . . We very much hope you can be persuaded to spend part of your holiday at your old home, the family school." Less than a week later, on February 14, after his regular morning rounds at the infirmary, Drury spoke to the school doctor of a peculiar numbness in his arm.

The symptom was diagnosed as coronary thrombosis; immediate care and an extended rest were prescribed. With his wife, Drury at once left St. Paul's for a hospital in Boston. Even the vice rector, Henry Kittredge, did not know until several days later why his chief had departed or that his absence might be prolonged. In fact the rector was to be in the hospital less than a week. From his bed he carried on his personal correspondence in the large familiar hand, penned a pre-Lenten message to the neighborhood congregation of the old chapel, and to a young secretary, Raymond Spencer, dictated letters on routine school affairs.[57] His family came to visit him, along with such an old friend as Henry K. Sherrill, the bishop of Massachusetts. As Sherrill turned to go, "I am a very shy person," Drury said, "but I just cannot help telling you tonight how much I love you." Two days later, in the early morning, word came to Bishop Sherrill, and to Henry Kittredge in Millville, that Samuel Drury had died.

PART III

CHAPTER ELEVEN

Worlds in Change
1938–1947

Aftermath

Like the first Coit, Drury died in the night. In neither case was the St. Paul's community prepared for the shock of a great captain's passing. Henry Kittredge's announcement in the Big Study, immediately after chapel, was greeted with uncomprehending silence. Drury had been so commanding a figure, had so dominated the life of the school, that it was almost impossible to imagine another taking his place.

The funeral, held at noon on February 23, found the chapel crowded with boys, masters, alumni, and friends of the school. The heads of other schools and representatives of the universities were there to pay tribute to a man who had been an exemplar in his role of schoolmaster and had so often challenged them with his fresh and powerfully expressed ideas. Roses, lilacs and camellias were on the altar—unseasonable, as had been his death. "O Pray for the Peace" was played in final tribute to a man who had never craved peace for himself, and indeed had feared that in the little Jerusalem over which he ruled there might be too much peace—or at least too much easy contentment. The last notes of the recessional, as they died away on the organ, were picked up by the chapel bells, and floated over the file of silent marchers mounting the hill to the school burying ground. There Bishop Dallas of New Hampshire intoned the committal service: "From henceforth, blessed are the dead."

Immediately after the service a trustees meeting was held at the bishop's house in Concord. Cornelia Drury, with characteristic dignity, sent word that her financial needs were adequately cared for and that no concern should be felt by the school. Kittredge was named acting rector, with the announcement to be made by the bishop that same evening in a masters meeting, and to the boys in the chapel. The memorial resolution passed by the board, bearing the mark of John Dallas's rugged Scots rhetoric, included in its praise of the late rector a tribute to the fortitude with which he had carried on "when misunderstanding made his position

257

Holding an assemblage of schoolboys in bemused suspense. *As acting rector, Kittredge reads reports in the Big Study.*

as rector trying and even hard.'' Thus to the end Drury remained a figure touched by controversy, his scars remembered no less than his accomplishments. He would have wanted it that way.

A permanent memorial to the fourth rector formed the substance of lengthy discussions at subsequent meetings of the board. A stained glass window in that part of the chapel he had helped created seemed unquestionably appropriate. Its details, however, were mulled over. At the meeting of October 1939, it was formally voted ''to substitute a pelican for the portrait of Dr. Drury.''* This was taken at the initiative of Cornelia Drury, one more instance of her common sense in all matters affecting the school.

Later a dormitory, bearing the fourth rector's name, was erected in the woods across the library pond. The building's homey scale and its Georgian architecture would have pleased Drury, but he might well have asked why it was situated so as to be invisible in the day's journeys about the school, and why its entrance was so obscurely placed. (He had himself been skilled at avoiding such mistakes.) Unfortunately, no one suggested

---

*Drury had sought out representations of the pelican in churches here and abroad, and favored it as a symbol of St. Paul's.

that the most fitting memorial would have been a series of scholarships for foreign students.

Meanwhile the search for a new rector went forward. Henry Kittredge seemed a likely choice—"the job could so surely have been yours,"[1] the chairman of the board wrote him afterwards—but Kittredge was a layman, and besides, he honestly did not want the post. Four months after Drury's death, the board elected a young clergyman, John Crocker, then chaplain at Princeton. Crocker turned down the offer—"It just seemed too big for me," he said years afterwards—[2]to become in due course headmaster of Groton, Endicott Peabody's successor. The needle swung again toward Kittredge. He was still reluctant, and began to think of a boyhood comrade and Harvard classmate, then a professor at the Episcopal Theological Seminary in Cambridge.

As early as 1926, Henry Kittredge had spoken of an anonymous friend to whom, he said, he went "whenever I am perplexed by questions of religion." And "I am perplexed by them very often," he added. Kittredge would explain his difficulty to this friend and expect a solution. "Usually I get one, but sometimes in the course of his answers he throws out disturbing conundrums that had never occurred to me."[3] That friend was Norman Burdett Nash; this first reference to him in school annals catches perfectly the image of a trenchant, probing mind, an intellect dissatisfied with easy answers, that the St. Paul's community was to know well.

Kittredge thought it inappropriate that he should put before the trustees the name of a personal friend. His wife suffered from no such constraints. Always outspoken, Gertrude Kittredge saw a good cause was at stake, and was additionally motivated by the conviction that her husband would be relieved to have the growing pressures dissipated. So she suggested Nash's name to members of the board, not (we may believe) without a glowing account of his virtues; there, for a while, the matter rested.

As acting rector, Kittredge stepped into the vacuum left by Drury's death with the apparent ease of one born to lead. His cheerful manner, his good-humored approach to even the most vexing problems, were what the school needed in this period of reorientation. To see him deal with a ruffled master, or a boy in some curricular or disciplinary trouble, was (as G. K. Chesterton said in another connection) like looking into the witches' cauldron and hearing a clear, cheery and educated voice saying it was a fine day. In morning reports he established a special rapport with a constituency that already knew him well. The angular gestures, the eyebrows quick to be lifted in humorous deprecation of some hot issue or as a warning of explosive laughter to come; the understated New England speech touched with the playfulness of Cape Cod neighbors; infre-quently—but not to be missed—the flashes of anger: all this made up a performance holding an assemblage of schoolboys in bemused suspense.

At first there was little to do but to keep the ship steady and to carry out faithfully the projects Drury had set in train. Even after the first shock had subsided, Kittredge thought of himself as the lieutenant of one he had greatly admired—"kind, formidable, unpredictable," he described him.[4] It was his habit, he told a friend, when the going was heavy, to close his study door and in the solitude to ask what Drury would have done in the circumstances. But he was too proud a figure not to be his own man, as he had been, indeed, ever since coming to the school. His annual reports for 1938 and 1939, showing him briskly taking charge, comprise a series of shrewd and sunny comments on school affairs and on the life of young scholars. The style would become well known within the school family and outside it; never did it move with livelier cadences than in these first flights as acting rector.

"At whatever point a boy starts his career at the school, whether early or late," he said, "he should immediately be made aware of the fact that he is expected to begin studying hard and steadily, whether he likes it or not, and to keep it up until he graduates." So much for the acting rector's attitude toward scholarship. But there were also leisure pursuits: the charms of the historic sluice, connecting the upper end of the school pond with Little Turkey, were eloquently set forth in the same report and were recommended to one and all. "It is an entirely unspoiled stream," we read, "running merrily, and at some seasons very swiftly, between wooded banks owned by the school. Here boys, poling their canoes up against the current on a May afternoon, and sailing down with it, dodging rocks and shaving fallen trees, can forget that the school exists and can return to it refreshed, as a man returns to civilization after a sojourn in the wilderness."

In the winter of 1939, a serious chain of illnesses filled the infirmary; happily, all the boys recovered. Kittredge, who with his wife had watched and worried through a growing crisis, emerged with his seemingly care-free attitude unshaken. "Two cases of scarlet fever," said he, "varied the monotony [of the winter term]; so did a number of cases of broncho-pneumonia. I have tried hard to persuade the medical profession to let us call this disease bronchitis, but they are too honest, or too scientific, or both; so the alarming word pneumonia must still be attached to this ail-ment."[5]

In due course the election of a new rector relieved Kittredge of his burden; at the same time he retired from his post as head of the lower school and moved to a large wooden house looking down on the sluice.

Here Mrs. Kittredge continued to dispense liberal amounts of tea—"two and cream, please"—while he returned to teaching and watched over the progress of a new administration.

The Nashes Come to Millville

At the November meeting of the board of trustees the choice of a new rector was discussed at length; and at a second special meeting, November 28, 1938, the trustees elected Norman Nash. Upon Nash's part there was little heart-searching before he accepted the post. In his late forties, he was a man who knew the world and knew his own mind. For twenty years he had been teaching Christian Ethics at the seminary, and no doubt he felt it time to put some of his principles to the test. The surroundings of a boys' boarding school would be new to him, but he was at home with young people and could count on his old friend Henry Kittredge to help him through difficulties.

To the school family Nash was entirely unknown, and much natural curiosity developed in regard to him. One alumnus, Chanler Chapman, took pains to search him out in the large and rambling clapboard house where he resided in Phillips Place, Cambridge, and was now waiting out 'the academic term until his new duties should begin. "All those years in the seminary, and his father's years before him," Chapman wrote with his customary effervescence, "the teaching of Christian Ethics, the reputation of a liberal and almost a radical, the very name Nash, and the drizzle and fog of a winter evening in Cambridge"—all were unpromising. "You couldn't help expecting a thin man, over-worked and under-nourished. You expect the ecclesiastical collar and bright, narrow eyes burning with Pauline doctrine." The shades of the house were up as Chapman approached. Within, he could see two men talking in a large study lined with books. A dog and a young girl—one of the two daughters and three nieces who would soon be moving to the rectory at Millville—appeared before him in the doorway. The dog had neither ears nor tail and he barked furiously.[6]

Shown without question or ceremony into the study, Chapman caught the name of the neophyte Episcopal clergyman who was making his exit. Kelly, it was—and Chapman saw vanishing all his preconceived notions of "twenty years with the Thirty-Nine Articles of Faith." Nash, to his pleasant surprise, was a tall well-fed man, with a ruddy complexion, irregular features and bright eyes. He was not even wearing the dreaded clerical collar. What followed was a haphazard stroll through the thickets of conversation. "I cannot help feeling," Chapman wrote, "that Mr. Kittredge is right. This man has simplicity and sincerity and humor. He seems to be mature without being 'set,' and twenty years of teaching Christian Ethics have not warped him.''

The trustees braced themselves for the whirlwind of the new rector's entrance upon the Millville scene. He had accepted the job on the understanding that he was a liberal and had ideas of his own which he was not likely to change. Kittredge assured the school body that Nash would bring ''a new point of view, new methods of procedure, a whole set of ideas to keep us in touch with the changing complexion of the times.''[7] ''When he meets the Begums of St. Paul's,'' Chapman predicted in his colorful imagery, ''the Hindu ladies of State Street and the Mohammedan queens of Philadelphia, the fat will be on the fire, the ship will shake.'' Nash never was as radical as all that, but for the seven years of his rectorship he indeed kept the place stirred up, his spirit of reform springing as much from directness and candor as from doctrine. Henry Laughlin, the board's

"We were grateful for his being on the bridge." *Norman B. Nash, fifth rector of St. Paul's School.*

witty chairman, would assert that having made Nash rector, he had no choice but to make him bishop in order to get rid of him.

In the rectory, soon filled with daughters, nieces, and the tailless dog, a buzzing intellectual atmosphere took over. Meals were served hospitably to a broad diversity of visitors and guests, but were always hurried, as if the rector could not spend himself on small talk or wait to get on to the next task. Mrs. Nash began taking in boys recuperating from illnesses, making the rectory a halfway house between their release from the infirmary and their return to full school life. "An angel of mercy,"[8] one of these remembered her to have been when, as a second former, he had sat awestruck at the family table, alone with the rector and Mrs. Nash, while the great man seemed lost in thought. The Nashes' tastes were plain; their motto was frugality. Those who remembered the gleaming brass andirons and silver candelabra of the Drury period, the books in their Levantine bindings, the fireplaces laid with apple wood upon a bed of pure white ash, would have found the place oddly informal. But that was the Nash way—the style of a Cambridge professor of Christian Ethics.

A Firm Hand at the Helm

The boys saw a preoccupied and rapidly moving figure, one who did not suffer fools gladly, and indeed sometimes seemed not to suffer them at all. Yet they respected the new rector and took in their stride his austere manner. "We seamen were far removed from the captain," one of them wrote; "but we were grateful for his being on the bridge and at the helm."[9] Students learned quickly to appreciate him as a just disciplinarian and rarely protested the expulsions he was forced to make. "Norman the Foreman" became his sobriquet. He was also known as "Norman the Doorman" because of the efficiency with which he concluded an interview once the business at hand had been disposed of. The sixth-form president during Nash's first year was a youth of unusual ability and promise, John V. Lindsay, who was to make a name for himself as congressman and mayor of New York. A fast friendship was early established. Lindsay remembered afterwards the care with which the new rector informed himself on every detail of student life and the sympathetic support he gave to Lindsay's own efforts.[10]

The autumn of 1939, when Nash took over, saw war break out in Europe. For a year it seemed a remote disturbance, one in which the fortunes of the United States—even less those of the small community of Millville—were not significantly engaged. At home the long ravages of the Depression years still showed in mass unemployment and a lethargic

economy. The new rector's first call was for stringency in school management. He asked the trustees to lower the tuition—a hitherto unimagin-
able request that was firmly turned down; he called for a greater spirit of
self-sacrifice and personal economy among the boys. Seeing foreign students forced to leave their homelands, he stressed the need for further
scholarship funds. At that time 17 per cent of St. Paul's students were
receiving aid, compared with 18 per cent at Harvard. A few years later the
proportion at St. Paul's was 19 per cent.

Reevaluation and retrenchment became the order of the day, in part
imposed by outward circumstances and in part by the rector's natural
inclinations. The old dairy farm, from which flowed the hundreds of
quarts of milk consumed daily by the St. Paul's constituency, was abandoned in favor of more economical purchases from New Hampshire pro-
ducers. The golf course on which Willard Scudder and his friends had cut
sporting figures, long a pleasant amenity of the school, was closed down,
and trucks were substituted for the remaining horse-drawn barges on the
journey to Long Pond. More important, the orphans' home—the only
physical structure at the school bearing the Coit name—was phased out.

The years had brought changes in social theories affecting the care of
homeless or handicapped children. The idea of keeping them in an institution, no matter how enlightened its management, gave way to their
placement in homes and families and to their attendance at public schools.
The orphanage in its later days had become something of an embarrassment. In the 1920s a boy was whipped severely for theft, and a hearing in
open court resulted in unfavorable publicity. By 1940, Coit House was a
residence for delinquent girls. Neither fact nor fancy ever linked St.
Paul's boys to these neighbors—the old "Biddery," lodging of the school
maids, had by contrast long evoked its share of libidinous thoughts. Yet
the orphanage seemed an unsuitable appendage to the school, and its removal to another site was discussed in trustees meetings.

During the war its ancient plant was used for the training of naval
personnel, the cellars stuffed with helmeted dummies of enemy soldiers
employed in mock warfare. Soon afterwards the outmoded buildings were
demolished and their site returned to pasture. Coit House became but a
legend, though the "little orphelings" and their somber residence had
once played so important a part in the life and philosophy of St. Paul's.

Change was coming on other fronts, too, and where it did not come
easily, Nash was happy to push it along. It was symbolic that early in his
regime there should have passed from the scene John Mercer, a man with
the longest record of service of anyone who had ever been employed by
the school. That old worthy had been brought in by Henry Augustus Coit
in 1874; he vividly remembered the fire that destroyed the first school

house, and had been known as a participant since then in every battle against floods, hurricanes, or other disasters of school life. For sixty-five years he had been actively engaged in work around the school grounds. The cottage opposite the school inn was his castle; the red barn, his treasury. From the latter, wearing a straw hat summer and winter, he distributed food to the dining rooms, counting his stores as if the devil himself were after them. His funeral in the old chapel, on what would have been his eighty-ninth birthday, seemed to many to mark the end of an epoch.

The notable group of old masters who had come to the school in the 1890s were at retirement age. Peck, Nelson and White withdrew in 1940 and 1941. By now the school had a pension system and a fixed retirement policy; Nash was spared the grumbling and sniping with which the old guard had greeted Drury's early years. Even so, there were difficulties in which the firm hand of the Doorman became manifest. One of these men found himself mortally offended by what he considered the rector's abrupt manner in dissenting from his views at a masters meeting; another judged himself to have been "forced" into unceremonious retirement, though age and deafness made him an unlikely teacher.

Traditionalists existed among the younger masters as well as the older. Graduates of the 1920s, now leaders on the faculty, openly asserted their lack of sympathy with the new administration's methods and ideas. A few of these formed a small group of mutually supportive dissidents, gaining credence for their views among gifted students, whose friendships they especially cultivated. Nash objected to this criticism. The school, he said, was too small a place to harbor even a "loyal" opposition. He also feared that cliques of the brighter boys would be set apart by a too-close relationship with these masters.

Meeting the problem head on in frank interviews with the men concerned, Nash made his views known. When a few of these men left, whatever personal wounds they may have borne, it was without the agitated repercussions that followed similar dismissals in earlier times. Drury, had he lived to witness these events, would no doubt have felt that his successor handled them better than he had done when young and still inexperienced. He would have appreciated the irony of seeing traditions and standards established by himself unduly venerated, as had been those of the Coits in his first years.

Nash looked impatiently on the curriculum (as he did on everything else), but the time was not ripe for a thoroughgoing revision. Throughout the Drury administration, basic subjects had remained to a large degree fixed; Kittredge's recommendation of many-sided teachers, rather than a multiplication of courses, continued to be the accepted doctrine of educational liberals. In the sixth-form year advanced students had the opportunity to study in small groups with some of the school's finest teachers, pursuing aspects of a subject far beyond the curricular requirements; but in lower forms the gate was still narrow and the way straight. A student coming in the early thirties from a progressive school in New York found himself baffled by the emphasis placed on Latin and by the absence of courses related to the arts.

Nash's contribution was not toward variety *per se,* but toward a greater stress on contemporary political and economic problems. The school's aim, he said in 1940, should be to teach the student "that history is now in the making, and that past and present are continuous stages in a living process, of which he himself is a part, and in which he must bear responsibility in years to come."[11] New courses in recent American history and in Western civilization brought the curriculum into closer relationship with the changing world outside. As the fateful autumn of 1941 advanced toward its climax at Pearl Harbor, it became evident that St. Paul's students—often in dramatic and tragic ways—were indeed to be part of history.

Parents and Sons

Many things were changing, but the nature of the young human animal does not change much from one generation to another, nor do the emotions of the parent in regard to it. Inevitably tension would arise between parent and offspring, and between home and school. The trauma of the child's separation from the parental environment had always been at the heart of the boarding school experience, a necessary precondition to the liberalizing, but often painful, rites of passage from infancy to adulthood. This was true when the school was essentially a family in itself, as under the first Coit. As it became a large and less personal institution, the relations of the two worlds could put strains on both sides.

Drury in his time had been much concerned with the influence of the home on the boy, and the influence of boarding school on the home – boy relationship.[12] Nash was more apt to take his charges as autonomous beings, challenged by duties and responsibilities of a society independent of the parental tie. He could be curt with parents; he concealed imperfectly his impatience with their limited knowledge of education and their special point of view toward their offspring. In one of his annual reports he did not hesitate to indicate disdain for a parent whose respect for the schoolmaster's life was questionable. "But he is an *able* person," Nash reported a mother as having exclaimed when it was suggested that her son might make a good teacher.

Yet in their own way, and often in mid-term encounters, parents and sons came to a natural though sometimes uneasy three-way relationship with each other and with the school. St. Paul's was always a pleasant place to visit, its landscape refreshing to the eyes of the city-dweller, and its inhabitants providing a pleasant change from the social circles in which they normally moved. A visit to Millville gave the worried parent a chance to check on the offspring's physical and intellectual growth, and to appraise his standing with the school authorities. The latter could be a trying experience. A mother of the 1920s told of having received in terror a suggestion from Dr. Drury that she drop in at his study. The rector began very solemnly, "Now as to Charley's Latin . . ." "Dr. Drury," rejoined the relieved mother, "I know nothing at all about Charley's Latin. I consider that matter to be entirely in your very capable hands."[13] The rector was taken aback, but the interview, dealing with the son's virtues and deficiencies, proceeded in an informal and agreeable manner.

In the late 1930s and early 1940s, before the vast changes wrought by World War II, the journey to Concord for a spring or winter weekend had its amusing aspects. A mother of this period has left a classic account, worth following because of its insights into the strange life of boys as well as for its lively image of the school. The trip from New York was then almost invariably made by train, on the old "State of Maine," from which the New Hampshire cars were uncoupled at Lowell, Massachusetts, in the middle of the night and (according to our good-humored guide) "were taken on a scenic tour of the yards, behind a switch engine driven by a novice engineer who had much to learn."[14] Arriving in the early morning at the cavernous Concord depot, the mother in this case relied upon the instructions of a first former who seemed under the impression she was anything but bright. "When you arrive at Concord," he wrote her, "get off the train and walk through the stashun [*sic*]. I have classes all morning so you may do what you like. You may want a bath"—this last a startling suggestion, adds the mother, "coming from a small boy so allergic to them."

The typical mother would install herself in the Alumni House, the agreeable small inn (at that time notably lacking in private baths) maintained by the school and standing at the entrance to its grounds. There she would knit and read through the long morning hours, awaiting the rather terrifying moment when her son would appear, scarcely recognizable—though having left home only a few months before—and surrounded by a formidable group of his peers. The most affectionate of sons would on these occasions greet his visiting parent with a casual "Hi."

To the mother whose account was cited above, the most awkward aspect of her visit was that she was constantly getting lost on the large grounds of the school. Her young escort would suddenly announce that he was going to some place "with a cryptic name like 'Big Upper' or 'Down Lower.'" Before she had time to ask him what he meant, he would have disappeared, leaving her to wander about like a derelict until he reappeared as suddenly as he had vanished, asking impatiently why she hadn't come along. Being thus rescued in the middle of one afternoon, the mother was informed she was being taken to watch the school hockey game.

The obvious place to watch the game, it seemed to her, was along the wooden barriers where the boys, colorfully dressed in their arctic clothes, were already gathering. But her own youthful hockey player seemed to think it was better that she be steered to a wooded peninsula overlooking the pond—to avoid, she supposed, having her fall down or otherwise make herself conspicuous. "A strange solitary figure silhouetted against the snow," she wrote, "I felt like the picture of Napoleon overlooking Moscow." Reflecting that her next visit was scheduled for the rowing season, she wondered whether, by way of making her inconspicuous, her son might place her in a tree.

So the weekend went by, highlighted by the much dreaded interview with the master in charge of studies. Steeling herself for this, the mother was in a severe panic, picturing him as a figure "somewhere between Erasmus and Zeus." "I was convinced that he would expel my son and me along with him, and my knees buckled as I approached his office, at the threshold of which my offspring turned tail and beat it."

"The cause of our panic," continued the mother, "proved to be a delightful, mild-mannered gentleman who with great courtesy asked me to be seated and plunged right into the matter at hand by remarking that my son's marks were not over-satisfactory—to which triumph of under-statement I acquiesced with sorrow." And so in due course came the inevitable time for parting. The train went off inexorably on Sunday after Evensong. Perhaps at the end would be a gleam of the filial affection the parent had come to fear was dead. In place of the now-familiar "Hi" (obviously inappropriate for a scene of departure) came a slightly bewildering "Be careful" . . . and then a sudden, unexpected hug.

Such journeys, however awkward for the parents and their sons, played a significant role in school life. How eagerly awaited! How quickly passed! Some gleam of new purpose would afterwards light the student's mind; and to the school these witnesses to an outside world, in the person of even the most confused or apprehensive parent, brought a fresh note in the long, otherwise unbroken termtime. The day of fleeting arrivals and departures by car would come after World War II, followed some years later by the freedom that allowed students to leave for weekends as they wished. But as the last days of the old order began to fade, the image remained of that indomitable parent, isolated on her promontory of snow.

Toward Redefinition

It was characteristic of Nash that after dealing summarily with practical necessities, he should have turned his mind to the basic intellectual issue: What purpose was being served by a school like St. Paul's? It was not, in his view, a question with an easy or self-evident answer. The public schools were then at a high educational level; in the future lay the disorders, the crowding and the falling standards of literacy which in the early 1970s raised questions about their capacity to educate effectively or to assimilate the youthful population. In 1940, to so rigorously honest a man as Nash it seemed plain that the private boarding schools were seriously challenged. "The conclusion has now become widespread in this country," he said, "that the independent school is merely a vestigial survival which will not last much longer."[15]

Nash's own conviction, as he looked forth from Millville upon the dark ideological movements of Fascism and Nazism, was that the independent school was not less necessary than it had been, but more. Caesar was ascendant, both in the form of demos and of dictator, making claims upon the whole man. To withstand these claims, to be an institution truly resistant, and resistant through a well-founded religious faith, was for him the modern destiny of St. Paul's.

From the beginning the school had been conscious of some special role in American society. This was not, as was sometimes supposed, to educate the rich, to redeem the sons of the industrial barons. The school's mission was to subject young men to a moral and rational environment, impressing upon their still malleable dispositions a particular image of virtue. Sometimes this was to be accomplished insensibly, under the spell of natural beauty and civilized personalities; sometimes through the forms of ceremonies and rituals. Upon these was superimposed a conviction of the Creator's immanent role in human affairs. Such a concept was adequate through the school's pastoral period, when God, almost like a Greek deity, was present at the feast as He was part of the young men's games and studies. But as the nineteenth century advanced, a new formulation seemed necessary. What, precisely, did religion have to do with education? And why did St. Paul's strive so consistently to combine the two?

The best of the early answers to these questions was given in 1888 by Samuel Eliot, speaking at the dedication of the new chapel. Education, real education, *must* be religious, Eliot contended. "No matter where it begins or where it ends, there is no phase of it so simple or so highly wrought that it can safely forego its relations with the infinite." Eliot proceeded to establish an unbreakable bond between the secular institution and a higher order. "Only as the light from heaven streams down upon and into the studies we pursue," he said, "can they be understood in all their completeness. Literature is not wholly itself, nor science, nor art, nor any branch of human learning, unless its divine connections are followed out; unless the subjects themselves, and the powers employed upon them, are accepted and used as the gifts of God."[16]

That redefinition of the school's religious base served for half a century and more. Ferguson was completely in accord with it; Drury, though his stress was most often upon the individual's personal relation with God, would have accepted it as a just application of religious faith to the specific problem of education. Preparation for the constricting college examinations might obscure the larger truth. Industrious pedagogues like Nelson or Peck might scoff at it. But in the school community at its best resided the conviction that the origins and the ends of learning extended somehow beyond the classroom—that "connections with the infinite" did indeed exist, of which the chapel services were but one form and one continuing manifestation. There, by and large, the matter rested, until widespread heresies in the political and educational worlds made necessary an attempt at restatement. The challenge was well suited to Nash's highly intellectual and unsentimental approach.

By 1940, amid the unfolding consequences of the Nazi creed, the secular ideal of citizenship no longer appeared adequate for the maintenance of a civilized social order. Allegiance given unquestioningly to a national leader was ending in atrocities accepted without overt dissent. "We are sure," said Nash, "that the man is more than the citizen, and indeed that only the man who knows himself as a member of the commonwealth which is eternal can offer the state a citizenship loyal, intelligent, critical."[17] Only a core of such men could preserve the state from the ancient idolatry of itself.

The individual, in the last analysis, must be independent; the institution within which his needs are met must be independent; and the independence of both must be founded on a secure religious faith. Given this approach, Nash stressed the name "independent school" rather than "church school." Truth, as he saw it, was always on trial. Searchers for truth could give no ultimate allegiance except to an ever-living God, superior to worldly powers.

To keep in balance the elements of faith and reason was, in Nash's view, the goal of the educator. Achievement of this goal could alone assure a school like St. Paul's a purpose serious enough to warrant its survival. Within an independent school, and under a clerical head, faith and reason could most effectively be made harmonious. The school without a religious center was defenseless against worldly tides. The layman as head, no matter how devout nor how closely linked with a school chaplain, invited the duality that Nash saw as so serious a threat in the modern world.

In anything but a truly independent school, he wrote to a trustee, it became all too easy for students, parents and faculty *"to segregate faith and to secularize knowledge."*[18] Nash's belief, explicitly and implicitly set forth, was to serve as an adequate grounding for St. Paul's until the tremors of the 1960s once again shook the foundations.

The War Years at Millville

World War II brought St. Paul's graduates out upon all the fighting fronts, in all the services and in all the ranks of command. From the little study inherited from Dr. Drury, Nash kept touch with a constituency he had barely come to know. "I had known, of course, that you carry forward the traditions and ideals of the school," an alumnus wrote from overseas,[19] "but to see that you can preserve, also, a warm and living bond between yourself and those of us who passed through in earlier years— that touches me very deeply." From Australia Samuel Eliot Morison, now a naval commander, wrote Nash that it was gratifying to learn the school was keeping *mens sana in mundo insano,* preserving the wisdom of the past "as exemplified by the Christian religion and the Classics." Winant was serving as ambassador in London, and at Anniversary in 1941, while England was undergoing alone its ordeal by fire, a special exercise was held to raise funds for this favorite alumnus and to express support for a beleaguered country.

To see young masters go off, and—when the draft age was lowered to eighteen—to watch sixth formers departing for training camp, was to create a feeling of frustration and of wistfulness in the older men. Duty, in Millville, wore during those days a dusty face. In an annual report in a year of far-flung fighting, Nash quoted the words of his predecessor: "Education," Drury had written, "is a practical, midstream mission, a call to the risky task of dealing with souls—souls in the making. Gladly aware that a little section of the battlefront is allotted to them, [schoolmasters] hopefully begin year after year, humbled by their failures, but cheered by the conviction that the work of a boarding school can be made one of God's causes."[20]

There was reassurance of a kind in such words, as there was magnanimity in the man who quoted them. Still, it seemed hard to carry on routine duties when so many of the St. Paul's family were engaged in the great actions of war. Gerald Chittenden expressed with poignancy the sentiments of the older masters, trying to keep touch with a younger generation:

> *What can we write that you would wish to hear?*
> *How change small beer for your full, ruddy wine?*
> *"We'll row this year. The ice is holding late.*
> *The willows by the pond are smoky green."*
> *Small beer, indeed. Yet once we, too, knew war,*
> *And through our talk of small, sweet changeless things*
> *You may, perhaps, smell snow off hot Timor*
> *Or hear the sweeps click, rhythmic, in Algiers. . . .*[21]

At the school, cutbacks of all kinds were put into effect. The remaining masters taught larger classes. The boys learned housekeeping chores and kept the grounds in place of men called to the front. Such an ancient (and already outmoded) custom as wearing starched collars on Sunday was discarded as laundry services were reduced. With gasoline rationed, horses were recalled from their honorable desuetude to draw the crews' barges to Long Pond, and for lack of fuel the power launches of the coaches gave way to one-man shells.

Amid the alarms of wartime even these arrangements failed to assure the continuance of rowing. Concord's water board, in an excess of patriotic enthusiasm, closed Long Pond; and the school sought in vain for other places where the shells might be launched. The Merrimack in its navigable portions was too swift; the peaceful waters of the Contoocook River were too far off; the Turkeys, too shallow and clogged with vegetation. In due course, the city council overruled the water board and a rowing season of limited duration was arranged. But a warning note had been struck. The school sooner or later would have to find a place for rowing less vulnerable than Long Pond to political and bureaucratic currents.

Millville was not immune to the wartime measures being taken elsewhere. Students were finger-printed; fire drills and air raid precautions were regularly carried out. Blackouts, the rector observed, were greeted with something less than enthusiasm by the boys when it was found that studies could proceed uninterruptedly in spite of them. On the surrounding hills, meanwhile, groups of masters kept night-long watches against possible enemy bombers. As in World War I, lawns were dug up for "victory gardens," and now coal was accumulated in massive piles, not adding to the beauty of the landscape but a reassuring sign in the face of frigid wartime winters.

A course in aeronautics was offered; Chittenden lectured on discipline and *esprit de corps*. But the rector cast a cold eye upon any signs of popular hysteria. In chapel he conspicuously refrained from calling on the deity to assure victory over the country's enemies; it was enough, he believed, to pray for steadfastness and courage.[22] He resisted as well the tendency to downgrade the traditional learning in favor of mathematics and engineering.

Sixth formers were then going directly into training; indeed many were graduating in special ceremonies at mid-year. What they failed to learn at St. Paul's, they were likely never to know. Even those who went on to colleges found them, as Nash complained, converted to training institutes for the armed services. More than ever, he felt, it was for St. Paul's to reaffirm its fidelity to humanistic values.

Nor did Nash relax the school's commitment to religious studies. He enlarged it, believing such studies to be a "vital part of a young man's preparation for war or peace."[23] To one mother who asked that her son be excused from Sacred Studies on the grounds that this course was not of "practical" use in military service, he replied that it was, on the contrary, extremely practical, being one of the means by which a young man's character was formed and his vision clarified. The mother's request was firmly rejected. The rector continued to teach his course on Christian Ethics, dealing with the old dilemmas of human conduct in vigorous, no-nonsense style. A new elective course in Christianity was introduced; it moved, Nash said, in "quieter waters remote from the war and an accelerated training." Drawing on advanced texts in theology and ethics, it was accepted, much to the rector's satisfaction, as an entrance credit by major universities.

Inevitably, problems of discipline arose. The ranks of younger masters were depleted; the number of applicants from which promising students could be selected was reduced; and boys in general were uneasy and restless. "Even the steadiest," Nash reported, "find it difficult to keep their minds on their work in times like these." An unusually large number of dismissals added to the turnover resulting from students departing for war. The upper school, with its numerous vacancies, was more than ever a place apart, and it became a predictable generator of trouble. As the *Horae* remarked facetiously, it was "practically a Ritz Hotel—minus some service and numerous other odd little improvements." Because of diminished numbers in the sixth form, almost everyone had as many rooms as he desired. Three so-called clubs, the Howdy Club, the Sheik Club and the Club Flamingo, consisted of groups of characters with whole suites at their disposal.

Of Valiant Youth

When, some years later, the time came to dedicate a memorial to those who had served in World War II, the alumnus orator of the occasion spoke of the dead who had once been boys at the school. "Had we but eyes to see," he said, "we could trace their footpaths beneath these trees. . . . Had we but ears to hear, we could detect the sound of their hurrying footsteps in the long corridors; the catch of their oars across the waters, or their skates over the black ice of the pond."[24] A few of these boys we can indeed almost see and hear. There was young Edward O. McDonnell, Jr., who, on becoming a pilot, brought his plane in low over the school, dipping his wings in salute. Two weeks later it was announced in chapel that he had fallen in combat over North Africa. On his last visit to the school he had spent an evening with one of his favorite masters, Gerhard R. Schade, reading classic texts in German.

Another, in letters happily preserved, leaves us the very tone and image of what it was to be young in those days. John W. Garrett, 2nd, came to the school in the autumn of 1939 and left in June 1942. He was an able boy, blessed in his home life, a good athlete and scholar, and he loved St. Paul's. In a way he speaks for a generation, for all those who, having outgrown youthful cynicism or rebellion, found happiness in the scenes and incidents of the last days before going to war. He speaks for the one hundred five St. Paul's graduates who gave their lives in the conflict.[25]

An enthusiastic but still immature fourth former, Garrett won a "demerit holiday" (a reward for good behavior): "we went cross country skiing," he wrote his family, "but after a twelve o'clock picnic lunch we were all so exhausted we could barely drag ourselves home. We spent the afternoon in bed." After his first Washington's Birthday: "How sad St. Paul's is now. . . . But the weekend certainly was fun. On Friday night we skated until about ten, out under the stars. The boys who had girls skating at their sides looked awfully embarrassed and self-conscious." At the end of the spring vacation, he grieved. "Woe is me! How low I feel! Each morning I think I am home, until that——bell wakes me up at 6:45. The first day was terrible. Nobody would concentrate except the masters. But with the coming of tomorrow we shall be in full stride, for ten weeks to come."

Through the next two years we watch the lad grow, his style lit by humorous perceptions and by a complete enjoyment of existence. As a fifth former, he climbs Jerry Hill in October. "Far to the north lay the White Mountains," he remembered. "Two of the highest peaks were snow-capped. . . . To the west, mountain rose above mountain to the Green Mountains and the Adirondacks a couple of hundred miles away. Concord, to the east, was clearly visible, and the Merrimack wound its sluggish course southward to the sea." The chapel tower and the power house smokestack could barely be made out above the trees in the hollow where St. Paul's was standing. "You can imagine what the sunset was over all this, reflected in the two lakes at the foot of the hill."

Later that same year he took part in a tournament of plays. "Our play, 'The Touchdown,' was about a last-minute victory of Wahoo College over Siwash. We of the cheering section were supposed to be utterly bored by the game and unconcerned with what went on. The dumb judge didn't get the point of our dead-pan faces, so he said, 'The Drury play cannot be called a play because of the remarkably stony faces of the cheering section.' After we had practiced for weeks! Well, it was lots of fun anyway." At the same time he was learning to study hard. "If I live through this week," he wrote just before exams, "I'll consider myself fortunate. If I pass, I'll probably die of shock."

"I've really enjoyed this term," Garrett tells his parents at the end of this fifth-form year; "and the sorrows and disappointments of other terms have paled into insignificance in the great happiness that has been mine for the two months past. But now at the end comes a twinge of regret that I have only one more year here. I have come to realize what a wonderful place the school is, in its location, in its boys, in its opportunities, in the companionship which one cannot help finding here; and in the realization that I have come to love St. Paul's. I did not want to come here, I fought the idea to the last ditch, but in the last two years I found out how terribly I underestimated the school and I am not ashamed to admit that I was wrong."

The sixth-form year, after a trip to Alaska in the summer, finds his sensibilities heightened. He speaks little of the war, but he sees St. Paul's with a vision sharpened by its looming presence. In November he describes in detail the last of the club football games. "I almost broke down and cried in the clubhouse after the game, as I took off my good old square-toed shoes, my pants, pads, and Old Hundred sweater for the last time—it was almost too much. It is very sad to think I'll never play football here again—after three years of it it is hard to realize that the last day has come and gone." Then the final Anniversary weekend came round. Again there is a vivid picture of the sporting events, this time the rowing races on Long Pond. The Halcyons (he was a Shattuck) won two victories by one-tenth of a second; two, by four-tenths of a second. "It was a heart-breaking afternoon for our side." Yet it was hard for the victorious Halcyons, too; their first crew failed by only two seconds to break the record. "It was too bad," Garrett wrote chivalrously, "that so much was so barely missed."

Three flags—the American, the Episcopalian, and the banner of St. Paul's—were "carried by the three red-heads of the sixth form," to make a colorful procession up the aisle at the Anniversary chapel service. "In two weeks we, too, shall take our places as alumni of St. Paul's," he wrote his parents. "Do you remember those letters I used to write in my fourth-form year—'You'll see great changes in me when I come home'?" And yet, he now adds, there is no change. "For St. Paul's is not a school which changes its students in a month or two—St. Paul's reaches down into the hearts of its boys; it plays upon their natures, their characters, their very souls—and these cannot be altered in a short time. Probably the changes will never be noticed. They will be shown, rather, in our children and our children's children—the friendship, the breeding, the open-mindedness, the sense of honesty and fair play and the desire to do and seek after what is right."

John Garrett graduated in June 1942. He entered directly into military aviation. Six months later a bomber he was piloting suffered mechanical failure and he brought the plane down in a crash landing. Of the crew of seven men, he alone was killed. He was not yet twenty years of age.

The Postwar Period

The war came to an end amid setbacks and disappointments on the military fronts as the Allies in the winter of 1945 repulsed the last German offensive in the Battle of the Bulge. The school resumed its normal course, but with its grounds and buildings showing the marks of inadequate maintenance, and with accumulated wartime deficits. Changes in student life—a greater informality in dress and less ready dependence on services once taken for granted—were not to be reversed. The young masters returned. The rectory, from which the Nash daughters and nieces had gone to war jobs and service with the WACs, became again a center of family life.

The educational system of the country had been permanently affected by wartime emphasis upon practical courses. Greek had been dropped from the college board entrance examinations—"a melancholy development," the rector wrote to Robert Peck, then living in retirement. The Bachelor of Arts degree was being offered for the first time without any Latin, and Latin was no longer a requirement for entrance to college. Nash commented somberly on "the parental disbelief in the classics, backed up by the failure of the colleges to encourage a classical program." "I cannot believe," Peck replied, "that the study of the classics will die. . . . There is still something to strive for beside making atomic bombs and calculating the trajectory of a rocket or a shell."[26]

The last year of the war had seen the students restless and frustrated. Disciplinary problems increased; scholarly standards declined. Nash spoke of "the mysterious process of maturation," and sought a cure for the unrest in what he called "the benevolent pressure of school life." "We do not propose to be less patient," he told the trustees, "but we hope that we can improve our guidance and correction."[27] Although the number of student applications had been disconcertingly close to the number of places available, Nash was disposed to drop students who showed no improvement in their marks after due warnings. Boys, even sons of alumni, were not to be admitted "to flounder through a year or two of discouragement and frustration." Yet on the whole he continued to be optimistic. What was a "good" year and what was a "bad," he asked, when things seemed to be at their worst. "In the day of judgment . . . we shall probably get plenty of surprises." At least there was enough of good and bad in each year, he added, "to keep one encouraged, and to prevent one from ever growing complacent."

In January 1946, Nash's election as bishop of Massachusetts was announced. No inner struggle seems to have accompanied the rector's decision to accept, as none had accompanied his decision to come to St. Paul's in the first place. He had felt for some years he had one more big task to do, and the bishopric was a natural progression. His work at the school could be considered complete. He had guided it through seven difficult years. War had forestalled most new initiatives; but his lively intelligence had helped keep the ship on course, and had enabled him to distinguish, almost infallibly, between the things that were transitory or fashionable and those that were likely to endure. The trustees, speaking in their final tribute of "the path through the school made by his vigorous and active step," did not misjudge the effect of his seven-year rectorship.[28]

The insignia of his office were laid upon Nash in Boston on February 14, 1946. A group of students went down to the service. Shortly afterwards a delegation of St. Paul's workers visited the bishop's house, where Mrs. Nash showed them around and served them "a beautiful meal" she had cooked herself.[29] The new bishop lived up to his reputation for boldness and independence. His first sermon was an advocacy of birth control as a means of family planning. In the 1950s, he took his stand against the malicious innuendoes of Senator Joseph McCarthy, personally defending several young clergymen of his diocese against charges of communism.

Bishop Nash practiced, as at St. Paul's he had taught, a citizenship "loyal, intelligent, critical."

CHAPTER TWELVE

A Layman Rules in Zion
1947–1954

Henry Kittredge's Hour

The school faced once more what Henry Kittredge had called a "broken" year; and once more he was called to the post of acting rector. It was a role with which he was becoming all too familiar. Not only had he filled the void after Drury's death; but in 1943, when Nash as a result of complications following a fall was unable to function for almost a full school year, he had taken over the burden from his friend. He was now fifty-seven years old. He had known the school intimately, in all its aspects, as had only a few men in its history. He was not—despite a certain diffidence of manner and an almost excessive enjoyment of his vacations on Cape Cod—an unambitious man; nor did Gertrude Livingston, his wife, lack the intelligence or charm to shine in the largest company. The example of the old professor must have been in the son's mind: that bearded, sprightly figure who had moved through his Cambridge world with an easy dominance and a widely acknowledged fame. This, if ever, was Henry Kittredge's hour.

The trustees felt the need for haste. The school in that uneasy post-war world, and after the earlier hiatus in leadership, could not afford to drift. The choice was complicated by the long tradition of a clerical head. There was nothing in the school's charter requiring a clergyman. The first rector elected under the original board of trustees had been a layman; the final choice of young Coit had been as much a matter of chance as of settled policy. Nevertheless, the tradition was firm. The post was offered to Charles L. Taylor, Nash's successor at the Episcopal Theological Seminary in Cambridge. When he refused it, the board turned once again to Kittredge. At a special meeting at the Yale Club in New York, on May 22, 1947, they elected him the sixth rector of St. Paul's. This time it was certain that acceptance would follow.

To a degree the new administration was bound to appear an interim one. Kittredge would have but seven years before retirement. His status

278

Henry Kittredge sets forth on a winter morning from the rectory.

THE SIXTH RECTOR'S GENIAL METHODS OF ADMINISTRATION

Dispensing "excuses" on a cricket holiday.

as a layman was thought to represent an interruption, not a break, in a long-established tradition. Yet the St. Paul's constituency looked to the rector with an affection and confidence that belied any thought of a *pro forma* choice. He knew the job, and beneath his easy manner were mature convictions about the nature of boys, the methods of teaching, and the destiny of the school.

"I don't believe that anyone so well qualified has ever been put in charge of a major boys' school in America," Henry Laughlin, then a member of the board, wrote Kittredge. He had perhaps been "eased into the job," as a result of the trustees' preference to continue with a clergyman at the head. "If the conditions had been in any way different, you would have burst into it instead." Laughlin concluded by expressing the hope that he would be a rector "as Drury and Coit were"—not a transition figure like Ferguson.[1] Such was Kittredge's intention also.

The Kittredge Style

The "Rector's Letter" in the spring issue of that year's *Alumni Horae* revealed the new voice sounding in Millville—a voice quiet and cheerful after Drury's epigrams and Nash's intellectual bombshells. "Truly spring comes slowly this way," he wrote to the school's parents and alumni. "And yet this morning as I walked to the school house, the air was warm, the sun bright, and a robin and a song-sparrow cheered one along the way. So we may call it spring until the next snowstorm."

The problem of the chapel worried Kittredge. He was, he said, "a humble learner in matters ecclesiastical."[2] Born and brought up a Unitarian, he was now confirmed as an Episcopalian; and he put in charge of the school's religious life a benign and industrious clergyman, Charles Webb, who had been at St. Paul's since 1926. Kittredge's own participation in the services would be remembered for his occasional addresses, always well written but delivered without the flair of his remarks on less formal occasions; and by the reading in loud clear tones, marked by echoes of a sea captain's commands, of certain oft-repeated prayers. He remained more at home in the Big Study than in the chapel, in the easygoing comments of "reports" than in ceremonies of worship. Yet he was, in the old phrase, "a believer"; his reticence and modesty in religious matters struck close to the uncomplicated faith of youth.

Kittredge was not one to push for material improvements, especially where his own comfort was involved. An eye to economy, as well as a deep-rooted reluctance to make personal demands, left the rectory in a state more satisfying to his New England conscience than his wife's tastes. In a plant suffering from wartime neglect there were more than the usual cases of leaky roofs, broken sewer lines and heating failures. Kittredge dealt with such problems as if they were part of a different world from that which normally concerned him, yet not without finding occasions for outbursts of his characteristic style. A crack occurred in the chimney of the power plant. "It took nearly ten thousand dollars," said he cheerfully to his board, "to plug that disastrous fissure."[3]

Kittredge's ideal image of the school was a happy place where boys, harassed by a minimum amount of regulations and penalties, would work hard and pursue a maximum variety of leisure activities. He cared for eccentricity, and he elevated tolerance to a major virtue. It was the school's aim, as he once expressed it, to attain "a genuine, natural, genial atmosphere," a condition to which most boys would respond, and which some would greet as a novelty "because they had never seen anything like it before."[4]

To a large extent he succeeded during his seven years in securing an air of relaxed cooperation. He would be criticized by certain of the masters for not providing leadership or definite goals. But he was convinced that leadership was a byproduct of a community functioning harmoniously, and was not imposed from above. As for goals, he assumed them to be so simple as to be self-evident. If they became complicated, they could only be illusory. Emphasis on method as opposed to substance, on procedure as opposed to underlying values, always distressed him. More accurately, it tested his forbearance and provoked his ironical humor.

The spread of academic achievement tests was, in particular, at odds with his philosophy. How could anything so unfathomable as the mind of a boy be weighed upon mathematical scales? "Not content with revealing what the pupil knows," he told a gathering of schoolmasters, "these experts have now discovered how to look into the seeds of time and prophesy what they will be able to do in years to come. We shall, no doubt, soon be able to determine by tests which of our boys are certain to turn into kind husbands and good providers, and which of the girls will become stars of the cinema."[5] The testmaker, he said on another occasion, stays in his lair. "He has never been in a classroom. He doesn't know any boys. He wouldn't like them if he knew them. Don't mistake me," Kittredge continued, good humor breaking through the unusual bitterness of his tone, "we buy the tests and use them. And some of our men believe in them."

(One of these men, a young master of whom Kittredge was particularly proud, had come to the school in 1942. He had, said the rector, a genius for getting hitherto uncollected facts into intelligible order. In charge of the registrar's office, he was actually making it possible to know how a form was doing academically. We are now very "scientific and up-to-date," Kittredge assured the trustees.[6] The name of the young administrator was William A. Oates, of whom more will be heard.)

Kittredge's own long career as a successful teacher gave him particular ideas about the academic side of the school. "We have little faith in pains and penalties," he declared in his first annual report as rector, "or in mechanical devices however ingenious." His aim was simple: to introduce more "liveliness" into recitations. He envisaged a school where boys would step across the threshold of a classroom—as not long since they had stepped across his—feeling an anticipatory thrill, and where each boy would leave the room "wiser and better than when he entered it." For a teacher to achieve these results, scholarly degrees and formal training were not necessary, he believed. "What he needs is imagination, vigor, and faith in the importance of his doctrine." Methods he would invent for himself as he went along; the best technique was that which suited a man's genius. "If he knows his subject thoroughly, he will at least have a chance of igniting a spark now and then in a youthful brain."[7]

Two classes of teachers Kittredge described in a private letter that showed well the man's style and his essential humor. One was "dry and dusty." No boy under him was allowed to loaf and few of them ever flunked. Almost none, on the other hand, emerged from his instructions with a true love of the subject being taught. There was another teacher, a bird of a different feather, one who was contributing much to the school by his gentility and scholarship. "He has no notion of discipline but goes through the day as though no boy would ever misbehave." He had the reputation of being very lenient. "He marks the boys easier than other teachers do; but I notice," said Kittredge, "that they do just as well on college examinations as those who have been prepared by the rest of us." Some of them even caught the idea of behaving themselves without being made to do so.[8]

As he professed a disdain for formal methods of teaching, so he treated lightly the principles of administration. Here he is discussing the delegating of authority. One of his aims, he had said, was to reduce so far as possible the inevitable stress and strain of school life for both masters and boys. "This was one of those broad and vague expressions into which one is sometimes betrayed in an expansive moment after a good dinner, and in truth I had at the moment no plan in mind for achieving this happy end. But none was necessary. The vice rector was there and obviously thought well of the idea, and in a week or two presented a plan . . . for bringing it to pass." So much for conventional rules of administration!

In regard to the boys, Kittredge took what seemed almost a perverse delight in praising the student who was less than brilliant in his studies or conformist in his habits. The "moon-cussers" of Cape Cod had always fascinated him—men who made it their way of life to gather in the booty from wrecked ships. Something of their waywardness would not, to his mind, be amiss in modern youth. To John Richards, in his retirement in Maine, Kittredge wrote of a vessel grounded in Chatham. The local boys had stripped her clean, doing as good a job as their fathers or grandfathers would have done; "apparently there is some life still, even in the rising generation."[9] To his Cape Cod neighbors he expressed in whimsical terms his regret that the boys of St. Paul's seemed to find life stale. There were no longer strange mascots among them, or examples of tattooing; even fishing had disappeared under the pressures of organized athletics.

Kittredge had a natural sympathy for such a lad as the representative of the third generation of Chapmans, John Jay Chapman 2nd. "A genial eccentric," he called him, a follower of family tradition—"an independent spirit, as friendly as the day is long, and a joy to the world, except when he neglects subjects which bore him."[10] In the same vein he praised eloquently those boys whose scholarship could not be called excellent. He liked "the plodders, a dozen or so in every sixth form, to whom geometry is a riddle and the understanding of a poem a battle against odds. . . . They are modest and cheerful, they are sympathetic supervisors in the houses occupied by younger boys; they are generous and sometimes distinguished athletes, and in every phase of the life of the school they pull their full weight. They leave the school a better place for their having been members of it."[11]

"We must be," Kittredge continued, "what Henry Adams called 'patient students of human error,' and if we persevere, by the time these willing workers have been in the school for two or three years, they will have learned the age-old problem of how to study well . . ." and will "pocket their diplomas with the rest."

From his wry appreciation of the odd boy and the misfit, Kittredge derived his hatred of intolerance in all forms. During World War II, instances of hazing had occurred at the school, and there was always below the surface of boarding school life the inclination toward brutal and unfeeling conduct. Even where hazing did not involve physical harassment, it could be subtly cruel. Humiliating nicknames were common. One master was known as "Creeping Jesus"; another as "Prosperity" because he was "always just around the corner." The seemingly innocuous sobriquet of "Deen" was applied to one boy because his complexion was thought to resemble wartime's Aberdeen proving ground. A master recalled seeing one lower former, after he had been mercilessly teased about his interest in minerals, dropping the precious stones of his collection one by one into the waters of the school pond.[12]

Against this trend in school life Henry Kittredge blazed away in school assemblies, and in an early annual report spoke out eloquently. "Youth is a cruel time," he said, "cruel and conservative." Happily the days were past when being a new boy by itself justified abuse. "But a vigorous ghost of their old savagery remains in the maltreatment to which queerness is sometimes subjected. To change this intolerance to tolerance, this cruelty to sympathy, is the schoolmaster's hardest duty—hardest and most important. Until it has been learned, a boy's Christianity is a hollow shell and the process of civilizing him has not begun."[13]

When discipline was required, Kittredge could be lenient—some thought too lenient. "We may indeed call ourselves children of a world in which a degree of frailty may still be found," he told the alumni. But the fact that he took so much of life on faith led him into swift and summary—occasionally too swift and summary—action when he felt his faith betrayed or the margin of his tolerance exceeded. A boy who incorporated into a *Horae* story the acronym for an indecent word (a word that would be used openly in the same journal a decade later) was hastily dismissed. Two masters who fell below his standards were let go with a minimum of notice, causing serious perturbation within the faculty. But matters of discipline were usually more happily dealt with. One year's sixth form, responding to the postwar boom in college applications, distinguished itself by getting the highest marks in the school's history. But their behavior, Kittredge reported sadly, "was not on a par with their industry."[15]

"A good many of them showed an unusual disregard for school rules. Two members of the form, indignant at the situation, began to stir up public opinion against it. Since there is always more good than bad in any group of boys, their efforts succeeded pretty well, and by the end of the year things were back about to normal."[14] Nevertheless, he concluded, the form would be remembered as one that worked hard but behaved badly. In short, the rector was hopeful, but he was also resigned in the face of the inevitable. Not for nothing did he inscribe in one of his commonplace books the epigram of Thucydides: "No man can pass judgment on Fortune."

Neo-Arcadian Days

St. Paul's did indeed seem a happy community under the rector's genial methods of administration. It was as if something of the school's early years had been recaptured. The terms went by smoothly; spring and autumn, and the hard test of winter, passed calmly once more amid traditional ceremonies, without heroic accomplishments as without disastrous setbacks. It was less a time of innovation than of agreeable accommodation and slow growth.

Events of school life were now observed by the editors of a school newspaper, the *Pelican,* with something of the flair and the attention to small detail that characterized the early scribes of the *Rural Record.* In 1945, a group of students had laid before Nash the plans for such a publication. There was "quite a long and detailed negotiation," one of them later recalled.[15] Nash undoubtedly foresaw that an innocent fledgling, the editors of which were mainly desirous of seeing in print a full account of their athletic exploits, could become a powerful instrument of social change. In any case he gave his permission, and the newspaper under its first editor-in-chief, J. W. Kinnear III (a future chairman of the school's board of trustees), started on an existence that was soon to challenge the century-old preeminence of the *Horae Scholasticae.*

The *Pelican* of the 1950s presented good-humored accounts of such occasions as the school dances, which the Kittredges helped make lively and colorful. The mid-term dance weekend of 1954 was the largest and perhaps the most sprightly ever held at the school. Seventy girls were on hand, brought from Concord in a hay wagon and deposited in the little building that had recently been erected at the edge of the school grounds in memory of Willard Scudder. Scudder would have enjoyed this use of the building, a restoration of the original Moses Shute cottage whose actual beams and timbers were still embalmed in the second story of the gradually decaying Middle. A blazing fire, burnishing the paneled, book-lined walls, illumined his portrait, an eternally dapper figure in its red Halcyon blazer, and warmed the newly arrived guests and their escorts. Preliminary greetings and assignments were completed and a light collation served. An informal dance, a sort of early discothèque, took place with music supplied (according to the *Pelican*) by "Peter Rabbit's handmade victrola."

Next day, a Saturday, there was a hockey game as there had always been, and the traditional Missionary Society Fair. It was "the gayest and most successful ever." Amid such innovations as a raffle for a portable radio, every old standby was included. One student foretold the future with "amazing foresight," while another guessed the weight of one and all—"only occasionally having trouble with the fair damsels visiting for the weekend." Meanwhile various couples circulated among the crowd, selling carnations at an unprecedented rate.

In the oak-ceilinged dining room of the upper school, with the founder and past rectors looking down from the wall, the weekend's principal entertainment unfolded. "As regards decoration," the *Pelican* asserted, "simplicity was the keynote."[16] The main chandelier served as a hub for sixty red and green streamers, "radiating to the more distant corners of the ballroom." Small tables, intimately lighted by candles, surrounded the dance floor. As the evening took its course, Mrs. Kittredge was very much in the midst of things, a delighted and delightful presence, knowing each girl (she had arranged for all seventy of them to stay at masters' houses) and not herself averse, in her husband's phrase, to "tripping the light fantastic" when invited by the young men.

Sunday brought its quieter amusements; until the evening came on, and after the brief, moving service in the dim chapel, all the girls were hustled off.

About this time the Thanksgiving Crawl was invented. A young instructor in Spanish and history, Señor José Antonio G. Ordonez y Montalvo, made his first run to Long Pond soon after arriving at the school. "I have loved it ever since," he said, "the trails, the water, the hills and fields, the little valleys, the peace away from school."[17] That first experience gave birth to the revival of cross-country running as a modern sport at St. Paul's—and was perhaps a harbinger of the craze for jogging that would sweep the country two decades later. It was known at that time, however, as "the crawl."

On Thanksgiving Day after chapel, under Señor Ordonez's direction, the crawl began with a ceremony on the chapel lawn, the participants joining in singing the first stanza of O God Our Help in Ages Past. This was done in order that all who took part might have the courage to finish. The intrepid group, leaving the chapel, rounded the lower school pond, crossed some fields and entered a dark wood, coming out at the foot of Jerry Hill and thence proceeding to Long Pond. The homeward trek, by another route, completed a circle of five miles.

The journey was interrupted by occasional incidents, such as one famous encounter with the "Mean Farmer" who ejected the crawlers from his fields with a pitch fork. The last stanza of O God Our Help was thenceforth repeated in this field in hopes of warding off this particular character; as it was on reaching Long Pond, for moral encouragement, and on the return in gratitude for having arrived. The whole circuit was made—and would be for years to come—at a slow jog, permitting ample opportunity to savor the changing views and the beauties of the November woods.

Kittredge deplored the disappearance of canoeing—"the saddest change that has taken place in the school,"[18] he remarked in a chapel address. But he found pleasure in the weeks long considered anathema at the school; the slush season of March when, as he said, "sports are largely unscheduled and the athletic program is casual and miscellaneous." That was a time when boys could develop their own talents and

"The saddest change." *Canoeing on the school pond had disappeared by the 1950s.*

follow their own fancy. And he encouraged the revival of one vanishing leisure-time pursuit, the building of huts in the school's wilder domain.

"It was a cheering sight to see last fall from the lower grounds," he reported, "a flag flying from a clearing on top of Prospect Hill, in front of a shack built and furnished by our boys. . . . Not so long ago a score of these shacks stood in various spots in the woods which surround us. A pleasant thing it was for masters to be invited to inspect the handiwork of the builders and to partake of tea or cocoa heated on a rusty, sheet-iron stove." Sometimes the builders had been botanists, sometimes ornithologists. Frequently they were neither, "but enjoyed the unsupervised and unscheduled hours."

A youth of ironical bent, graduating in 1948, caught accurately in a memoir in the *New Yorker* the spirit the rector sought to foster. He recalled the feeling of ease and casual abundance at the school—"showers that ran in a never-ending stream of hot water, food of such extraordinary delicacy that it could frequently be eaten without ketchup." There were teachers, even, who seemed to have taken up their task "with at least a semblance of vocation"; there were "lots of trees and grass, and woods, and ponds. We used to skip football practice some afternoons to go roaming through the woods at the back of the playing fields, looking for a supposed secret way to a nearby village, but it was nice crashing through the woods, even in November . . . even when the sun went down very early and the trees were bare and the ground hard, and everything in the world seemed brittle—except us, I think."[19]

So these neo-Arcadian years went by. "A friendly, industrious and profitable year," Kittredge termed one of them, guided by a vigorous council under what he called "the finest group of masters the school has had in a long time."[20] (They were on the young side, their average age thirty-seven; and a larger proportion were married than would have been the case a decade earlier.) The sixth form of a couple of years later was characterized by "friendliness, cheerfulness and imagination." It was not, the rector asserted, imagination of the highest sort, such as inspired Milton or Michelangelo; rather the lower order of imagination that enabled Defoe to describe in detail the furnishings of Robinson Crusoe's cabin.

Sixth formers that year were "full of suggestions for making their lives pleasanter." They were resourceful, too, moving a game which was destroying the grass, to another site, where "it destroyed the grass just as successfully"; and they were sociable, inviting masters and their wives to join a newly instituted coffee hour. "This genial point of view," Kittredge concluded, "set the fashion for the younger boys, with the result that the year, by and large, was a very pleasant one."

On a spring evening Kittredge observed the boys strolling in front of the rectory, at about the pace, he averred, "one may suppose the peripatetic philosophers to have set themselves when, with heads thrust forward and hands clasped behind their backs, they wrestled, as they walked, with thoughts beyond the reaches of their souls." It is good, he added, "for all of us to be here at such a time."[21]

The Concord neighbors found themselves being wooed by invitations to Millville's lectures and entertainments; even the faculty wives were included in school events, with the rector's wife revealing herself to be an early devotee of women's liberation. At a masters meeting addressed by the new school psychiatrist, the wives were invited. "We are getting very liberal with the ladies, I may say," Kittredge wrote to the chairman of the board, "but then they have long been admitted to the smoking rooms of steamers."[22] Parents came and went and adapted themselves to the mood of the school. The rector, in a talk to Cape Cod neighbors, might deplore their seeming omniscience about educational matters, but he was pleased by one father who quoted his son's letter to the effect that there were three athletic clubs and that he had been chosen "a Simian." The father replied that he had always suspected this to be the case.[23]

"Even the trustees must like the place," the rector wrote to his old friend John Richards. "They are prolonging their traditional sojourn by twenty-four hours and are also shifting the scene of the mid-winter meeting from Boston to here. So be it. We shall do our best to make their visits pleasant."[24]

The Trustees Turn Southward

Kittredge had been rector only three years, and his retirement was still four years away, when the trustees began an active search for his successor. They were determined that there should be no interval of uncertainty and that the new head should be thoroughly prepared and indoctrinated.

The search had its colorful and striking moments. On a Sunday in 1951, John R. McLane, a board member of almost thirty years' standing, stopped by for the morning service at All Saints Episcopal Church in Atlanta, Georgia. The congregation was large and represented some of the city's wealthiest citizens; about six hundred that morning had turned out to hear the rector preach. After the service the rector lingered at the door of the church, an imposing figure in white vestments, greeting parishioners. Presently he turned to the stranger watching on the sidelines. McLane introduced himself. He had come, he said, to talk to the rector about the post of headmaster of St. Paul's School. Matthew Warren was hurrying off to lunch; the rest of the day was entirely full; but he gladly volunteered to converse with the stranger while disrobing. He was, he said, strongly disinclined to leave All Saints.[25]

Did he know the famous Concord school? Yes, said Warren; he had long summered on the New Hampshire seashore at Little Boar's Head (a name which generations of St. Paul's boys would transform into an off-color spoonerism); and he had once motored over to see the St. Paul's chapel. He remembered little of the visit, except the image of a window—in what he later learned was the rectory—being thrown open and the curtains floating in the summer breeze. Unfortunately, for it might have been a pleasing link in the chain of history, Drury's face was not framed in the casement.

But Warren recalled an occasion when Drury had come to preach in the 1930s at the church in Chestnut Hill, Pennsylvania, where he was himself a young curate: the immense anticipation before the visit, the congregation crowded with St. Paul's alumni, the unforgettable voice and presence. An impression had been formed in Warren's mind which now, perhaps, unconsciously began to work its effects.

At about the same time, a member of the Yale Corporation, Charles Dickey, was inquiring of his fellow member, Bishop Henry Sherrill, whether he knew of any man to succeed Henry Kittredge at St. Paul's. Yes, replied Sherrill, there was one man—in Atlanta.[26]

Presently other emissaries from St. Paul's were making the journey southward. On October 1, 1951, Laughlin and Dickey, the board's two most influential members, invited the rector of All Saints to dine at a leading Atlanta hotel. The rector insisted that he be the host, and that the dinner be held at the Driving and Riding Club, inner sanctum of Atlanta's élite, of which rectors of All Saints Church were members, apparently, by divine right. "Gentlemen," said Warren, as they settled down in their comfortable surroundings, "I am a drinking man. If you have no further interest in me that is all right. But I am now going to order a martini." Laughlin and Dickey confessed that in the expectation of a dry evening they had fortified themselves appropriately before coming to the club. In the circumstances, however, they were pleased to accept another drink.

Conversation during dinner was along general lines, but afterwards the three withdrew to the rectory in the exclusive residential section of Atlanta's Ansley Park. Dickey opened the conversation abruptly. "Do you like boys?" he asked. "Name me one," said Matthew Warren, "and I'll tell you whether I like him or not." If the trustees were looking for a man who loved boys in general and in the abstract, he was not for them.

Warren was interested in education—that he could not deny. He talked of his earlier work in St. Louis, where he had been a leader in the educational activities of the Episcopal church, of the Sunday school at All Saints where attendance had grown during his rectorship from one hundred to three hundred students. He had some very definite convictions regarding the relationship of religious and secular learning.

The three men talked until well past midnight. It was evident that the dialogue had not been concluded. Rather against his will, Warren was persuaded to make a visit to the school. If he showed the least interest, he protested, to that extent he was straining the bonds that tied him to his Atlanta congregation. But he went nevertheless, with his wife Rebecca; and the opportunity to look over the school was turned to his embarrassment into a sort of royal passage.

In Philadelphia, in New York, in Boston, there were stopovers, with small luncheons or dinners at which the mightiest of St. Paul's alumni came out to look over the man who might be the school's next head—and to put subtle pressures upon him as well. Finally in Boston he borrowed a little Ford from Henry Laughlin and, as if to prove his independence, went first to Groton where his older son was a student.

Thus he came in due course to St. Paul's. The Kittredges, who knew what was up, received him and his wife with their usual hospitality at the rectory for lunch, and then showed him around the happy kingdom over which they presided. But Matthew Warren was strangely depressed. The place looked to him "over-grown and run down." Compared with the tidy environment of Atlanta, the well-kept lawns and neatly clipped bushes of Ansley Park, the effects of wartime economies and deferred maintenance showed distressingly; many of the school's buildings seemed old and out of date. To the Warrens' critical eye the rectory, in particular, appeared shabby. The little Ford had barely passed from the school grounds before Rebecca said, "Don't take it. It will be too much."

At a special meeting of the board on December 16, 1951, Matthew Madison Warren was elected the school's seventh rector. He accepted, on the understanding that he would assume office in June 1954. In the meantime he would spend a year studying theology at Union Theological Seminary, would visit schools abroad, and would come to St. Paul's as vice rector for a year of on-the-job training. In the end St. Paul's did indeed absorb Matthew Warren, deeply and wholly. It changed him. But during the third longest of the school's rectorships, amid times of extraordinary turbulence, it would never prove "too much" for his faith or his reforming zeal.

Manipulating the Inevitable

Events during the Kittredge years were not lacking, but for the most part seemed to happen without great stir, as if generated by the same Fortune that regulated the seasons or the unpredictable dispositions of boys. "We don't have to invent changes," said the rector in an address to the alumni. "They are pushed on us by circumstances. All we have to do is keep limber and manipulate the inevitable."[27]

World War II, the GI Bill of Rights, shortages of men and materials and then the postwar boom, had all left their mark on school life. Some of these forces resulted in curricular changes—a new emphasis on art and music instruction, a course in public affairs and American democracy; also in an increase in scholarships, abolition of the old waiting list for admissions, and preparation for a college scene so highly competitive as to cast its shadow backward over the last two years of study at school. Still other changes occurred in the buildings and the physical environment of the school.

The first postwar construction project was a war memorial, which the trustees and alumni, after prolonged discussion, determined should take the form of an auditorium. The old gathering place atop the gymnasium, built in 1879, had long since outlived its usefulness. Drury was said to have declared that the only kind of music he liked was loud music, an opinion that may have been reinforced by the fact that anything less was in danger of being drowned out by the squeaky chairs and creaking floors. There remained the question of site and the style of the proposed structure. The architectural firm of Ralph Adams Cram was engaged, but the heavily adorned Gothic style of their design, and its suggested location upon the site of two small clapboard cottages (one the former home of James Potter Conover), caused the plans to be rejected and the contract canceled.

A second proposal, by Richard A. Kimball, was accepted. Ignoring the street as an organizing concept, as well as the Olmsteds' advice to group buildings around the valley of the sluice, Kimball placed a massively scaled pseudo-Georgian building behind the school house, on land sloping toward the lower grounds, once the site of the school piggery. Later, flanked by buildings for science and mathematics, the auditorium wold be part of an academic quadrangle, handsome enough in itself but breaking the scattered and informal siting that gave the school grounds their special character. Unfortunately, the porticoed entrance to the auditorium occurred at its eastern end (not, as could well have been the case, at its center), thus orienting the building toward the new Dunbarton road and causing the audience to debouch in a direction contrary to the flow of school traffic.

Difficulties in raising funds for the structure, combined with lingering shortages and increasing prices, put off the dedication until June 1951. The alumni, upon entering at last, found themselves in a beautifully detailed antechamber, with the names of the war dead engraved upon a large panel of slate. (No sculpture, this time, broke the cool abstraction of the tribute.) Beyond, an auditorium sloped comfortably. It was large enough to hold the entire school but, like most multi-purpose halls, would prove poorly suited to some of its varied functions, while acoustically it left much to be desired.

A further initiative in the building field almost ended in disaster. At their meeting of January 1952, the trustees, for reasons of economy and in order to reduce maintenance costs, voted to demolish the old chapel. First building to be erected by the school, gift of the founder and embodiment of treasured memorials, here the first rector had inspired generations of St. Paul's boys. The chapel was still serving for smaller school services and as a place of worship for the surrounding neighborhood. The decision to tear it down was reversed that autumn under protest from masters and from a comparatively few alumni, young and old. That it should have been taken in the first place is significant. It suggests the materialistic values at work in the postwar world, together with the decline of the religious impulse in school life. It suggests, also, a basic disorientation of spirit. A school confident of its future would not have come so close to forgetting its past.

The country was at that time passing through the ordeal of the Korean War, the first national conflict unsupported by the generous and romantic ardors of youth. This was not yet Vietnam, the repercussions of which, upon St. Paul's and virtually all other educational institutions, would be shattering. But it was a portent of things to come. Kittredge summed up the reactions of the students: "They see themselves in combat and it depresses them."[28] How different from the zeal with which the young had faced the wars of 1917 and 1941! "These are at best troublous times for youth," the rector continued, "calling for unusual sympathy and understanding from us all." They were troublous times, too, for

The decision to tear it down was reversed.
The old chapel in a photograph of the 1950s.

American society, and for the little group of trustees, gathered in Millville, who cast their vote against the old chapel.

A matter less emotionally complex for the school was presented in 1951 by the closing of Long Pond to recreational use. Those clear waters had been found during the summer to be polluted. The pollution soon disappeared and the alarm of the citizens abated. Politically, however, the issue would not die. In March 1952, a climactic hearing was held, with so large a crowd of citizens in attendance that the meeting was moved from City Hall to Concord's largest auditorium. It was, according to one witness, "the hottest hearing in Concord's history."[29]

Devotees of fishing sided with the school's interest in rowing; the board of trade and the majority of local doctors called for a reopening, and the city council had voted in a tie—thus requiring the hearing. Speaking extemporaneously, Kittredge made an eloquent argument citing the school's involvement in the Concord community (which he had himself done much to vitalize): the attachments formed in seventy-one years of mutual dependence; the economic benefits of school-provided jobs, purchases, and bank deposits; the courtesies extended to the citizens through use of the school ponds and tennis courts in summer; and the school camp harboring annually some fifty Concord boys. All was in vain. Passions were beyond the appeal of reason. "A small minority," cried the opposition, "wants to play in our drinking water." Three weeks later, the vote of the council went 16–4 against both boating and fishing on the pond. St. Paul's faced the end of one of its most salutary and long-lived sporting activities.

Kittredge characterized the day of April 14 as "one of the gloomiest I can remember." Not only had the council's vote on Long Pond been adverse. In addition, he had been forced to expel two fifth formers for exploding gunpowder in the backyard of the Middle. "It's a pity," he told the chairman of the board, "they didn't explode it indoors and blow the old crate to smithereens."[30]

Preparations against the closing of Long Pond had, however, been in the making for more than two decades. Under Drury's imperial drive, virtually all the land surrounding the two Turkey ponds had been purchased by the school. His last annual report suggested autumn rowing. Where? "I speak as a fool," he wrote—quoting St. Paul and using the word "fool" with overtones of divine innocence. "It is an eleven-minute stroll, a seven-minute jog-trot, a four-minute bicycle spin from the chapel to a suitable point on the shores of Big Turkey."[31] Now was the time to put this prophetic vision to the test.

As soon as the frost was out of the ground, a road to Big Turkey was cleared, branching off the old road to Dunbarton. A number of big pines along the shore were cut down to make a dock; a pile of sawdust, left over from the lumbering operations following the hurricane of 1938, was leveled to make a place for spectators. Launches and shells were brought down from Long Pond—some of the latter actually carried on foot by rowing enthusiasts—and racks were built for them under the trees. "We are making the best of Turkey," the rector wrote, "and a very fair best it is."[32] The course was considerably shorter than that which had long been rowed; much of it was in shallow water, strewn with floating debris. But it served, and it kept the tradition of Race Day alive. Monumental public works, necessary to convert the course into one truly adequate for the St. Paul's crewmen, would have to wait for another day.

In this period came large—and mostly unanticipated—additions to the school's endowments. No one was more surprised than Henry Kittredge when he turned out to be the beneficiary of more sizeable gifts than any rector before him. He did not think of himself as a fund-raiser. When he was head of the lower, a wealthy alumnus had indicated his desire to make a gift to that part of the school where he had received his first instruction and his greatest delight. Kittredge said he would like to think the matter over, and when he returned to the prospective donor, suggested that for the lower school study a new dictionary would be very welcome. Now, in his rectorship, more than dictionaries began to flow in.

In rapid succession a bequest of $1.5 million came from Edward S. Harkness; nearly half a million was added by a bequest of Hamilton Fish Webster, a graduate of the golden 1870s, to increase scholarship funds. Most extraordinary, a fabulously wealthy lady who had never visited the school, Sylvia Wilks, upon dividing her estate among various institutions, left the little colony at Millville $2 million the richer. Over these accretions Henry Kittredge presided, bemused and impressed. An alumnus congratulated him at the conclusion of a particularly successful year: "But will there ever again be such an avalanche of coin?"[33] It seemed unlikely.

The Changing of the Guard

The autumn of 1953 found Matthew and Rebecca Warren installed in Hargate beside the old mill stream. As rector-elect, Warren received his training by taking part in various school activities, teaching two divisions of Sacred Studies, and ministering to the old chapel congregation. It was not, either for him or for Henry Kittredge, a comfortable arrangement. Looking back on this period, Warren commented on how much easier it was to be rector than to be waiting awkwardly in the wings. As for Kittredge, "The year is still young," he wrote Laughlin a little apprehensively, "but so far nothing but sweetness and light between Matthew and me."[34] And a little later: "He and I have not had a single row." The two Warrens were "as busy as bird-dogs," he reported, and were impressed by the fast pace of school life. "I suppose it *is* fast," he commented, "compared with the pace of an Atlanta parish." Matthew, having recently been in charge of a parish of some eighteen hundred souls in a city undergoing rapid social and economic transformation, would have read these words with wry amusement.

It was a credit to both men that the year ran out peaceably. Between them they agreed that the rector-elect would not involve himself in current policies. During discussion at a masters meeting, he refused a request to give his opinion on a vital issue. On the other hand, he would be consulted when anything affecting his forthcoming administration was being decided. The one occasion when the two men came close to a quarrel shows Kittredge in a characteristic light. At a meeting of the admissions committee (there was only one meeting at that time, compared to the daily meetings over a period of months twenty years later) the name of a certain candidate went around the circle. From each of those present he received a negative vote. All looked to the rector. "He's in," said Henry Kittredge.[35]

Warren had been present but had kept his silence. The next day, feeling this was a decision affecting him and his future, he went to see Kittredge. But he got nowhere. "He's in," Kittredge repeated, and that was the end of that. (The student in question passed through St. Paul's, but in college broke under scholastic pressures.)

For the rector there was coming, as there had for others before him, a season of last things. At a crowded dinner at the Plaza in New York, alumni and their wives gathered to express their affection for the Kittredges. Displaying the gifts of the raconteur that had for so many years made her a luminous presence at the tea table (and a star upon the stage of the Master Players), "Patsy" Kittredge charmed the audience. Then it came time to introduce the rector. The toastmaster announced somewhat apologetically that a sum of money was being presented to Henry in the form of a check, rather than as the more tangible gift the committee had hoped to purchase. "Have no worry, my friend," said the rector as he rose to respond. "There is nothing that so warms the heart of a New England schoolmaster as a little cold cash." Henry Kittredge told stories about boys he remembered and the evening was a great success.

At the end there was no apparent emotion, no strain in the farewells. The future of the school seemed secure; Kittredge was delighted by the thought of retiring to his beloved Barnstable. After forty years of daily responsibility in a boys' boarding school, the prospect of idleness was, he said, "sheer heaven."[36] From John Richards came a homely elegy:

Barnstable is built with her boots in the bay—
There will dwell a teacher who has put his texts away . . .

The parting gift of the trustees was a pair of marine binoculars, through which the ex-rector could observe the free life of the birds, or perhaps keep a weather eye for any wrecks that might pass his way. Upon this son of Harvard, Yale conferred an honorary degree. "Humane in instinct," it described him, "gifted with humor, wise in administration." The *Herald Tribune* noted the retirement of a great teacher. He threw out in abundance, it said, those "generous hints" which could be considered the substance of all true education. "His subject was English, but it might have been almost anything, for the example of the man, the wisdom implicit in his bearing and action, was the contribution which inspired above everything else his students' minds."

At Barnstable the little house on Pine Lane, to which he had gone so avidly for refreshment and rest during his years of work, became the center of life through the four seasons. It was a rambling sort of place. The living room with its heavy black beams and large chimney was the original structure dating from the early eighteenth century; beyond this, later additions stretched out, built and paid for as royalties from his books came in. A little apart was his study, with its large desk, its books, its walls covered with prints of sailing vessels. Here, in letters written in his elegant small handwriting, he kept touch with his many friends, and with the fruits of a wide reading filled the pages of his large, leather-bound "common-place books." Behind the house was the barn, where he would go over lovingly, like a man sorting out his treasure, the pieces of driftwood he collected on the beaches.

Matthew Warren sent him down firewood—good New Hampshire logs, not the Cape Cod scrub, to serve in the long winters. Family and old boys came by. He returned rarely to the school, and when he died in 1967, at the age of seventy-seven, it was as one who, having enjoyed life fully, was ready to depart.

CHAPTER THIRTEEN

Era of Reform
1954–1964

A Marked Man

Matthew Madison Warren was a West Virginian, born and bred. His family's home was in Beckley (population, 3,000); there, among eight children of whom he was the youngest, he grew to early manhood. It would one day be of importance to St. Paul's School that he carried in his veins the blood of forbears known for their staunch independence—slaveholders, to be sure (in a society of slaveholders), but insistent that none should be sold nor any slave families broken up. For Warrens of the Civil War generation, the arch-enemy was Jefferson Davis.[1]

The Beckley high school knew a bright lad when it saw one. Matthew was graduated at fifteen. Too young to enter college, he continued to study Latin with his high school teacher, passing beyond Vergil through Ovid and Horace. For two years he took odd jobs. These included work in the printing office of a local newspaper, in the engineering department of a coal mine, and playing the Wurlitzer organ at the local movie house. Altogether his was a happy youth, surrounded by family affection, in an environment providing mental stimulus as well as the unstructured time that allows a boy to grow and to become himself.

At seventeen this secure world was shaken by his father's sudden death. A prominent banker and newspaper owner with interests throughout West Virginia, he left an estate encumbered by debt. Before Matthew could seriously contemplate the effect of financial reverses on his own life, a wealthy aunt—inheritor of western lands—stepped forth to assure the payment of his educational expenses, and indeed to make him one of the better-off students at the University of West Virginia.

At the university he sailed through easygoing years. Tall, quick-witted, an accomplished piano player, he was well known on the campus, and he managed, over severe competition, to win the heart of a dazzling Phi Beta Kappa student from Smithfield, Pennsylvania. "The college got little out of me," Warren said years later, "but I got Rebecca Guiher."

Within this confident, outwardly superficial youth the sinews of purpose were forming. He began to catch a glimpse of something beyond college pleasures and easy success; slowly, under a wise counselor, he came to the determination to enter the ministry and then to become a pastor-educator.

To marry while a student at the Virginia Theological Seminary was not permitted; a three-year engagement was stretched to six. After graduation, Warren's rise within the church was rapid. His first post was under Malcolm Peabody, son of Groton's Endicott Peabody, in St. Paul's Church in the wealthy Philadelphia enclave of Chestnut Hill. From Peabody, Warren learned much in matters both pastoral and social, and he came to cherish him as one of his pantheon of teachers and mentors. Afterwards he was called to a parish church in Macon, Georgia; he established the Educational Center for the Diocese of Missouri, and in 1945 stepped into the rectorship of All Saints in Atlanta.

The post was a rich prize, one that could well have consumed the energies of an ambitious man for thirty years. The church's large congregation contained the cream of Atlanta's powerful and wealthy citizens. The city itself was growing rapidly, from some 300,000 when Warren arrived to a million a decade later. Under outstanding mayors it was becoming a model of enlightened southern attitudes toward the black citizenry. The rector strained relations with his own vestry by pushing to integrate his church and by inviting black ministers to preach. Despite controversy, he remained a popular figure. The Matthew Warren of this period was described by *Time* magazine as "a kindly, angular six-footer, who can play both Bach and Boogie-Woogie on the piano and likes to give big coffee parties after church."[2] "As an adversary," it was said by a church paper, "he can be formidable."

Not thirty years, but seven, was the span allowed Warren for his ministry at All Saints. At forty-two he was a marked man; major opportunities, including calls to the deanship of a western cathedral and to a bishopric, were among the possibilities before him. He dug himself deep into the Atlanta community—a man of destiny, but not yet convinced where destiny might lead. And then at one Sunday service a stranger appeared in his congregation, a trustee of St. Paul's School in Concord, who spoke to him quietly while he was disrobing. . . .

Driving Hard

"You drive a very spirited horse and it will be hard for the poor old trustees to keep you in sight . . . I do not believe that the world can, or should be, remade in less than the statutory seven days." So wrote, with a slight note of warning, the chairman of the board, Henry Laughlin, at the end of the new rector's first few months.³ Warren had come into office determined to push a program of modernization and reform at St. Paul's. For more than a decade maintenance had been deferred, new construction had been postponed. Economy had been the watchword under Nash and Kittredge, both in the school's administration and in demands made upon its constituency. After having been $1,400 for twenty-two years, tuition fees had remained at $1,600 since 1947. Apart from the war memorial, no general drive for funds had been conducted among the alumni since the 1920s. A school capable of meeting the new educational and cultural needs of the time was Warren's goal. This required, in his view, an outward aspect reflecting the institution's traditional pride and its underlying wealth.

The rectory, first of all, was to be refurbished. "I hope it has not been a shock to you," Warren wrote Laughlin, after he had seen the new arrangements. "We found it impossible to stop anywhere, as the house doesn't lend itself to working here and not working there."⁴ Not only had basic repairs been undertaken, but the whole building had been redecorated. Worn Oriental rugs gave way to wall-to-wall carpeting; new upholstery took the place of somber and slightly frayed velours. The large desk at which Drury had labored was moved to an upstairs room, and the library was to be used for meetings and social gatherings rather than for lonely meditations.

The house, at least in its lower floor, was now more a public than a private place. The whole was indicative of the new rector's determination to bring a modern look to the school. What he said about this first renovation—"We found it impossible to stop anywhere"—would characterize his administration in many fields.

To increase the tuition seemed to Warren a cardinal necessity. For Nash, the objective had been to lower it; he cared to make the school more accessible to the kind of middle-income families he knew in Cambridge, and to impress on the sons of the wealthy from Pittsburgh and New York the need for austerity in their life styles. Nash was gently but firmly rebuffed by the trustees, already hard-pressed to meet the school's operating expenses. Warren, with his insistence on an increase, ran into no less sturdy opposition. He carried the day for his cause, but not without coming into conflict with Henry A. Laughlin, chairman of the board.

Laughlin was president of Boston's influential publishing house, Houghton Mifflin, and a member of a family whose name was prominently associated with big steel. In his large and beautifully appointed Georgian home in Concord, Massachusetts, he would bow before the family portrait over the mantlepiece with filial piety, combined with a practical respect for his forbear's laudable ability to make money. Henry Laughlin in

"You drive a very spirited horse." *The seventh rector, Matthew Warren,
with Rebecca Warren in the rectory garden.*

Now more a public than a private place. *The rectory in the school's modern phase.*

all his relations with other men, and in his general view of the world, was detached, witty, and given to a charming irreverence. He had a deep love for St. Paul's, coupled with a determination that it should not change too rapidly or too conspicuously from its old ways.

Coming onto the board in Drury's administration, a personal friend of the rector, he found the appointment "too wonderful to be true." "Dear old friend," Drury wrote him in response, "it meant so much to all of us at the rectory to have you beneath that roof. The school and that house are always to be yours."[5] The letter was signed "Ever affectionately." Drury died nine months after it was written, and Laughlin never gave his heart in quite the same way to any of Drury's successors. Following Reeve Schley as chairman in 1952, he looked on Nash as a brilliant stranger, and treated Henry Kittredge with deferential courtesy, always faintly uneasy lest Henry grow more fond of Barnstable than of Millville.

About Warren he had at first some reserve. His punctilious sense of style was offended when twice in the same letter Warren used the expression "you may be sure," and when his thanks for a small gift seemed excessive. The two men, after taking each other's measure, contrived a relationship of hard-hitting candor that makes their correspondence lively reading. Beneath the outward "joshing" there was to develop over the next years a true affection. As these aging warriors faced the uncertainties of the period, a care for each other—reinforced by friendship between the two "Beckies," their wives—would continue after Laughlin's retirement until his death in 1977.

For the present, on the question of a tuition raise, Laughlin's convictions were firm. He, and other members of the board, saw in a low tuition the preservation of something old and fundamental in the St. Paul's tradition—a denial of the idea that the school was only for the rich, and a suggestion that even the rich should not flaunt their wealth. Warren countered with the argument that St. Paul's should at least charge as much as other comparable schools and that it should live in a manner befitting its constituency. The less advantaged, in his view, should have access, not through a tuition kept artificially low, but through ample scholarships provided by increased endowment and more highly organized annual giving. Scholarships, he foresaw, would pay the entire tuition of a certain number of deprived students—including in some cases their clothes and travel money—and ought not to be considered merely a means of mitigating the tuition load on hard-pressed middle-income families.

The school Warren envisaged was one where the rich would be pressed to give, and from which the poor would not be excluded. In addition, he wanted higher tuition to pay for faculty salaries raised to what he considered a competitive and also a dignified level. He could never be persuaded by the argument that perquisites provided by the school, such as free housing, meals, and full scholarships for qualified sons of faculty members, were a substitute for adequate salaries.

At the board meeting of January 1955 the rector won his victory, as important for what it symbolized of his attitude and approach to education as it was in its effect upon the immediate budget. Over Laughlin's reluctance, the annual fee was raised from $1,600 to $1,800. Subsequently, Laughlin instructed the school's business manager to hold up the announcement. Warren was furious. A heated telephone conversation took place, and next morning Laughlin, having come up from Boston, was at the door of the rector's study. The confrontation cleared the air. Afterwards there was full, if sometimes stormy, cooperation; and Warren, from that day, was plainly marked to be a strong rector.

A Building Program

Warren's next attack was upon the physical condition of the school plant. In his first annual report he pointed out that Dr. Ferguson's final, urgent advice had been the building of a new Middle. "It is my somewhat shaky hope," said Warren, "that similar requests from me will not be so delayed." The Middle was, indeed, in the process of being demolished when he became rector, and he rejoiced in seeing its successor rising upon the same site. A report, undertaken at his initiative by a nationally known management and planning firm, judged the days of the lower school and the Big Study to be numbered. In time, and in their own way, both would disappear. For the moment Warren was more interested in a major—and for the school quite radical—construction project.

This was the building of a modern exercise house, a gymnasium with an indoor "cage" for sports. How could such a thing be necessary? For generations it had been part of St. Paul's folklore that in an abundance of outdoor space and a vigorous and bracing climate, God had provided everything essential to the physical development of young men. A gymnasium might be a useful annex for such limited purposes as gymnastics or early rowing on the machines, but the suggestion that the New Hampshire weather was not always ideal, and that there were weeks when outdoor sports were impossible, was not immediately welcomed.

Skepticism was heightened when it was discovered that central to any new exercise house would be facilities for basketball—"Not basketball!" cried a sizeable minority of the trustees—and that central locker rooms and showers for the whole student body would be provided. The latter was in direct contravention of the long-established custom of having boys keep their "old clothes" in their rooms, to which they imparted a characteristic, and nostalgically remembered, odor.

The school's hundredth anniversary was to fall in 1956; Warren proposed that the principal fund-raising activity connected with the event be devoted to financing the new exercise house. The trustees were at first dubious. Was not such an objective too narrow for so grand an occasion? Laughlin was "flabbergasted" by the amount of money that would have to be raised for the purpose—approximately $3 million. In the Alumni Association, opposition developed to a project so much at odds with cherished illusions. The alumni agreed, however, to raise the money on condition that the trustees determine to what purpose it should be used. By this time the trustees had been persuaded by Warren's insistent logic that an exercise house was an indispensable need of the school.

So the new gymnasium was built. It stood sensibly on the main route between the center of the school and the lower grounds, an unadorned, barnlike structure of cement block, to which was attached a sort of over-sized Quonset hut containing a fine space for track, tennis and other sports. Besides the basketball courts in the main building there were specialized facilities for boxing, wrestling, shooting and other diversions. The Gates Room, a handsome central space, was well adapted to entertainment of visiting teams and to other school functions.[6] As much as anything else, this building symbolized the seventh rector's concern for modern social values and his sympathy with the mores of contemporary youth.

Other building enterprises followed. Structures that had withstood staunchly the usage of years were refurbished room by room. Hargate, the dining hall for the Middle School, was elaborately made over into an art center; the lower school study was converted to a dormitory named for Nash, and the gas house converted to a freezer locker and then to a post office. The old upper was demolished, and to the rear of the new upper school were added two handsome dining halls, thus centralizing all kitchen facilities. Three new dormitories, for sixty boys in all, each with a house for a married master and rooms for a single, were then proposed by the rector.

These were envisioned as standing in an apple orchard at the western end of the school grounds. The trustees engaged a well-known contemporary architect and planner, Edward Larrabee Barnes, who recommended that they be placed, instead, at the center of the school: low, recessive structures of dark brick extending from either side of the historic rectory. By this scheme, subsequently adopted, the school was saved the universal plight of mid-century towns and cities—proliferation at the extremes while the center became progressively more vacant.

Building on sloping land which the Olmsteds had judged to be unfeasible, Barnes reemphasized the main street of the school's earliest years.

A major act of construction remained. The lower school, built in the late nineteenth century on the site of the original school house, was an imposing pile loved by many, but in its Dickensian austerities, its echoing hallways and high, draughty dormitories, unlikely to win the hearts of visiting parents or their offspring. Warren was determined the building should be replaced by one more habitable and sunny. Barnes was again employed as architect, contriving for an adjacent site an oddly composed series of forms which again strengthened the main axis. An interior street ran down the center, connecting separate dormitories, masters' houses and apartments. The building's expressive shapes, said one alumnus, made it look like something which had been dug out of the ground.

The building was named Kittredge, recalling the man who had made the old lower a place of vivid delights. His widow, coming from Barnstable for the dedication in 1969, declared she liked it all, and regaled lower schoolers of that day with tales of great events during the years she had lived there. Boys of the first and second forms trudged back and forth across the lawn separating the old and the new buildings, carrying belongings from their abandoned alcoves. "And then the great mass of the old lower was forever dark," it was recorded, "except in the memories of the hundreds who had dwelled there during its seventy-eight-year history."[7]

Toward Racial Integration

Progress appeared also upon a different front.

When Warren was still rector-elect, before he moved to Concord, Charles Dickey had stopped by for the night at Little Boar's Head. "If you integrate the school," he asked suddenly, "how will you do it?"[8] Warren replied he did not know, but he felt he should not begin with a black student. The matter was left open, but Warren knew he had the support of the trustees in his ultimate decision.

In December 1956, Warren sent a memorandum to the board informing them that the Reverend John Walker, of St. Mary's Church, Detroit, would become a history teacher at the school the following autumn. Five candidates had been interviewed and Walker was unquestionably the best. "The unusual aspect of the situation," the rector continued, "is that Mr. Walker is a Negro."

Thus, at a stroke, Warren broke the color line that had existed at St. Paul's. The school's admission policy had made no discrimination in regard to race, but the fact that black boys were unlikely to apply was accepted as a fact of life. To search out a few and to make them bear the burden of being first seemed to Warren a dubious procedure. A black master, on the other hand, would be mature and would be able to meet whatever strains occurred. He would, moreover, prepare the way for students of his own race.

John Walker, whom Warren chose for this role, was an appealing young man, then in his early thirties: articulate, gentle in his ways, and with a clear sense of where he, and his fellow blacks, were going. The boys found in him a first-rate teacher and a sympathetic counselor. From the alumni came a few—surprisingly few—outcries of dismay. More widespread, perhaps, was the feeling that Warren had become a "controversial figure"; but the rector had grown used to that in Atlanta and it did not faze him. Walker left in 1966 to become canon of the National Cathedral in Washington and then bishop of Washington. He returned often to the school to confer with minority students, and in 1972 became a member of its board of trustees.

Two years after Walker's coming to the school as master, the first black student, Luther Hilton Foster, took his place in the St. Paul's community.

The Religious Dimension

Warren was a man of action; but he was above all an educator, a moralist, a social philosopher. He stepped into the role of rector determined to fill it in all possible dimensions: a manager and administrator, the director of a sizeable physical domain, but more than that—a lord spiritual of the realm, ready to face up to the most threatening of secular powers.

From the beginning, he felt that the school was part of an America undergoing vast social strains. The unappeasable drive for civil rights had already begun in the South. He knew that the school could not escape the implications. And he sensed, too, other revolutions in the making: the growing disillusionment of youth with an inherited order that did not seem to answer its varied, often inexpressible needs; the drive for women's rights; the urge for personal fulfillment through art; and the increasing recognition of the role of sexuality in the development of the young human being. Warren was not a reformer in the sense that he wanted to seize on any one of these and ride in some particular direction. But he was a seer, delicately attuned to emerging issues; and he was a practical ruler who saw their consequences for his little realm, no longer secure against the penetrations of change.

"Our task," he said at the beginning of his rule, "relates to a nation's necessity and a culture's hunger."[9] And to the students in a first Labor Day Letter, he presented the school's responsibility to the individual in terms that the young were only beginning to understand. "Come to us with a high sense of the importance of your own 'self,' and the importance of other 'selves' who are here," he said. Then he added the religious implication. "Remember that the significance of 'self' is the gift of God who made us after his own image." St. Paul's, he maintained, had never been concerned with creating the single type, whether marked by dress, interests or beliefs, and now more than ever, individuality was to be recognized and cultivated. "Surely there is no 'self' which the school and the church does not recognize as being unique, precious and important."

The religious dimension was, in his judgment, paramount. It was through religion that the gifts and graces of youth, the animal spirits of healthy human beings, could be brought to serve ideal ends; it was in chapel that the polarities of old and new, of tradition and change, could be reconciled. Yet adolescence, he realized, was not an essentially religious time. "Young men in their teens feel confident, they are vigorous, their lease on life seems to be permanent. . . . How hard it is to call on a Saviour when you don't feel you need one."[10]

This sympathy with the dilemma of youth did not leave him, even in the hardest times. As the students turned increasingly against the Christian experience and view of life, he believed they were searching rather than being wholly negative. "I personally do not feel our students are trying to get out of anything," he said, when the agitations turned against chapel attendance. "The truth is, they are trying to get more significantly into something."[11]

The hundredth anniversary was not only the occasion for a drive for funds. Significantly, it was the occasion also for a reevaluation of the place of the church school in contemporary society. It was early determined that the crucial year should not be celebrated by showy events, but by an enlargement and deepening of the school's traditional ceremonies. In the autumn term Robert Birley, the headmaster of Eton, took up his residence at the school and led a continuing seminar on values implicit in modern secondary education. In the spring, Anniversary was planned on a large scale, attracting an unprecedented influx of alumni and their families. Bishop Henry Sherrill, so long a friendly power behind the school, preached the sermon in a chapel crowded to its last seat, with an overflow in the cloisters and the old chapel. At luncheon afterwards, in a tent beside the pond, the St. Paul's family paused—before dispersing in a cavalcade of autos—to hear from an alumnus an evocation of the great names, the enduring images, of the school's past.[12]

But it was in the autumn of the anniversary year that the most far-reaching event took place. This was Matthew Warren's own, and he planned it with the ardor of a churchman and a scholar. A symposium on

In a chapel crowded to its last seat. *Procession at the hundredth Anniversary service.*

Detached, witty and with charming irreverence. *Henry Laughlin, Chairman of the Board, with Matthew Warren, 1956.*

the future of the church school brought representatives from two dozen schools to hear the world-famous theologian Paul J. Tillich present an original and stimulating paper on the relations between religion and education.[13] What Tillich said that day would be read and debated over the country and in educational institutions throughout the Western world. Two decades later, when traditional concepts had been shattered, educators and churchmen would still be reading Tillich's message. Did it hold the light they were seeking? Or had time made necessary some new formulation of the answers—and indeed of the questions—which Tillich propounded?

The theologian's approach was radical and contemporary in that it saw doubt, not as antithetical to faith but as an essential element within it. Biblical and Protestant faith, he declared, "must be seen as *comprising itself and the doubt about itself.*" For this reason there was risk inherent in every act of faith, and from every risk arose the need for a kind of existential courage. Put in another way, humanism and religion were not at odds. Modern Christianity embraced the humanist's principle of identifying Christ with the universal Logos—the existence of everything that is: the question *and* the answer. It thus opened up all human possibilities and provided opportunities for the individual to develop in ultimate freedom.

The church school Tillich saw as a kind of laboratory, in which the largest issues of the relationship between Christianity and culture, the church and the world, could be brought into a preliminary equilibrium. What Tillich called the "inductive method" was the way to that equilibrium, and it was best exemplified in the growth of the young person. The youth begins in a state of "dreamy innocence" of critical questions, a state not of long duration in contemporary culture and one from which, while it lasts, he should not be awakened. But with questions must come answers; from symbols must come truth. "The great task of the religious educator is to transform the primitive literalism with regard to religious symbols into a conceptual interpretation, without destroying the power of the symbols." Throughout civilization, and through the length of a man's life, these stages of transformation would proceed.

Thus Tillich at the school's Anniversary, as had Eliot and Nash in their day, confronted the essential nature of religious education. No one had done it in more radical terms or with so fundamental a comprehension of the humanist tradition. Nevertheless, the sweeping secularization of the 1970s would make Tillich's formulation appear too narrow. Did "religious symbols" still exist to any meaningful extent? Could one any longer describe the task of education as the process of transcending them? Tillich would undoubtedly have answered that what he meant by religious symbols are part of human development and are independent of historic Christian forms. The child, and then the man, moves from primitivism to truth in every generation; truth always involves both faith and doubt, and always carries traces of its divine origin.

The Pressure of Numbers

As an educator, Warren was challenged by a wholly new situation: the generation of children born immediately after World War II had come to school age and were knocking in unprecedented numbers at the doors of secondary, and then higher, educational institutions. It was a generation whose fathers had benefitted from the GI Bill of Rights, which opened to them the college experience as World War I had made high school education almost universal. Now all were set on getting a higher education for their own children, and getting it, so far as possible, under conditions of excellence.

For St. Paul's, this meant an end to the dearth in applications that had troubled Nash and Kittredge through the 1940s and 1950s. Nash knew years when the school sank below desired numbers. Kittredge would admit cheerfully that, in his attempts to fill the school, he was "scraping the bottom of the barrel." He created a new post, Director of Admissions, and dispatched the incumbent to drum up trade in communities more distant and more varied than those from which St. Paul's had drawn its clientele in the past. Now Warren's problem was that of choice and selection. He set up elaborate screening procedures; and the westward trek of his admissions officers was more to make certain that St. Paul's was getting the best of the available pool of youngsters than to ensure that its places were filled.

Inevitably, competition arose between the sons of alumni and the new crop of applicants. The practice of admitting students on the basis of early applications—the "waiting list" that had so constrained and troubled Drury—had faded into disuse, and the individual's capacity to benefit from the St. Paul's experience became the ruling criterion. From the school's older constituency came cries of outrage as "favorite sons" were rejected by the admissions committee.

As early as 1955, Laughlin was writing Warren: "As the pressures become greater I become convinced that St. Paul's School has a larger obligation to its alumni . . . than has seemingly been recognized by the [admission] decisions this year."[14] Warren was unrepentant. Indeed, he saw that pressures in the times ahead would be "well nigh unsupportable," and for the following year he promised little in the way of "less torture." The chairman's suggestion that he and the rector sit down "very quietly," he termed euphemistic—as if any consultation on this subject must be noisy and inconclusive.

Yet Warren was deeply imbued with the sense of St. Paul's as a community, an organic structure embodying the past as well as the present, a place where young men, varied in their gifts and their approaches to life, could learn from each other. He was not intent (despite charges to the contrary) on making St. Paul's a mere powerhouse of the intellectual élite. To admit boys clearly capable of academic work of a high order was, of course, desirable—"a good school," he said, "is one hard to get into, hard to stay in, but ever so valuable if you do."[15] Yet proven academic ability was but a single element in the decisions of the admissions committee. If St. Paul's needed scholars, it also needed artists, debaters, good writers, athletes, as well as those whose development was still a matter of promise and hope. Excellence, to be a meaningful concept, meant excellence over a wide diversity of fields, and not in studies alone.

"We have not sought to comb the country for the very ablest boys attainable," Warren assured the alumni, "nor have we used scholarship funds to entice the unusually able boy to our school."[16] Scholarships had been used, rather, to make it possible for all those selected by the admissions committee—the academically brilliant and the less brilliant—to come to St. Paul's. Moreover, Warren remained a strong advocate for maintaining the two lower forms, though selecting still-immature and unproven boys put St. Paul's at a competitive disadvantage with four-year schools. He liked to develop relationships between the youngest boys and those in the upper forms, even if the youngest did not always turn out to be the brightest. He was insistent, too, that the lower schoolers' soprano voices were indispensable to the school choir.

At the other end of the scale, admissions to college, the postwar flood of students was also causing difficulties. As the colleges found their applications soaring, the mediocre student, however worthy and attractive in himself or as a member of the community, was often denied admission. The same alumnus who would have been the loudest in his outcries had his son been turned down by St. Paul's now took out on the school his sense of grievance if the boy failed admission to the college of his choice—which was often the college of the father's choice. The school encouraged consideration of a wide list of colleges hitherto unvisited by Concordians; but these, finding themselves suddenly favored by the boom in applications, were sometimes more narrowly insistent on high academic grades than the larger and more famous institutions.

The problem was illustrated in the relation of St. Paul's (along with other independent schools) to Yale. The rise in the standards of public education, combined with the growing anti-élitism of the times, made the

high schools an inviting field for recruitment. Yale's highly visible director of admissions, R. Inslee (Inky) Clark, liked to point out that the Bronx
High School of Science could alone provide 200 applicants yearly of the
highest intellectual caliber, while he maintained direct contact with 3,000
out of 25,000 secondary schools in the country. To lean too heavily on
such schools as St. Paul's and Choate—whatever their past connections
with Yale—seemed to him foolish as well as unfair.

Besides, there was an old complaint about students from St. Paul's:
that although they showed high grades on admission to Yale, they often
finished poorly. At college, said one critic, they would suffer "not orgias-
tic self-destruction, but rather a nonchalant, unhurried delinquency."[17]

In vain Charles Dickey, member of both the Yale and the St. Paul's
boards, exerted his influence. Warren, meeting with Yale's president,
Kingman Brewster, found the kind of respect one strong man feels for
another, but was not able to change the immediate situation. In 1965, the
admissions to Harvard and Yale were eighteen and six respectively; in
1967, nineteen and seven. Both of these figures were low compared with
those of an earlier time.

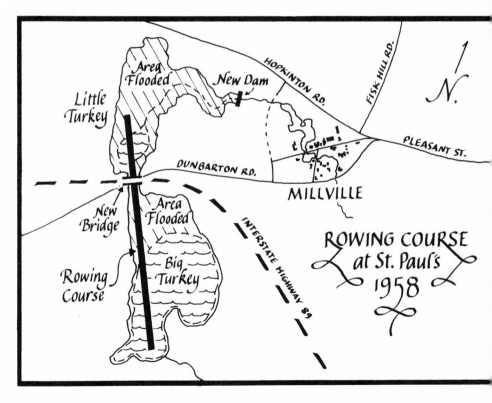

The Curriculum Reexamined

Within the school, discontents with the forms and substance of education began to be expressed in the early 1960s. Disciplinary problems at school and dropouts from college were early warnings of shockwaves to come. Sensing the new mood, Warren in 1961 initiated a broad inquiry into the St. Paul's curriculum—the term "curriculum" being interpreted to include not only the academic program but all the rules and procedures affecting work at the school. At a two-day faculty meeting before the autumn term of 1961, the heads of departments presented the substance of their courses to a panel of outside advisers. Before Christmas the panel was reconvened, and discussion groups of masters and students met throughout the year. The explosion of contemporary knowledge was discussed; the ferment in science; the revolution in mathematics as well as the changing attitudes of students.

Subjects which had once been contained under a familiar heading, such as a modern language, now extended into broad literary and cultural by-ways. The method of teaching a language included a specialized language laboratory, a proliferation of advanced special courses, and flexible student–teacher relationships. Underlying everything was an awareness of intellectual standards well beyond those required of previous student generations. The bottom half in scholarly rank were, by 1960, equal in ability and achievement to the ablest boys of a decade earlier.

The results of this reappraisal showed themselves in a broad increase in student options. The "holy five" of the ancient curriculum—mathematics, English, science, language, and history—would ultimately break down into a list of almost a hundred choices. No less important was a residual feeling that nothing in school life was beyond reconsideration, provided it led to a more congenial atmosphere for learning. Warren saw the danger of merely adding quantitatively to the students' workload. What was necessary was to reassess fundamentals and to make the additions qualitative. He saw the need for more continuous stretches of free time, for providing opportunities for more independent work, more reading, more writing, more specialization when that would be beneficial; and, not least, more leisure for a boy "to explore the notion of himself."[18] Mealtimes, for example, would become flexible; study hall and even athletic requirements would be reduced.

Two major curricular innovations were introduced: the first, independent studies for St. Paul's sixth formers; the second, an Advanced Study program for New Hampshire high school students during the summer months. The first of these, independent studies, allowed students in their last year to free themselves from normal academic routines and, under the direction of a master, to work on projects of their choosing.

Sixth formers would soon be found working in Concord's health and mental institutions, examining an issue of seventeenth-century theology, painting a picture or building a musical instrument, teaching Latin in an elementary school, or assisting a legislator in Washington.

Warren's imagination went beyond this. He conceived of a school where students would spend a year or more abroad, returning to Millville as to an intellectual and spiritual home, where they could validate their experiences, renew their friendships, and shape future plans. Such a school would be numerically a good deal larger than the St. Paul's facilities could contain, with students coming and going, never all of them in residence together at one time.

The second innovation, the Advanced Studies program, touched the regular students only indirectly, but it was of major importance in itself and it would significantly affect the St. Paul's curriculum. The school grounds, deserted in summer, suggested the possibility of a session for highly motivated students from the New Hampshire high schools. Under Alan N. Hall, in 1958, the first such session was launched, with a hundred students from fifty-two public and parochial schools. They lived as a community in school dormitories and under the normal school routines of chapel, athletics and extracurricular activities. The school's ablest teachers stayed to instruct them, along with carefully selected masters from other secondary schools. A group of interns, at college or recently graduated, derived their first teaching experience within this challenging atmosphere. The students were pushed hard, taught to study intensively and to take responsibility for managing their own time. When the six-week course was over, most of them felt they had grown a yard; many, previously undecided, were inspired to go on to college.[19]

The fallout of the summer session was felt by the school in improved relations between Millville and the New Hampshire community; it was felt, also, in revitalized methods of instruction. If the Advanced Studies program benefitted from the St. Paul's traditions and procedures—and not least from the beauty of the physical surroundings—the school's regular students benefitted from a deepened philosophy of teaching. In the highly condensed courses of the program, with most of the sessions running for several hours at a stretch, it had become necessary to engage in conceptual thinking, to probe to the heart of a matter rather than to drill the student in peripheral details. This reaching for fundamentals had been one of the chief desiderata of the 1961 curricular review.

For the summer session of 1961, thirty-five girls were admitted to the program. The number was chosen because it conveniently filled one regular school dormitory. The reinterpretation of the word "student," to include the female as well as the male, was undertaken for reasons that were beginning to be felt throughout the private schools. The Middle was the residence of this first contingent—the new Middle, unfortunately. One would have liked to imagine, as the girls took over their rooms, the groans of the old building where Willard Scudder and Charles Knox had once lived.

The presence of these girls, wrote Matthew Warren, "added greatly to the interest of everyone, particularly the boys."[20] This conclusion was not forgotten by the rector, who was already contemplating a fundamental change in St. Paul's School, compared with which the other side effects of the Advanced Studies program would seem minor.

A New Pattern of Athletics

Winds of change—winds which Warren was seeking to anticipate and to meet—manifested themselves also in the field of athletics. Through the 1950s and 1960s, long-established patterns of athletic competition were breaking down for reasons that alumni and trustees found difficult to understand. Basically, the same forces were at work as elsewhere in the school—a desire among the students for wider options and new forms of activity; and there were perhaps also present preliminary and unexpressed symptoms of that desire to confound their elders which was to show itself so strongly before the 1960s ran out. So hallowed an activity as football began to lose its appeal. Soccer, and then lacrosse, became increasingly popular. Most significantly, the club system of intramural sports, cherished in Millville for three-quarters of a century, showed signs of obsolescence.

It was easy, at first, to assume that the rector, as a newcomer and not himself athletically inclined, had failed to grasp the nature of the club system. But when a committee of the trustees was appointed to look broadly into the athletic program, they observed for themselves what had already been reported by the administration. Regulations still made sport compulsory for all, but a greater variety of activities were being pursued, and a large number of games were being played against outside schools. At the board meeting of April 1958, the value of the club system, at least as the exclusive form of athletic competition, was reexamined. The minutes of that meeting record "a lengthy discussion without conclusion."

Two years later, a second trustees committee reported. Acknowledging the existing system to be unsatisfactory, it proposed a varsity team for each sport, with intramural contests taking place only between the lower teams. Could the clubs survive, being thus relegated to a second place? Could the varsity players escape the injurious effects of being elevated to the rank of stars? The committee's recommendations were tabled, but the forces at work could not be halted. In the next years various changes were effectuated as the students became more conscious of their interests and more articulate in promoting them.

These changes were not in the direction of increased emphasis on sports. This was no return to the athletic craze that had dominated St. Paul's and other schools at the start of the century. If more games against outside schools were advocated, it was less because of a desire to create a star system than to curb the isolation in which St. Paul's was felt to exist. At other levels the spirit of competitiveness was damped down. A profusion of "minor sports" evidenced the students' growing emphasis on individuality, and the athletic schedule became increasingly complex, as the curriculum already had been fragmented. By the late 1960s, organized sports were no longer compulsory for all students. Top players of squash and tennis were being given "letters" indistinguishable from those given to the giants of the football and hockey teams.

In two areas, hockey and rowing, major commitments were made to strengthen sports long associated with St. Paul's. A group of alumni, feeling the school teams to be at a competitive disadvantage with schools that could begin their practice early on artificial ice, proposed a modern rink. The trustees at first demurred. A rink would be expensive to maintain. Also it would imply that the Millville climate had deteriorated, not being so frigid as it was formerly. The rink was built with special contributions and named for Malcolm Kenneth Gordon; but it was found subject to mechanical woes requiring a second effort at fund-raising to enclose it against the wind and sun. In the end, the school teams found themselves playing indoors on artificial ice expertly maintained. The rinks on the school pond were reduced from six to three, and often these would not get set up before mid-January.

As for rowing, it had to be accepted that banishment from the waters of Long Pond was irreversible. Yet the makeshift arrangements on Big Turkey were unsatisfactory. A dam built to raise the level of the waters resulted in complaints of flooding from the few remaining owners of riparian lands, and still failed to meet the need for a full-length, unobstructed course. A challenging opportunity was presented when a new, limited-access highway was planned by the state. With results as beneficial as those achieved when the Hopkinton and Dunbarton roads were relocated under Drury, state authorities were persuaded to skirt the school and build a bridge at the narrow neck of land between Big and Little Turkey. In return for the donation of land, the bridge was designed with spans sufficiently wide to permit crews to pass beneath. The school then undertook to dredge and widen what had been a marshy stream connecting the two ponds. In 1958, the Turkeys were united in one sweep of unbroken water, offering the prospect of an ideal rowing course within easy walking distance of the school (see the map on page 312).

The crews first rowed the new course on Race Day, 1958, with spectators cheering from a wooded promontory downstream from the new bridge. Unfortunately, the troubles of the earth-shapers were not at an end. As so often when the course of nature is altered, unforeseen difficulties arose. The banks of the channel between the two Turkeys slipped, requiring repeated and expensive dredging. Floating islands of algae and debris formed in Little Turkey. Logs cut after the hurricane of 1938, submerged for protection against rot, now rose unwanted to the surface. Finally, severe droughts in 1964 and 1965 so reduced the water-table that the city of Concord laid pipes from the school's new rowing grounds to Long Pond, pumping precious supplies out of the Turkeys.

Not until the late 1960s was the new course stabilized, and secure for the time being against outside demands.

With spectators cheering from a wooded promontory. *Race Day at Turkey Pond.*

The Fire Within

The night of January 21, 1961, was one of the coldest in New Hampshire's twentieth-century history, twenty-five degrees below zero. At evening the school was gathered in Memorial Hall, absorbed in a film, *Shake Hands with the Devil.* In the Big Study a single master, the art teacher William Abbe, was in his apartment when he noticed smoke rising through the hall outside. He knocked at the doors of the few apartments carved from the old labyrinth of classrooms; finding no one there, nor anyone elsewhere in the building, he called the fire department, grabbed a few of his possessions, and escaped to the outdoors.

Across the street, at the rectory, Matthew Warren was still unaware of the fire working its way through the walls of the Big Study. On the threshold, alarmed and shaken, Abbe stammered out the news. Seizing him by the shoulders, Warren demanded assurance that no one was trapped in the gathering smoke and fire.

It was already too late to save the building. Firemen battled against the insuperable odds of sub-zero temperatures, the water from their hoses freezing in grotesquely formed icicles, while the interior became an inferno. Late in the night, flames creeping unseen in the vault of the cloisters were discovered by one of the boys who, by giving alarm, undoubtedly saved the chapel. The night, despite its coldness, was still; even a slight wind would have spread the destruction. Awed by the fury of the conflagration, students, faculty, and all the school community stood silently in the arctic cold. "There was nothing to do," wrote one student to his parents, "but to stare unbelievingly for an hour or so at that magnificent wreck, which continued to throw 200-foot flames into a pitch-dark night, and then to go home and to convince one another that it was true."[21]

The next morning, encased in ice, the ruins of the old building lay forlornly at the center of the school. The Big Study had outlived its usefulness—classrooms, the rector's study, many of its former services had been transferred to other buildings; but it had stood as an important focal point and gathering place. Besides the few masters' apartments and a dormitory to accommodate the more youthful of returning alumni, it contained the lofty study hall, paneled and refurbished as a memorial to Dr. Ferguson, which had served as an antechamber to the chapel and as a place to gather afterwards for reports. The "tuck shop" and post office below, the arcade and the brick terrace in front, made it a visible point of attraction where knots of boys could be found at all hours. With the building's destruction, a subtle disorientation, an extended search for new patterns of traffic and assemblage, would mark the school's life for several years to come.

Fire had thus struck a second time at the heart of St. Paul's. Unlike the burning of the school house in 1878, this conflagration had no clearly ascertainable cause. Here was no bolt from heaven, but a more subtle force working from within. The investigations following the fire, the protracted questioning of individual boys, created a severe breach in morale; and when two minor and hastily arrested blazes subsequently developed, nerves were drawn taut. The origin of the fire was never officially determined. Writing five years later, Matthew Warren commented that the condition of the school was a happy one: for the first time no student in residence had been on the scene during the fearful January night; none had lived through its demoralizing aftermath.

The fires of 1878 and 1961 both tested the faith of the community, and the tests were characteristic of the different centuries in which they occurred. One was a blow of nature, comparable to that which destroyed a farmer's store of grain or flooded his fields; the second was from within, apparently the result of a human failing. Coit had gathered the strength of the community and had displayed his own rugged force in combatting the blow and making a new beginning. For Matthew Warren, as for all the leaders of his generation, the task was more difficult. No longer was the wrath of a righteous God to be appeased or to be suffered with faith. The challenge was more complex—a culture imbued with contradictory and often self-destructive impulses. It had to be faced, at best, with a devout intelligence.

As the troubles of the next decade gathered, that January night would seem to be symbolic of the way communities suffer for reasons they only partially comprehend, and from which they recover in ways not capable of being foreseen.

CHAPTER FOURTEEN

A Darkling Plain
1964 – 1969

Halfway Mark

In the autumn of 1964, Matthew Warren left for a sabbatical, spending the winter and the following spring in Rome and Greece. He had been rector ten years; he foresaw seven or eight years before retirement. On the eve of his departure, he told the trustees of three major objectives he hoped to accomplish in the time remaining. These were: replacement of the old lower school by a modern building; establishment of a girls' school in close proximity to St. Paul's; and creation of a foreign residency program as part of the regular curriculum. The new lower school was indeed built; the latter two aims were diverted by rapidly developing events. The St. Paul's to which Warren returned was a changed, or changing, school; and the sabbatical turned out to be a watershed in his rectorship.

The first ten years had been a time of modernization in all aspects of school life: in administrative procedures; in the physical plant; in studies, sports and leisure activities. Newly established fellowships (named for the donor, Mrs. William H. Conroy) brought stimulating visitors to spend more or less protracted periods at the school, meeting with students in formal and informal sessions. The option of spending a year abroad, and growing emphasis on the enjoyment of art, freshened the old Millville airs. Nevertheless the remaining years of Warren's tenure were to be a time of slow-burning discontents culminating in outbursts at the end of the decade. It may seem paradoxical that revolution should thus have followed reform. In fact, students of social history have found the great upheavals almost invariably to occur when liberties are in process of being enlarged and when the lot of the population has already been improved.

Events at the decade's end, subdued and small-scaled though they were, followed a classic pattern. As in major revolutionary movements, a small group of intellectuals was the precursor of later, drastic acts. As in other such movements, too, the liberal leader who had foreseen the cataclysm and moved to avert it was branded with the mark of an old order.

The "revolution" at St. Paul's, 1968–1970, would be significant in its long-range results. However vague many of the students' immediate demands, they grew out of a determination to create a new kind of community. From the pain of the time, from its unpleasant and (occasionally) its amusing aspects, came such basic residues as coeducation, the secularization of the social order, new forms of study, a new athletic system, and a new approach to discipline. Warren stood at the center of the maelstrom, giving it meaning and dignity; but he paid the price reformers have invariably suffered in similar historic situations. He was himself too intelligent—as the students were on the whole too fair-minded—to let the growing tension develop into a personal confrontation. But as events of the second half of the 1960s unfolded, the seeds of personal tragedy were implicit.

By 1964, Warren had settled into the saddle of his "high-spirited horse": a rector in the grand manner whose mark on St. Paul's would evidently be deep. In the eyes of the students, he preserved the monarchical character of his greatest predecessors. But he was a monarch of a very modern kind, exceptionally sensitive to current states of mind and skilled in contemporary techniques of management and administration. He appeared a forbidding figure, standing tall, clear in his views, a man ready to listen but, when a matter had been settled, not to be lightly contradicted.

The chapel was for him, as it had been for the first Coit and for Drury, the stage on which his personality was manifested and his authority defined. From the rector's stall at the rear of the long chapel, he overlooked a congregation every one of whose members he knew intimately and over whose lives, in their spiritual as well as their material aspects, he held sway. His sermons were brief and direct. If they lacked the ultimate magic of eloquence, they were grounded in a lucid faith and spoke clearly to shared experience. After the daily service, in the ceremony of "reports," he was the image of a man briskly and competently in charge. If the students did not "love" this rector, they respected, and trusted and, not infrequently, feared him.

Tempering this fear was awareness of another side of Warren's nature, the quality of being both modest and vulnerable. Students and faculty observed his energies sometimes slacken and his disappointments become visible. Then he could be "ogrish" and amiable by turns. Even before events of the late 1960s had put him through the fire, he understood the innate paradox of communal life: the need of the best of human beings was to live in close interdependence, yet they were fated by this interdependence to hurt and bruise one another. Free communication would be won, he realized, at the cost of many psychological scars. This was written into the nature of things. The most one could pray for, in regard to oneself and others, was that no one would be permanently damaged by such encounters.

He bore, as the students sensed, his own burden of hurts. They saw him go off on Sunday evening, after a hard week, for a period of recuperation at Little Boar's Head; and in the rectory, in meandering discussions or relaxed at the piano, they found—perhaps unexpectedly—a friend with whom they could sympathize. Beside, there was always Becky Warren, open, fiercely loyal to her husband, and with a warm feeling for growing boys who want so badly, she wrote, "to be finished, to feel completed."[1]

The board of trustees looked on Matthew Warren with respect for his powers and with some apprehension because of his relentless drive for change. Most of them were less keenly attuned than he to the rumble of growing unrest. Having attended the school when it was a relatively isolated place, they were not all readily convinced that the struggle for civil rights, or the assassinations and wars of the 1960s, were dissolving the bonds of tradition. To them, Warren seemed to push forward with unnecessary haste.

In 1960, Henry Laughlin had retired as chairman. By his wit, which reinforced an underlying conservatism, he had kept the board at the thin edge of excitement and conflict. "The meetings must indeed be dull," he wrote Warren from exile, "if no one can stir in you the spark of controversy."[2] A year later, Charles Dickey retired. Cautious on fiscal matters, he, too, had often restrained Warren; but it was impossible ever to think of Dickey as anything but a youthfully enthusiastic friend. "In his life with us he has taught much about simplicity and its grandeur," Warren wrote of him in his annual report of 1963; "about wisdom and its depth . . . about good humor and its healing powers."

William H. Moore became chairman, to be followed in 1966 by Amory Houghton, Jr. They were both of a new generation, younger men than Warren, and they bearded the rector circumspectly. Within the board there was still the voice of influential dissent. Thomas Rodd watched with distress many of the changes pushed through by Warren. He played a role on the board similar to that of a Schley or an Ingersoll under Drury; while Percy Chubb brought to the rector the same kind of personal support, combined with luminous good sense, as had Perkins in an earlier generation.

From Cape Cod, Henry Kittredge wrote in characteristic vein of the board now in control of St. Paul's affairs. He was struck by the new "youth and vigor." It was very different from his recollections of early years, when trustees were characterized by "ear trumpets, crutches, frock coats, high button shoes."[3] Whether the members of this new board

He bore, as the students sensed, his own burden. *Matthew Warren in the chapel.*

were possessed of the wisdom which would enable them to guide the school through a period of severe testing, only the experience of the next ten years could show.

Warren's vice rectors, as he left for his crucial sabbatical, were Ronald J. Clark and William A. Oates. A fervent teacher of mathematics and an enthusiast for educational innovations, Clark was also proficient in squash, winning the hearts of successive generations of student players—male, and in due course female, too. He came to the school under Kittredge in 1939, and would retire more than forty years later with his zest as a teacher undiminished. Oates, his tenure going back to the Nash era, had emerged from the registrar's office to take over, under Kittredge, the key post of admissions officer.

Storm Warnings

The annual report for 1963, marking Warren's first decade as rector, set the stage for the years to come. Still the builder and innovator, he was beginning to give increasing attention to the mood of the school and to the impingement of outside events upon its life. "The revolutions and the revolutionary movements," he said, "have caught up with the United States. We and our students at the school cannot be isolated from the convulsions in the South. . . . The boys are suffering the same pain, the sense of shame or anger or fright anybody else in the country feels in the face of the same specter." The rise of bitterness he saw at an all-time high; and this bitterness, he warned, "is the most dangerous result of the resistance to the rise of the Negro's demand for equality."

Warren did not perceive at this juncture the degree to which such bitterness would penetrate St. Paul's; but by 1963 there were already signs of restlessness within the student body. Several severe disciplinary cases occurred. Complaints were being heard of "lack of communication" within the school community both in regard to student–administration and student–faculty relations. St. Paul's was a closed society, complained the *Horae,* striking what was for it an unusual note. The school was not so much closed against the world—that could not be. But it was closed, said the editor, "like a Pandora's box," against discontents within.

While both the *Horae* and the *Pelican* were beginning to express radical sentiments, a new mood of anti-élitism in the national media angered and confused the students. Issues of *Esquire* and *Holiday* carried articles pointing to St. Paul's as the archetype of the snobbish "preppie" stronghold. "The Paulies," declaimed *Esquire,* "are deeply yet intuitively convinced of their membership in a self-perpetuating community of the Elect."[4] Some students were resentful of such attacks. Visiting the school as a Conroy fellow, the noted journalist James Reston was astonished to find how different was the substance of things from the popular image being disseminated. But others within the school, often the more brilliant students, took such verdicts to be the awful truth and began to demand changes of one sort or another.

The classes graduating from St. Paul's in the years 1964–1966 constituted in themselves a kind of early warning system. Their impulses were undirected and their discontents inchoate, yet in their bohemian ways they were possessed of symptoms beginning to be common throughout the youth culture. Among them was a student, the son of an old St. Paul's family, given to a passionate immersion in the works of Marx and Lenin. His adviser warned that he was neglecting his assigned studies; but "I do not believe," he added sensibly, "that we can forbid boys to read books." One was an actor gifted beyond the ordinary; his roommate was of a brilliant, probing mind, searching through dark ways for human relationships he never fully succeeded in attaining. Another of this group—tall, somber, the grandson of a famous novelist—crowded a few brief years after graduation with arcane

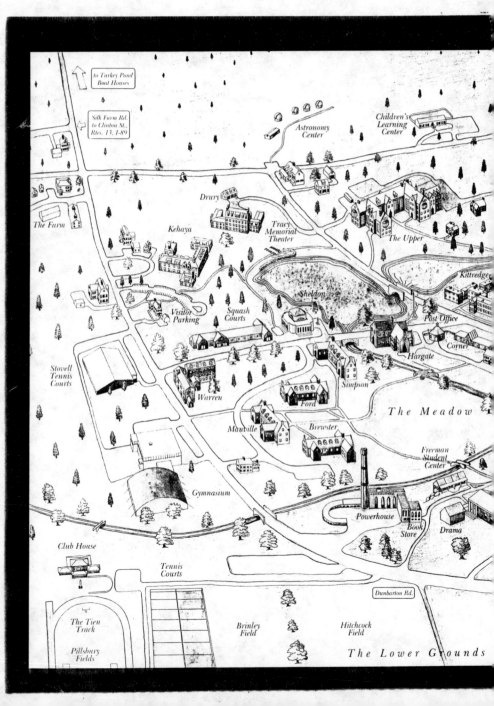

to Turkey Pond
Boat Houses

Silk Farm Rd.
to Clinton St.,
Rtes. 13, I-89

Astronomy
Center

Children's
Learning
Center

Drury

Kehaya

Tracy
Memorial
Theater

The Upper

The Farm

Kittredge

Sheldon

Visitor
Parking

Squash
Courts

Post Office

Corner

Hargate

Stovell
Tennis
Courts

Warren

Simpson

The Meadow

Ford

Mauville

Brewster

Freeman
Student
Center

Gymnasium

Powerhouse

Book
Store

Drama

Club House

Tennis
Courts

Dunbarton Rd.

The Tien
Track

Pillsbury
Fields

Brinley
Field

Hitchcock
Field

The Lower Grounds

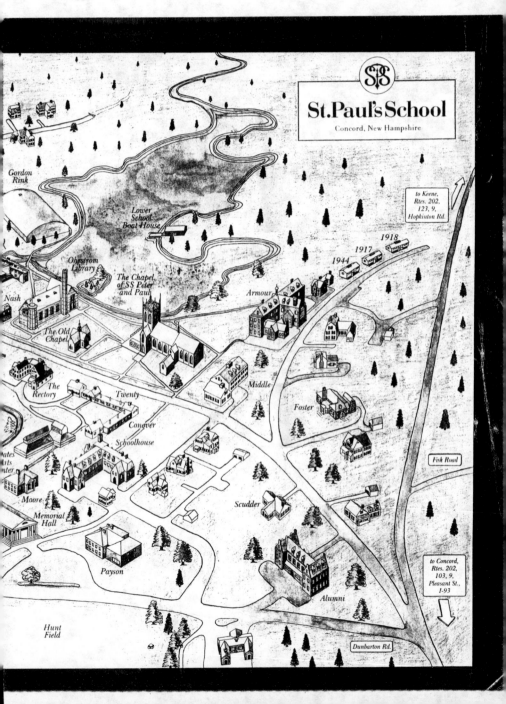

St.Paul's School

Concord, New Hampshire

Gordon Rink

Lower School Boat House

Ohrstrom Library

Nash

The Chapel of SS Peter and Paul

The Old Chapel

The Rectory

Twenty

Conover

Schoolhouse

ates rts nter

Moore

Memorial Hall

Payson

Hunt Field

Armour

Middle

Foster

Scudder

Alumni

to Keene, Rtes. 202, 123, 9, Hopkinton Rd.

1918

1917

1944

Fisk Road

to Concord, Rtes. 202, 103, 9, Pleasant St., I-93

Dunbarton Rd.

learning, and, when it seemed plain the world was not going his way, shot himself.

In the same period came the student who was later to create the widely read cartoon strip, "Doonesbury"—a quiet and personally unhappy member of the community, with a strongly individualistic outlook on the world. He combined—as to a greater or less degree did many of his compeers—passive disillusionment with belief in an unexplained residue of decency and hope in the world.

The *Horae,* always a sensitive indicator of intellectual trends, was taken in charge by a highly talented group of editors, adept in the play of ideas and full of experimental zeal. More prophetic than occasional outbursts of criticism or dissent was a pervasive sense of things coming apart. The traditionally staid cover of the school magazine burgeoned in bright colors and abstract designs; its fiction was suddenly marked by macabre themes. Where there was humor—and it seemed to many there was not humor enough—it was obscure and sardonic in tone.

The year of the rector's sabbatical saw arriving at the school a promising young master, in tune with the developing mood. A graduate of Groton and Harvard, a veteran of the Kennedy Peace Corps, Gerry E. Studds was a powerful teacher, capable (as Winant had once been) of opening to

"Was St. Paul's ceasing to be a Christian community?" *John Walker about to leave Concord.*

boys in his history classes the drama of unfolding events. He made scholars; he also made disciples and converts. A new student appeared as well that year, assigned to the same house in which Studds had his apartment, a chubby bespectacled lad, the son of a prominent public servant. Edmund L. Resor and Studds formed a friendship that was to hold fast during the four years remaining to each of them at the school. As his adviser, Studds was soon writing to Resor's parents of the quick mind and capable intelligence of their offspring. These two, the boy and the master, were to play important roles—one in the limelight, one by subtle influence—in the events of 1968 and 1969.

For the time being the rector was far from these nascent developments, and the reports of his two vice rectors were less prophecies of things to come than they were vivid and often amusing glimpses of the school at this juncture—a society in precarious stability as it approached the waterfall of revolt. While Warren basked in the Rome sunshine, the temperature at Millville fell below zero for ten consecutive days. The ante-chapel during morning services was forty degrees, and the cold seeped into the long nave. "There is a spirit of the medieval church around," Clark wrote. "You would have done penance in your chapel seat." No boys had worn their overcoats to service, but scarfs and long haircuts had been in evidence. "I'm sympathetic to long haircuts at the moment," he wrote.[5]

As winter passed, the inevitable slush season set in. "Already a notice has been read to the effect that boys should stay out of the mud," Clark informed his absent chief; "but as usual the mud seems to have some attraction for them." Flu hit heavily, and at one time forty boys were in the infirmary. One Saturday night, "at a particularly raucous movie," the boys misbehaved. The president of the sixth form arose and sharply rebuked the audience. So effective was he that for two weeks afterwards the hall remained quiet, to the point where "even amusing parts of the movie were no longer laughed at."

Some hard disciplinary cases were dealt with, and Oates noted that the school was marked by an emerging temper: "a bit more freedom of expression," he described it, and "more willingness to back up opinions with actions." Matthew Warren pondered these last words, coming from one whose judgment he trusted, as he passed the spring of 1965 amid the departed glories of a classical civilization.

Discontents in the Nation and the School

The rector returned to St. Paul's to find that "a bit more freedom of expression" was an understatement for the current mood. As in all the independent schools, students were hearing the beat of a rapidly developing youth movement bent upon self-assertion and the challenging of old values. The original causes of this mood lay outside the school and were to prove international in scope. They included the rise into public consciousness of new groups—blacks, Puerto Ricans and other minorities; disillusionment with the fruits of a materially prosperous, highly technological civilization; and, increasingly, the impact of such outside events as the assassinations of John Kennedy, Robert Kennedy, and Martin Luther King, Jr. On top of everything else was the Vietnam War, a holocaust seeming to spring directly from the bankrupt values of the generation in power. Here were unraveled and made explicit the results of technological supremacy, reliance on force, and the suppression of alien ideologies.

Within the youth movement the reaction was, essentially, one of passive resistance. Extreme individualism reinforced the disenchantment with accepted values and withdrawal from established patterns of competitive success. The country-wide revolt of youth extended from refusal to serve in Vietnam to taking refuge in hallucinatory drugs. It included such symbolic manifestations as outlandish clothes and hairstyles, the playing of loud "rock music," and a general disregard of social rules. Occasional outbursts of violence betrayed the basically passive nature of the dissent; fleeting commitments (such as participation in Eugene McCarthy's presidential campaign of 1968) brought youth out into the political arena. Only with time—and then with many unconvinced holdouts among the young, and many unconquered garrisons—would the generations once more arrive at a natural accommodation.

To St. Paul's students, the full dimensions of the generational revolt were not immediately apparent. They were traditionally conservative; they thought of themselves as being somewhat apart from the conventional patterns of youthful behavior. Within their own small world, however, they began to be conscious of undue restraints. The regimen of school life was in many aspects unchanged from what it had been forty years before. Successive liberalization of the school rules, beginning with Drury's reforms, still left students within a web of regulations and prohibitions more strict than anything in the world outside. These they were expected to bear in loyal compliance with the needs of the institution. Now it began to be asked whether the needs of the institution were not subordinate to those of the individual.

The options available to the St. Paul's student were painfully narrow—or at least it appeared so to the young emancipators of the 1960s. In the patterns of life imposed by the school—in the choice of courses, in the ways of spending free time, in opportunities for associations with representatives of minority groups and of the opposite sex—the school seemed to be imposing its own values rather than letting the individual make a choice. So, while some sought the novel right of importing pizzas from town and others sought relief from the requirement to engage in athletics or even to attend chapel, almost all became engaged in seeking freer personal expression.

As in most revolutionary situations, the original impulse was confined to a small minority. The group of brilliant intellectuals graduating in the mid-sixties stirred a ferment that put its mark on those occupying the chief positions of power a few years later. A series of strong—and strongly individualistic—sixth-form presidents held office in the late 1960s and early 1970s. Activists, ambitious to make names for themselves as well as to bring St. Paul's into the mainstream of country-wide educational developments, they were in close and friendly contact with young, politically conscious members of the faculty. Discontent had passed from being smart to being popular; from the intellectual to the political realm.

Even in 1968, however, the number of students concerned with radical change, whether in the school or in American society, was a minority. Opposition to Vietnam was slow in developing, and many went through the school enjoying without question—as students had done for more than a hundred years—the slowly unfolding rewards of Concord life. New Hampshire's spring still came with dazzling beauty, and friendships between the boys, or between boys and masters, paid their rich dividends.

The president of the sixth form of 1966, William S. Moorhead 3rd, wrote to Matthew Warren a letter speaking the thanks of many. He praised the "frankness and intellectual probing" with which religious studies had been handled. He acknowledged the sense of real participation in decision-making, and praised the faculty. "Though they differed, I could see they cared enormously for the boys," young Moorhead wrote. "More than ever during my last year, I was really enjoying everything, even the trying moments, because I was feeling everything deeply." This came at a time when the school administration was being accused of obscurantism and oppression.

A graduate of the form of 1966, Nicholas Gagarin, evoked in *Wind Song,* a novel written while he was still a student at Harvard, the bittersweet emotions of a final spring in Millville. Gagarin was one of the rebels against the old order, but his hero senses all the complexities of a generation in transition. "This was the end of four very good years at St. Paul's in which he had learned and grown. It was always good," he mused, "when something comes to an end. It is sad as well, but it is good to experience the completeness of one period and to know that you are moving on to another. . . ." Then the youth faced the year's final ceremonies:

He wondered if he would cry as he sat in the chapel waiting for the service to begin. . . . He had been in the chapel hundreds of times in the last four years. He had said prayers here, sung hymns, and been confirmed an Episcopalian. There were many occasions on which he had hated the chapel. . . . And there had been lots of mornings when at 8:29 he had found himself among the last rush of boys scrambling to get in before the large wooden doors swung closed. But to do something for the last time brings out special emotions. As the bad memories faded away, [he] felt a great tenderness inside him. The chapel was lit in candle-light. The congregation rose to sing the Last Night hymn. . . .

The Administration's Response

Matthew Warren's response to the growing dissidence did not take the form of looking for culprits or trying anything so futile as forcible suppression. It was his determination, instead, to go forward along lines he had been pursuing from the start. He had not struggled to integrate a church in the South in order to preside over a segregated school in the North. He had not fought to modernize St. Paul's in order to stop when the need for modernization seemed greatest. He returned from his sabbatical with redoubled zeal, more than ever convinced of the revolutionary nature of the times.

His annual reports from this time on alternate between warnings to the trustees of tensions and possible upheavals, and appeals to the students for a common faith. "The question which comes to mind day after day," he said, is whether "we are able to change our habits of thought, our inbred prejudices and predilections, our preferred view of ourselves and our world. We must do so . . . quickly enough to help our young people live fruitfully and sensibly." "There appears to be no end to the restlessness," he wrote a year later, "and our own community is not, nor should [it] be, unaffected."

Warren had long since formed his own view of the nature of youth, a view at once severe and compassionate. Childhood, as he saw it, was a time of life when God is multiple, "when standards are frequently pagan and when all things are of interest but no one thing demands all of one's loyalty." But with adolescence came a temper nearer to Judaism—"a life in which there is one unqualified God of strict law, swift punishment, and one holy nation."[6] It was to the representatives of such a "nation," ardent in their pursuit of what they conceived to be the right, intolerant and often humorless, that he addressed his appeals. Far from being sentimental about young people, Warren could be wily and even hard, but he never failed to respect the dignity of their strivings or to deal with them as responsible individuals.

Now he sought for time—time in which communication might be facilitated and understanding enlarged; time that might allow old and young the better to understand each other and the nature of their changing world. But time seemed to be one thing that was everywhere lacking. Almost no one, he remarked sadly, had even the time any more to climb Jerry Hill.

In the past, Warren pointed out, men had not known enough about the environment outside their immediate experience. "Now we know too much, too quickly, and without time to think." Distant wars, violence in the streets of American cities, were as near as one's own hand. Academic communities had been realms permeated by "the serenity of time"; they had once provided a setting "for casual, almost desultory movement, where the scholar matures with few distractions at a leisurely pace, in the company of others of like mind and equal quietude."[7] Now all that seemed to have passed. In place of what had once been a natural process of understanding, communications between human beings had to be deliberately, even formally, organized.

"From the rector's point of view," he said, "there is little that cannot be discussed and ultimately there's nothing that need be hidden." But communication had become more elusive than the normal give-and-take of community discussion. It had become as much a nonverbal as a verbal transaction. Attitudes, gestures, emotional states conditioned it, as well as "the character of the person making statements and our accumulated experiences through the years with each other." "We must struggle," he was saying by 1967, "by every device we can manage, for ever richer conversation, verbal and nonverbal."

Toward the Cataract

Accustomed to act quickly, Matthew Warren in these critical years persuaded the trustees to accept a number of fundamental and dramatic changes in school life. These included unlimited weekends away from school and experiments in reducing the required number of chapel services. On occasion, Sunday Evensong would be omitted and attendance on Wednesdays and Saturdays was made voluntary. Perhaps only a churchman could have initiated this step, so radical in its transformation of long-standing practices—as only a southerner could have moved so effectively toward integration. Requirements for seated meals, enforced study hours and formal rules of dress were also relaxed, in moves to slacken the pressures of school life and permit the individual more freedom of choice.

To encourage fundamental reconsiderations of policy, the administration called upon the Harvard Business School to work out a series of "cases" dealing with school issues. At long sessions prior to the beginning of a new academic year, students and faculty, led by Harvard-trained experts, played roles and followed hypotheses to divergent conclusions. Efforts to increase the number of black students were set on foot at the same time. In conjunction with other independent schools, and with financing from major foundations, promising black youngsters were sought out in city ghettos and given stepped-up training in academic subjects. Scholarship funds were made available to cover their tuition, as well as their clothes and incidental expenses. By 1967, the student body at St. Paul's included eleven U.S. blacks, one African, and two American Indians. Small though this representation of minorities still remained, its ideas and values provided a heady ingredient within the school's traditional mix.

Warren was also prepared to move toward coeducation, but he delayed as various methods were discussed within the board of trustees. Soon after becoming rector he had raised the issue, supported at that time by only a small minority of the board. Apart from complex problems within the school, coeducation was bound to create problems among the alumni, already apprehensive because of the swift tide of change. Heavy capital expenditures, moreover, appeared necessary to alter so fundamentally the nature and make-up of the school. Yet Warren never gave up the idea. The student world, as he saw it, depended for its health upon a depth of human relationships not capable of being satisfied within an all-male community. The comparatively isolated location of St. Paul's made contacts with girls particularly difficult. And basic to everything else, in Warren's view, lay the problem—hitherto largely ignored at St. Paul's—of youth's sexual development.

The boy of fifteen, Warren had written in an early annual report, "is becoming increasingly self-consciously sexual, which is really not to be wondered at, but which many adults and especially his parents wish he wouldn't." Later he commented on the surprising extent to which maturity had been hastened in contemporary society. In its physical development, youth was now a year or eighteen months in advance of earlier generations. Admission of girls to the Advanced Studies program had been a cautious preliminary step in coeducation; and now, bringing to the school the noted sex educator Dr. Mary Calderone—"Nothing you ask will shock me," she said—was another novel foray for the times. Meanwhile board discussions continued upon the feasibility of establishing a co-ordinate school for girls on property adjacent to the existing school buildings.

St. Paul's was moving forward—moving at an unprecedented rate.

Still, there were signs that not all was well within. Reporting on the year 1966, Warren noted "a chilly attitude" on the part of sixth formers. "Many sixth formers really don't want responsibility," he quoted one student as saying; "they would prefer to associate with each other and let the rest of the school take care of itself." He pleaded for a deeper sense of interdependence. The school's hope and faith, he said, were profoundly involved in community life; in shared experiences, and in responsibilities freely accepted. Looking back, one sees that the students were in fact anxious to accept responsibility—but on their own terms. Within a year of Warren's plea they would find it within themselves to act decisively. Hindsight shows their "chilly attitude" to have been part of a silent, still-unarticulated refusal to play the game under existing rules. The year 1966, with its mute withdrawals, was a direct prelude to the outspoken dissent of 1968.

In the spring of 1966, John Walker, the first black master, was about to leave Concord to become canon of Washington Cathedral. In a farewell article, he described St. Paul's as an institution that, under Matthew Warren's leadership, had grown in depth of feeling and in human interaction. More optimistic than the rector himself in judging this period, he nevertheless showed between the lines an awareness of the same gnawing problems.

Was St. Paul's, he asked, ceasing to be a Christian community? Did the widely prevalent dissent from rules, and particularly from acceptance of religious forms, mean that the school was changing its basic character? Arriving as a young master in 1957, Walker had judged St. Paul's to be a Christian school, not because of its daily chapel services or because of the number of clergymen on the staff, but because the students cared about others. "The caring for others," he said, "became an act of worship." And so it might be even in 1966. "Wherever there is love, concern, and a genuine attempt to understand each other, there is the Church." St. Paul's, he concluded, would remain a Christian school "insofar as it seeks to induct its members into relationships where love becomes a possibility, and is in evidence much of the time."[8]

Walker thus subtly rebuked the bitterness and the anti-religious tendencies then current at St. Paul's. With echoes of Tillich, he opened the way for a new synthesis and reconciliation.

Matthew Warren's sixtieth birthday was celebrated in the autumn of 1967. Classes were suspended, refreshments and cakes were served. On the chapel lawn a crowd gathered round the rector, to shake his hand and to congratulate him. The party was generally considered a success. "It's not quite a be-in," one student was heard to remark, "but it's better than going to class.''[9] After that, amid outward calm, the seasons advanced in their normal course. "It was an entirely good [school] year," Warren wrote to his old friend Henry Laughlin, "up to the last ten days of the term."

The calm was deceptive. Events of the outside world were surging against the once-secure walls of the school. In 1967 occurred the first death of a St. Paul's alumnus in the Vietnam War. Stephen D. Kelsey, Jr., had been an outstanding athlete and a cheerful presence in the school community. He died in one of his first days of battle, during a jungle raid. A death as swift as it seemed senseless made him one with a long line of Americans disappearing into the abyss of Vietnam's suffering.

New Hampshire that winter provided a testing ground for the forthcoming presidential race. The Democratic senator, Eugene J. McCarthy, entered early into the primaries on an uncompromising anti-Vietnam platform. Richard Nixon and George Romney, holding divergent attitudes on Vietnam, followed him. All three came to St. Paul's and submitted to questioning by the students. McCarthy's strong showing in these primaries led to President Johnson's decision not to run for another term; it was a signal for Robert Kennedy, with his capacity to reach and stir a vast constituency of the underprivileged, to enter the race.

McCarthy appealed to the prevailing mood of youth. Something "cool" in his approach to political problems, something aloof and disillusioned in his wit, were as important in winning allegiance as his outright stand against Vietnam. For his sake young recruits from the colleges shaved their beards and cut their hair, appearing in a guise reassuring to voters of the Granite State. At St. Paul's, Gerry Studds was prepared to play a major role in his primary campaign. A carefully argued letter from the senator requested the rector to give Studds leave of absence. Warren refused. "We are not in a position," he wrote curtly, "to have faculty leave at midstream." It was, perhaps, his one tactical error in this difficult period. Studds, already a lightning rod for student discontents, turned his frustration and disappointment against the school. Meanwhile, the atmosphere grew tense. In April, Martin Luther King, Jr., was assassinated, and a month later, in a hotel kitchen in Los Angeles, Robert Kennedy lay mortally wounded by an assassin's bullet.

On the night of King's death, the rector walked out alone over the school grounds. At a distance from the center he came upon a group of black students huddled miserably together. "You fellows have your troubles," he told them sympathetically. "They're killing off our leaders," was the freezing reply, the few words carrying the bitterness and the fearful apprehensions of the hour. When Concord planned a memorial service on the steps of the State House, Warren announced that he and his wife would lead a march on foot. Two hundred boys and masters joined them, moving in silence down the same path that Henry Coit and his brother had taken as they led the school to services for Lincoln. Significantly, a sizeable minority now chose not to follow the rector, walking by themselves behind Ryckman King, the president of the sixth form.

The Sixth-Form Letter

In May, pent-up, simmering emotions blazed out. A letter signed by eighty sixth formers and by an equal number of fifth formers set forth with astonishing bitterness the students' complaints about the school.[10] Posted on various bulletin boards—as Martin Luther's heretical theses had been nailed to the door of the cathedral in Wittenberg—the three-page, single-spaced letter was in its contents and method of promulgation a defiance of authority, convention, and civility. In a community that for more than a hundred years had lived by tacit understandings and freely accepted restraints, the letter was more of a shock than open violence might have been. Words had always been important at St. Paul's, and now words struck with the force of physical blows.

The document, characterized by one master as "bruising and ruthless," pictured the school as a mindless institution, imposing on its members a regimen of indignities and oppression. Boys and masters, it was contended, found themselves subjected to a power structure allowing no expression of personality, and fatally inhibiting "spontaneity, openness, honesty and joy." The masters were held to be either obsequious in their deference to the administration or aloof from the concerns of the students; those few with whom there could be discussion about serious matters were under threat of being excommunicated by their superiors. Whatever progress in reform had been made over recent years was judged to be minimal: integration was a token gesture; independent studies programs were a sham. "We are tired of being politely listened to," the manifesto concluded, "of being told that our ideas are interesting and promptly being forgotten."

The rector was away, at a board meeting of the Virginia Theological Seminary, when the letter was promulgated. A delegation of students waited on his return and presented him with a copy. He was offended that the expression of discontents should have occurred in his absence, but his immediate reaction was to take it less personally than had been expected of him. For years he had known controversy and had learned to stand his ground. "As a third form composition in English," he said of the letter, "I'd flunk it." The next morning he called together his vice rectors, Oates and Clark, together with a small group of his most trusted advisers. They met unobserved in a rear office in the school house. "Is there anything going on in this school you know of and I do not?" was his first question.

Reassured on this point, he turned to ways of meeting the situation. To expel the ringleaders was one choice, for which there was some support within the group. Warren's mind went back to what he had heard of the spring of 1923, when Drury, at the very end of the term, had expelled the top leaders of a defiant sixth form. For him, this was not an answer. "These were my people," he reflected many years later. "If I sent them home I would not be able to find a way of dealing with them."[11]

The faculty, meanwhile, found itself angry and divided. On one side were the older masters, for whom the students' indictment was a blow even harsher than for the rector. They had been less directly involved than he in the management of the slowly developing crisis, and were less prepared for a rhetoric devoid of traditional courtesies. They had labored to instruct these boys; most of them had thought they were reaching the deeper levels of youth's confidence and understanding. How could they have been so mistaken?

Many of these masters suspected their younger colleagues of having stirred up and exploited, for their own advantage, the feelings of the students. Gerhard Schade, successor to old Spanhoofd in learning, in wit, in his love of the German language, told a hastily summoned masters meeting that he discerned a "mephistophelian craft" at work. The smoke that had choked and paralyzed the school was not, in his view, the kind of smoke that signifies a real fire. It was, rather, a "psychedelic" smoke, the output of a "smoke-machine." "A very few dedicated and extremely able masters," he declared, "have developed such an apparatus, and they, together with a few boys, have collaborated daily in order to perfect it."[12]

In the privacy of the same masters meeting, Señor Ordonez made an aristocrat's eloquent appeal for unity. "If the walls are not to come down between us," he told his colleagues, "we must exercise more charity with each other, and, just as important, stop this undignified gabble with the very young." In the life of Europe he had known two traditions, the Socratic and the Christian. "The Socratic tradition stands for freedom of thought; the Christian tradition guarantees the integrity of the human person. The Socratic tradition means truth; the Christian tradition, charity. I stand, for what it may be worth, on these traditions, and in my years remaining in this place, if wanted to remain, I shall stick to my two traditions. I have found no other worthy substitutes for them."

Such was the old guard of 1968—proud, indignant, hurt. An unusually large number of younger masters stood against them, feeling the uncertainties and the opportunities of their time, persuaded that the students, often little removed from them in age, were on their side. In Europe that spring, André Jacq, one of the most engaging of St. Paul's teachers, brooded upon the revolution of which the events in Millville were only a fleeting shadow. Democracy, he wrote to Matthew Warren, had partly transcended class distinctions; it was now attempting to transcend distinctions of age. In its extreme and youthful enthusiasm, the revolution was breaking down all the compartments of the social structure. "It knows no *a-priori,* no determinism in ideas, emotions, age, culture. . . . Its only permanence is change. It has a short memory and a long view. It is fluid, rushing forward like a new-born river—and going where? To lose itself, it believes, some day, in an Ocean of Love." St. Paul's, Jacq added, might never again be what it was before the crisis occurred. "Violent evolution is cruel . . . yet the world of tomorrow could be the better for it."[13]

The community had been deeply shaken—boys set against masters, masters against their colleagues. To Warren's lasting credit, he kept it from being damaged irreparably. At the same time he kept the controversy from degenerating into one between himself and the dissidents. A few days after the sixth-form letter had been launched, its principal authors acknowledged it to have been overstated, but they justified its rhetoric on the ground that it had stirred people up. A more constructive series of proposals was issued. At the same time the school administration showed itself ready to treat the situation seriously, and to try to get at the root of the trouble as the students saw it.

Two immediate opportunities presented themselves. In a few days the trustees would be gathering for the regular spring meeting. For the first time in the school's history, students were invited to attend—a group of four from the fifth and sixth forms. Among these was the outgoing president and his newly elected successor. In attendance also were a number of younger masters who shared in the general malaise and had been openly involved with the chief student protestors. Discussions with the students ran on through the morning, and the masters remained late into the afternoon. The tone was respectful on both sides, though with unfamiliar outspokenness on the part of the students and faculty representatives. Reporting to the alumni at the Anniversary celebration next day, the chairman of the board, Amory Houghton, Jr., declared that "The trustees consider that the importance of the suggestions [offered at the trustees meeting] merit prompt and thorough consideration."

The second opportunity for dialogue was a review of the curriculum, already scheduled for the summer. Warren seized upon this, enlarged the participation, widened the range of subjects to be considered, and deepened the tone of candor and commitment. Eighty boys remained for two days after the normal closing of school to help determine the agenda, now redefined by the sixth-form letter, to include everything that happened to a student between entrance and graduation. Six students and six members of the faculty then met for six weeks during the summer.

To reconsider the processes of life together at St. Paul's, Warren had said, would require "infinite patience and laborious hours." No one questioned this when the report had been completed, least of all Matthew Warren himself. He wouldn't want to repeat the performance, he confided in privacy. "If heaven is good, and I truly believe it is, I won't be made to do it again in this world."[14]

The report, ready for the school when it reconvened in the autumn of 1968, called for implementing many of the changes recommended in the sixth-form letter. These included an easing of all school rules, voluntary chapel on Sunday, coeducation, elimination of numerical grading, and a greatly extended and more flexible program of studies. Beneath the recommendations was a general insistence that the students of the school be treated as fully mature individuals, capable of determining their own goals and standards within an environment free of moral and religious presuppositions.

"A Rough Time Ahead"

The school had come through the immediate crisis of 1968. Words had done their worst; but St. Paul's seemed ready to go forward. When the rector promised that although not everything in the curriculum committee's report would be adopted, everything would be considered, his words were taken in good faith. Student–faculty committees were appointed to weigh every aspect of the summer's recommendations, and the prompt adoption of many of them—actually an extension of the rector's reform program of 1966 and 1967—showed that the administration was in earnest.

The following academic year was, nevertheless, one of turmoil. Having gained a new freedom to speak and act, the students were resolved to make use of it. They saw the universities in a state of radical upheaval; they saw the country and the world in the clutch of seemingly uncontrollable forces, and they were convinced that at St. Paul's they were part of a significant experiment in individual growth and social reorganization.

The president of the sixth form, in the traditional address to the school at the beginning of term, set the tone. Edmund Resor spoke of the palpable excitement in the air. "By becoming involved in appropriate changes at St. Paul's," he said, "we gain some understanding of change in the rest of the world, and by changing ourselves with the school we can grow in such ways that we will be able to do something about the world."

Warren rightly saw "a rough time ahead." "Concessions will have to be made to the revolution if we are to continue to exist," he wrote in a private letter.[15] His old friend, Forbes Mackintosh, head of Loretto School in Scotland, drew the moral clearly. "You and I (and our generation of teachers)," he wrote Warren, "have encouraged young people to think for themselves and 'to prove all things.' It is not for us to complain when the process of proving produces in them a disgust for much of what they find."

With the support of the trustees, the rector took steps to safeguard the school against such physical violence as ripped apart the fabric of Columbia and Harvard. Yet he never quite lost his belief in good will and reason. At the conclusion of the summer's curriculum review, he wrote to the alumni that the discussion had been "generally healthy" and would produce in the end an atmosphere of "greater trust, greater frankness, and genuine understanding." Before reaching the end, however, there was to be a long way to go.

Threats to boycott the chapel, various forms of disobedience and affronts to authority, continued among a portion of the student body. Long hair and disheveled clothes became a mark of being "with it." Drugs, then pervading the high schools, began to make their appearance at St. Paul's. The school, according to one neutral student, was "afflicted with the rabies of revolution." Attempts were made to classify everyone as "radicals" or "reactionaries." Accusations of "selling out" were leveled against anyone showing signs of cooperating with the administration.[16]

The *Pelican* remained a forum for the most excited rhetoric. Even the philosophical Forbes Mackintosh was shocked. There had been "some rumblings" at Loretto, he wrote Warren, but nothing like what was being regularly expressed at St. Paul's. "From what I can make out," he said of the *Pelican* articles, "nobody loves anybody and everyone has a crack at everybody else." The tone of articles referring to the faculty he characterized as "pretty unpleasant."

"Adolescents," quoted the *Pelican,* "are among the last social group in the world to be given the full nineteenth century Colonial treatment." What many people did not realize, it continued, "is that youth today is *different from any previous generation*—they are more active, more interested in the world around them, and more eager to improve the things they disapprove of." Then, in a fine flourish, that young Danton concluded: "It no longer does any good to ignore this growing force; it does no good to talk down to youth, for they must be listened to. . . ."

Parents were no less perplexed than the school administration. To the mother of a student leader, the rector wrote that it would be impossible to conceive of a more "difficult" young man. The mother replied that she agreed entirely. At the Parents Day symposium of that year, fathers and mothers heard their offspring declare heretical sentiments and ideas. At

Long hair and disheveled clothes became marks of being "with it."
A group of students at Anniversary, 1970.

least one of these parents admitted that, for the first time, he began to understand his son. He was himself, he declared, "very much a square and very conservative," yet, hearing the discussion, he sensed that "maybe democracy is working here a great deal better than it seems to be working outside."[17]

There were some lighter moments in the midst of the tensions and signs of happier things to come. The boys wanted girls—and so the school took steps to bring a group of them to Millville. In the winter of 1969, arrangements were made for a brief exchange with Concord Academy in Massachusetts. The boys waited impatiently to see what sort of girls they would be. "It is naturally expected," said the *Pelican,* "they will be young, lovely, and vivacious." Not surprisingly, they were.

The chapel was the symbol of much that the students of 1969 resented. Not only was attendance required, but the building's very presence, inescapable at the center of the school grounds, suggested something fixed and immutable, representing values descended from an ancient tradition outside themselves. The *Pelican* fumed because the rector insisted that, even if individual students chose not to pray, they were expected to rise and to kneel with the rest of the congregation. "The rector's views on behavior in chapel," said the editorialist sharply, "disregard student feeling." Yet even here a light was beginning to shine through. Sixth formers took charge of the services in morning chapel; several brief plays were presented in the nave, and a new liturgy was coupled with a jazz mass. These occasions were decidedly pleasant, though some disappointment was expressed in the *Pelican* because "the Lord's Prayer remained as it had been for several hundred years, and so did the Nicene Creed."

In secrecy, during the autumn of 1969, the students constructed a brightly painted sculpture of fourteen-foot-high letters spelling the word "LOVE." In the pre-dawn hours of November 1, at the opening of Dance Weekend, the separate pieces were assembled on the chapel lawn."LOVE not only stated the mood of the weekend," said one youthful commentator, "but much of what today's youth seeks." An *agapé* service was celebrated in front of the sculpture by school clergy, accompanied by guitars and folk music, and with students and their dates in attendance.

An alumnus, seeing a picture of the event, was horrified and irate. "How easily shocked you are," replied the rector. "Love," he admitted, was a four-letter word, but "I think it has good scriptural background." For the students, at any rate, the passing of bread and wine had at last become something real. "A spirit grew during the course of the service that got me out of my hang-ups," said one. The experiment was repeated several times in the early mornings of the following spring. "I don't hear of any joy in this group," a visitor on Parents Day had complained. "The things I remember at school and college were the funny things that happened." To which one of the students replied, "If you want to see some joy come to the *agapé* feast tomorrow. You come as you are, you play guitars, you sing and dance and you are just happy to be alive."[18]

The alumni, as they returned for Anniversary in the spring of 1969, were not fully aware of the scope of disturbances within the school. Many were inclined to criticize the rector for the precipitousness of recent changes. They were at once enlightened and shocked when the president of the sixth form rose to make the annual address at the alumni meeting. Sturdy, freckled, peering out at the world through dark-rimmed glasses and crowned with a shock of red hair, Edmund Resor made it clear that, in his view, the revolution was not over. His remarks were bitter in tone and unyielding in their assumption that youth knew the answers. The administration, he maintained, was concerned more with the school as an institution than with the individuals who composed it. "I say now that I would advise any brother or friend of mine not to come here unless I was convinced the basic conflict between the people and the institution had been resolved in favor of the people."[19]

Alumni stood around afterwards in offended groups. This seemed to be a different school from the one they had known. To those who had followed developments closely, it was evident that much time and effort would still be required before St. Paul's reestablished itself as a fully functioning community.

CHAPTER FIFTEEN

A New Community
1969–1979

A Process of Choice

The trustees were confronted once again by the need to search for a new rector. By 1968, Matthew Warren was approaching the age of retirement. If anything like the schedule followed in his case were to apply to his successor, it was not too early to begin. That summer the board appointed a search committee. In January 1969, in a letter to the school community, Warren took the position that a new rector, when he was chosen, should assume office promptly. He looked back on his own long incubation as a highly unsatisfactory period for him personally; moreover the times did not allow any weakening of authority. He was tired, he told the trustees; he had brought the school through a severe crisis, but only at the cost of physical and psychological strain. To preside over the dismantling of a social order, laboriously and lovingly constructed, to remain tolerant while every value was questioned and challenged, had not been easy.

Amory Houghton, Jr., chairman of the board, addressed the school in February 1969, announcing the initiation of the selection process. The quest for a new rector would be nationwide; emphasis would be on finding a clergyman, if possible; sensitivity to the feelings and desires of youth was a paramount consideration. Students and faculty were then invited to join the discussion at a meeting of the trustees. Several of the students felt that, as then constituted, the role of rector was too all-embracing, with too much power and too much control over detail concentrated in one man. Could not authority be divided between a rector, a dean of students, and a school chaplain? As for the personality of a new rector, "a father figure," it was declared by one, "is the kiss of death."[1] Others saw the need for someone who identified with the students, rather than for one who overawed them.

By the following summer, though no demonstrable progress had been made in finding a new man, Warren was more than ever convinced that a

342

change in leadership would be timely. "I have the feeling we will not be at St. Paul's for long now," he wrote to a friend. "People of my age and my disposition are not the fellows to be meeting the current struggle."[2] In December of that year he slipped on the black ice of the school pond (the third rector to fall prey to the ever-present hazard of Concord's weather) and, through the following months, suffered the painful aftereffects of a concussion.

The trustees, meanwhile, had been narrowing their search. At the school was a man to whom in their deliberations they kept returning. The vice rector, William Oates—under Nash "the new man in history," looking like a college undergraduate, "and a very attractive one";[3] under Kittredge the still-youthful wizard of the registrar's and the admission's office—had assumed an increasingly important role. The death of his wife after a long, stoically borne illness in 1965, leaving him with three growing sons, had deepened within him, behind a cheerfully brisk exterior, natural currents of understanding and a feeling for the cares of others. Warren strongly supported this aide and protégé, and encouraged him to remain at the school when offers for other posts were being received.

When on February 2, Houghton announced in chapel the election of Oates as the eighth rector, the choice was greeted by the whole community with approval, and with the sense that this was an almost predestined succession.

Matthew Warren, holding to his determination that a new rector should take office promptly, set his own retirement for March 15, the end of the winter term. He went out with the honors due his extraordinary services. Not always understood by the school constituency, he had carried out his tasks with immense vision and energy—a reformer, an innovator, a wise counselor of youth; and at the end, an undaunted leader through a time of storm. On the morning of Sunday, March 8, the chapel was crowded at a special service to mark his retirement. The emotions of the hour were expressed within ancient forms—invocations that had been said at the school for a hundred years, hymns that carried their message of hope and of time's defiance. No sermon, no eulogy, broke into the solemn ritual of prayer and music. "O God, thou summonest the prophets and the apostles to speak in thy name and to walk with thee."[4] Thus spoke the celebrant. And the family of St. Paul's responded: "Halleluiah, Amen."

In perspective, Warren stood with the greatest of the school's rectors: with Coit, who had established it; with Drury who had restored it. No less dramatically than these he had played his part, driving the school forward to meet the claims and expectations of a new age. He suffered the fate of pre-revolutionary leaders—to be identified with the old after having acted powerfully to create a new order. With dignity Warren bore the

A strong sense of authority was not lacking. *William A. Oates, rector.*

misunderstandings of his position, strengthened by religious faith and by a sophisticated grasp of historical forces.

Summing up the Warren years in the alumni magazine, the school's outstanding teacher of history, Carroll McDonald, put the matter definitively. That the school withstood, relatively unscathed, the impact of 1968 and 1969, he wrote, "is due to the care with which Matthew Warren rethought the long tradition inherited from his predecessors and to the extent to which he made the school a more integral part of the larger community."[5]

Oates's Youth and Early Career

William Armstrong Oates was born in 1916 in Aberdeen, South Dakota (population, 16,000). His father, starting out in life as a schoolteacher, married a former student of his, a girl from Rockport, Illinois. For many years he held the post of business manager at the state college. His wife bore him five children, one of whom died in infancy. The future rector of St. Paul's was the middle child, flourishing in a congenial family atmosphere and in a community alive to a variety of novel educational ideas. He started kindergarten at the age of three and went through high school with honors.

The town of Aberdeen was part of a vanishing rural America. South Dakota had become a state only in 1889; Oates could recall the excitement of seeing the road before his family's house paved for the first time. The young man had traveled to Chicago, but had never been farther east, when he formed the determination to go to Harvard. No family ties led him in that direction; no family pressures were exercised. He set foot for the first time in Cambridge when he made his entrance as a freshman. "I thought Harvard provided the best education," he said years later, "and I wanted to go there."[6] Aberdeen saw little of him after that. His father retired to California, and Oates spent most of his summers working in Cambridge—he achieved professional skills in shorthand and typing—to pay for his education.

As a sophomore he entered Eliot House, whose master at that time was the redoubtable "Frisky" (Roger B.) Merriman. The young man from South Dakota made friends with the Merriman family and with other faculty members in his chosen fields of history and English literature. A year abroad on a scholarship; a period after graduation getting his Master of Arts in English; and he was ready to try his wings as a teacher. Merriman's son, Roger, offered him a job at Shady Side Academy in Pittsburgh. There, in the autumn of 1941, he arrived with his bride of a few months. The work did not seem very challenging, nor were the financial arrangements favorable; the younger Merriman was anxious not to put obstacles in the way of his ambitious young recruit if opportunity elsewhere presented itself.

During part of his summers as a Harvard undergraduate Oates had worked at "Mowgli," a camp run by A. F. Elwell. Youthful experience as a scout served Oates in good stead, and Elwell proved a remarkable man, almost for the first time making summer camp a genuinely educational discipline. In Oates's life he became a formative influence. The skeins of fate now began to draw together, for Elwell in 1906 had roomed at Harvard with two future rectors of St. Paul's, Henry Kittredge and Norman Nash. It was natural for Elwell to write the latter; Oates went to Concord to be interviewed and was offered a post teaching history. In September 1942 he moved with his wife and his oldest son, then three months old, to an apartment in the upper school.

Twenty years later, on a partial sabbatical, Oates moved restlessly after his wife's death between Concord and Cambridge, carrying forward studies he had long pursued during summer vacation. Working on his thesis for an Ed.D., he formed the habit—which was to stand him in good stead throughout his rectorship—of arising at five in the morning to begin writing. Emotionally detached from many of the school's problems at this time, he considered accepting offers that were coming to him from his Cambridge friends: the superintendency of a large school district, the executive directorship of a foundation. Then Matthew Warren told Oates one day he was submitting his name to the trustees for consideration as the next rector. Within twenty-four hours of the completion of his doctoral thesis, the storm of May 1968 broke out. Oates was drawn back into the center of school affairs, and a new chapter opened before him.

Houghton called Oates in January 1970 to tell him the trustees had elected him the school's eighth rector. He asked for twenty-four hours to consider, but there was never any doubt in his mind that this was the work for him. He had known St. Paul's for more than twenty years; he had participated in every aspect of school policymaking and administration. As a researcher he had considered carefully the problems of contemporary education. Moving into the rectory in the spring of 1970, he saw clearly the task ahead.

Baptism by Fire

Outside events did not change their course, nor moderate their speed, when Oates took over. The invasion of Cambodia, undertaken without warning or public debate, fired the Vietnam opposition to a fever heat. As demonstrations mounted on college campuses, the administration in Washington showed itself out of sympathy with the country's youth. Amid mounting tensions, four students were killed when the National Guard opened fire on a protesting group at Kent State University. St. Paul's, like other secondary schools, was thrown into turmoil. Oates moved decisively, with the authority that comes of power newly granted, making clear his own attitude of responsiveness to the students.

At the height of the Cambodian crisis, classes were suspended to make way for seminars devoted to the underlying issues of Vietnam. A number of students traveled by bus to Washington to take part in protests over the shootings at Kent State. For a while, in that turbulent spring, St. Paul's seemed to be in an almost continuous series of committee meetings. Emerging values were brought to bear upon every problem and every institution, from the broadest issue of international life to the most intimate and parochial.

Oates acted as a man presiding at the creation of a new order. The students accepted his good faith, warmed to his obvious sympathy with their aims, and on occasion even heeded his advice. What he granted in the way of new freedoms they looked upon less as the departure from old traditions, or as concessions won by force, than as proof of his participation in an educational order freed from prescribed limits. It seemed that everything could be worked out anew, and that in whatever was done, the sense of the student's individuality, and of the validity of personal experience, would be decisive.

In one of his first public statements, Oates explained the three "streams of interest" which he saw converging at St. Paul's. First was an intense concern with the individual psyche, a feeling for the growth from within that makes each person unique in his perceptions and understandings. No longer, Oates declared, was it being asked, "What shall I do?" but "What shall I do with myself?"[7] The second stream was an intimate awareness of change within the person in process of development from youth to adult. Each student was seen as being at a different stage along this mysterious path. External indications, such as age or behavior, were less significant in revealing the point arrived at than private convictions, often unfathomable to the outsider. "How do I know what I am going to do?" exclaimed one of these students when pressed to reveal his plans for the coming summer; "I don't even know who I shall *be*."

Finally, the rector detected an increased sensitivity among the young, showing itself in care for each other (and occasionally, even, in concern for members of the adult world!) and in a striving for deeper relationships and more meaningful communications. This student sensitivity extended to the natural world of objects and things, as in the sudden awareness of ecology; and to their own bodies, as in cultivation of the dance, in concern for what they ate, and in efforts to extend their mental perceptions.

The radical individualism of the new approach seemed in sharp contrast to the traditional role of the school's rector. In fact, the contrast was more apparent than real. Oates's mild and cheerful countenance, his eager receptiveness to new ideas and practices, were undergirded by a quiet sense of authority. He remained in this time of crisis, and throughout his administration, a strong figure at the center. No matter how wide-ranging or how prolonged a discussion he might encourage, the final decision on questions large and small remained with him. What saved him from confrontations was his evident sympathy with the feelings of modern youth, and his exercise of a variety of techniques to defuse opposition and induce consent to his ultimate decision.

He would share with faculty and students the agony of search, even the pains of indecision, and just when it appeared that further groping would be unbearable, he would announce a sane and generally acceptable solution. This patience and empathy, combined with clear willingness to take final responsibility, effected a workable compromise between the republicanism of the new students and the traditionally autocratic nature of the school's governance.

Oates's immediate appointment of Philip Burnham and John H. Beust as vice rectors confirmed his style. Burnham had been head of the English Department for fifteen years, having succeeded faithful John Richards in that position. A quizzical and enthusiastic teacher, of a disposition not easily ruffled, Burnham continued until his retirement in 1978 to handle issues involving faculty and curriculum with open-minded ease. Beust had been head of the Science Department. To budgetary and administrative matters he brought the cool and meticulous judgment especially sought by a rector with long experience in management.

A Fuller Integration

A demand of the more socially conscious students was for a larger number of blacks and representatives of the third world. The recruiting drive undertaken jointly by independent schools had run out of steam by the end of the 1960s. After Martin Luther King, Jr.'s, assassination, St. Paul's initiated a new effort of its own, supplemented by ample scholarship grants. By 1972, the number of blacks at the school had risen to thirty-nine. Although this was not enough to satisfy the more articulate among the white students (their formula was a representation proportionate to that in the country as a whole), it was sufficient to bring about a decisive change in the atmosphere of Millville.

These new black students were children of the civil rights movement, reared among urban tensions of the 1960s, and strongly imbued with an urge to express themselves and their culture. Symbols of conformity, like conventional dress or ways of speech, they rejected with passionate intensity; whereas the white students rejected them lightly, as one part of their search for a more free existence. The simmering discontents of the whites were intensified, and were given a firm moral base, by the minority elements.

On their part the blacks, reluctant to conform, were also at first reluctant to mix with the white students. As in other educational institutions they sat at their own tables at mealtimes, demanded their own dormitories, and tended to set up a coterie around black masters. The strong sense of community at St. Paul's, one of its oldest and most firmly established features, somewhat mitigated these divisions. But in the spring of 1971, the discontents of the blacks became articulate, much as the discontents of the whites had exploded three years earlier.

The president of that year's sixth form, Nicholas Shorter, was disturbed by what he felt to be a continuing malaise. He called a meeting of the student body, taking the unusual course of setting no agenda and suggesting no topic except the general atmosphere of the school. As the unstructured discussion faltered, blacks seized the center of the stage. In heated language they declared they were not fully accepted at the school, that they were bound by regulations they found hateful, and that the curriculum ignored their interests. In a gesture of defiance, a resolution not to wear ties or jackets was adopted by them and supported by a considerable number of white students.

Next day, a Saturday, masters were confused and divided as they faced the dilemma of ejecting large numbers of students from their classes or of acquiescing in a plain contravention of the rules. For the rector it was a test of authority. After the contest of wills had proceeded inconclusively over the weekend, he summoned the chief black leaders to his study. This time there were no committee meetings to prolong the discussion, no attempts to decentralize the decision-making process. Oates confronted the students with an ultimatum: Either they would obey the rule in regard to dress or they would suffer consequences damaging to their careers and to their future ability to act as spokesmen for the black cause. They would all be expelled immediately and he would make sure that their records would be permanently marked.

It was a gamble—and it paid off. The students could persuade themselves that they had made their point and thus retreat with reasonable honor. The next day, jackets and ties were again in evidence. But an additional push for change had been provided, the consequences of which became evident in the following months. To the assembled school that spring the rector announced that the rules in regard to dress were being relaxed; henceforth a wide latitude would be permitted, so long as everything met the standard of being "neat, clean, and in good repair." At the same time the curriculum began to show a marked increase in attention to black authors and to the contributions of blacks to American civilization.

By the later 1970s, the blacks and their third world allies were making a contribution to the community through all the normal channels. The separatist pressures gave way to cooperation in sports, publications, the performing arts, and not least in the leadership of the sixth form. In the social sphere, friendships and associations became the rule.

Yet to be black at St. Paul's remained, for those who set themselves to experience it, a test of courage and understanding.[8] The minority student left a familiar environment and faced challenges for which little in the previous experience of the black boy or girl had been a preparation. Such students returned to a world inevitably grown somewhat strange to them, to hear taunts from those who had chosen a different path. However great the benefits of education at an independent school, or however rich an individual's memories, it was hard to identify afterwards with a place so essentially alien. It would be remarked sadly that younger brothers or sisters rarely followed in the footsteps of a black who had attended St. Paul's.

As the minorities in the school represented increasingly an emerging middle class, and as they came from integrated schools, tensions relaxed. But St. Paul's did not lose its sense of admiration, or its gratitude, for these young people. They had ventured much in becoming part of a community which they diversified and enriched by their presence.

The "Girl Problem"

Contrary to what might be supposed, St. Paul's boys had not, prior to 1970, been entirely ignorant of the female sex. "I've seen girls before," remarked a fifth former, when asked how he viewed a forthcoming exchange with Concord Academy. "I only hope they aren't brains," added a precocious third former.[9] But these girls, at the rim of the students' universe, were never entirely real. Aloof and dazzling, they were imported for the rituals of Dance Weekend or known fleetingly during vacation. The ideal St. Paul's date, *Esquire* reported maliciously but not wholly inaccurately in 1964, "is a 'looker,' usually boarding-school bred, dresses tastefully and yet a bit differently *à la mode,* has a vaguely conventional air and doesn't laugh too loudly." The students became acquainted with these dates, the article continued, at holiday parties and during summers on the Cape. "They also know color-fold-out-girls, locker-room fantasy girls and, occasionally, New York prostitutes hunted up in vacation-time groups."

The traditional school answer to the "girl problem" had been to provide elementary sex instruction in one form or another. Dr. Shattuck, in whose genial disquisitions on the subject young Scudder found "nothing new," came regularly to the school in the nineteenth century. Later, Drury took a candid but peremptory approach. "This of all others is the place [for sex education]," he declared; "now of all periods is the time."[10] The best way to treat the issue was, in his view, "to have it into the sunlight once for all and wholly; once to say everything about it, and then to say nothing more."

The trouble was, growing boys could not be prevented from having further thoughts. Myths persisted at the school of chemicals added to desserts and vegetables to damp their interest; on at least one occasion Drury personally oversaw a collection of suggestive magazines being consigned to the fiery furnace of the school power plant. Still, the thoughts persisted. From the days of the Swedish maid-servants of the nineteenth century until the period after World War II, when most school servants vanished amid economy drives and social change, the hope persisted that some particularly demure lasses might turn up in Millville. (As might have been foreseen, those hopes were disappointed.) In schoolboy fantasies, and no doubt in homosexual episodes—though surprisingly few of the latter show up in the school's records—the primal urge continued to manifest itself.

Activities carried on during vacations provided problems of their own. Drury was appalled at the holiday practices of the youth of his time. What was one to expect of a boy, he asked, "when we know that he has turned night into day, dancing any sort of dances until any hour?"[11] Dances at the school, on the other hand, had a long tradition. The first mention of one occurs in 1861, when four "ladies" came out from town and music was provided by a local fiddler. Later occasions, formally organized and carefully supervised, became an important and pleasant aspect of school life.

Looked forward to eagerly, Dance Weekend left memories to warm the long winter term. With what feelings of expectation, for weeks afterwards, the student approached his post office box, and with what trembling fingers he turned the dial! But by the 1960s, in an atmosphere of greater freedom between the sexes, interest in the highly structured dance weekends fell off. Attempts to overcome the effects of the school's isolation by inviting girls more often ran into the dead end of student indifference. "More dances," said the *Pelican* in 1967, "will only produce more frustration."

There was indeed, despite many touching and romantic overtones, something dreadfully artificial about these occasions. "Having a girl is absolutely vital," wrote Nicholas Gagarin in his novel *Wind Song*. "You are absolutely nothing unless you have one." But "having one" raised all sorts of problems. "I shall never forget the panic of waiting at the Concord station, late one Friday afternoon, for the train from Boston to arrive," Gagarin continued. "It was not a general panic, but a very specific one: What the hell was I going to say to her?" This might sound funny, but for the young swain it was not funny at all at the time. "When you have met a girl only once in your life, and spent eight months of the year out of sight of any girl at all, and when you suddenly find one thrust upon

They also knew fantasy girls. *A young musician of the mid-fifties.*

you—well, it is pretty easy to panic." Gagarin considered writing topics of conversation on his shirt sleeve, but didn't, fearing his date would notice.

Now all this was about to be changed. Coeducation had been one of the clear recommendations of the curriculum study group of 1968. The idea, linked to the women's liberation movement and to the current revolution in sexual mores, was in the air. Colleges and universities that had long been sacred precincts of the male sex were becoming coeducational. Yale and Princeton had already succumbed, and Harvard was at last recognizing Radcliffe students as entitled to its regular diploma. Andover and Exeter would soon go coeducational. Was St. Paul's to lag behind?

Among the revolutionaries in Millville, in the autumn of 1969, some doubts were expressed when it was proposed to follow the brief experiment of the previous year with a winter-long exchange with Dana Hall. These doubts were doctrinaire and tactical. Was the administration, asked the *Pelican,* seeking to supply a "pacifier"? Were the Dana Hall girls being brought in to dissolve the unity of the student body? Above all, what would happen to the crucial issues of personal appearance—the long hair, the patched clothes—when girls began to exert the charms of their presence?

Coeducation was recognized overwhelmingly, nevertheless, as being in keeping with the students' long-range interests. It was fitted to the ethos of a place like St. Paul's, that had long sought to perfect a common life where shared interests and learning experiences reached far beyond the classroom. The trustees, when they voted in May 1970 to admit a substantial number of girls not later than the autumn of 1971, did not consider they were changing the essential character of the school. They knew, however, they were taking a step bound to assure for St. Paul's an atmosphere different from anything that had prevailed in the first 114 years of its history.

The Girls Arrive

The trustees were aware, also, that they were moving in a manner unusually precipitous. The effect of girl students upon the deportment of young men, upon their study, sports and leisure habits, had been observed in two exchanges during the winters of 1969 and 1970, as well as during the Advanced Studies programs of numerous summers. But no surveys had been undertaken on the requirements for capital expenditures, on the long-range implications for the size of the school, the composition of the faculty, the number of student applicants and other questions that trustees usually worry about.

Until the time of final decision, it had been presumed that coeducation would ultimately be achieved by the establishment of a co-ordinate girls' school within the boundaries of Millville. But the board, instead, took the direct and dramatic step of recognizing that girls were part of the human race. With the school opened to a new class of applicants, the girls showed up in reassuring numbers. Admitted into the heart of the school on an equal basis with the boys, they took their place as full citizens in the republic of St. Paul's.

Matthew Warren had brought the school to the border of the promised land. It now fell to the new rector—barely a few months in office—to lead the tribes across. Oates undertook the task with zest. The myriad details of organization and recruitment he handled with the efficiency that had served him well as vice rector for administration. In January 1971— well ahead of the deadline set by the trustees—nineteen girls arrived in Millville as regular students of the school. Not since the first women arrived in 1619 to cheer the struggling colony at Jamestown had representatives of the female sex been so eagerly awaited. Their coming coincided with the lowest sub-zero temperatures in more than fifty years. It was a condition that might have been created to try their hardihood or to prove the warmth of the school's welcome. Neither the girls nor the school failed the test.

The first girl students formed an interesting group, representative of the new and the old within the school's constituency. It included two black students, Loretta M. Jacobs and Lee Ella Bouton. The presence among them of Julia Anne Jordan spoke of the school's continuing link with Concord. Mary Bryant Bigelow was the great-great-granddaughter of Samuel Huntington, the trustee who had played so important a role in the search for a first rector. Elizabeth Rose Morison was related in the same way to the long-tenured trustee Samuel Eliot, and in addition was the granddaughter of Samuel Eliot Morison. It was her great-grandmother who in 1878 had visited the rectory over Washington's Birthday, on a visit that might be characterized as the school's first tentative, unplanned experiment in coeducation. Upon these nineteen girls now fell the task of taking their place in an environment hitherto dominated exclusively by the male sex.

They were expected to be themselves, while being looked on by four hundred young men as exotic strangers. They were challenged to be competitive without seeming aggressive, and to be friends with each other without rejecting the friendship of boys. In the beginning there were at most one or two girls in a classroom, and they tended to be discreetly silent. A shyness among the boys they occasionally mistook for unawareness of their presence. In the nooks and crannies of the school there

Nineteen girls arrive in Millville. *The first group was representative of the old and new within the school's constituency.*

lingered unfortunate phrases to suggest that girls had not come at all. For a year following their arrival, the *Horae* continued in each issue to state that it was published "by the boys of St. Paul's School"; and in reports, "boys" absences continued to be noted, regardless of the delinquent's sex.

By the spring of the first year, however, relationships had been defined and solidified. The fact that the girls formed so small a minority was less troubling to them than to the several hundred boys who competed for their attention. "Now that we have girls," declared one sensible observer, "the need is for more."[12]

There was also a need for women teachers. By the autumn of 1971, six were members of the faculty. Roberta Tenney, earliest friend and counselor to the pioneers of the previous January, stayed on to become one of the school's top teachers of history. She was soon joined by Virginia Deane, who was to be named a vice rector in 1975. Miss Deane had strong ideas of her own on what coeducation should mean. Coeducation, she wrote soon after arriving, was usually interpreted as the education of the two sexes in the same facilities and with the same opportunities. But that was only the beginning: "The real challenge of coeducation is the education of each sex about the other."[13]

Such a goal, sensitive and subtle though some of its implications might be, was well suited to St. Paul's with its interacting community built on more than intellectual attainment. It was suited also to the mood of the 1970s. The new order was composed of students who cared about each other, respecting the uniqueness of personality, their own and that of their friends. In these circumstances each sex was prepared to be "educated about the other," within the constraints generally accepted by their society.

The change to coeducation had been accomplished without capital expenditures, except for a wall to divide the girls' locker room from the boys' in the gymnasium. The girl students took seats in the chapel or the classrooms as if they had always been there, and occupied rooms in one or more of the school's regular dormitories. As their numbers increased, however, the overall size of the school became a matter of concern. To cut down sharply upon the number of boys admitted would be to alter the character of the school and to disturb relationships with the alumni body. The problem was partly resolved by increasing the number of students to just under five hundred. But the pressure on admissions remained great, as more girls of high qualifications applied, and as the objective of a sixty to forty proportion between boys and girls came to be tacitly recognized.

The difficulty was alleviated by the decision of the trustees to make St. Paul's a four-year school. Termination of the all-boy lower school, so long a place of affectionate nurture and admonition, a focus of responsibility for upper formers and a refuge for the sons of families broken by divorce or engaged in careers requiring long absences from the country, was a choice not easily made. "How many opening-day tears and fears," wrote a master, "how many feuds and fights and feeds" would end with the departure of the school's youngest boys.[14]

By 1970, the lower school had in fact undergone transformations that weakened it as a separate entity within the school. Its students, lodged in Kittredge, went to a new dining hall in the upper school for their meals and to the school house for their studies. When the lower school ceased to exist in the autumn of 1973, older students overflowed the momentary vacancy it created. Its former alcoves converted to rooms, Kittredge took its place as a popular, centrally located dormitory.

Toward 1980

By the 1970s, the form and spirit of a school keyed to a new age had fully emerged. Abolition of the lower school had not only provided place for a larger number of girl students but had encouraged the freer atmosphere of a school composed entirely of a higher age group. The ideal of flexibility and adjustment to individual needs prevailed throughout. Strict divisions

Presiding at the creation of a new order.
Oates, with Chairman of the Board Amory Houghton, Jr.

An atmosphere different from anything that had prevailed in the first 114 years of the school's history.

between forms gave way before the wider option in course selection and as the result of a housing system that mixed students from the fourth to the sixth forms. Movement back and forth between Millville and the outside world was constant. A dozen students would be absent, some spending a year abroad, some working elsewhere for a term or more while engaged in independent study programs. Weekends away, or trips for athletic or cultural events, were a regular part of school life.

Nowhere did the principle of choice show itself more sharply than in the curriculum. Academic requirements for the school diploma were revised, widening the passage, in the rector's words, "through which students travel in their efforts to make knowledge their personal possession."[15] Courses in the languages and in science had, of course, been greatly expanded since the nineteenth century, and "special classes" for advanced students had enlarged the curriculum's traditional content. Yet even under Warren's curricular revisions, the departmental structure remained largely unaltered. Now the arts became one of the regular departments, with studio courses for academic credit—in drama, music, dance, crafts—being accompanied by historical and analytical studies. "Human Relations," too, became a major grouping, emphasizing the growth of personality in all its aspects.

Other departments saw important changes in the content of their courses. The department of religion superseded the old "Sacred Studies"; its approach was comparative and undogmatic, with strong emphasis on moral choices as exemplified in literature and contemporary life. Under the enthusiastic leadership of George A. Tracy, the study of Greek and Latin continued, no longer as a basis of all other learning but as a means of inquiry into the nature of civilization and a method of intellectual discipline. It was not unusual, in the St. Paul's of the late 1970s, to find a hundred students taking Latin and Greek, with an advanced group reading St. Mark in the original. History and English between them offered some seventy course choices. "American Advertising" took its place beside "Shakespeare"; "Women in History" beside "Practical Politics."

In this new community, the concepts of law and of justice were decisively made over. The presence of girl students removed the last vestige of the military analogy which Joseph Coit had seen lying below the surface, making possible a fuller expression of a "free system." Rules were reduced to a minimum, and their enforcement was the result of an authority widely diffused among students and faculty. The rector ceased to be an unchecked, arbitrary power working in mysterious ways.

In one of his annual reports, Oates defined discipline at the school as "a relation between people, usually with . . . one person directing, or leading, or helping another."[16] The element of "help" was often paramount in a disciplinary situation, and was recognized by the students, who saw their own role in the process as that of guiding a friend as much as enforcing a rigid code. Under the school's "developmental" philosophy, the capacity to deal effectively with advice or punishment was one of the important variables among students of different ages, sexes, and rates of growth. Discipline became itself part of education, rather than an extraneous force in conflict with it.

In 1975, Oates reported on the school's successful adaptation to all aspects of coeducation. The number of girl students had grown from 114 in 1972 to 149 and 177 in the two following years. Before the school had reached the latter number of boys, twenty years of its history had passed! There were then sixteen full- and part-time women teachers. The first woman trustee, Elizabeth W. Loomis, had taken her place on the board. The headmistress of Rosemary Hall, Mrs. Loomis was the widow of a St. Paul's graduate and the mother of two of its alumni. The girls were show-ing their proficiency at sports. In field hockey they had suffered but one defeat in three years. In soccer, basketball, squash, lacrosse, tennis and crew they were also distinguishing themselves. (The boys had also had winning seasons in an even wider range of sports.) Girls were now elected regularly to take their place among the officers of the sixth form, as well as in extracurricular organizations.

In 1974, Amory Houghton, Jr., resigned as chairman of the board (he would soon be busier than ever, soliciting major gifts for the school's endowment). His successor, Samuel R. Callaway,[17] represented the forces of experience and continuity. But younger members were elected—the youngest by far in St. Paul's history. Benjamin R. Neilson had been president of the sixth form in 1956, and in the critical year 1968 he became a trustee. Walker Lewis had also been an outstanding student president; he was twenty-seven when he first took his place among the group sitting informally around the rectory living room, spring and fall, much as they had conducted their deliberations in the days of the first Coit.

Growing deficiencies in the education offered by public high schools—the residue of the urban problems of the 1960s—were resulting during this time in a larger-than-ever stream of applicants to the indepen-dent schools. St. Paul's was in the forefront of those feeling the pressure. The year 1974 saw the largest number of visits to the school by prospec-tive students and their parents, the largest list of candidates—of boy can-didates and girl candidates—heretofore experienced. Those records were to be regularly surpassed in the following years.

The trustees and the alumni undertook at this juncture a drive for $30 million, all but a small part of it to be marked for endowment.[18] The unprecedented size of the goal was based on a realistic assessment of economic trends over the next twenty years. Rising costs were already eating at the financial substructure of many private institutions. Only a larger endowment could enable St. Paul's to maintain its standards of excellence and the diversity founded in part on liberal scholarships, while maintaining a reasonable tuition level. An economic recession slowed the first part of the drive, and its end was delayed. But in February 1980, at a dinner in New York it was announced that the goal of $30 million had been surpassed. The new funds, given and pledged, exceeded the school's total endowment as late as the 1960s.

One immediate result of the drive was the pledge of an anonymous donor of funds for a major investment in the performing arts. Half of a promised multi-million-dollar gift was to be used to house drama, music and dance; the other half to be used for endowment of these programs. It was hoped that by this endowment the school would in the future be saved from the tendency, universal among educational and other institutions, to make the arts the first to bear cuts in times of economic retrenchment.

These buildings formed the major construction program of the 1970s. Designed by Hugh Hardy and associates, their combined bulk threatened to place a disproportionately large structure on the landscape, or one situated remote from the academic heart. But the drama workshop—a space filled with platforms, bridges and catwalks—was added inconspicuously to Memorial Hall, where the performing arts had long been focused. Separate music and dance facilities, united below ground, were slipped into the midst of other classroom buildings, completing encirclement of the sluice's little valley.

In November 1978, the new drama building saw its opening night. Many details were still unfinished; the ground outside was muddy in a late rain and piled high with materials used in construction of the two adjacent buildings. No ceremonies marked the first use of the facility. But as students, in a production of *A Midsummer Night's Dream* which they had themselves organized and directed, made their entrances to music—descending and reascending from the various levels of this modern stage structure—it was clear that this was one more important manifestation of change at St. Paul's.

The performing arts, now highly developed and pursued for academic credit, were an intrinsic part of St. Paul's as it moved toward the one hundred twenty-fifth anniversary of its founding. Here was sensitivity, articulateness, individuality; here was a reaching for excellence in visible and classic forms. The new community—like the new theater—was one where many talents could find expression, according to the stage of development each student had attained, within a framework of caring and mutual support.

CHAPTER SIXTEEN

Epilogue—Past and Future

Independent schools in the United States were established to meet various needs, from providing rural surroundings for children of the urban rich to importing the civilized customs of British education. Institutions, however, tend to be changelings: they outgrow their original aims and live on to serve new purposes. By the last quarter of the twentieth century, the independent schools appeared to have a secure place within secondary education. Their freedom and variety allowed them to experiment without governmental hindrance; they were able to guarantee discipline and intellectual rigor within an educational environment that could too often provide neither.

These independent schools had developed an ambiguous, but on the whole friendly and respectful, relationship with the institutions of higher learning. The colleges would have liked to boast of an ever-larger dependence on the public school system; but they recognized that the graduates of the private schools, now drawn from a wide variety of backgrounds, were well qualified and serious, and were trained in the basic skills that public education seemed unable to impart. At the same time, in their advanced courses, and in the growing sophistication of their scholarship, these schools offered a challenge to the undergraduate curriculum— indeed a threat to the validity of the whole undergraduate career. Sandwiched between the upward pressures of the independent schools' sixth form and the students' urge for early entrance into professional training, the four-year college was being forced to reconsider the whole question of its relevance.

Within this framework, the independent schools flourished. They drew able students in increasing numbers. They recruited faculties that pushed beyond the traditional upper limits of secondary education. Voices could still be heard asking whether the independent schools had a function and could endure; but the question—at least for the time being—seemed to have been resolved. While the public schools contended with the seemingly insuperable problems of the inner city, or with legislatures bent on short-sighted economy, the maintenance of the private system seemed more essential than ever as the guarantor of excellence and of educational innovation.

Two factors clouded the horizon of these private schools: inflationary trends, and the intensified search of local communities for new revenues. Intolerably high tuitions, acerbated by tax policies overstepping the long-established immunities accorded educational institutions, could pose a fatal threat. The more fortunate of the independent schools found relief in increased support from graduates and parents, particularly for enlarged endowments. They existed within communities where, despite recurring agitations, public officials recognized the interdependence of town and gown.

St. Paul's was among these fortunate schools. By the end of the 1970s, it was favorably situated within the overall educational system, within the community, and in the regard of its own constituency. The question that remained—and that stands tantalizingly at the end of this narrative—is the degree to which it had maintained its historic identity. Was it the same school Dr. Shattuck had watched grow from tentative beginnings? That Ferguson and his successors had nurtured through good and through difficult days? Or had it changed so deeply in the last quarter century as to make its long history—however moving or colorful it might be—irrelevant to the living generation?

Students of the 1970s, looking back, indeed felt that the year 1968 had brought about a sharp break in the fabric of St. Paul's history. Like all who had known at first hand the aftereffects of revolution, they viewed the past as across a wide gulf, seeing their own existence cast in a new mold. A visitor from an earlier epoch, returning to find so much that was strange in Millville, might well have agreed with these students. The casual dress and manner of the St. Paul's family, even in such previously sacred surroundings as the classroom and chapel; the easygoing relations among students and between students and their instructors; the haphazard meals and the constant comings and goings, would have made the place almost unrecognizable. The visitor would have got the impression of a community of carefree wayfarers, or perhaps thought he had landed in a medieval town.

The chapel, though it stood in its old magnificence, would have seemed to Coit or even to Nash an unfamiliar place. Still central to the school, it performed its functions in ways they would have found difficult to understand. The serried ranks in which students had once entered and departed, all of one sex and all similarly clothed, had given way to a

Chapel had become, not part of the answer, but part of the search.
The rector reading reports from the rector's traditional stall.

straggling, multicolored procession. In winter, students arrived at their seats clad in cumbersome outdoor gear, often with packs on their backs, as if they were about to embark upon an arctic expedition. Spring brought out, in visible and often picturesque forms, the romantic liberations of the season. Within the chapel the habit of "lolling," which an earlier rector had found so insupportable, was not unknown.

Mistrust of authority, inherited from 1968, pervaded the chapel services, as it did other aspects of school life. Truth was believed to exist not in preordained rituals or forms, but in the perceptions of individuals, according to their experience and their personal insights. Chapel had thus become, not part of the answer, but part of the search; and even the search had to be largely unforced and voluntary. Christian dogma, like all other dogma, was obsolete; even the symbols of the old religion were employed sparingly. Instead, students organized services of thanks in the chapel, or expressed their pleasure in existence by singing folk songs or playing the flute; they listened to brief talks, in most of which secular experiences were shared. On winter mornings, when it was too cold to gather outside on the steps of the chapel, the rector made school announcements from his stall at the rear of the long, dimly lit nave.

Had St. Paul's in fact been cut off from its past? That the events of 1968 had left an ineradicable mark upon its life could not be denied. The revolution had been real, and its effects were continuing and profound. But even the most far-reaching of such historical changes leave unshaken many of the old landmarks of a society. At St. Paul's, though young men and women had broken with the past, the past still spoke to them in an accumulation of tacitly received wisdom, in names and images, in the physical surroundings of the New England landscape. The school was still, in Tillich's phrase, "a community with symbols." In those symbols were embodied answers to the questions of human existence and its meaning. The young person, often at the very moment when he or she felt most free of external influences, was guided by an inheritance only partly sensed.

St. Paul's had begun as an experiment in liberal education. At the beginning, the influence of Round Hill had been at least as strong as that

Past and future remained a seamless web.
The dam site where the school's history began.

of Flushing Institute; the ideas of Jefferson and Rousseau, as those of the patron saint. Even in periods when the religious aspect was most marked, secular values of community life were not neglected. William Oates presided over a post-1968 school not less a part of the St. Paul's tradition than the medievalism of Henry Coit's last phase. The "developmental" philosophy espoused by Oates had been at the heart of many of the rituals and ceremonies of early years; and through the 1970s, when "inductive" education was branded a thing of the past, students were being led more subtly than they knew into ways by which earlier generations had found understanding and joy. More than in most educational institutions, the events of 1968 at St. Paul's had been a true break with the past; more than in most, the past and present were cut from the same cloth.

Moving about St. Paul's in the spring of 1979, one was tempted to feel that the school had reached an apex. This was a busy and apparently contented community, enlightened within and secure in its relations with the external world. After periods of prosperity and times of testing, it had reached this happy elevation. What would happen next?

However tempting it may be to suppose one has reached the end of history, history teaches us to be wary of such judgments. St. Paul's in the late 1970s could be viewed as a kind of modern utopia, but even utopias have their day. This school would be no exception. Other rectors, other trustees and teachers—above all, other students—would make it over by degrees, while events in the outside world were exerting their force.

Perhaps in the future the drift will be toward an ever-larger freedom, a liberalization of codes and rules beyond those now envisaged. Or, in the way things have of turning back upon themselves, it may be toward reassertion of a stricter sense of order and discipline. A myriad new arrangements are within the realm of possibility, as all things are tested by experience and by time. The life of the colleges is in flux, as is that of the schools, and beyond these lie the expectations of a constantly evolving social order. "We walk, and we work, by faith," wrote Samuel Drury. By faith St. Paul's would continue to define itself and to deepen its insight into the lives of young men and women.

Acknowledgments

Materials on St. Paul's School are abundant but are greatly in need of the attention of a trained archivist. In the school library five different locked rooms or cabinets store uncatalogued printed and manuscript material; in the school house are another five. These latter include personal letters of the rectors, trustees, masters, alumni and parents, as well as some documents, such as trustees minutes, not open to general inspection. I have had full access and have drawn, with special permission where necessary, from all sources.

In the search, in addition to names mentioned in the Introduction, I have been greatly aided by Raymond Spencer, secretary to five rectors. Joseph A. Manley, school librarian, and Ann Louise Locke, assistant librarian, have been enormously patient in answering my requests for information. Phyllis Robinson has helped me in a thousand ways and has applied to this history the eye of a sympathetic outsider. Christine Shipman Doscher has again been a faithful and persevering typist.

William Abbe, of the St. Paul's faculty, has kindly consented to the use of one of his woodcuts for the endpapers of this book; R. Brooke Roberts, a graduate, has drawn the maps.

It is not possible to record my gratitude to many masters now at the school as well as to some who are retired; to students who have enlightened me both directly and indirectly; and to alumni and alumnae who have answered my appeals on specific matters. No one who works in this field, however, can fail to express his debt to the late Arthur Stanwood Pier, whose graceful history of St. Paul's, published in 1934, laid the groundwork for subsequent research. His chapters on the Drury regime he wrote under the severe handicap of dealing with contemporary events while the chief actor was still alive. Fortunately, the tale was taken up by Roger W. Drury, in *Drury and St. Paul's—The Scars of a Schoolmaster*. The son writes of his father with affectionate discernment and rare candor.

A. H.

Bibliography

━━━━━━◆◆◆◆◆◆━━━━━━

Books, Pamphlets and Articles

The reader is asked to refer to this list when short titles are given in the Notes.

ACOSTA, NICHOLS. *Forty Years More.* Groton, Mass.: Privately printed, 1976.

ADAMS, CHARLES FRANCIS. *Richard Henry Dana—A Biography.* Boston: Houghton Mifflin Co., 1890.

ALLIS, FREDERICK S. *Youth from Every Quarter—A Bicentennial History of Phillips Academy.* Andover, Mass.: The University Press of New England, 1979.

AYRE, ANNA. *The Life and Work of William Augustus Muhlenberg.* New York: Harper and Bros., 1880.

BALTZELL, E. DIGBY. *The Philadelphia Gentleman.* Glencoe, Ill.: The Free Press, 1958.

BARRETT, JOHN SPENCER. "The Round Hill School," *Proceedings of the American Antiquarian Society,* April 1917.

BARZUN, JACQUES, ed. *Selected Writings of John Jay Chapman.* New York: Farrar Straus and Cuddahy, 1957.

BELLUSH, BERNARD. *He Walked Alone—A Biography of John Gilbert Winant.* Paris: Moriton, 1968.

BENSON, ALBERT E. *History of St. Mark's School.* Cambridge, Mass.: Privately printed.

BIRMINGHAM, STEPHEN. "The New England Prep School," *Holiday,* June 1964.

BOUTON, NATHANIEL. *History of Concord.* Concord, N.H., 1856.

BRACKMAN, JACOB. "The Gospel According to St. Paul's," *Esquire,* June 1966.

BROOKS, VAN WYCK. *New England Indian Summer 1865–1915.* New York: E. P. Dutton and Co., 1940.

CHAPMAN, CHANLER A. *The Wrong Attitude, A Bad Boy in a Good School.* New York: G. P. Putnam and Sons, 1940.

CHAPMAN, JOHN JAY. *Learning and Other Essays.* New York: Moffat Yard and Co., 1910.

COIT, HENRY AUGUSTUS. "An American Boys' School—What It Should Be," *The Forum,* September 1891.

————, *School Sermons.* New York: Moffat Yard and Co., 1909.

COIT, JOSEPH HOWLAND. "The School's Ideals." An Address delivered on the third Sunday after Easter by the Rector, 1897.

[————, and SHATTUCK, GEORGE CHEYNE.] *Memorials of St. Paul's School.* New York: D. Appleton and Co., 1891.

CONOVER, JAMES POTTER. *John Hargate: 1856–1907.* The Alumni Association of SPS, 1907.

————. *Memories of a Great Schoolmaster.* Boston: Houghton Mifflin Co., 1906.

DANA, RICHARD HENRY, JR. *Speeches in Stirring Times* and *Letters to a Son*. Edited by Richard Henry Dana III. Boston and New York: Houghton Mifflin Co., 1910.

DARWIN, BERNARD. *The English Public School*. London and New York: Longmans Green and Co., 1929.

DAVIES, JOHN. *The Legend of Hobey Baker*. Boston: Little, Brown and Co., 1966.

DRURY, ROGER W. *Drury and St. Paul's—The Scars of a Schoolmaster*. Boston: Little, Brown and Co., 1964.

DRURY, S. S. *James Potter Conover: An Appreciation*. Pamphlet published by the *Horae Scholasticae*, 1932.

———. *Schoolmastering, Essays in School Engineering*. Boston and New York: Houghton Mifflin Co., 1910.

EDMONDS, JOHN B., ed. *St. Paul's School in the Second World War*. The Alumni Association of SPS, 1950.

ELIOT, EMILY. *Diary of a Visit to St. Paul's School*. New York: The Uphill Press, 1967.

FERGUSON, HENRY. *The Journal of . . . , Jan. to August 1866*. Hartford: Privately printed, 1924.

FLINT, WILLIAM W. *Historical Sketch of Coit House, Formerly the Orphan's Home of Concord, N.H.* Concord, N.H.: The Rumford Press, 1930.

FUESS, CLAUDE M. *An Old New England School: A History of Phillips Academy, Andover*. Boston: Houghton Mifflin Co., 1917.

GAGARIN, NICHOLAS. *Windsong*. New York: William Morrow & Co., 1970.

GAITHORNE-HARDY, JONATHAN. *The Old School Tie—The Phenomenon of the English Public School*. New York: Viking Press, 1978.

HALL, EDWARD TUCK. *St. Mark's School, A Centennial History*. The St. Mark's Alumni Association, 1967.

HARRISON, HALL. *Life of John Barrett Kerfoot*. New York: James Pott and Co., 1886.

HOVEY, RICHARD B. *John Jay Chapman, An American Mind*. New York: Columbia University Press, 1959.

HOWE, M. A. DE WOLFE. *John Jay Chapman and His Letters*. Boston: Houghton Mifflin Co., 1937.

KEYSER, R. BRENT. *The Fifth Form of 1878*. Baltimore: Privately printed, 1917.

KINSMAN, FREDERICK JOSEPH. *Salve Mater*. New York: Longmans Green and Co., 1920.

KNOX, JAMES C. *Henry Augustus Coit*. New York: Longmans Green and Co., 1915.

LAMBERTON, JAMES M. *An Account of St. Paul's School*. Concord, N.H.: Privately printed, 1898.

LYFORD, JAMES O. *History of Concord, N.H.*, 2 vols. Concord, N.H.: The City Government, 1896.

MCCRACKEN, WILLIAM D. "St. Paul's School," *New England*, June 1897.

MCLACHLAN, JAMES. *American Boarding Schools: A Historical Study*. New York: Charles Scribner's Sons, 1970.

MACKAY-SMITH, ALEXANDER. *Sermon Preached on the Fiftieth Anniversary of St. Paul's School*. Concord, N.H., 1906.

MASON, JULIAN. "Owen Wister—Boy Librarian," *Quarterly Journal of the Library of Congress*, October 1966.

MASSACHUSETTS HISTORICAL SOCIETY. *Pro Bono Publico, The Shattucks of Boston,* 1871.

MATTHEWS, T. S. *Name and Address—An Autobiography.* New York: Simon & Schuster, 1960.

MORGAN, WILLIAM DAVIS. *The Architecture of Henry Vaughan.* Ph.D. dissertation, University of Delaware, Newark, Del.

MORISON, SAMUEL ELIOT. *One Boy's Boston—1887–1901.* Boston: Houghton Mifflin Co., 1962.

OLDHAM, BASIL. *A History of Shrewsbury School, 1552–1952.* Oxford, Eng.: Basil Blackwell, 1952.

OLMSTED BROTHERS, Landscape Architects. "Report to Frances H. Appleton, President of the Alumni Association, St. Paul's School," 10 Sept. 1898.

PERRY, BLISS. *Richard Henry Dana, 1851–1931.* Boston: Houghton Mifflin Co., 1933.

PIER, ARTHUR STANWOOD. *St. Paul's School, 1855–1934.* New York: Charles Scribner's Sons, 1934.

———. "Years Ago," *Horae Scholasticae,* 1932.

POTTER, HENRY C. *Sermon Preached by the Bishop of New York, April 28, 1895 in Memory of Rev. Henry Augustus Coit.* The SPS Alumni Association, 1895.

PRESCOTT, PETER S. *A World of Our Own—Notes on Life and Learning at a Boy's Preparatory School.* New York: Coward McCann, 1970.

ROOS, WILLIAM. *The Hornet's Longboat.* Boston: Houghton Mifflin Co., 1940.

SCUDDER, HORACE E. "A Group of Classical Schools," *Harper's,* October, 1977.

SHATTUCK, FREDERICK. *The Centenary of Round Hill School.* Boston: Privately printed, 1924.

SIZER, THEODORE R. *The Age of the Academies.* New York: Teachers College, Columbia University, 1964.

———. *Secondary Schools at the Turn of the Century.* New Haven: Yale University Press, 1964.

SPILLER, ROBERT E., *et al.,* eds. *Literary History of the United States.* New York: The Macmillan Co., 1959.

SWIFT, AUGUSTUS M. *Derwent Coleridge—Scholar, Pastor, Educator.* New York: Charles F. Roper and Co., 1883.

TOLAND, E. D. *The Diary of . . ., 1920–1945.* Concord, N.H.: Privately printed, 1946.

WARD, JARED. *St. Paul's School, 1954–1974—A Case Study in Institutional Change.* Cambridge, Mass.: Harvard College, 1978.

WARREN, MATTHEW M. "Speeding Up the Bright Ones," *Atlantic Monthly,* June 1962.

WEAVER, GEORGE. *The History of Trinity College.* Hartford: Trinity College Press, 1967.

WENDELL, BARRETT. "Samuel Eliot," *Proceedings of the American Academy of Arts and Sciences,* vol. 34, 1898.

WHITRIDGE, ARNOLD. *Dr. Arnold of Rugby.* New York: Henry Holt and Co., 1928.

WILLIAMS, MYRON R. *Story of Phillips Exeter.* New York: 1967.

WISTER, OWEN. "Dr. Coit of St. Paul's," *Atlantic Monthly,* CXLIII, 1926.

———. Introduction to *St. Paul's School in the Great War.* The Alumni Association of St. Paul's School, 1923.

ZABRISKIE, ALEXANDER Z. *Bishop Brent—Crusader for Christian Unity.* Philadelphia: The Westminster Press, 1948.

Manuscript Collections

Titles are listed alphabetically and referred to in shortened form in the Notes. Additional typed documents, theses, and so on, are referred to individually in the Notes. The Sheldon Library, here and in the Notes, refers to the library of St. Paul's School.

Administrative File (Records of official school correspondence, including many personal letters of the rectors). St. Paul's School Administrative Office.

Alumni File (Records of alumni and alumnae, mostly pertaining to years at the school but containing some vital later information). St. Paul's School Alumni Office.

Chapman (John Jay) *Papers* (Important correspondence with S. S. Drury, Owen Wister, and other school figures). The Houghton Library, Harvard University.

Collection of Letters Given by Samuel Eliot Morison (A number of these nineteenth-century documents relate to St. Paul's). The Boston Athenaeum.

Coit (Charles Wheeler) *Recollections of St. Paul's School* (See Chapter Two, note 8).

Dickey (Charles S.) *Papers* (Correspondence with the rectors and with fellow trustees by an influential board member of the mid-1900s). The Sheldon Library.

Drury (Samuel Smith) *Papers* (An invaluable collection including diaries, personal correspondence and manuscripts). The Sheldon Library.

Kittredge (Henry Crocker) *Papers* (Spotty but revealing collection of the sixth rector's letters, notes for addresses, commonplace books, etc.). The Sheldon Library.

Letters Concerning the Founding of St. Paul's School (Typewritten copies of letters from the letterbooks of George C. Shattuck in the collection of the Massachusetts Historical Society; running to the 1870s, but most detailed for the years 1855–1857). The Sheldon Library.

Miscellaneous Letters Concerning St. Paul's School (A random collection mostly from the 1860s and 1870s). The Sheldon Library.

Rural Record (Handwritten journal of school events kept by various masters from 1857 to the early twentieth century). The Sheldon Library.

Scudder (Willard) *Diaries* (Running from his days as a student in the 1880s to near the end of his long mastership in the 1930s, these provide, amid much trivia, important light on school events). The Sheldon Library.

Shattuck Papers (Letters of the founder, George C. Shattuck, and his son George B. Shattuck, as well as other members of the family—a number referring to school affairs). The Massachusetts Historical Society.

Trustees Minutes (Beginning in the Ferguson regime early in the twentieth century, these documents are unrevealing in the first decades but come to life under the skillful hand of John R. McClane, clerk of the board from 1918 to 1952). St. Paul's School Administrative Office.

Wister (Owen) *Papers* (A significant collection with much material on the school during Wister's student years, 1874 to 1878, and some interesting documents after his graduation). The Library of Congress.

Notes

Books and manuscript sources previously listed in the Manuscript Collections and Bibliography, when cited in these Notes, appear in shortened form under the author's name. The following abbreviations are used in the Notes for persons and publications frequently cited:

AH   August Heckscher
ALH   *Alumni Horae*
AR   Annual reports of the
            rectors
GBS   George Brune Shattuck
GCS   George Cheyne Shattuck
HAC   Henry Augustus Coit
HCK   Henry Crocker Kittredge
HF   Henry Ferguson
HS   *Horae Scholasticae*
JHC   Joseph Howland Coit
JJC   John Jay Chapman
MKG   Malcolm Kenneth
            Gordon
MMW   Matthew Madison
            Warren
NBN   Norman Burdett Nash
OW   Owen Wister
RR   *Rural Record*
SPS   St. Paul's School
SSD   Samuel Smith Drury
WS   Willard Scudder

Introduction
1. J. R. Bishop, *HS*, December 1877.
2. Chanler Chapman to AH, 22 March 1978.

Chapter One, The Founding: 1855
1. The reference in this paragraph to lingering patches of snow is from JHC, *The School's Ideals*. Most accounts state that three boys were in the carriage with the Coits, but the weight of evidence indicates that young Frederick Shattuck

was already at the farm. The presence of the dog is attested to in GBS, *HS*, April 1906.

2. Lyford, *Concord History*, p. 1322. Doubts about the provenance of the "pre-revolutionary" cottage are resolved in John Rexford, *ALH*, Summer 1954. No house stood on the Millville land when Moses Shute bought it in 1817 for $22, but the cottage appears to have been moved from another lot purchased in 1818. The present-day Scudder House is a replica of this cottage.

3. Suggestions for the name of the venture included "The Millville Grammar School" and "Croswell College," the latter in honor of the founder of Boston's Church of the Advent. The name St. Paul's School was chosen by Dr. Shattuck and was never seriously in doubt. In this paragraph the quotation, "a small beginning," and the subsequent biblical allusions are from HAC, "The True Immortality," in *School Sermons*.

4. Invaluable background on this and on nineteenth-century education in general is in McLachlan, *American Boarding Schools*. See also Barrett, *The Round Hill School*, and *Outlook of the System of Education at Round Hill*, published anonymously, Boston: The Steam Power Press, 1831. In the Sheldon Library is a unique volume containing memorabilia of the school and portraits of many of its graduates.

5. Barrett, *supra*, p. 10.

6. The Shattuck family history is related in *Pro Bono Publico*, Boston, The Massachusetts Historical Society.

7. GCS, Jr., to GCS, 15 July 1827. The two letters that follow are J. G. Cogswell to GCS, 20 July 1827, and GCS, Jr., to GCS, 4 Feb. 1827. All are in the *Shattuck Papers*.

8. These quotations are from Barrett, *The Round Hill School*, pp. 10 ff.

9. Shattuck, *The Centenary of Round Hill School*, 1924.

10. Cited in Pier, *St. Paul's School,* p. 3. Pier gives no sources, and the whereabouts of this letter from Coit to his parents is unknown.

11. Kerfoot diary, March 1830; cited in Harrison, *Life of Kerfoot*, p. 8.

12. SPS *Annual Statement, 1858*.

13. [GCS and JHC], *Memorials of St. Paul's School*, p. 15.

14. Carlton Chase to GCS, 23 Oct. 1855, *Letters Concerning the Founding*.

15. Lamberton, *St. Paul's School*, p. 50.

16. Carlton Chase to GCS, 10 March 1855, *Letters Concerning the Founding*.

17. The search for a rector, described in the following pages, is based on *Letters Concerning the Founding*. Individual quotations are not cited except where there may be some likelihood of uncertainty.

18. Paragraph based on letter of Carlton Chase to GCS, 23 Oct. 1855, *supra*.

19. The phrase "He found his bride" was proposed in 1931 by Dr. Drury for a memorial plaque in the Lancaster church but was rejected by the vestry as too romantic. The more prosaic "Here he met his wife" was substituted. Clifford C. Twombley to SSD, 30 Jan. 1931, *Administrative File*.

20. W. B. Peters to GCS, 23 and 27 Dec. 1855, *Letters Concerning the Founding*.

21. GBS, *HS*, April 1906.

22. The fourth rector first pointed out that this psalm was appointed to be read on April 3. "Thus Coit must have spoken," Drury wrote, "as with pious faith he laid the foundations." SSD, *AR*, 1911. The words were set to music by Channing Lefebvre for the school's one hundredth anniversary.

Chapter Two. *In Arcadia: 1856–1866*
1. Carlton Chase to GCS, 19 Dec. 1856, *Letters Concerning the Founding.*
2. In this paragraph, the fate of the little dog is in GBS, *HS,* April 1906; the end of "old Kate" is in *HS,* December 1860; the death of Peters is told in HAC to GCS, 7 Jan. 1862, *Letters Concerning the Founding.*
3. *RR,* 1 Dec. 1857. Emphasis added. The *Rural Record* exists in four handwritten folio volumes in the Sheldon Library. An indispensable source for the school's early years, the *Record* was kept anonymously by Francis Chase from 1856 to 1862, John T. Wheeler to 1872, Hall Harrison to 1874, and Augustus M. Swift to 1879. A gap of nine years occurs, then the entries are carried on by various hands until 1890, and then by J. M. Lamberton and Willard Scudder. The Scudder volume is missing.
4. JJC, "The Influence of Schools," in *Learning and Other Essays.*
5. Mackay-Smith, *Sermon on the Fiftieth Anniversary.*
6. The manuscript is in the Sheldon Library. Dated 1852, it belonged to Mrs. Coit's mother; later recipes are added in another hand, presumably her daughter's.
7. GBS, *HS,* April 1906. The subsequent observations in this paragraph, written when George Shattuck was a student, are from a letter to his sister Eleanor Shattuck (15 May 1858) in the *Shattuck Papers.*
8. The description of the school house, and of its art works (below), is based on Chapter I of an undated manuscript, *Recollections of St Paul's School,* by Charles Wheeler Coit, elder son of the first rector. Pier, in writing his *St. Paul's School,* had access to it. Like him, I owe much to this crucial source, though I felt free of restrictions that Coit placed on its use and that prevented Pier from citing it directly. Its whereabouts unknown, the manuscript lay in the administrative files of the school until being rediscovered in 1978.
9. Students referred to the cellar lavatory as Moab and to the bootroom as Edom—as so often drawing for schoolboy jokes on knowledge of the Bible. "Moab is my washpot; over Edom have I cast out my shoe." Pier, *St. Paul's School,* p. 21.
10. Traditionally thought to come from St. Augustine, a St. Paul's scholar traced the words to the 53rd Epistle of St. Jerome. Frederick J. Kinsman, *HS,* June 1926.
11. George Shattuck, in a letter to his sister, quotes the farmer, Woodbury Flanders, to this effect. Young Shattuck thereupon asserts that the bell "sounds as sonorously as there is any necessity for." GBS to Eleanor Shattuck, 10 Jan. 1857, *Shattuck Papers.*
12. A. M. Day, *HS,* April 1861.
13. JHC, *The School's Ideals.*
14. Information on Concord's development and its physical features is drawn from Bouton and from Lyford, Concord's historians of 1856 and 1896 respectively. Uses of the Merrimack at mid-century are picturesquely portrayed in a lithograph in the New Hampshire Historical Society, Concord, dated 1853, taken from a painting by G. Harvey.
15. Helpful research on the mills of Millville was done in 1977 by SPS students under Richard F. Davis of the History Department. A summary is in *ALH,* Summer 1978.
16. Bouton, *History of Concord,* p. 542.

17. Thus: "Four smart shocks" (1870); "The heaviest earthquake shock ever remembered" (1882); "two heavy shocks" (1884); "earthquake at 5:09 a.m." (1887); "a severe shock" (1889). As late as 1978, an earthquake registered 3.5 on the Richter scale. These facts are of some relevance in connection with the establishment of nuclear power plants.

18. *RR*, 15 Jan. 1857. The following pages rely heavily on the *Rural Record*. Quotations from this source are not cited, except where the text may leave some uncertainty as to the source or the date.

19. *RR*, 18 April 1857.

20. *Ibid.*, 25 April 1857.

21. *Ibid.*, 15 Oct. 1857. The entry is in the rector's hand. To this day the prayer read in chapel on the last night of a term contains the intercession that "none who come here may go away unimproved."

22. *Ibid.*, 29 June 1858.

23. *Ibid.*, 25 Jan. 1859.

24. The Rev. S. R. Johnson to Bishop Kerfoot, 7 Feb. 1867; cited in Harrison, *Kerfoot*, p. 479.

25. *RR*, 12 Sept. 1858. The entry is in Coit's hand.

26. The best translation of these untranslatable lines is by George Chapman, *ALH*, Spring 1954: "Hail, Mother, dearer than blessed light dawning / Loved of our hearts more than pleasures of morning / Comrades, with voices free / Sing in her praise . . ."

27. Quoted in Robert H. Bancroft, *HS*, June 1910.

28. Robert H. Bancroft, *ibid*.

29. This was obviously not the rector but a younger brother, William N. Coit, who was at the school for a few years prior to 1860 as curator, or keeper of the grounds. He constructed the white fences with granite posts, surviving in some places to this day. Students, as might have been expected, were prohibited from sitting on these fences.

30. *HS*, June 1910. The article is anonymous but was evidently written by Willard Scudder.

31. *HS*, January 1862 and November 1863. The author of the article on insects in the next paragraph is M. S. Davidson.

32. George S. Mumford, *HS*, June 1910.

33. OW, "Dr. Coit of St. Paul's," *Atlantic Monthly*, 1926.

34. *RR*, 1 Feb. 1862.

35. The poet of this occasion was Robert H. Bancroft; the orator, J. Louis Stebbins. Texts are in *HS*, July 1860.

36. Harrison, *Life of Kerfoot*, p. 324. The chapter from which this is taken, XII, was written by Joseph Coit.

37. Whittingham to Kerfoot, 7 March 1865; cited in *ibid.*, p. 383.

38. *Ibid.*, p. 56.

39. *Ibid.*, p. 318.

40. At this same momentous time, Dr. Muhlenberg made his one recorded visit to the school: "A man of so holy, devoted and useful a life, of such shining deeds and treasured words"—so the recorder characterized him (25 May 1865). Muhlenberg preached at Confirmation and twice on Sunday; "in a few earnest and affectionate words," he bade farewell to the school on which his influence had been strongly stamped.

41. Richard Henry Dana III. The letter is cited in Bliss Perry, *Richard Henry Dana*, p. 35.
42. HAC to GCS, 20 April 1862, *Letters Concerning the Founding.*
43. HAC to GCS, 28 Feb. 1862, *ibid.*
44. In 1870 it was widely supposed that Coit would be elected bishop of New Hampshire. He apparently had little desire for the post, to which William W. Niles was elected. Pier, *St. Paul's School,* p. 93.
45. This letter is dated 18 Aug. 1867; quoted [GCS and JHC] *Memorials of St. Paul's School,* p. 130.
46. Pier, *St. Paul's School,* p. 49.
47. James Barnes, ''A Look Back,'' *HS,* June 1910.
48. *RR,* 4 Feb. 1869

Chapter Three. Vintage Years: 1866–1874
1. T. M. Rochester, *HS,* October 1872.
2. The lack of approval is shown in an icy letter to Owen Wister, a favorite former student. ''I have been much grieved and shocked about you,'' the rector wrote when the young man confessed to religious doubts. ''While I cannot cease to care for you . . . I cannot feel that your relation to the school or to myself is the same as that of one who holds fast to the faith.'' HAC to OW, 8 July 1884, *Wister Papers.* Coit could snub former students of whose conduct he did not approve. ''Indeed,'' Chapman wrote him (in Coit's later years), ''those stories have been so frequent that I supposed not only that you did not feel tenderly toward old boys, but that you had sometimes felt bitterly toward some of them.'' JJC to HAC, 2 Nov. 1894, *Chapman Papers.*
3. A full account of Coit House, from 1866 to 1930, is in Flint, *Historical Sketch of Coit House.*
4. Charles P. Parker, *HS,* December 1868.
5. Conover, ''Early Days at the Home,'' *The Church Fly Leaf,* Diocese of New Hampshire, October 1915.
6. C. P. Parker, cited in Flint, *Historical Sketch of Coit House,* p. 6.
7. OW to Frances Ann Kemble, 22 Nov. 1874, *Wister Papers.*
8. Cited, Flint, *Historical Sketch of Coit House,* p. 3.
9. CWC, *Recollections of St. Paul's School,* Chap. IV.
10. *RR,* 5 May 1873.
11. From an article, unsigned, in *HS,* May 1871.
12. CWC, *Recollections of St. Paul's School,* Chap. IV.
13. The letters quoted in this and the following paragraph are in *Miscellaneous Letters Concerning St. Paul's School.*
14. These figures are given in McLachlan, *American Boarding Schools,* p. 182.
15. Cited [GCS and JHC], *Memorials of St. Paul's School,* p. 130.
16. GBS in *HS,* June 1910.
17. As recalled by George W. Douglas, *ibid.*
18. R. H. Dana II, quoted in Perry, *Richard Henry Dana,* p. 38.
19. CWC, *Recollections of St. Paul's School,* Chap. III.
20. A. N. Littlejohn to HAC, August 1877, *Miscellaneous Letters Concerning St. Paul's School.*
21. Oldham, *A History of Shrewsbury School,* p. 61. The description of Keat in the following paragraph is from Darwin, *The English Public School,* p. 112.

22. Darwin, *The English Public School*, p. 131.
23. Adams, *Richard Henry Dana*, p. 2.
24. John E. Ordway in Lyford, *History of Concord*, p. 1,247.
25. Whitridge, *Dr. Arnold of Rugby*, p. 18.
26. Cited in Ayre, *Muhlenberg*, p. 136.
27. See A. M. Swift, *Derwent Coleridge, passim.*
28. Knox, *Henry Augustus Coit*, p. 21.
29. For the characterization of Swift, I owe much to CWC, *Recollections of St. Paul's School*, Chap III. See also Pier, *History of St. Paul's School*, pp. 109 ff., and Knox, *supra*, p. 21. Swift's entries in the *Rural Record*, 1874 to 1879, attest to his warmhearted enjoyment of life. A letter to a boy recently graduated reinforces the impression: "Of course I ought to be correcting three hundred examination papers *but I'm not.* I'm tired of being informed that Alcibiades was young, profligate and handsome. And as for the adverbial adjunct to the predicate, I simply loathe it. Are you aware that today is an Ember Day? *Litany.* We don't intend to be discouraged." 4 Nov. 1883, A. M. Swift to OW, *Wister Papers.*
30. From a Boston newspaper account preserved in *RR.*
31. HAC to JJC, 19 Jan. 1877, *Chapman Papers.*
32. Cited in Hovey, *John Jay Chapman*, p. 10.
33. JJC, 'The Influence of Schools," in *Learning and Other Essays.*
34. Cited in Mason, "Owen Wister—Boy Librarian," in *Library of Congress Quarterly.*
35. Julian Mason, *supra,* first documented Wister's relationships with his grandmother and with Hall Harison. I owe much to this source.
36. Most of the letters quoted in the following pages can be found in Mason's article, *supra*. I have used a few others from the *Wister Papers.*
37. Dana's letters are in Perry, *Richard Henry Dana.* The father's letters to the son are in Dana, *Speeches in Stirring Times.* Perry draws on an unpublished autobiography by R. H. Dana III in the Dana Papers, Massachusetts Historical Society.
38. Cited in Perry, *supra*, p. 30. After the disappointment recorded here, Dana gave his collection of birds' eggs to a fellow student. That was not the end of his trouble. "It has given your mother great distress," the father wrote. "She has associated you with that collection. . . .She shed a great many tears over it, and said that if you should die, or leave her, she would always want them [the eggs] to remember you by." 25 Feb. 1866, cited in Perry, *supra*, p. 46.
39. The account of the fire is from Dana's unpublished autobiography, cited in Perry, *supra*, p. 47.
40. A typewritten copy of A. Mackay-Smith's diary for 1867 is in the Sheldon Library. The diary has its dark side, indicating that forms of hazing were not absent from the school. "We got Wey and Clark and tied them and hung Wey up by a rope"; or again, "Payne and I tied Wey and Clark up."
41. OW, *HS*, June 1935. Wister's essay was to have been an introduction to a collection of *Horae* verse, which he did not finish editing.
42. JJC, "The Influence of Schools," in *Learning and Other Essays.*
43. From Dana's unpublished autobiography, cited in Perry, *Richard Henry Dana*, p. 45.
44. *RR*, 3 Sept. 1866.
45. Richard D. A. Parrot, *HS*, June 1921.

46. The description here and through the following paragraphs is based on *RR,* 7 June 1871.

Chapter Four. At the Turning Point: 1874–1878
1. JH to GCS, 27 June 1874, in *Letters Concerning the Founding.*
2. [GCS and JHC], *Memorials of St. Paul's School,* p. 128.
3. H. A. Neely to HAC, 13 Feb. 1873, in *Miscellaneous Letters Concerning St. Paul's School.*
4. *Oxford Companion to American Literature,* New York: Oxford University Press, p. 204.
5. The manuscript of Eliot's journal, 1857 to 1894, is in the Boston Athenaeum. The journal is unfortunately scant in direct references to St. Paul's. On his period at Trinity, see Weaver, *The History of Trinity College.*
6. S. Eliot to HAC, 26 July [no year] in *Miscellaneous Letters Concerning St. Paul's School.*
7. Eliot in old age is portrayed in Wendell, "Samuel Eliot," *Proceedings of the American Academy;* also in Morison, *One Boy's Boston,* p. 3.
8. In the Beineke Library at Yale I have examined with awe the water-stained notebook containing the original manuscript of this journal. The story of the voyage is graphically told in Roos, *The Hornet's Longboat.* An interesting sidelight is that the voyage made Mark Twain famous. Stationed in the Sandwich Islands as a correspondent for the *Sacramento Union,* Twain rose from a severe illness, had himself transported by stretcher to the hospital sheltering the survivors, and interviewed them. He stayed up all night to write the story, and his article was thrown aboard a state-bound schooner as it was pulling away from the pier. His account, the first of the miraculous rescue, was reprinted across the country. See Albert E. Stone, Jr., "Mark Twain and the Story of the *Hornet,*" in *Yale University Library Gazette,* April 1961.
9. Mrs. Coit's letter, and the account on the following pages, is from Emily Eliot's journal, the manuscript of which was presented to the Sheldon Library by her son, Samuel Eliot Morison. (A limited edition of this journal was printed by AH and Charles C. Heckscher, *Journal of a Visit to St. Paul's School,* New York: The Uphill Press, 1967.) The days of Feb. 22 to Feb. 29 are also chronicled in *RR.* Wister's "little play" was titled "I've Written to Brown." *HS,* March 1878.
10. Coit's two letters to the parents, here and below, exist in printed form in the Sheldon Library.
11. E. D. Tibbits to OW, 22 May 1878, *Wister Papers.* The later record of this outstanding form, with comments on the school's history, is in Keyser, *The Fifth Form of 1878.* (Students at this time were usually graduated from the fifth form; Wister in 1878 was staying on for a sort of postgraduate year, in what became known as the sixth form remove.)
12. The basic source for the burning of the school house is CWC, *Recollections of St. Paul's School,* Chap. V.
13. The historic table was subsequently placed in the common room of the new school house, where it was permitted to be used only by advanced students in mathematics. It is stored today in the school's red barn. See MKG, *ALH,* Autumn 1965.

Chapter Five. The Age of Faith: 1878–1895
1. CWC, *Recollections of St. Paul's School,* Chap. VI.
2. St. Paul's had inspired the founding of other schools. When Joseph Burnett, whose oldest son had been to St. Paul's, wanted to enter a second son, he found the lists crowded. Coit suggested that since he had five more sons he start another school. This Burnett did, establishing St. Mark's in 1865 with a nephew of Bishop Kerfoot as its first rector and a St. Paul's trustee on its board. Benson, *History of St. Mark's School,* p. 11. In 1894 Endicott Peabody in turn used St. Mark's as a model for Groton.
3. HAC, "The True Immortality," in *School Sermons.*
4. Cited in McLachlan, *American Boarding Schools,* p. 195.
5. CWC, *Recollections of St. Paul's School,* Chap. VI.
6. Article by John MacMullen, 1881, reprinted as a pamphlet now in Teachers College Library, Columbia University.
7. Cited in McLachlan, *American Boarding Schools,* p. 129.
8. This and the following paragraphs are based on the Willard Scudder diaries, beginning 25 Jan. 1882.
9. HAC, *School Sermons,* p. 241.
10. Wister's remarks, in manuscript form, are in the *Alumni File.*
11. JJC, "The Influence of Schools," in *Learning and Other Essays.*
12. OW, "Dr. Coit," in *Atlantic Monthly,* 1926.
13. Knox, *Henry Augustus Coit,* p. 20.
14. CWC, *Recollections of St. Paul's School,* Chap. VI.
15. Knox, *Henry Augustus Coit,* p. 20. These paragraphs also draw on Kinsman, *Salve Mater,* Chap. I.
16. JJC, "The Influence of Schools," in *Learning and Other Essays.*
17. Kinsman, *Salve Mater,* p. 25.
18. HAC, *School Sermons,* p. 278.
19. CWC, *Recollections of St. Paul's School,* Chap. VI.
20. HAC, "The True Immortality," in *School Sermons,* p. 173.
21. Morgan, *The Architecture of Henry Vaughan.*
22. Samuel Eliot, *Address in the Chapel of St. Paul's School,* Sept. 21, 1886.
23. CWC, *Recollections of St. Paul's School,* Chap. VI.
24. Flint, *Historical Sketch of Coit House,* p. 15.
25. CWC, *Recollections of St. Paul's School,* Chap. VI.
26. Eliot, *George Cheyne Shattuck, A Memorial Address,* Concord, N.H., 1893, in the Sheldon Library.
27. Conover, *A Memoir of John Hargate,* pamphlet in Sheldon Library.
28. Quoted in *RR,* 4 Feb. 1895.
29. JJC, "The Influence of Schools," in *Learning and Other Essays.*

Chapter Six. This Troublous Life: 1895–1906
1. This letter is among those given by S. E. Morison to the Boston Athenaeum.
2. The views expressed in this and the following paragraphs are from [GCS and JHC], *Memorials of St. Paul's School,* pp. 139 ff.
3. Paragraph based on Pier, *Years Ago,* one of a series of pamphlets published as supplements by the *HS* in 1932.
4. Brooks, *New England Indian Summer,* p. 416.
5. *Ibid.,* pp. 422 and 433.

6. On Andover's crisis see Allis, *Youth from Every Quarter.* On St. Mark's in this time of trouble, see Benson, *History of St. Mark's School.* Exeter was particularly turbulent between 1884 and 1894. An early Exeter historian describes student life in this period as "vicious and harmful"; Williams refers to these years as "Exeter's dark ages."

7. Excerpts from the Flint diary appear in *ALH,* Spring 1971. The reference to laudanum is dated 23 May 1896.

8. This paragraph is based on MKG, *HS,* Spring 1940.

9. The origin of these clubs goes back to 1859, when two cricket clubs, Hercules and Venus, were formed. The name Venus was rejected as inappropriate, and the clubs were quickly re-formed into Isthmian and Olympic. These in turn became Isthmian and Old Hundred. The 1888 football clubs were first Mohican, Rugby and Delphian. When it was decided to apply the tripartite club system to all forms of sport, the Isthmians took over Mohicans; the Old Hundreds took over Rugby; the Delphians continued under their existing name. To this day every new boy or girl, on entering the school, becomes an Isthmian, Old Hundred or Delphian.

10. A lively, journalistic account of Baker's exploits is in Davies, *The Legend of Hobey Baker.*

11. Pier, *St. Paul's School,* p. 298.

12. A printed history of the "Bogi" (1908) in the Sheldon Library gives much of the information on the secret societies, here and on later pages. See also Pier, *supra,* Chap. 15.

13. Quotations are from the typewritten report of the Olmsted Brothers to the president of the Alumni Association, 1898, in the Sheldon Library. A later report on planning and landscaping the center of the school appeared in printed form: *Report on the Physical Development of St. Paul's School,* by Grover Atterbury and Frederick Law Olmsted, 1932, also in the Sheldon Library.

14. The famous old cottage was preserved, more as a practical matter than an act of piety. Moved to the far side of what was to become the new Dunbarton road, it serves to this day—unnoted and unsung—as a lodging for school employees. It is the oldest building in Millville and, though much altered from its original form, the only one to have been part of the school at its founding.

15. Theodore Roosevelt to MKG, *HS,* October, 1898.

16. Morison, *One Boy's Boston,* p. 79.

17. *Diary of Edward D. Toland,* p. 22. Toland, who graduated in 1904, writes well of this early period. Later diary entries, made when he was a master, were written (in his own words) "to preserve a record of the *shortcomings of the school administration under Dr. Drury," Diary,* p. 2 (italics in the original). They are highly prejudiced and colored by deep personal animosity.

18. Pier, *St. Paul's School,* p. 262. Pier knew this period at first hand, and the account in Chap. 13 of his book is excellent.

19. Pier, *supra,* p. 113.

20. Toland, *Diary,* p. 22.

21. The letter is in the collection donated by S. E. Morison to the Boston Athenaeum.

22. Conover, *John Hargate.*

23. This version of Coit's touching rejoinder is in Conover, *ibid.* See also Pier, *St. Paul's School,* p. 196.

24. Conover, *ibid.*
25. *HS,* June 1906.
26. The quotations are from JJC, "The Influence of Schools," in *Learning and Other Essays.*

Chapter Seven. Interregnum: 1906–1910
 1. Comments attributed to Scudder in this and the following paragraphs are from his diaries for 1907 to 1908. The diaries are a particularly valuable source for this period.
 2. Account based on Scudder diaries. No minutes of the standing committee meetings were kept.
 3. J. H. Coit, 2nd., to HF, 9 June 1907. Correspondence between Ferguson and the younger Coit is in the *Administrative File.* This file, to which the author has had unrestricted access—sketchy in Ferguson's administration but very full under his successors'—constitutes an indispensable source for the school's history in the modern period.
 4. *HS,* Feb. 1922.
 5. HF, *AR,* 1907.
 6. Again, information on the activities of the standing committee of the Alumni Association comes from the well-informed comments in the Scudder diaries. Minutes of the meeting of the Alumni Association of 6 June 1907, strongly asserting support for Kinsman, indirectly confirm the dissidence of a minority.
 7. Kinsman to the secretary of the Alumni Association, 11 July 1907, *Administrative File.*
 8. Kinsman, *Salve Mater,* p. 5. The first chapter of this brilliant apologia gives a vivid picture of the school in the late 1880s.
 9. Kinsman, *ibid.*
10. Ferguson's remarks to the trustees, and through the following pages his comments on management of the school and on education, are from his annual reports, 1907–1911. Ferguson initiated this invaluable series of publications, continued by his successors. He was also responsible for having the board, for the first time, keep minutes of its meetings.
11. The *Drury Papers* include the correspondence with Bishop Brent quoted in this section. When source and date are self-evident, I have not cited specific quotations. R. W. Drury, in *Drury and St. Paul's,* first unfolded the narrative sketched here.
12. SSD, Diary, *Drury Papers,* 8 Dec. 1924.
13. HF to SSD, undated. This letter is in the *Administrative File,* unlike the others in this correspondence, which are in *Drury Papers.* Conceivably, it was not actually sent.
14. *HS,* Feb. 1924. The article is unsigned but was undoubtedly written by Scudder. A full account of the occasion is in R. W. Drury, "Wilson at St. Paul's," *ALH,* Spring 1974.
15. Quotations from the speech are from a fragmentary text in the Concord *Monitor,* 3 June 1909; in *The Papers of Woodrow Wilson,* Princeton, N.J.: Princeton University Press, vol. 19, pp. 226 ff.
16. Ferguson's farewell included a characteristically discreet and generous gift, added to many he had made anonymously during his years as rector. Reflect-

ing his own efforts to keep the school on an even keel financially, he donated $24,000 to be used as the rector's collateral fund for borrowing such monies "as may be necessary for the prompt transaction of the daily school business." The trustees learned of the gift "with deep emotion" (Trustees Minutes, 2 June 1911). In 1882 Ferguson had been the donor of the Ferguson Scholarships, of which Scudder and Kinsman were among the first winners.

Chapter Eight. The Way Restored: 1911–1919
1. The original program of this production, 21 Sept. 1898, is in *Drury Papers.*
2. R. H. Macdonald to MMW, 1 April 1964. *Alumni Files.*
3. Cited in R. W. Drury, *Drury and St. Paul's,* p. 9.
4. *Ibid.,* p. 11.
5. Dr. Locke to Bishop Lawrence, 16 Nov. 1907, *Drury Papers.*
6. Zabriskie, *Bishop Brent,* pp. 35, 159.
7. Quoted in Charles Wiggins, "Samuel S. Drury," *ALH,* Spring 1938.
8. Cited in R. W. Drury, *Drury and St. Paul's,* p. 56.
9. C. Brent to Cornelia Wolcott, 6 Oct. 1910, *Drury Papers.*
10. Robert W. Potter, *ALH,* Spring 1938.
11. Unsigned article, *ibid.*
12. SSD to Robert P. Perkins [no date], *Administrative File.*
13. It was the custom for the rector, at the autumn meeting of the trustees, to read his report to the board. Subsequently, often with emendations or omissions, the report was printed. Unless otherwise noted, Drury's statements to the board are from the printed source. In this and the following paragraphs, quotations are from SSD, *AR,* 1911.
14. SSD to HF, 6 Nov. 1911, *Administrative File.*
15. SSD, *AR,* 1915.
16. *Ibid.,* 1912.
17. The infirmary was given to the school by George A. Armour as a memorial to his son Edmund Armour, who had died of infantile paralysis during the school year.
18. Sermon notes, Spring 1914, *Drury Papers.*
19. SSD, *James Potter Conover* (a pamphlet published by *HS,* 1932), p. 12.
20. This letter and others referred to and quoted in the following pages are from the *Administrative File.*
21. SSD, *James Potter Conover, supra,* p. 12.
22. Correspondence between Milne and Drury, drawn upon here and in subsequent paragraphs, is from the *Administrative File.* Most of Milne's letters and memoranda are undated but run between 1911 and 1920.
23. Details of the boxing match, and the rector's reaction to it, are in C. Chapman, *The Wrong Attitude,* pp. 116 ff.
24. Memorandum, C. C. Monie to SSD, *Administrative File.* The three boys involved were L. K. Garrison, S. S. Jarvis and M. T. Mellon.
25. The account of the SPS Special Versus the Colonial is drawn from letters from Milne and Monie to the rector, in the *Administrative File.* Scudder's diary provides additional details.
26. The quotations in this and the following paragraph are from SSD, *AR,* 1915.
27. C. D. Dickey, Sr., to SSD, 14 April 1914. This, and Drury's reply, are in the *Administrative File.*

28. Drury's statements are from a handwritten manuscript in the *Administrative File,* set down in preparation for the trustees meeting. They do not appear in the printed text.
29. Gordon's letter is in the *Administrative File.*
30. SSD to James C. Knox, 20 July 1917, *ibid.* Similar versions were sent to other protestors.
31. Letters in this paragraph are in the *Administrative File:* T. Nelson to SSD, 9 July 1915; SSD to R. Peck, 14 Aug. 1915; SSD to G. P. Milne, 13 Aug. 1933.
32. SSD to H. Richards, 25 April 1916, *ibid.*
33. Paragraphs on Winant are based on Bellush, *He Walked Alone;* T. S. Matthews, *Name and Address;* M. M. Melone, *Herald Tribune Magazine,* 25 Sept. 1935.
34. Quotations from *Kittredge Papers* and from letters in the *Administrative File.*
35. Wister, *St. Paul's School in the Great War,* Introduction.
36. The R. S. Conover letters are in the *Alumni File.*
37. Junius B. Wood, *Chicago Daily News,* undated clipping in the *Alumni File.*
38. G. Frazer, Boston Herald, December 1962, quoted in Davies, *Legend of Hobey Baker,* p. xvii.
39. Drury-Spanhoofd correspondence is in the *Administrative File.*
40. Pier, *St. Paul's School,* p. 338.
41. Henry Marquand, *Poems,* privately printed, p. 6.
42. In this paragraph, Drury quotations are from SSD, *AR,* 1918. The Chapman letter (22 Sept. 1918) is cited in Howe, *John J. Chapman,* p. 335.
43. SSD manuscript notes, *Administrative File.*
44. *Ibid.*

Chapter Nine. Schoolmaster as Prophet: 1919–1929
1. J. C. Knox, *HS,* April 1906.
2. Ben R. C. Low, *Darkening Sea,* New Haven: Yale University Press, 1925.
3. WS to SSD, 12 Aug. 1910, *Administrative File.*
4. SSD to Robert P. Perkins, 23 June 1919, *Drury Papers.*
5. Material in this paragraph from *Wister Papers.*
6. Chanler Chapman to SSD, 27 Sept. 1919. The handwritten letter, ten pages in length, was acknowledged by Drury as "a wise letter in spite of your whimsical wildness—which I like." Both letters in the *Administrative File.*
7. Minutes, Trustees Meeting, 3 Oct. 1919. A copy of the letter to the Knoxes is in the *Administrative File.*
8. SSD to J. G. Winant, 9 August 1919, *ibid.*
9. This statement, Drury's only attempt at electioneering, appears in the *Concord Monitor,* 1 Oct. 1923. The reference to Winant's hat is SSD to J. G. Winant, 12 Nov. 1936, the *Administrative File.*
10. This, and the reference to St. Crispin's Day, are from Matthews, *Name and Address,* p. 150.
11. JJC to SSD, 11 Nov. 1917, cited in Howe, *John Jay Chapman,* p. 327.
12. Diary, 10 Aug. 1923, *Drury Papers.*
13. R. W. Drury, *Drury and St. Paul's,* pp. 83 ff. I am much indebted to the account given here of the critical Trinity offer.
14. SSD to W. Barclay Parsons, 21 April 1921, *Drury Papers.*
15. The Brent letter to Drury, in the *Drury Papers,* is dated "Manila, II Epiphany, 1910." The later comment is from the same source, 4 May 1921.

16. Drury, *James Potter Conover,* p. 12.
17. Quotations in this paragraph are from a postcard from Robert Soutter and a letter from William C. Breed, both addressed by the students to their families, in *Drury Papers.*
18. The student quoted is Jefferson Fletcher, *ibid.*
19. In this and the following paragraph, letters from Chapman, J. H. Coit, 2nd., and Gordon, *ibid.*
20. *New York Times,* 12 June 1921.
21. C. Brent to SSD, 3 June 1921, *Drury Papers.*
22. The text of Drury's address at the alumni dinner is in *ALH,* January 1922.
23. C. Brent to SSD, 26 April 1923. The Drury quotation in this paragraph is from his diary, 11 May 1921; both in *Drury Papers.*
24. SSD to E. G. Kendall, 12 May 1925, *Administrative File.*
25. A text of this canceled letter, dated 22 May 1924, is in the *Administrative File.*
26. SSD to JJC, 19 May 1914, cited in R. W. Drury, *A Man's Life.* (This typescript, in the *Drury Papers,* is an early version of *Drury and St. Paul's.*)
27. SSD to R. P. Perkins, 30 June 1910, *Drury Papers.*
28. JJC to SSD, 17 Feb. 1919, cited Howe, *John Jay Chapman,* p. 359.
29. Levi H. Greenwood to Charles D. Hart, 26 Feb. 1920, *Dickey Papers.*
30. C. D. Dickey, Sr., to SSD, 10 April 1910, *ibid.*
31. J. M. Goetchius, "The Alumni Fund Dinner," *ALH,* May 1921.
32. R. W. Drury, *Drury and St. Paul's,* p. 171.
33. Diary, 20 Oct. 1923, *Drury Papers.*
34. The Stokes-Drury correspondence, dating between 1924 and 1928, is in the *Administrative File.*
35. The Morison-Drury correspondence dates between 1928 and 1933, *ibid.*
36. Anecdote, C. D. Dickey, Jr., as related to AH.
37. SSD, *AR,* 1924. Ten years earlier, Chapman had characteristically written the rector that St. Paul's was in danger of getting "all the New York rich. . . . But Peabody of Groton drew the poison on himself and saved us." JJC to SSD, 5 Dec. 1913, cited in Howe, *John Jay Chapman,* p. 263.
38. WS to SSD, 2 Sept. 1919, *Administrative File.*
39. F. B. White to SSD, 2 Sept. 1919, *ibid.*
40. Memorandum, C. C. Monie to SSD, [undated].
41. For an account of this incident see R. W. Drury, *Drury and St. Paul's,* pp. 158 ff. Additional material is from the *Drury Papers* and the SPS *Alumni File,* as well as background from the Scudder diaries.
42. Robert L. Pruyn to R. W. Drury, 18 July 1961, *Drury Papers.*
43. Pruyn to SSD, 17 June 1923, *Alumni File.*
44. F. B. White to SSD, 29 April 1923, *Administrative File.*
45. Diary, 14 June 1925, *Drury Papers.*
46. The quotations in this section are from Drury's diary for the summer of 1923.
47. The quotations in this and the following paragraphs are from Drury's annual reports, 1924–1926.
48. *Time,* 20 May 1929.
49. The quotations in this paragraph are from John Richards to SSD, 20 May 1929, and Oliver Stonington to his parents, 21 May 1929, both in *Drury Papers.*
50. Paragraph based on AH recollections.

Chapter Ten. Augustan Age: 1929–1938
1. SSD, *AR* 1914.
2. J. V. Merrick to SSD, 5 May 1928, *Administrative File.*
3. C. E. Ingersoll to SSD, 28 Aug. 1926, *ibid.*
4. In a Greek aphorism, the sculptor gave a thoroughly pagan interpretation of the work: "That men may be content to live, the gods have hidden from them that it is sweet to die"—*St. Paul's School War Memorial,* a brochure in *Wister Papers.*
5. Quoted in R. W. Drury, *A Man's Life* (typescript in *Drury Papers*), p. 327.
6. II Kings 4:10.
7. A. W. Williams and J. Mayor, *HS,* December 1925.
8. C. C. Monie to SSD, 15 July 1934, *Administrative File.*
9. A. P. Stokes to SSD, 6 Nov. 1924, *ibid.*
10. J. H. Coit, Jr., to SSD [no date], *ibid.*
11. SSD to A. S. Pier, 2 Nov. 1929, *ibid.*
12. J. H. Coit, 2nd., to SSD, 24 Nov. 1914, *ibid.* The ensuing quotation is SSD to C. D. Dickey, Sr., 27 Oct. 1915, *Alumni File.*
13. JJC to SSD, 11 Feb. 1916, cited in Howe, *John Jay Chapman,* p. 319.
14. J. G. Mumford, *HS,* April 1906. The quotation about Winant is from Bellush, *He Walked Alone,* p. 4.
15. J. C. Knox, "Francis Marion Crawford," *HS,* May 1909.
16. The quotations are from letters in the *Administrative File.*
17. In this and following paragraphs, except where indicated, quoted remarks are from letters in the *Administrative File.*
18. Chanler Chapman, *The Wrong Attitude,* p. 129. In the following paragraph, the glimpses of Lay and Spanhoofd are from this source.
19. SSD, *AR,* 1929.
20. Recollection of AH. The letter in the same paragraph is from Whitney Dickey, as quoted in Charles D. Dickey, Sr., to SSD, 2 May 1913, in the *Administrative File.*
21. HCK, *AR,* 1929.
22. Chanler Chapman, *The Wrong Attitude,* p. 57.
23. Matthews, *Name and Address,* p. 154.
24. The particular discussion described in this and the following paragraph is based on an article by Scudder, *HS,* October 1925.
25. WS to SSD, 4 May 1920 and 3 Sept. 1929, *Administrative File.*
26. Reference to the "Alcoholic Ward" is based on the fact that victims of chicken pox were regularly rubbed with alcohol. Letter is WS to AH, December 1931.
27. J. V. Merrick to SSD, 9 April 1928. This and the following letters are from the *Administrative File.*
28. WS, *HS,* October 1928.
29. C. C. Monie to SSD, 20 July 1926, *Administrative File.*
30. The Drury-Kittredge correspondence is in the *Administrative File.*
31. James M. Byrne, *ALH,* Spring 1967.
32. The anecdotes in this paragraph are from *ALH,* Spring 1967.
33. This and the following paragraphs are from HCK, *ALH,* December 1926.
34. R. H. Lederer, *ALH,* Summer 1967.
35. J. Richards, Memorandum, 7 Oct. 1964, *Administrative File.*
36. Articles from *HS:* R. R. Roberts, Jr., April 1923; G. R. Clarke, June 1926.

37. As related to the author by Mrs. Richard Eaton; and SSD, *AR,* 1931.
38. Matthews, *Name and Address,* p. 158.
39. S. H. Iams, Jr., *HS,* February 1928.
40. Unsigned, *HS,* December 1926.
41. R. W. Drury, *Drury and St. Paul's,* p. 80.
42. Diary, 21 Jan. 1924, *Drury Papers.*
43. The quotations are from Barnard, *Gently Down the Stream,* pp. 32 and 33; Matthews, *Name and Address,* p. 160.
44. M. Heckscher, Jr., *HS,* June 1934.
45. SSD, *AR,* 1933. The ensuing quotations are from the annual reports of the mid-thirties.
46. Barnard, *supra,* p. 31.
47. The Drury quotations in this paragraph are from SSD, *AR,* 1931; SSD to G. Hawtrey, September 1932; and SSD to J. Richards, 28 Aug. 1934. The two latter are in the *Administrative File.*
48. M. K. Gordon, *ALH,* July 1936.
49. SSD, *AR,* 1937.
50. *Ibid.*
51. SSD to G. Alington, 16 Nov. 1937, *Administrative File;* and SSD, "The Rector's Letter," *ALH,* December 1937.
52. The text of Drury's speech is in *ALH,* July 1936.
53. Cited in R. W. Drury, *Drury and St. Paul's,* p. 280.
54. In a letter to J. Simpson, 9 Feb. 1938, in the *Administrative File,* Drury reports on what he told trustees at their winter meeting.
55. SSD, *AR,* 1937.
56. In this paragraph, letters are C. W. Coit to SSD, 23 Aug. 1937; R. Coit to SSD, 11 Jan. 1938. In the next paragraph, reference to "the lengthening days" is SSD to C. W. Coit, 7 Feb. 1938, written in Drury's last week at the school. All are in the *Administrative File.*
57. A handwritten copy of Drury's pre-Lenten message was brought to the school by Mrs. Charles Webb, widow of the former chaplain, while the author was working on this section. It is now in the *Drury Papers.* Drury's remark to Bishop Sherrill is quoted in R. W. Drury, *Drury and St. Paul's,* p. 288.

Chapter Eleven. Worlds in Change: 1938–1947
1. Henry Laughlin to HCK, 21 Jan. 1949, *Administrative File.*
2. Notes for a chapel talk, 1926, *Kittredge Papers.*
3. HCK, *ALH,* Spring 1953.
4. HCK, *AR,* 1938.
5. *Ibid.*
6. The quotation and remaining description of Nash in Cambridge are based on an unpublished typescript by Chanler Chapman in the *Alumni File.*
7. HCK, *AR,* 1939.
8. David King to AH, 15 Feb. 1978.
9. *Ibid.*
10. J. V. Lindsay to AH, 21 May 1978.
11. NBN, *AR,* 1939.
12. Cf. Drury, *Fathers and Sons,* 1930; also *School, Home and Company,* 1933.
13. Recollection, anonymous source to AH.

14. Cornelia Otis Skinner, "Ordeal for Sons," *Nuts in May,* New York: Dodd Mead and Co., 1950. Quotations in remainder of the section are from this source.
15. NBN, *AR,* 1941.
16. Samuel Eliot, *Cornerstone Address,* 21 Sept. 1886. Printed copy in Sheldon Library. The version given here is slightly condensed.
17. NBN, *AR,* 1941.
18. NBN to Alexander Whiteside, 2 Nov. 1938, *Administrative File* (italics added).
19. AH to NBN, 21 June 1944; also S. E. Morison to NBN, 14 Jan. 1940, both in the *Administrative File.*
20. Quoted in NBN, *AR,* 1941.
21. Gerald Chittenden, *Letter to a Graduate,* 1943. Unpublished typescript, *Administrative File.*
22. The author is indebted to Gerhard R. Schade for this detail and other helpful information on the Nash years.
23. NBN, *AR,* 1941; later quotation in this paragraph, *ibid.*
24. An inscribed copy of Ranald H. Macdonald's address at the dedication of the auditorium hangs in the memorial entranceway. Also in *ALH,* September 1951.
25. A typewritten copy of John Garrett's letters to his family, written while at St. Paul's, is in the *Alumni File.*
26. NBN to Robert Peck, 25 June 1946, and Peck's reply, *Administrative File.*
27. NBN, *AR,* 1945.
28. Minutes, Trustees Meeting, January 1963.
29. From an unsigned longhand account by a school employee, *Administrative File.*

Chapter Twelve. A Layman Rules in Zion: 1947–1954
1. Henry A. Laughlin to HCK, 2 June 1947, *Administrative File.*
2. Quoted in *New Hampshire Churchman,* October 1954.
3. HCK, *AR,* 1949.
4. Notes for remarks at a masters meeting, *Kittredge Papers,* 1935.
5. Address, Tuition Plan, Luncheon Forum, 17 Feb. 1945; also address before the New Hampshire Private School Teachers. Both manuscripts are in *Kittredge Papers.*
6. HCK, *AR,* 1948.
7. *Ibid.,* 1947.
8. *Ibid.,* 1953.
9. HCK to F. B. White, 19 Aug. 1936, *Administrative File.*
10. HCK, typed recommendation to Harvard, 8 Feb. 1944, *Alumni File.*
11. HCK, *AR,* 1951.
12. AH interview with Ronald J. Clark. Clark's perceptions of the Kittredge era were a source of vivid enlightenment to the author.
13. HCK, *AR,* 1947.
14. HCK, *AR,* 1948.
15. J. W. Kinnear III to AH, 11 June 1979. Editors, in addition to Kinnear, editor-in-chief, were W. S. Edwards and D. L. Hopkins, Jr. The first issue of the *Pelican* was dated 19 Sept. 1945.

16. *Pelican,* 16 Feb. 1945.
17. The description of "the crawl" is from an article by Jose A. G. Ordonez, *ALH,* Autumn 1971.
18. Notes for a Chapel Talk, 1947, *Kittredge Papers.* The two following Kittredge quotations are from HCK, *ALH,* Spring 1954, and Notes, *supra.*
19. Michael Arlen, *New Yorker,* 11 April 1970.
20. HCK, *AR,* 1953.
21. HCK, *ALH,* Spring 1954.
22. HCK to H. A. Laughlin, 21 Sept. 1951, *Administrative File.*
23. It will be recalled that the three athletic clubs were Delphian, Old Hundred and Isthmian.
24. HCK to J. Richards, 30 Sept. 1953, *Administrative File.*
25. Details in this and the following paragraphs are from AH interviews with Matthew Warren at North Hampton, N.H., May 1978. Events are corroborated in correspondence in the *Dickey Papers.*
26. C. D. Dickey, Jr., Memorandum, 5 Sept. 1941, *Dickey Papers.*
27. New York Alumni Dinner, November 1947. Manuscript in *Kittredge Papers.*
28. HCK, *AR,* 1951.
29. *Concord Monitor,* 25 March 1952.
30. HCK to H. A. Laughlin, 15 April 1954, *Administrative File.*
31. SSD, *AR,* 1937.
32. HCK, *AR,* 1952.
33. AH to HCK, 27 June 1951. The school's endowment in 1951 stood at approximately $7 million, up from $2.3 million twenty-five years before, notwithstanding the intervening Depression. Trustees were at pains to argue that the need for further giving was not obviated as a result of the recent windfalls. See "Financial Picture of St. Paul's School," memorandum by C. D. Dickey, Jr., 27 April 1951, *Dickey Papers.*
34. HCK to H. A. Laughlin, 29 Oct. 1953, *Administrative File.*
35. Anecdote from AH interview with Warren.
36. HCK, *ALH,* Spring 1954. Lines by John Richards are from the same source.

Chapter Thirteen. Era of Reform: 1954–1964
1. This section's account of the seventh rector's early life is drawn largely from AH interviews with Warren.
2. Cited in "New Rector for St. Paul's," *New Hampshire Churchman.* October 1954. The quotation immediately following is from the same source.
3. H. A. Laughlin to MMW, 29 Dec. 1954, *Administrative File.*
4. MMW to H. A. Laughlin 7 Oct. 1954, *ibid.*
5. SSD to H. A. Laughlin, cited in R. W. Drury, *Drury and St. Paul's,* p. 402. Laughlin's reserves were expressed in a letter to Charles D. Dickey, Jr., 24 Oct. 1951, *Dickey Papers.*
6. The Gates Room was donated by the family and friends of Thomas S. Gates 3rd, who died in a fire while skiing during the winter vacation at Mount Tremblant, Quebec.
7. *SPS Newsletter,* 17 Nov. 1969.
8. MMW to AH, 29 Aug. 1978.
9. MMW, *AR,* 1956. Other quotations in this paragraph are from the rector's "Labor Day Letter," 1954, one of a series addressed annually to the students.

10. MMW, *AR,* 1955.
11. MMW, *AR,* 1966.
12. "The Anniversary Sermon," by Henry Knox Sherrill, and the "Anniversary Address," by August Heckscher, appear in *ALH,* Summer 1957.
13. Tillich's address, "The Theology of Education," was first printed in *The Church School in Our Time—A Symposium,* St. Paul's School, 1957. In the following paragraph, italics added.
14. H. A. Laughlin to MMW, 3 May 1955. Warren's reply is dated 6 May 1955. Both are in the *Administrative File.*
15. MMW, *AR,* 1954.
16. *Ibid.,* 1961.
17. Brackman, "The Gospel According to St. Paul's," *Esquire,* June 1966.
18. MMW, *AR,* 1962. This annual report gives a full account of curricular changes.
19. On the Advanced Studies program, see MMW, "Speeding Up the Bright Ones," *Atlantic Monthly,* June 1962.
20. MMW, *AR,* 1961.
21. P. H. Heckscher to AH, 24 Jan. 1961.

Chapter Fourteen. A Darkling Plain: 1964–1969

1. Rebecca Warren, "Rug in a Teapot," *ALH,* Spring 1960.
2. H. A. Laughlin to MMW, 12 Oct. 1960, *Administrative File.*
3. HCK to MMW, 10 Oct. 1961, *ibid.*
4. The two articles referred to are Brackman, "The Gospel According to St. Paul's," *Esquire,* June 1966; Stephen Birmingham, "The New England Prep School," *Holiday,* February 1964.
5. Letters quoted in this and following paragraph were written to Warren by Oates and Clark, January–March 1964. All are in the *Administrative File.*
6. MMW, *AR,* 1955.
7. *Ibid.,* 1967.
8. J. T. Walker, *ALH,* Summer 1966.
9. *Pelican,* 4 Oct. 1970.
10. The "sixth-form letter" does not appear in printed form. A text is in the *Administrative File.*
11. This account, including direct quotations, is from AH interviews with Warren, May 1978.
12. The quotations from faculty speeches are from texts in the *Administrative File.*
13. A. M. Jacq to MMW, 11 Aug. 1968, *ibid.*
14. MMW to C. D. Dickey, Jr., 2 Aug. 1968, *ibid.* The earlier quotation in this paragraph is MMW, *Letter to the Alumni,* 14 July 1968.
15. MMW to H. A. Laughlin, 28 June 1968, *Administrative File.* The following quotations, Forbes Mackintosh to MMW, 12 June 1968, *ibid.*
16. C. A. Bradshaw, "A Student's View," *ALH,* Spring 1969.
17. Quoted, *SPS Newsletter,* 17 Nov. 1969.
18. Quoted, *ibid.* Letter at start of this paragraph is MMW to F. C. Church, 27 Jan. 1969, *Administrative File.*
19. The text of Resor's address is in *ALH,* Summer 1969.

Chapter Fifteen. A New Community: 1969–1979

1. Minutes, trustees meeting, April 1969.
2. MMW to C. D. Dickey, Jr., 26 Aug. 1969, *Administrative File*.
3. NBN to G. Alington, 26 Sept. 1942, *ibid*.
4. See "A Special Order of Service at the Time of the Retirement of the Seventh Rector of the School," the Sheldon Library.
5. J. Carroll McDonald, "Invitations to Maturity—The Rectorship of Matthew Warren," *ALH*, Spring 1970.
6. This quotation, and many of the facts in this section, are from AH interviews with Oates, November 1978. On 22 Dec. 1976, Oates was remarried to Jean Carolyn Matson.
7. Cited in McDonald, *supra*. The quotation "How do I know . . ." is from an anonymous student to AH.
8. For what it meant to be black in the 1970s, see *Through Our Eyes*, by the Third World Coalition, ca. 1975, the Sheldon Library. I am indebted to conversations on this subject with R. H. Lederer and to correspondence with Robert Hall.
9. Quotations from *Pelican*, 9 Feb. 1965.
10. SSD, *AR*, 1913.
11. *Ibid*. The reference to the "four ladies" is in *RR*, 27 Dec. 1861.
12. "School in Action," *ALH*, Spring 1971.
13. Virginia S. Deane, "Opportunities of Coeducation," *ALH*, Autumn 1971.
14. Alan N. Hall, "The School in Action," *ALH*, Summer 1971.
15. W. A. Oates, *AR*, 1971.
16. W. A. Oates, *AR*, 1972. See also George R. Smith, "The Discipline Committee and Its Work," *ALH*, Spring 1977.
17. At the trustees meeting of April 1979, Callaway was succeeded by James W. Kinnear III, founder of the *Pelican*.
18. The drive was headed by Ralph T. Starr, president of the sixth form, 1944.

Index

Page numbers in *italics* indicate illustrations.